The Loyalists
of Quebec
1774-1825

A Forgotten History

Printed in Canada

Published under the auspices of the Heritage Branch —
Montreal of the United Empire Loyalist Association of Canada.
This book may be obtained from the Association at 700 Casgrain
Ave., St. Lambert, Quebec, J4R 1G7

Price-Patterson Ltd.
Montreal, Quebec, Canada
ISBN 0-9691262-4-7

Dedication

In memory of David M. Stewart,
philanthropist, "animator" and real friend and
supporter of Heritage Branch — Montreal,
of the United Empire Loyalist
Association of Canada.

The Loyalists of Quebec
The Forgotten Heroes

CONTENTS

The Loyalists of Quebec

Introduction

by Hereward Senior

While 1776 marks the founding of the American republic, the year 1783 earmarks the beginning of Canadian society. If the revolution had been a total victory there would today be a single state in North America. Canada as we know it presently was the result of the determination of French Canadians to preserve their heritage and the resistance of the Loyalists to the revolution.

At the cessation of hostilities in 1783, the 100,000 or so Canadien were the majority of surviving British subjects in America. They occupied the Saint Lawrence gateway to Canada, but without the reinforcement of some 35,000 or more Loyalists to occupy and defend their flanks west of the Ottawa and in the Maritimes, they could hardly have hoped to survive.

The defeat of the Crown forces in the southern colonies was much like the defeat of the French forces in the Seven Years War. It presented a challenge. For the Canadien the challenge was to preserve religion and culture within the framework of British political institutions. For the Loyalists, to provide an alternative to the American revolutionary system with its republican civil religion and total repudiation of its European connections.

This challenge was accepted by the Loyalists who by coming suddenly and in large numbers advanced the economic development of the Maritimes and what was then Western Quebec, by several generations. In so doing they strengthened the case for a continued British military presence in North America and gave French Canadians time to develop a political defence of their cultural heritage.

As the winners write history, the Loyalists have never received much sympathy outside of Canada, and even in Canada the national liberal school of historians assumed without investigation that Loyalists were the subservient tools of authority, impractical romantics, or reactionaries. British Whig or Liberal historians had no sympathy for those called Tories, and British Tories had little interest in American history.

In American patriotic literature the Loyalists first appear as traitors to the American cause. This was followed by more sympathetic American historians, like Lorenzo Sabine, who saw the Loyalists as decent conservatives, potentially useful citizens of the republic, needlessly alienated by revolutionary persecution. In recent years more socially minded and less sympathetic historians have found Loyalists too set in their way of life to meet the needs of the changing times. Such interpretations cannot explain how tens of thousands of such people were able to cope with exile, to create a workable North American society within the framework of a British political system.

Some recent historians see Loyalists as liberals reacting against mob violence, or even socially subordinate classes, like slaves and tenant farmers who instinctively oppose a revolution led by their exploiters. With few exceptions, most American historians still see the Loyalists as opponents and victims of an historically necessary revolution, which, whatever the cost, advanced the interests of mankind.

Bernard Bailyn, dean of American revolutionary historians, has in his recent *Life of Thomas Hutchinson, Royal Governor of Massachusetts*, entered a note of doubt about this assumption. Having lived through the '60s when scholars who publicly dissented from the student revolution were subjected to mob violence, Bailyn could see in the revolution the suppression of political dissent.

The Declaration of Independence was a beacon to dissenters everywhere, so much so that dissenters throughout the world had no interest in how its authors were dealing with their own dissenters. In a century when so many have been driven into exile in the name of a new social and political order, it is useful to have a second look at the Loyalists who in their own time were the casualties of revolution.

The revolution was one of the great upheavals on this continent. It drove about 80,000 into exile out of a population of 2,000,000. Many went to England and the West Indies, as well as to Canada. Only 100,000 in a population of 25,000,000 were driven out of France during the French Revolution. Most had returned to France by the restoration in 1815. There was no restoration in America, but there was Canada, which continued to attract American settlers into the 19th century. Among them was the Massey family, who though not Loyalist in ancestry, became Loyalist in spirit.

It is difficult to find a comprehensive definition which would include all Loyalists. We do know that they represented a fair cross-section of the population, weighted a little on the side of minorities. They felt in various degrees the organized wrath of the revolutionary party. Those who spoke publicly against the revolution were tarred and feathered and many suspected of secret opposition were subject to surveillance from vigilance committees.

Loyalists found it difficult to believe in the strength of arguments employed by those who did not tolerate public debate. They saw the revolution as the work of a party rather than of a people, and felt they were as much American as those whom they opposed. Monarchy, which was the form best understood by the Indians, and the only system most of them had ever lived under, appeared more American than a republic, which seemed more associated with classic scholarship than the world they lived in.

This volume deals with a particular group of Loyalists — those that were resident in the Montreal District. Our first purpose is to discover who they were and list their names. Our second is to give an account of their origins, and finally to make an estimate of their contributions to the history of the province and the city.

CHAPTER 1

Montreal in the Loyalist Decade 1775-1785

by Elinor Kyte Senior

In the decade from 1775 to 1785, Montreal experienced four distinct inundations of peoples, each producing repercussions that rocked political attitudes, created new fears, shook old alignments, restricted trade temporarily and, in some cases, provided new jobs. When Col. Guy Johnson and other tenants of Sir John Johnson quit the Mohawk Valley in Upper New York to head for Montreal in the summer of 1775, they represented the first large contingent of refugees to flee to the northern City from the civil tension that was rampant in the American colonies[1]

Before the year was out, some 2,000 Americans of a different stamp headed for the same City, intent on seizing it.[2] Within another two years, such a wave of British and German regular troops swept into the city, overflowing into billets in the surrounding district, that Montreal's population of 6,275 was

---

[1]See anonymous letter dated Quebec, Oct. 1, 1775, cited in Abbé H. Verreau, *Invasion du Canada, Collection de mémoires recuilles et annotés* (Montreal 1873) 354; see also Simon Sanguinet, Le Témoin Oculaire de la guerre des Bostonnais en Canada dans les Années 1775 et 1775," *ibid.*, 41.

[2]Stuart R.J. Sutherland, "Richard Montgomery," in DCB, iv, 547.

dwarfed by comparison.[1] These troops made up the army of
7,900 under Major General John Burgoyne that was to bring the
American rebels to heel. Its defeat at Saratoga on Oct. 12, 1777
turned another tide of refugees northward — men, women and
children who rejected both the overtures and threats of the
leaders of revolt. These were to be the most permanent of the
Loyalist refugees streaming into the Montreal district in this
decade of turbulence.

The City towards which these uprooted Americans headed
was a walled one containing 659 homes whose occupants were,
for the most part, French-speaking Roman Catholics.[2] It was a
city of limestone houses, roofed with tile-like shingles of cedar
or boards, very susceptible to fire. Floors were of clay, covered
with flat stones. Three fires in the City in the 1760s had gutted
208 houses and a number of public buildings, including the
newly-constructed barracks located at the top of Jacques Cartier
Square, which had to be rebuilt.[3] Within the walls were four
Roman Catholic churches, a hospital and a small jail.[4]

Among the City's inhabitants was a smattering of English-
speaking traders and settlers whose numbers did not increase
significantly in the decade from 1764 to 1774. In 1764 there were
about 100 families in addition to the British garrison of some
500 soldiers.[5] Ten years later there were but 93 Montreal traders

---

[1]James Stokesbury, "John Burgoyne," DCB, iv, 114.
[2]Louise Dechêne, "La Croissance de Montréal au xviiie siècle," in Revue
d'histoire de l'Amérique française, 27, no.2, (September 1973), 164.
[3]Wood, Storied Province, ii, 685-86.
[4]See map according to P.L. Morin, Montreal, at the end of the French regime,
and Sketch of Montreal, c.1760, by D. Pomarade, in Wood, ii, 664 and 680.
[5]Rev. Samuel Bennett, Regimental Chaplain to Society for the Propagation of
the Gospel, Nov. 19, 1764, in H.C. Stuart, History of the Church of England
in Canada, (Three Rivers 1893), 24.

to sign the petition asking for the repeal of the Quebec Act that had confirmed French civil law and the Roman Catholic religion in the Province. The indignant signees, who wanted an elected Assembly and hoped to get rid of French civil law, included almost the entire male English-speaking population, with the exception of a few government officials such as Postmaster and Sheriff Edward William Gray.[1]

What was significant about this small group of "old subjects," as the incoming traders were called, was that they became assimilated linguistically into the much larger French community. Thus, as American refugees began to filter across the boundary line into the Province from 1775 on, they found themselves not only in a new country, but among people speaking a strange language. In their pleas for government help, these refugees spoke of their plight when trying "once more to begin the world again and shift for myself," as one explained, "which at best must be hard, being in a strange country and unacquainted with [the] language."[2]

The larger French-speaking community in which the Loyalists found themselves was headed by men like the Sanguinet brothers, Simon, Christophe and Joseph; by Trottier Dufy-Desaulniers; St. George-Dupré; Pierre Panet; and Pierre Guy with some of the old noblesse such as François-Thomas de Verneuil de Lorimier, Luc de la Corne, Joseph de Longueuil, and François-Marie Picote de Belestre. These men, like the wealthier English merchants such as Thomas Walker, had

---

[1]Petition to His Majesty, George III, Nov. 12, 1774, in Adam Shortt and Arthur Doughty, **Documents Relating to the Constitutional History of Canada, 1759-1791** (Ottawa 1907), 415-16.

[2]Petition of Hugh Munro, River du Chine, to Abraham Cuyler, late Mayor of Albany, Dec. 21, 1782 (National Archives of Canada (NAC): Haldimand Papers, henceforth HP, MG21/B214/I/374).

homes in Montreal and farming estates in the nearby countryside. Walker was by far the leading merchant in the City. An enterprising and pugnacious man, he left England for Boston in 1752 and then moved to Montreal in 1763, where he soon established highly successful links in both the fur and wheat trades.[1] His elegant Montreal home was the Bécancourt Manor, later owned by James McGill on Notre Dame Street. It was here, while Continental troops occupied the city in 1775-76, that Walker entertained the American commissioners Benjamin Franklin, Samuel Chase and Charles Carroll, the latter remarking that Walker's home was "the best built, and perhaps the best furnished in this town."[2] Walker's country estate was at l'Assomption, northeast of Montreal, where, as a wheat buyer and speculator, he gained considerable influence in the rural area surrounding Montreal.

This was the area that in the 1770s had experienced a wheat boom, attracting men like Walker, and Americans such as the brave provincial officer Moses Hazen, and Boston lawyer James Livingston, who became a wealthy grain merchant at Sorel.[3] There was also Hazen's one-time timber partner, Samuel Mackay, the son of a Scottish lieutenant. By 1774 the farmers along the Richelieu accounted for three-quarters of the 300,000

[1]Lewis H. Thomas, "Thomas Walker," in DCB, iv, 758-59.

[2]Charles Carroll, Journal of Charles Carroll of Carrolltown, during his visit to Canada in 1776, (Baltimore 1876), 93; see also plan of the Chateau de Vaudreuil and its entourage 1760, in Wood, Storied Province, ii, 678.

[3]For Hazen, see Allen S. Everest, Moses Hazen and the Canadian Refugees in the American Revolution (Syracuse 1976), 3-14; for Livingston, see Shortt and Doughty, Constitutional Documents, 1759-1791, 456.

bushels of wheat being exported to European markets.[1] It is not surprising then, that one of the American commissioners, Carroll, should remark that "These are the rich men in Canada; the seigneurs are in general poor." Carroll continued. "It is conjectured that the farmers in Canada cannot be possessed of less than a million sterling in specie — they hoard up their money to portion to their children; they neither let it out at interest, not expend it in the purchase of lands."[2]

Nor is it surprising that one of the spokesmen for the French community of Montreal before and during the American occupation of the City in 1775-76, Simon Sanguinet, emphatically asserted that "les Canadiens...préférant de garder la fidelité qu'ils doivent au Roy de la Grande Bretagne — refusèrent entierement d'entrer dans leurs querelles [American], au contraire ils s'attacherent plus que jamais à cultiver leurs terres et à augmenter leurs commerces à l'abri d'un acte du parlement de la Grande Bretagne qui leur assuroit la paisible possession de leurs biens — le libre exercise de leur religion, la participation aux employs civils et militaires — leurs anciennes lois rendues, exempts de payer aucunes taxes — les limites du Canada fixées, en un mot le titre de citoyen anglois — Ces faveurs accordées par le Roy et le Parlement de la Grande Bretagne rendoient les Canadiens la plus heureux peuple de l'Univers."[3]

These words were echoed by another Frenchman, Hector St. Jean Crevecoeur, the former soldier of Montcalm, who settled

---

[1]Memorial of British merchants trading into Quebec, Feb. 8, 1786, in Shortt and Doughty, **Constitutional Documents**, 542; see also Carroll, **Journal**, 96, he gives figures for 1771 of 471,000 bushels, two-thirds imported from this area.
[2]Carroll, **Journal**, 98.
[3]Sanguinet, Le Témoin Oculaire, in Verreau, **Invasion du Canada**, 2-3.

in Orange County, New York. In the colonial society of pre-revolutionary America he found a "great American asylum...united by silken bonds of good government, all respecting the laws, without dreading their power, because they are equitable...we are the most perfect society now existing in the world."[1] In other words, two members of the French community in North America found their respective British provinces as close to Utopia as they could wish.

Indeed, when an agent of the Continental Congress, John Brown, came to Montreal in March 1775, his Puritan susceptibilities were a little shocked at the levity of society. Men and women were playing whist, billiards and other gambling games. He was taken aback when one young lady boldly asked, after being introduced to him, if he was married and whether he intended to take someone home with him. Another wanted to know if Montreal women were more handsome than Boston ladies. Apart from these flippancies, he found the girls had "honest hearts and sensible minds, were good housekeepers, singing at their work, and the men, whether married or expected to be, were gay, merry and happy." He thus confirmed Sanguinet's opinion of the general contentment of the Canadiens. Not only did they now have the Quebec Act assuring them political and religious privileges, even their drinking habits had been carefully attended to by British merchants. Discovering that the "inhabitants of Canada under the French government were accustomed to Red French wine as their Common Beverage," merchants had looked around for a cheap substitute to avoid the heavy English duties on French wine. They found that red wine from Catalonia was the

---

[1]Cited in William Nelson, **The American Tory**, 171.

"nearest in point of Quality" and straight away began importing some 2,500 to 3,000 hogshead annually.[1]

By 1781, 73 of these British entrepreneurs possessed land in Montreal.[2] Outside the city, 16 seigniories, described as "some valuable country," were also in the hands of recently-arrived British merchants.[3] Thus, small as the English-speaking population was in Montreal from 1774 to 1784, they represented a growing land-owning and, for the most part, increasingly wealthy group, able to speak and work in French.

For those who were Protestant, they could attend services in the Recollet chapel, conducted by the French-speaking Swiss chaplain to the troops, David Chabrand Delisle. Delisle's command of English improved little over the decade that Loyalist refugees were pouring into the City, but this was not an immediate problem to the refugees. They could attend occasional services conducted by two Loyalist regimental chaplains, Reverend John Stuart, a former Anglican missionary to the Mohawks, and Reverend John Bethune, a Presbyterian minister who became chaplain to the 84th Royal Highland Emigrants,[4] however, both had moved to the upper province by 1787. Thus, by 1789, when the City's Protestant population had

---

[1]Memorial of British merchants trading into Quebec, Feb. 8, 1786, in Shortt and Doughty, **Constitutional Documents, 1759-1791,** 542.

[2]"Declaration du fief et seigneurie de l'isle de Montréal au papier terrier du Domaine de sa Majesté en la Province de Québec en Canada, 3 février 1781," in Claude Perreault, **Montréal en 1781** (Montreal 1969).

[3]Case of the British Merchants trading to Quebec, May 1774, in Shortt and Doughty, **Constitutional Documents,** 363.

[4]Robert Campbell, **A History of the Scotch Presbyterian Church, St. Gabriel Street** (Montreal 1887), 25-28; Governor to _____ April 8, 1785, (NAC: MG11/Q24/I/72); see also Petition of Rev. John Stuart to Haldimand, Dec. 31, 1783 (NAC: MG21/B215/2).

increased to 1,800, half of whom were Anglicans, a clamour was raised for an English-speaking clergyman.[1] The Loyalist Bishop of Nova Scotia, Charles Inglis, responded by appointing missionary James Marmaduke Tunstall as an assistant to Delisle. Inglis made it clear that "Mr. Delisle remains as he was, the first minister...he is to preach in French at such stated times as shall be judged expedient; he is also occasionally to preach in English, though not often. Mr. Tunstall is...the regular preacher."[2] Thus, Protestant Montrealers, their numbers expanded by the Loyalist immigration, succeeded in 1789 in securing an English-speaking clergyman.

A large number of French Roman Catholics — Canadiens, as they were called both by themselves and by the English newcomers — formed a considerable part of the Montreal merchant community. Of the 16 firms trading out of Montreal to the upper country by 1782, nine were English and seven French.[3] Three years later there were 34 Montreal companies engaged in this trade, 18 of them French.[4]

A number of Jews such as Lazarus David, Jacob Kuhn, Levy and Ezekiel Solomons, and the Judah brothers were also part of the Montreal merchant community. Small as their numbers were, they formed the first congregation in Canada, Shearith

---

[1]John S. Moir, **The Church in the British Era**, (Toronto 1972), 43; Wood, **Storied Province**, ii, 683.

[2]Christ Church Cathedral Archives: Minute Book Register, July 1789 — May 1802, see entries dated Aug. 23 and July 15, 1789.

[3]See list of Canots to the Pays en Haut, June 2, 1782 (NAC: MG21/B130/II).

[4]See list of Montreal Merchants trading to the upper country, April 2, 1785 (NAC: RG41A1/28/9066).

Israel, at Montreal in 1768[1] Like the merchant community as a whole, the Jewish group was divided politically. Young David Salesby Franks, a cadet member of the Jewish family that held the contract for supplying the local British garrisons,[2] was ready to overlook those who splattered black paint over the bust of King George in Place d'Armes and hung a necklace of potatoes and a wooden cross around the neck, with the inscription "Voilà le pape du Canada et le Sot Anglois."[3] The incident became a cause célèbre, occurring as it did on April 30, 1775, the night before the Quebec Act came into force.

Few Montrealers doubted that the perpetrators hoped to create bad feeling between the English and French of the City. Yet the combining of the Pope and the King in the insult puzzled the well-affected in Montreal. They crowded around the desecrated statue the next day to watch the soldiers wash the black paint away, remove the cross and necklace, and post a reward for the discovery of the culprits. British military authorities tended to blame members of the English community, while Picoté de Belestre exclaimed loudly that the author of the outrage ought to be hanged. Franks boldly replied that no one should be hanged for so little. Infuriated, de Belestre tweaked his nose, whereupon Franks struck de Belestre such a blow that he was knocked to the ground. Others interfered to separate the two. The next day de Belestre, still indignant, swore out a warrant against Franks, who was

---

[1]Esther Blaustein, Rachel Esar and Evelyn Miller, "Spanish and Portuguese Synagogue (Shearith Israel), Montreal 1768-1968," in **Transactions**, The Jewish Historical Society of England, 1969-70, xxiii, 1971, III.

[2]Carol Whitfield, **Tommy Atkins, the British Soldier in Canada 1759-1870**, (Ottawa 1931), 33.

[3]Sanguinet mémoire, in Verreau, **Invasion du Canada**, 24.

imprisoned without bail. Tension ran so high in the city that a
second fight broke out between a member of the old French
noblesse, Le Pailleur, and another member of the Jewish
community. Le Pailleur charged that the Jews in Montreal had
disfigured the King's statue. Levy Solomons angrily denied it
and threw Le Pailleur to the ground. Like Franks, Solomons too
was arrested but was released on bail.[1] Nor did the incident end
there. Later, "enemies of Government...pulled down the King's
bust, cut off the Head and threw it in a pump well," until it was
found and fished out by James Cusack, a captain of the bateaux
in Col. Guy Johnson's contingent of Loyalists that arrived in
Montreal in the midst of these bitter outbursts.[2]

Thus, by mid-spring of 1775, the quarrels of the southern
colonies had generated tensions in the City and soured relations
to some extent. While most British merchants, who had earlier
supported petitions praying for a local Assembly and a repeal of
the Quebec Act, now drew away from the more radical
merchants such as Thomas Walker, James Price, Charles Hay
and Joseph Bindon. French-Canadian merchants and
shopkeepers kept clear of all entanglements. They did not so
much as send a single observer to the coffee house meetings in
February and April 1775 when American agents appealed to
Montreal merchants for support.[3] This was the state of
Montreal when Capt. Moses Hazen of St. John's burst in upon it
in May 1775 with the staggering news that not one, but two
separate American raids had been made on Fort St. John's, its
small garrison captured, and booty taken off. Hazen rushed on

[1] _____ to H. Finlay, May 6, 1775, **ibid.**, 335-36, for details of these fights.

[2] Petition of James Cusack, Montreal, April 20, 1782 (NAC: MG21/B214/318-21);
the bust is now in the McCord Museum.

[3] Sanguinet mémoire, in Verreau, **Invasion du Canada**, 21.

to Quebec City to bring Gov. Carleton the first report of enemy action along the Richelieu.[1] News of the close approach of the Americans threw Montreal into a state of alarm. From the City, Madame Benoist wrote hurriedly to her brother at Quebec, the Hon. François Baby, informing him that "La mauvaise volonté du plus grand nombre des Canadiens, et qui n'était que trop manifeste, obligea le colonel [Templer, commanding officer of the 26th Regiment] de menacer de faire sauter la ville par les poudres sy on ne voulait pas se garder."[2] Merchants like the former French royalist officer, Pierre Guy, dismayed at the poor response to the call for militia volunteers from among his countrymen, hoped that the Americans "nous laissent tranquilles, car il n'est pas necessaire de te dire combien leurs mouvements nous ont fait du mal et ont interrompus le commerce."[3]

These letters show that the American quarrels were also affecting trade and that, initially, French as well as English Montrealers showed little enthusiasm for taking up arms to defend the outposts along the Richelieu River, upon which the ultimate security of the City depended. If these fell Montreal fell, for the City, open on three sides and commanded from the rear by high ground, was impossible to defend.

By May of 1775, Carleton was only too well aware of the extent of treasonable activity being carried on between American military leaders and their sympathizers in Montreal. So bold were the latter that one of them, Joseph Bindon, crossed the St. Lawrence in the same vessel as regulars being sent to

[1]Carleton to Dartmouth, Montreal, June 7, 1775 (NAC: MG11/Q11/184-89).
[2]Mme. Benoist à Baby, May 25, 1775, in Verreau, Invasion du Canada, 305; see also Sanguinet mémoire, 37.
[3]Guy à Baby, Montreal, June 19, 1775, ibid., 306.

relieve Fort St. John on May 18th. At Longueuil, Bindon secured a horse and hastened to St. John's to warn Ethan Allen, the American leader, and his 80 raiders of the approach of the troops. Allen's first plan was to ambush the British detachment but, as daylight drew near, they prepared to decamp, having given Bindon a letter addressed to James Morrison and other Montreal merchants "friendly to the cause of Liberty" asking them to sell him armaments and rum.[1]

Bindon met the regulars on his return just outside St. John's and told their commanding officer, Major Charles Preston, that a great number of Americans were at the fort. Preston urged Bindon to return with them to St. John's so that in the event they were overpowered, he could carry intelligence to the commanding officer at Montreal, Col. Templer. Bindon demurred, explaining that he had an important letter for Montreal, and was allowed to proceed. The regulars reached St. John's just as the rebels were re-embarking, and there was a brief exchange of fire before the raiders got away. Bindon hurried on, reaching Montreal, where his report of gunfire at St. John's so alarmed the populace that they expected Ethan Allen and his men at their gates momentarily.

The garrison commandant beat an alarm for all inhabitants of the City and suburbs to gather at the Recollet chapel to decide the best means of defence. Enthusiasm to take up arms was unbounded. In the midst of the discussion Templer received word from Preston of what had transpired at St. John's, including Bindon's treachery. Yet it was not until the troops returned from St. John's that action was taken against him and then it was ineffectual. The enraged soldiers seized Bindon

---

[1]Carleton to Dartmouth, June 7 and Aug. 14, 1775 (NAC: MG11/Q11/184-191); Sanguinet mémoire, in Verreau, **Invasion du Canada**, 29.

while he was sitting on merchant Richard Dobie's gallery and led him to the pillory. Officers interfered to prevent injury to Bindon, and the next day indignant merchants sympathetic to Bindon met at Sutherland's coffee house where they raised a cry against the military, saying that the insult offered to Bindon by the troops could happen to others.[1] In a surprising turn of events Col. Templer replied that he would see that "justice was done to the soldiers." They were saved from punishment by the intervention of several "honnetes gens anglois et canadiens" who asked mercy for the soldiers. As for Bindon, none doubted his guilt. Yet he was let off to bide his time until he could welcome the American invaders six months later.[2]

Carleton hurried to Montreal on June 7th, 1775. Here he perused with dismay intercepted letters. One was from Benedict Arnold to Montreal merchant and Justice of the Peace Thomas Walker, written on May 24th. In it Arnold blatantly asked Walker to supply him with advice "from time to time of the number of Troops with you, their Movements and Designs if possible ... and if joined by any Canadians or Indians."[3] Yet, Carleton dared not clap any of these suspected merchants into jail. Instead he declared martial law and wrote a long and gloomy appraisal of the City and the general state of the Province. "The Noblesse of this neighbourhood (Montreal) was called upon to collect their inhabitants to defend themselves," he wrote to Secretary of State Lord Dartmouth, "but though the Gentlemen testified great zeal, neither their entreaties or their example could prevail upon the people. A few of the gentry,

---

[1]Sanguinet mémoire, in Verreau, **Invasion du Canada**, 31-32.
[2]Carleton to Dartmouth, June 7, 1775 (NAC: MG11/Q11/184-86); Sanguinet mémoire, in Verreau, **Invasion du Canada**, 33 and 80.
[3]Enclosure, Carleton to Dartmouth, June 7, 1775, (NAC: MG11/Q11/196).

consisting largely of the youth in this place and its
neighbourhood, formed a small corps of Volunteers under the
command of Mr. Samuel Mackay and took post at St. John's.
The Indians showed as much backwardness as the Canadian
peasantry."

Carleton's troop disposition was even more distressing.
"Not 600 rank and file fit for duty upon the whole Extent of this
great River." he declared, "not an armed vessel, no place of
strength, the ancient Provincial Force enervated and broke to
pieces, all subordination overset, and the minds of the people
poisoned by the same hypocrisy and Lies practiced with so
much success in the other provinces and which their emissaries
and friends have spread here."[1] The prospects for defence were
bleak. Nevertheless, Carleton ordered Major Preston back to St.
John's with a party of soldiers to build redoubts to enclose the
barracks and the large stone house that had been leased to
Moses Hazen and his partner, Lt-Col. Gabriel Christie.[2] Earth
ramparts enclosed by a water-filled ditch surrounded the fort
which was protected by palisades that projected out into the
ditch to prevent an escalade. Such fortifications were meagre,
but they were better than nothing. Carleton also sent a party of
Indians forward into the woods between Isle aux Noix and St.
John's to watch for intruders, but warned the commandant at
St. John's "not to depend upon them so far as to omit taking the
same precautions as you would observe were there no such

---

[1]Ibid., 186; see also **Journal of the Most Memorable Occurrences in the
Province of Quebec**, in Seventh Series of Historical Documents, Literary and
Historical Society of Quebec, 1905, 12-13.

[2]Fernand Ouellet, "Gabriel Christie," in **DCB**, iv, 149-151; see also Everest,
Moses Hazen, 16-21.

people,"[1] an early indication of Carleton's cool attitude towards employing Indians. His last security gesture before returning to Quebec City was to order an armed schooner to be built as quickly as possible at St. John's for use on the river.[2]

On July 16th Montreal was again thrown into a fever of excitement with the sudden appearance of the first of the Loyalists, Col. Guy Johnson, a 36 year-old native of Ireland, who had succeeded Sir William Johnson as superintendent of the northern Indians. With him came the cream of the Indian department from the Mohawk Valley — Col. Christian Daniel Claus, John Butler, Gilbert Tice, Peter Johnson, Sir William's half-Indian son, and the Mohawk chief, Joseph Brant. They were followed by a flotilla of bateaux, captained by James Cusack, carrying some 200 wives, children and other white settlers, and what was more impressive, 300 Indian warriors and their families, amounting in all to 1,500.[3] Guy Johnson's young wife, Mary, a daughter of Sir William Johnson, was not among them. She had died suddenly at Oswego early in July while her husband and other Department officials were conferring with the Iroquois to procure their pledge to protect the St. Lawrence-Lake Ontario supply route against rebellious Americans.

Fatigue and the tension of the past four months had taken their toll on Mary as she saw her husband and two small daughters increasingly surrounded by hostility at their home

---

[1]Carleton to Preston, June 8, 1775 (NAC: MG23/B10).

[2]Prescott to Preston, Aug. 31, 1775 (NAC: MB23/B10).

[3]Jonathan G. Rossie, "Guy Johnson," in DCB, iv, 393-94; Carleton to Dartmouth, Aug. 14, 1775 (NAC: MG11/Q11/222-224); see also A.G. Bradley, Lord Dorchester (Toronto 1928), 88; George Stanley, Canada Invaded (Toronto 1973), 32-33; Verreau, Invasion du Canada, 41 and 354.

near Fort Johnson in the Mohawk Valley. Guy Johnson, heir to
Sir William's mantle, was the top British official in the area,
and as such was singled out by the Tryon Committee of Safety
as their most formidable opponent. Tough and contemptuous,
the new superintendent of the northern Indians had done little
to allay their fears. He fortified his home, Guy Park, located near
present-day Amsterdam, New York, and his armed retainers
were known to stop and search travellers suspected of sympathy
for the radicals at the Philadelphia Congress. In Schenectady,
rumours flew that "Colonel Guy Johnson would come down
the river with five thousand Indians and cut us all off."[1]
Another uproar ensued when the Tryon Committee of Safety
got hold of a letter calling on the Oneidas to come to Guy Park
to join the Mohawks in saving the Johnsons from "the Boston
people."[2]

Matters reached a crisis in May, 1775, when Col. Guy
Johnson, with his two brothers-in-law, Col. Christian Daniel
Claus and Sir John Johnson, broke up a meeting of local radicals
who were overly enthusiastic for the "rebels" who had fired on
the King's troops at Concord and Lexington. While a number of
Sir John Johnson's tenants provided the strong-arm squad for
the raid, Guy Johnson mounted a high porch and harangued
the crowd on the virtues of loyalty and good order. He did not
go unchallenged. One of the crowd interrupted, calling him a
liar. This was too much for Guy Johnson. He grabbed the man
by the throat. A general melee ensued during which the

---

[1]Cited in Codman Hislop, **The Mohawk** (New York 1948), 158.
[2]**Ibid.**, 159; for a copy of this intercepted letter and other letters of Guy Johnson,
see William L. Stone, **Life of Joseph Brant-Thayendanegea: including the
Border Wars of the American Revolution** (New York 1838), i, 63-70.

interrupter was thoroughly trounced and the crowd took off. That round went to the Johnsons, but the overawed forces, some of them members of the Committee of the Palatinate District of New York, complained bitterly to the Committee of Safety at Albany. "The Scotch Highlanders, who were Roman Catholics," they reported, "have armed themselves to the number of 150, ready to aid in the suppression of any popular outbreak in favour of the growing cause of liberty."[1] Those who favoured popular outbreaks had a vested interest in getting rid of any force that threatened to suppress them. "Johnson's dogs," they dubbed the tenants. Nor were the Highlanders strangers to rebellion. These were men of Glengarry and Knoydart, Scotland, who had emigrated to Tryon County two years earlier at the invitation of Sir William Johnson. Gentlemen of the Macdonell clan - Aberchalder, Leek, Collachie and Scotas, some of whom had been out in '45 — led the large migration.[2] Barely having begun to improve their leased land holdings on Sir William's large estates, they did not relish taking orders from the anti-Johnson party that styled itself the Tryon Committee of Safety. If there was to be a fight, they would take their stand under the Royal standard with Sir John Johnson, who had succeeded to his father's estates when the latter died suddenly in the midst of a great Indian conference in

For Col. Guy Johnson the winds of rebellion blew even more strongly. As heir and superintendent of the Indian empire of Sir William Johnson, he understood the need to gain

---

[1]See reports of the Provincial Committee of the Palatinate Districts of New York to the Committee of Safety, Albany, May 18, 1775, cited in Stone, **Life of Brant**, i, 54.

[2]For a discussion of this migration, see J. A. Macdonell, **Sketches, Glengarry in Canada** (Montreal 1893), 8-13.

the active support of the northern Indians to the Crown. Moreover, both he and Sir John were aware of the overtures being made by rebellious elements to the Indians both above and below the border of the province of Quebec. Thus, as hostility towards him increased and rumours flew that he would be seized by New Englanders, Guy Johnson made swift plans to quit the Mohawk Valley for Oswego to confer with the Indians there and thence to Montreal where he hoped to persuade the Caughnawagas to support the Crown. Moreover, he had to deal with a jurisdictional dispute about the Canadian command of the Department which had been brewing since the death of Sir William. Col. Daniel Claus had been named deputy agent of the Canadian Indians under Sir William, but Carleton supported the appointment from Quebec of the half-pay officer, Major John Campbell, as superintendent of Indians for the Province.[1]

Carleton, wishing to lessen the Johnson influence over the Indian Department in Quebec, was not anxious to see the affable and competent German — Daniel Claus — who was fluent in several Indian dialects, resume his residence in Montreal and consolidate his position within the Indian empire of the Johnsons.[2] Thus, as the storm clouds darkened in the southern Colonies, forcing the first contingent of Loyalists into Quebec, there were undertones of conflict between the leaders of this first American exodus and the top government officials at Quebec City. This was to colour joint action against the American rebels, who began to invade the Province almost as

---

[1]Carleton to Dartmouth, Aug. 14, 1775 (NAC: MG11/Q11/222); see also Douglas Leighton "Christian Daniel Claus," in DCB, iv, 154-55.
[2]DCB, iv, 155

as soon as Guy Johnson, Daniel Claus and the other refugees reached Montreal.

On arriving, the Indian Department officials immediately went to Caughnawaga at Sault St. Louis where the Iroquois told them of their alarm at the rebel action so close to their own lands and their awareness that Carleton was none too pleased with them. Indeed, one of the part-Indian, part-black residents, known as Louis Le Nègre, who had taken a strong pro-American stance, travelled back and forth over the frontier, bringing flattering messages to the Indian chiefs from American military leaders.[1] Louis Le Nègre had even gone to Boston and Cambridge, where he was warmly received by George Washington, who was anxious to get his advice about how to keep "the seven Nations from takg up Armes against the Americans."[2] Louis was back at Sault St. Louis when Col. Johnson, Claus, John Butler and the Mohawk chief, Joseph Brant, arrived to try to persuade them to "take up the Tommy Hawk...Against the Americans."[3] Present, too, was the Jesuit priest, Father Joseph Huguet, whom the Indian Department officers feared, for it was believed that Huguet, if not preaching disloyalty, was at least encouraging the Indians to be neutral.[4]

Thus Johnson and Claus faced a fearsome Indian council, and it was only with great skill that Claus was able to counter the eloquent arguments of Le Nègre by reminding the Indians of past injuries received at the hands of the southern colonists. Before his harangue was over, Claus succeeded in arousing

---

[1]Mémoire, de Lorimier, in Verreau, **Invasion du Canada,** 247.
[2]Deposition of Collo. Louis, c.1776 (NAC: MG23/B3/folder 3/139).
[3]**Ibid.**
[4]Jospeh Cossette, "Joseph Huguet" in **DCB,** iv, 375.

them to the point that they "determined of attacking and laying waste the New England Frontiers."[1] However, he urged them to attend a congress at Lachine to declare their sentiments personally to the Gov. Carleton.[2] This congress was attended by all Indians who had accompanied Guy Johnson and Claus from the Mohawk Valley and Oswego, as well as those from Caughnawaga, making a total of some 600 Indians, according to Simon Sanguinet's estimate.[3] After four long days of debate from July 26th to 29th, their decision was to take up the hatchet against the Bostonians. However, Carleton insisted that they must not take any action without his express permission and, when on scouting expeditions, they were not to fire on Americans unless fired at first.[4] Johnson and Claus were dumbfounded. They did their best to convince Carleton that the Indians must be given some leeway, but he refused to loose the Indians on the frontiers and the Congress broke up with shades of irritation on all sides. Carleton sent off a letter in a huff to Lord Dartmouth. "As Colonel (Guy) Johnson intends residing in this province," he snorted, "I could wish his rank and command were more clearly described." As for the Indians, he reported, "they all promised great things. It is at present absolutely necessary to gain them and perhaps at all times, though at a very considerable expense, but they are not to be depended upon, especially by those in a weakly situation."[5] Thus Carleton's hesitation about employing the Indians partly

---

[1]Cited in Stanley, **Canada Invaded, 1775-1776**, 33.

[2]Sanguinet says the congress was held at the Recollet Church, see Verreau, **Invasion du Canada**, 41.

[3]**Ibid.**

[4]**Ibid.**, 40.

[5]Carleton to Dartmouth, Aug. 14, 1775 (NAC: MG11/Q11/222).

stemmed from financial considerations as well as for humanitarian reasons.

The Governor's intransigence threw such cold water on the Indians' enthusiasm that eventually many of those who had come to Montreal with Joseph Brant made their way back to the western frontier at Niagara with John Butler. As for the Caughnawagas, most returned to Sault St. Louis, but a small party under François-Thomas de Verneuil de Lorimier set off for the border to reconnoitre. On August 22nd, they encountered an American party near Lacolle River. In an exchange of gunfire several Indians were wounded while the American leader, Capt. Remember Baker, was killed, beheaded and his head carried back triumphantly to Montreal, along with intelligence reports found on him.[1] These confirmed the extent of Louis Le Nègre's activities on behalf of the rebels at Caughnawaga. With the Indian attack on Baker and his party, the Americans began to increase their pressure on the Caughnawagas to remain neutral. This prompted a number of Indian officials, including Capt. Gilbert Tice; Walter Butler, a son of John Butler, and Peter Johnson, Sir William's half-Indian son to join the military force at Fort St. John, to keep a close eye on Sault St. Louis and its Indians, and to accompany Indian scouting parties that were scouring the countryside along the Richelieu River.[2]

In Montreal, Guy Johnson grew restless and disgruntled at what seemed to be Carleton's inaction. His fears mounted as he watched merchants not only selling liquor to the Indians and stripping them of their clothing but what was worse

---

[1]Verreau, **Invasion du Canada**, 41; see also Mémoire de Lorimier, 246; see also Lt. Col. R. Prescott to Major C. Preston, Aug. 31, 1775 (NAC: MG23/B10).
[2]Stanley, **Canada Invaded, 1775-1776**, 34.

"propagating also many dangerous reports among them, telling them they approved of the rebels coming, as it was for the interest of the Colony."[1]

But what was more disheartening for well-affected Montrealers and Caughnawaga Indians was that Johnson refused to cross the St. Lawrence again to use the weight of his name and position to counter American overtures to the Indians. To Loyalist Montrealers like Simon Sanguinet, Johnson's conduct seemed "assez singulière, car il avoit tant de peur qu'il ne se croyoit pas en sureté de coucher dans la ville de Montréal — il couchoit toujours à bord d'une frégate mouillée devant la ville de Montréal — et ne voulut jamais aller à St. Jean ou les Sauvages le demandoient absolument — se qui les auroit engagés à rester aux retranchements de St. Jean." [2] There is a temptation to believe that Johnson was still sulking over the splitting of the Canadian Indian command. This was part of the picture. But there was also the loss of his young wife just a few months earlier and the aftermath of the unpleasant months in the Mohawk Valley, and his flight to Montreal only to find the City and its surrounding area also in turmoil.

Another man in Montreal who was seething with indignation against Carleton was the prominent 64-year old merchant and Knight of St. Louis — Luc de la Corne. A former royalist officer, he was one of those who counted more than ten Indians among his household slaves.[3] The family dynastic ties reached in every direction. His eldest daughter had married Claus's rival in the Indian Department, Major John Campbell. De la Corne had been eager to raise militiamen in his seigneury

---

[1]Ibid.

[2]Sanguinet mémoire, in Verreau, **Invasion du Canada**, 46.

[3]Pierre and Madeleine-Dionne Tousignant, "Luc de la Corne," **DCB**, iv, 425-9.

north of Montreal to help protect the Province against the invaders. When potential recruits at Terrebonne, Lachenaie, Mascouche and Repentigny proved reluctant to mobilize, de la Corne's strong-arm methods raised a hornet's nest instead. Some he threatened to imprison. A few he slapped around a bit and finally he announced that regular troops would come to enforce his orders. The habitants, accustomed to fifteen years of relief from this sort of impressment into military service, dug their heels in and complained so bitterly that Carleton intervened. To his humiliation, de la Corne was rebuked and a British regular officer sent to reassure the protesting habitants.[1] De la Corne threw up his hands and decided the only, or, at least, the sensible thing to do was to negotiate with the incoming Americans and this he did, along with six or seven friends, through Caughnawaga spokesmen. Though he knew of de la Corne's indiscretion, Carleton turned a blind eye to it, just as he did to much of the activity of the Montreal merchants friendly to the Americans. It may have been temporarily the wiser course, but it left Loyalist Montrealers perturbed that the "disaffected" in the City went unpunished.[2]

When the Continental army of 1,400, under the former British officer who had served at Louisbourg and Quebec, Richard Montgomery, crossed the Quebec frontier on September 4th, 1775, it entered a territory where Indians, Montrealers, merchants and habitants, governor and garrison, were all uncertain as to whether defence was feasible. Carleton had already sent the majority of his meagre force of regulars — some 512 — to Fort St. John, together with about 100 local

---

[1]Gustave Lanctôt, **Canada and the American Revolution** (Toronto 1967), 58; Sanguinet mémoire in Verreau, **Invasion du Canada**, 38-39.

[2]Sanguinet mémoire in **Invasion du Canada**, 38, 50-53.

officers and volunteers, and about the same number of
Indians.[1] Regular officer Major Preston was in overall
command. Lt. Samuel Mackay, who had undertaken the
temporary relief of the fort in May after the first American
surprise attack, was one of the few British provincial officers at
the fort. With him were a group of 30 volunteers whom he had
raised at his own expense, composed almost entirely of
Canadians.[2] Mackay's volunteers, both those who had served at
St. John in May and those with him throughout the two-month
siege in the fall, represent the first contingent of Quebec
Loyalists, that is, these were men who took their stand under
the Royal standard, ready to do battle against all within or
without the Province in arms against the legal government.
They differed from their American counterparts only in the
final outcome of the war. American Loyalists were defeated
while Quebec Loyalists enjoyed ultimate victory for their
Province did not succumb to the revolutionaries.

Command of the local Indians at Fort St. John fell to the two
de Lorimier brothers, François-Thomas de Verneuil and Claude
Nicolas-Guillaume, both of whom, like Luc de la Corne, spoke
a number of Indian dialects, and could disguise themselves so
well as Indians that they were able to slip in and out of the fort
as intelligence agents all during the siege.[3] The American
Loyalist, Capt. Gilbert Tice, was in charge of the Mohawks at the
fort.

---

[1]Stanley, **Canada Invaded**, 35; Mémoire de Berthelot, in Verreau, **Invasion
du Canada**, 229.

[2]Samuel Mackay to General Allan Maclean, March 23, 1778 (NAC:
MG23/B43).

[3]Mémoire de Lorimier, in Verreau, **Invasion du Canada**, 247-48, 256.

As the rebel vessels neared the fort, making for a landing out of reach of the fort's cannon, Major Preston ordered the two de Lorimiers and Capt. Tice to take a party of 97 Indians out to prevent the Rebels from disembarking. Thus a party of 100 men, almost entirely Indians, crept through thick undercover to oppose the landing of 1,400.[1] Their opening burst of fire sent the enemy scurrying for cover, but in the subsequent exchange of sniping during the day, Tice was wounded in the thigh, an Indian chief was mortally wounded, and seven other Indians were killed. The Americans were driven back by the combined action of the Indian party and the guns from the fort which eventually got in range.[2] Yet it was largely a victory for the de Lorimiers and their Indian warriors and all acclaimed it as such. Indeed, churches in Montreal resounded with Te Deum as a thanksgiving "pour ce succès inattendu."[3]

However, this initial action had its negative aspect. Though led by two members of the old French noblesse and by one of the Loyalist refugees from the Colonies in revolt, the Indians resented the fact that the British regulars and volunteers remained within the fort throughout the day-long engagement. As they carried their dead warriors back to Sault St. Louis for burial, more and more Indians from the fort joined them, so that only a handful remained within the palisade and the prospect of Indian neutrality increased. The positive aspect of the engagement was that young Montrealers demanded Carleton's permission to march to St. John's to aid in its defence. Up until then Carleton had said that they must remain

---

[1] Ibid., 248.
[2] Stanley, **Canada Invaded**, 39.
[3] Mme Benoist to François Baby, Sept. 9, 1775, in Verreau, **Invasion du Canada**, 311-12.

to defend the City but, with the news of this repulse of the Rebels, he permitted those who wished to volunteer to proceed to St. John's.[1] It was then that 120 Canadiens, 6 British residents and perhaps as many as 300 Indians, under the command of Joseph de Longueuil, left the City, among them lawyer Thomas Walker,[2] a Loyalist cousin of the more notorious disaffected Thomas Walker, soon to be arrested. According to Simon Sanguinet, this contingent of Montreal Loyalists was made up of "plusiers negociants riches qui abandonnèrent leurs familles et leur commerce."[3]

A second contingent of volunteers, raised by Montrealer Picoté de Belestre, headed towards Fort St. John by way of Sorel.[4] These men were from various parishes: Rivière de Loup, Quebec city, Three Rivers, Mascouche, St. Geneviève, Varennes and St. Eustache.[5] There were 20 "officiers et gentilshommes," that is, Canadians who had served as officers under the French crown. Besides Samuel Mackay, there were three other "volunteer" officers: Capt. Joseph-Michel Legardeur de Montesson, Luc Schmitts and Daniel Robertson as well as 16 militia officers from Montreal and Three Rivers, and 10 rural militia officers, all of them Canadians.[6]

These two fresh contingents at St John's represented the second distinct group of Quebec Loyalists to take up arms in

---

[1]Ibid.

[2]Ibid.

[3]Sanguinet mémoire, in **ibid.**, 43.

[4]Mme Benoist to Baby, Sept. 9, 1775, in Verreau, **Invasion du Canada**, 313.

[5]Liste de Messieurs les officiers et Gentilshommes Canadiens qui ont servit en qualité de voluntaires sous les ordres de Mr. Bellêtre et pris Prisonniers dans la Garnison de St. Jean sous le commandement du Major Preston, Nov. 5, 1775 (NAC: MG11/Q11/284).

[6]Ibid.

defence of the Country. Their arrival at the fort led to unwarranted optimism which was soon dampened when a party, led by de Longueuil, was surprised by the American invaders. The Rebels killed and scalped the volunteer Iroquois interpreter, Porteous, and wounded Chevalier de La Bruyères.[1] From then on the commandant, Preston, was instructed by the commanding officer at Montreal to consult Picoté de Belestre "whenever it may be found necessary to send detachments to harass or attack the Enemy."[2] Preston's superior officer, Col.Richard Prescott, who remained in command of the skeleton garrison in Montreal, was high in his praise of de Belestre "...an officer of experience and perfectly acquainted with the manner of carrying on War in this country," he wrote, one of the few times during the year that British officers showed perception about the local situation and the usefulness of Loyalist volunteers.[3] But by then it was too late. With the ambushing of this party of Canadians and the slaying of Porteous, all the Indians deserted the camp.[4] The defenders left at the fort numbered in all, including women and children, about 1,300.[5] The Indians had been an uncertain factor, blowing hot and cold as to which side they would support, if any. Habitants south of the St. Lawrence faced similar problems. As more and more invaders spread over the countryside, paying hard cash for provisions and circulating pamphlets in French

---

[1]Sanguinet's mémoire, in Verreau, **Invasion du Canada**, 43; Mme. Benoist to Baby, Sept. 12, 1775, **ibid.**, 314.

[2]Prescott to Preston, Sept. 11, 1775, (NAC: MG23/B10).

[3]**Ibid.**

[4]Mémoire de Lorimier, in Verreau, **Invasion du Canada**, 247; Mme. Benoist to Baby, Oct. 3, 1775, **ibid.**, 316; see also Hey to Lord Dartmouth, Sept. 17, 1775, in **Constitutional Documents**, 459.

[5]Stanley, **Canada Invaded**, 51.

inviting farmers to join them, habitants welcomed the trade and hard cash, and some 500 went so far as to enlist in two rebel battalions formed by James Livingston and a wigmaker from Quebec, Jeremy Duggan. The existence of these "rebel" regiments meant that Quebec was beginning to reflect the state of insurgency that existed in the sister Colonies. Thus the American rebel military leaders grew bolder.

With most of the regulars and Loyalist volunteers bottled up in St. John's and the Indians neutralized, Ethan Allen determined to by-pass St. John's and storm Montreal on September 25th, 1775, using some of the newly-enlisted local partisans. Thus arose the second chance for well-affected Montrealers to take up arms. For the American Loyalists who had reached the City in July, it was an opportunity to show their solidarity with the Quebec Loyalists. Yet what happened in Montreal as American raiders neared has had mixed reports. The most-quoted witness, Simon Sanguinet, tersely asserted that "Les citoyens sortirent de Montréal au nombre d'environ trois cents canadiens et trente marchands anglois. Le reste des marchands anglois ne voulurent point y aller. C'est là où on reconnut le plus overtement les traîtres."[1]

Sanguinet's testimony cannot be dismissed lightly. He was well-affected to government and admired Carleton even though he criticized his hesitation in taking the offensive against the invaders. Yet Sanguinet was irritated by the conduct of the British traders in Montreal — first for their advocacy of a repeal of the Quebec Act, and by the traitorous conduct of a small party of traders. His pique may have led him to overstate the case against the entire British merchant group. When Montrealers left for the relief of St. John's, Sanguinet claimed

---

[1]Verreau, **Invasion du Canada**, 50.

that "Les marchands anglois refusèrent d'y aller nettement."[1]
Yet Mme. Benoist says that there were six British traders among
those who marched, not many it is true, but some. Moreover,
Carleton was opposed to having Montrealers go to St. John's
and permitted the move only under heavy pressure from the
Canadians. Thus, it was likely that the British merchants
thought it more prudent to abide by Carleton's wishes. But once
the Rebels were at the gates of Montreal, the time had come for
these traders to show their colours.

Sanguinet's figure of 300 Canadians and 30 British is
contradicted by a Canadian who participated in the skirmish
with the Americans. Charles de Lanaudière, Carleton's aide-de-
camp, reported that about 200 Loyalist volunteers and 36
regulars formed the defence party under the command of Major
John Campbell of the Indian Department.[2] De Lanaudière's
figures are confirmed in the most recent scholarship, George
Stanley's *Canada Invaded*, which puts the figures at 34 regulars,
120 Canadians, 80 British traders and 20 officers of the Indian
Department.[3] The picture that emerges, then, is that about an
equal number of Canadians and British sallied forth through
the Quebec Gate to meet the notorious Green Mountain Boy
and his Canadian cohorts, the British representing almost the
entire merchant class then resident in the City, and the
Canadians representing about one-twelfth of the male French-
speaking population of Montreal.

The surprising development in this initial attack on
Montreal was that neither Col. Guy Johnson nor Daniel Claus,
nor indeed Carleton nor the commandant of the garrison, Col.

---

[1]Ibid., 43.
[2]De Lanaudière to Baby, Sept. 28, 1775 (ibid., 316).
[3]Verreau, **Invasion du Canada**, 46.

Richard Prescott, accompanied the defenders. Johnson and Claus kept to their vessels, partly as a result of continuing ill-feeling over the quarrels within the Department and the fact that a subordinate officer, Major John Campbell, was to lead the defence force.[1] There was a second reason. Johnson and Claus were appalled at the defenceless state of the Province with only 600 regulars available for field duty. Indeed Claus attributed the habitants' reluctance to fight to this fact.[2] Others of the American Loyalists were willing to fight, come what may. It was one of Sir William Johnson's half-Indian sons, Peter, to whom Ethan Allen was forced to surrender his sword when the raiders were overpowered.[3] Yet the eyes of Montrealers were on the leader of the American Loyalists, Guy Johnson. That he remained outside the Loyalist coalition that assembled at Place d'Armes gave Montrealers and Indians reason to ponder what their own response should be to the invaders at the gate.

For most Montreal French-speaking Roman Catholics, the whole quarrel between Great Britain and its Colonies in the south was becoming more and more puzzling. With Ethan Allen's defeat, militia volunteers poured into the City from the countryside eager to offer their services to Carleton to push the invaders out of the province.[4] But when Montrealers urged him to send mounted volunteers to round up the retreating raiders Carleton refused.[5] It is true that the parade of the notorious Ethan Allen through the streets of Montreal to a

---

[1]Sanguinet mémoire, Verreau, **Invasion du Canada**, 50.
[2]Col. Daniel Claus, Memorandum of the Rebel Invasion of Canada, 1775 (NAC:MG11/Q13/49).
[3]Wood, **Storied Province**, ii, 690.
[4]Sanguinet mémoire, in Verreau, **Invasion du Canada**, 54-56.
[5]**Ibid.**, 51.

prison ship produced a sensation. This setback for the Americans and the fact that they still had not seized Fort St. John gave some encouragement, but as winter approached it was clear to all that the small force at St. John's could not prevent the eventual descent of the Rebels on the City unless Carleton armed the local volunteers. Gestures were made in this direction, but proved ineffectual and too late.[1]

Fort St. John fell on Nov. 2 after a siege of almost two months, described by a beleaguered Loyalist, Antoine Juchereau-Duchesnay, who "essuyé la plus grande misère que j'aie eue dans tous mes campagnes."[2] Twenty defenders had been killed, another 23 wounded.[3] Those who survived were herded into bateaux on their way to prisons in the southern Colonies. Among the 79 Canadians were two knights of St. Louis, de Belestre and Capt. Montesson. For Samuel Mackay, his second-in-command Capt. Monnin, and their 30 volunteers, it was the beginning of "four months in a loathsome dungeon" in Hartford, Connecticut. When Mackay and five of his men escaped, they travelled through 200 miles of enemy territory in 29 days, learning, like many of the later fleeing Loyalists, what it was like to survive "eight days on a dog's carcase."[4] At the time of the fort's surrender there were two Indians within the fort, both of whom shared the fate of the other captives.[5]

---

[1]Stanley, **Canada Invaded**, 58-60.

[2]Duchesnay to Baby, dated Fort Jean, 2 novembre 1775 (Verreau, **Invasion du Canada**, 320).

[3]Ibid., 78; see also Stanley, **Canada Invaded**, 62.

[4]Samuel Mackay to General Allan Maclean, March 23, 1778 (NAC:MG23/B43).

[5]Liste de Messieurs les officiers et Gentilshommes qui ont servit en qualité de volontaires sous les ordres de Mr. Bellêtre, et pris Prisonniers dans la Garnison de St. Jean sous le commandement du Major Preston, Nov. 5, 1775 (NAC: MG11/Q11/284).

Most of the Canadians were released from prison by 1777, but some were unable to cross the frontier to return home. They languished in the strange Colonies, cursing their fate and stupidity at being made captive. Juchereau-Duchesnay was one of these. Writing from Albany in January, 1776, to urge François Baby to arrange his exchange for an American officer, he lamented only that he had not left Fort St. John "quand j'ai vu que l'on ne parlait que de se rendre," an indication that others must have managed to slip away from the fort while the negotiations were going on between Major Preston and Gen. Montgomery.[1] Another Canadian officer, Antoine de Bellefeuille, when given his parole on condition that he would not bear arms against the Americans, found his way to Detroit where he assisted Gov. Henry Hamilton in the attack on Vincennes and was once more captured. Sent to prison in Virginia he "shared a tedious imprisonment" in Williamsburg jail with Gov. Hamilton, the officer whom Carleton had sent to quell the ruckus provoked by Luc de la Corne's strong-arm methods to mobilize militiamen at Terrebonne. In letters to his father, de Bellefeuille spoke warmly of Hamilton, "qui ... me tient lieu d'un second père."[2] Released a second time, he made his way to New York, carrying warm recommendations to Sir Henry Clinton from the still-imprisoned Hamilton who asked Clinton's help for de Bellefeuille "should an occasion present of his reaching Canada."[3] Not only did de Bellefeuille find friends

---

[1]Juchereau-Duchesnay à Baby, Jan. 31, 1776, in Verreau, **Invasion du Canada**, 324.

[2]Antoine de Bellefeuille to his father, dated New York, Dec. 11, 1780 (McGill University, CH227, S205); for Hamilton, see Elizabeth Arthur, "Henry Hamilton," in **DCB**, iv, 321-24.

[3]Henry Hamilton to Sir Henry Clinton, Oct. 1, 1779 (McGill University: CH227, S205).

among the Loyalists in the Colonies, he also secured contacts with those within the revolutionary orbit. Thus Benjamin Davis of New York could write to his brother Edward, in Boston, to ask his aid for de Bellefeuille, "as he is a friend of mine for whom I have esteem...should he be taken and carried to Boston...I recommend that...you would use your influence that every indulgence may be shown him."[1] These letters show that de Bellefeuille moved about from city to city in the hope of regaining entry to Canada and that as a Canadian he had one advantage in that people in high places, both Loyalist and Patriot, were willing to help him.

These captives, like Samuel Mackay, Antoine Juchereau-Duchesnay and Antoine de Bellefeuille, together with the volunteers who warded off Ethan Allen's attack on Montreal and those who successfully defended Quebec City during the long winter of 1775-76, were the undisputed "Loyalists" of the province of Quebec. To Samuel Mackay goes the title of the first Quebecer to take up arms against the rebellious colonists, for he was a volunteer with Major Preston's detachment of regulars sent to St. John's on May 18, 1775, "to chastise," as he recalled, "the presumptuous rebels who retired before our arrival."[2] When Preston's party returned to Montreal, it was Mackay who remonstrated with the Montreal commandant on the need to garrison this fort. Col. Templer's reply was that he simply could not spare any men for St. John's. It was then that Mackay secured Templer's permission to raise a number of volunteers. With these he returned to St. John's to hold the fort until Carleton arrived in Montreal and ordered Preston back with

---

[1]B. Davis to E. Davis, July 19, 1781 (**ibid.**).

[2]Captain Samuel Mackay to General Allan Maclean, March 23, 1778 (NAC: MG23/B43).

most of the regulars then in the Province, thus confirming
Mackay's appraisal of the absolute need of securing this fort. In
this sense, Mackay was the first Quebec Loyalist.[1]

In the early years of the American revolution, those men
who volunteered their services in defence of the established
government were known as Royalists by their friends and as
Tories by their enemies.[2] They not wait to see which side
appeared to be winning before they took their places under the
Royal standard. Those who became prisoners of war were
anxious and ready to resume the fight against the
revolutionaries as soon as they succeeded in getting back to
Quebec. Antoine de Bellefeuille, for instance, had a "grande
envie de ma donner entièrement à l'art militaire." He wrote his
father from New York that Gov. Hamilton "fait son possible
pour me procurer une place et...s'il ne peut me placer ici, il
écrisa au Général Haldimand en ma faveur."[3] Juchereau-
Duchesnay was furious at his prolonged exile in Albany.
Fearing that he would not be included among the officers of the
new Canadian companies being raised by Carleton in 1776, he
did not hesitate to write and express his strong opinion that
"Tous les officiers qui se sont montrés bons sujects devraient, ce
ma semble, s'attendre à la préférence." By these he meant those
who had commanded at St. John's and were now in exile —
particularly de Belestre, de Longueuil, de Lamorandière, de

---

[1]Ibid.

[2]See Sanguinet mémoire, in Verreau, **Invasion du Canada**, 93, for a
contemporary discussion of these terms; see also Justin Smith, **Our Struggle
for the Fourteenth Colony**, ii, 506.

[3]Antoine de Bellefeuille to his father, Dec. 11, 1780 (McGill University: CH227,
S205); see also David Lee, François Lefebvre de Bellefeuille, **DCB**, iv, 465-66.

Boucherville, de la Valtrie, de St. Ours, de Rouville, D'eschambault, de Lotbiniere and, of course, himself.[1]

In selecting the officers for the Canadian companies, Carleton kept these men in mind and commissioned de Rouville, de Boucherville, D'eschambault, de Salaberry, de Tonnancour, D'Ailleboust Cuisy and Noyelles de Fleurimont, all captured at St. John's and imprisoned in the southern Colonies.[2] These officers were just as jealous of their rights and as ready to take offence at any slight as were the American Loyalist officers whom Carleton later commissioned and authorized to raise troops from among their countrymen who were escaping into Quebec from the rebellious Colonies. Samuel Mackay, for instance, was miffed in 1777 when Carleton put him in charge of a company of Canadians without commissioning him. This was one of the three companies of 100 militiamen each that Carleton drafted under Capts. de Rouville, de Boucherville and Monnin, the first conscripts under the British regime. This calling out of only three companies under the new militia act was tokenism writ large. Burgoyne's needs for his army were monumental — at least 1,000 men were required for transport duty alone, but Carleton's policy was to draft a minimum of men at first in order to "reconcile them by degrees to what the French government had deemed an indispensable duty," that is to serve as soldiers defensively or offensively as required by government.[3]

---

[1]S. Juchereau-Duchesnay to François Baby, Jan. 31, 1776, in Verreau, **Invasion du Canada**, 324.

[2]Return of officers of the Canadian Companies raised in 1776 by Sir Guy Carleton (NAC: HP, MG21/B167/ii/369-370).

[3]Gustave Lanctôt, **Canada and the American Revolution** (Toronto 1967), 164-65.

Thus Mackay found himself once more in the thick of a delicate military situation, when he was put in charge of the conscripted men as they arrived at the Recollet monastery in Montreal where they were put under normal military discipline — unable to leave barracks without permission.[1] This was an unaccustomed restraint which they were reluctant to put up with. As desertions soared, Carleton riposted with an order that two married men would be drafted from the parish of each deserter.[2] In this manner the three companies were soon filled. One company under Mackay was detailed to accompany Col. Barry St. Leger on his attack on Fort Stanwix. The other two were attached to Burgoyne's army marching south to attack the Colonies in the Lake Champlain area. Mackay sent his company ahead under two subordinate officers while he returned to Montreal to insist upon his commission. When Carleton refused, Mackay threw up his command, and joined Burgoyne's army as a volunteer.[3]

Thus Mackay marched southward with the huge army that included 400 Indians under the command of another disgruntled Montrealer who was in Carleton's black books ever since he had flirted with the rebels in the fall of 1775. This was Luc de la Corne, who had ample reason to rue any thoughts of collaborating with the invaders. They had exiled him from the City and then ordered him to Philadelphia where he was imprisoned.[4] Like Mackay, de la Corne chose to march as a volunteer. So, too, did 175 others, including Major John

---

[1]Sanguinet mémoire, in Verreau, **Invasion du Canada**, 143.

[2]Lanctôt, **Canada and the American Revolution**, 164-65.

[3]Mackay to Maclean, March 23, 1778, (NAC: MG23/B43); see also Sanguinet mémoire, in Verreau, **Invasion du Canada**, 144.

[4]Pierre and Madeleine Dionne-Tousignant, Luc de la Corne, **DCB**, iv, 428.

Campbell, and many of his staff.[1]   Mackay's star was in the ascendant under Burgoyne who recognized his leadership qualities and raised him to command the corps composed of American Loyalists whose commander, Col. Francis Pfister, fell during the disastrous Bennington affair when troops sent to garner provisions for Burgoyne's army were cut off.[2] Mackay's command of this largely American corps, which contained a few French-speaking Quebecers too, linked Quebec and American Loyalist military men for the first time. His American officers were men who would take the lead in the future American Loyalist corps re-organized in Montreal under Sir John Johnson — captains such as Samuel Anderson, Robert Leake, John and Henry Ruiter and William Mackay, lieutenants such as Coenradt and Harmon Best, John Howard, Edward Carscallion, and the Canadians - Peter Le Gras (Pierre La Grass) and Anthony Le Chena (Antoine Chennette), sergeants David Dulmage, Jacob and Everhart Weager, and corporals William Coenradt, Jacob and Peter Detlor and James Perigo.[3] Mackay was one of the few commanders who managed to get his corps away before the convention of Saratoga when Burgoyne's entire army, described by de la Corne as "one of the finest ...(the) country had yet seen," laid down its arms.[4] On his return to Canada, Mackay and his corps were ordered to

---

[1]Mémoire de Lorimier, in Verreau, **Invasion du Canada,** 288; Lanctôt, **Canada and the American Revolution,** 165.

[2]Mackay to Maclean, March 23, 1773 (NAC: MG23/B43).

[3]A muster roll of the corps of Loyal American Volunteers raised by the late Colonel Francis Phister (Pfister) of Hosack, and commanded by Captain Samuel McKay (Mackay) 14 April 1778, Chataugaye (Chateauguay) (NAC: HP, MG21/B167/I/172, 109-112).

[4]Cited by Tousignant, Luc de la Corne, DCB, iv, 427.

quarters on the Châteauguay River where they "spent a tedious winter" longing for action.[1]

If Mackay was the first Quebec Loyalist, then the Chevalier de Lorimier was the second and probably the most valuable and steadfast of all. He was with Mackay at Fort St. John in the summer of 1775, moving in and out of the fort and throughout the infested area disguised as an Indian, and acting as a scout and intelligence agent for Carleton. When the Governor attempted an ineffectual relief of Fort St. John that autumn, it was de Lorimier who commanded the 800 volunteers and Indians in Carleton's force.[2] During the occupation of Montreal, de Lorimier was feared and flattered by the American commandant, Gen. David Wooster. Wooster had been with Sir William Johnson when the troops under Amherst first entered Montreal in 1760. With Sir William, he had been quartered in the de Lorimier home and became friends with the family.[3] Thus, when Wooster returned to Montreal as conqueror a second time, he sent word to de Lorimier that he had nothing to fear from the American invaders. Unlike the pro-American party within the City — men such as Joseph Bindon, James Price, William Haywood, Levy Solomons, François Cazeau, Thomas Walker, Moses Hazen, Samuel Jacobs and Pierre du Calvet, all of whom became part of Wooster's administrative and provision team[4] — de Lorimier kept his distance, preferring to remain on his farm at Lachine.[5]

---

[1]Mackay to Maclean, March 23, 1778 (NAC: MG23/B43.)

[2]Mémoire de Lorimier, in Verreau, **Invasion du Canada**, 260.

[3]Ibid., 263.

[4]Sanguinet mémoire, Verrreau, **Invasion du Canada**, 80 and 92; Petition of Levy Solomons to Congress, Nov. 15, 1784 (NAC: MG23/B3/folder I); Sheriff Edward William Gray to L. Solomons, Aug. 22, 1776 and same to Pownall, March 23, 1780 (NAC: MG23/G113/ii); Memorial of Officers, Merchants and

The American commandant soon felt waves of hostility within the City and rightly suspected plots. Loyalist emissaries like Joseph Papineau and Capt. Lamothe frequented the City, bringing intelligence to the Loyalists and carrying news to Carleton at Quebec.[1] Others such as the wealthy and influential British trader, Jacob Jordan, kept de Lorimier informed of affairs in Montreal.[2] Thus, when Wooster determined to disarm and arrest a number of prominent Montrealers and send them to prison in the Colonies, he ordered a general assembly of citizens at the Recollet chapel. Two of the pro-American merchants, James Price and William Haywood, were sent as his spokesmen to order militia officers and magistrates to surrender their commissions or face imprisonment. Alerted by Jordan of this meeting, de Lorimier hastened to Montreal to attend and took the lead in defying the American authorities. In the midst of harangues by Price and Haywood and the confusion that ensued when American soldiers seized one citizen who spoke out against the measures, de Lorimier jumped up on the pulpit shouting "Ecoutez —braves citoyens — j'ai été conquis par les

Traders in behalf of themselves and other refugees from Canada, Philadelphia, Jan. 24, 1784 (NAC: MG23/B3/folder I); Allan S. Everest, **Moses Hazen and the Canadian Refugees in the American Revolution**, (Syracuse 1976), see especially 30-45; for names of Canadians in rebel American army, see (NAC: MG23/B3/folder 3/17 and folder 4/21); Pierre du Clavet to Congress, Sept. 15, 1785 (NAC: MG23/B3, folder ii); Justin Smith, **Our Struggle for the Fourteenth Colony** (New York 1907), ii, 560.

[5]Mémoire de Lorimier, in Verreau, **Invasion du Canada**, 262; (NAC: MG23/B27 and MG23/B19).

[1]**Blockade of Quebec in 1775-1776 by the American Revolutionists**, 1905, Seventh Series of Historical Documents published by the Literary and Historical Society of Quebec, 53; Verreau, **Invasion du Canada**, 98, 124, 283.

[2]Mémoire de Lorimier, in Verreau, **Invasion du Canada**, 262; see also A.J.H. Richardson, Jacob Jordan, **DCB**, iv, 402-03.

— j'ai été conquis par les troupes britanniques — j'ai deux commissions du Roi de France. Le gouvernement anglois ne me les a jamais demandées — je n'ai pas l'honneur d'en avoir du Roi Georges — mais si j'en avois — jamais les pouilloux du Congrès ne mettroient la main dessus."[1]

Spurred on by de Lorimier and Cuthbert Grant, Montreal militia officers and magistrates refused to give up their commissions. These included the colonel of the Montreal militia, Thomas-Ignace Trottier Dufy-Desaulniers, Lt. Col. Neveu Sevestre, and Major St. George Dupré, Sheriff Edward William Gray, the three Sanguinet brothers, Lawrence Ermatinger, James McGill, Nivard St. Dizier, and Pierre Panet, all of whom soon found themselves arrested and on their way to imprisonment at Fort Chambly. Other Montrealers had already been exiled — such as Luc de la Corne and Legislative Councillor John Fraser, the latter had volunteered to ward off Ethan Allen and his raiders.[2] Even the Superior of the Sulpicians, Etienne Montgolfier, was ordered seized, but the wife of James Price had the good sense to urge Wooster to leave Montgolfier alone.[3]

For his insolence, de Lorimier was ordered by Wooster to prepare for exile to New York, but he escaped on snowshoes to St. Regis and thence to Fort de la Galette (Oswegatchie) where Capt. George Forster of the 8th Regiment had a detachment.[4] Here he was involved in Forster's successful attack against the American outpost at the Cedars, undertaken on the

---

[1]Ibid.

[2]Memorial of John Fraser to Major General Schuyler, Albany, Feb. 4, 1776 (NAC: MG23/B3/folder 2).

[3]Verreau, **Invasion du Canada**, 95.

[4]Mémoire de Lorimier, **ibid.**, 264-67.

anniversary of Ethan Allen's attack on Fort St. John. With de Lorimier, who led the preliminary attack, was William Johnson, the part-Indian son of Sir William Johnson. Young Johnson stepped forward on de Lorimier's invitation and offered to share with him the glory of advancing against the American position as an example to the Indians who had demurred advancing, saying "Cet honneur appartenoit aux troupes du Roi," a taunt made derisively because the troops under Forster had taken up the rear.[1]

De Lorimier and Johnson remained among the friendly Indians of St. Regis for a month awaiting developments in Montreal and Quebec City, receiving bits of news from courier Joseph Papineau. As the invaders prepared to vacate the City when news reached them that British reinforcements had arrived at Quebec City from Great Britain, they indulged in wholesale looting.[2] Their final act of fury before heading for the border was to set fire to two large piles of fuel-wood, but Montreal Loyalists managed to extinguish them. It was at the height of this activity in Montreal that St. Regis and its people were startled by the arrival of Sir John Johnson with a party of Indians and some 170 tenants from the Mohawk Valley, emaciated after 19 gruelling days through the wilderness.[3] After

---

[1]Ibid., 273-74; for identification of Molly Brandt's father as white, see Matilda Schieffelin to her parents, John and Ann Lawrence; d. Navy Hall, opposite Fort Niagara, Dec. 4, 1780, in New York Genealogical and Biographical Record, 1941, vol. 72, 122.

[2]Sanguinet Mémoire, in Verreau, **Invasion du Canada**, 132-3; for Arnold's exoneration of charges of pillaging, see Everest, **Moses Hazen**, 45.

[3]Mémoire de Lorimier, **ibid.**, 284; see also memorial of Sir John Johnson to Commissioners appointed to enquire into the losses of American Loyalists, in Sir John Johnson, **The North American Johnson** (London 1963), Appendix III, 90; Petitions of Walter Sutherland, Aug. 31, 1779, and John Bracken, Nov. 19,

a brief rest, Sir John pushed on to Montreal, where he arrived on June 16, 1776, at the head of some 500 Indians, Canadians and Scottish tenants a few hours before British troops reached the City from Quebec, and not long after the last of the American troops had fled. Thus it was a party of American Loyalists who first reached the liberated City.[1] They found it almost deserted. Out of a population of over 6,000, scarcely 400 inhabitants were still within its walls. Most had fled the previous fall as soon as they saw the British troops embarking for Quebec City.[2] For most, this movement of the regulars out of the City had been the most disheartening. One of the few women who remained watched them forlornly from the walls of the City. To her brother at Quebec City she wrote "Je t'avoue que cela m'affligea plus que l'approche des Bostonais."[3]

With the arrival of the leader of the western New York Loyalists, Montreal Loyalists became overshadowed by their American counterparts. Even the part Montrealers played in the defense of the Province in 1775 and later in the offensive measures under General Burgoyne in 1777 tended to become blurred and forgotten as merchants and citizens returned to their homes and watched a steady stream of American refugees crowd into the City, along with ever-increasing numbers of British soldiers. However, the services of the Quebec volunteer officers and soldiers could not be entirely neglected. A number of them received land grants in recognition of their services, though it is not clear from existing records that all who served

---

1972 in (NAC: HP, MG21/B214/I/133 and 362-63); both these men came through the forest with Sir John Johnson.

[1]Sanguinet Mémoire, in Verreau, **Invasion du Canada**, 80.

[2]Ibid.

[3]Mme Benoist to her brother, François Baby, Nov. 3, 1775 (**ibid.**, 317).

were compensated. A list of such soldiers and officers, published in the Public Archives Report for 1891, does not contain the names of all the volunteers who were at Fort St. John, for instance.[1] Conspicuously missing from the list was François-Thomas de Verneuil de Lorimier who, after the liberation of Montreal, was a volunteer with Burgoyne's army and was invalided back to Montreal, suffering a grievous leg wound that turned gangrenous.[2] It was likely de Lorimier who received 1,200 acres of land west of Johnstown, present-day Prescott.[3]

Some provincial officers received half-pay until their death, but again it is not clear that all volunteer officers were so lucky. Still getting half-pay in 1828 were five Quebec veterans of 1775-1783: Jacques Hervieux, Joseph Boucher Labroquères, J. M. de Tonnancour, Joseph de Varennes and Joseph Vigneau.[4] Perhaps most of the reduced Canadian officers had died by 1828, but Vassel de Montviel did not die until 1843. He was still serving as militia Adjutant General of Lower Canada and had been an officer in Hertel de Rouville's company in 1776. Yet he

---

[1]Retour des personnes qui se sont trouvées dans le Blocus de St. Jean et d'autres dans l'affaire de Bennington à qui Milord Dorchester veut bien accorder des terres pour récompense de leurs services, Quebec, July 3, 1788, in **Public Archives Report**, 1891, see Douglas Brymer's report to John Carling, 1-3.

[2]Mémoire de Lorimier, Verreau, **Invasion du Canada**, 292-94.

[3]See Surveyor John Collins' map of New Johnstown, Aug. 27, 1790 (NAC: H12/440), listed as Cornwall but more likely present-day Prescott.

[4]List of American officers who were reduced in the years 1783 and 1784 and paid by the Commissariat from Jan. 1, 1828, May 16, 1835 (RG8/C634A/108); see also Return of Officers of the Canadian Companies raised in the year 1776 by Sir Guy Carleton (NAC: HP, MG21/B167/Pare 2/369-370).

was not listed among the half-pay provincial officers in 1828.[1] Other categories of Quebec Loyalists existed. These included the officers and men of the Provincial Marine — men like Commodore Jean-Baptiste Bouchette, Commander Hypolite La Force, and John Schank.[2] They kept the lake and river vessels on the move, carrying out such chores as getting Carleton safely out of Montreal to Quebec under the mouth of American-captured cannon. In a special category of undisputed Quebec Loyalists were the couriers, men like Joseph Papineau and Lamothe (Lamotte), who moved from New York to Montreal and Quebec, camouflaging themselves in the snow under white blankets as they neared Canadian sentries sympathetic to the Americans, and bringing a mixture of information, rumour and gossip to Carleton which, if not always accurate, was often cheering.[3] Still other Loyalists were the 51 Canadians who enlisted in the ranks of the 1st Battalion of the Royal Highland Emigrants and served throughout the remaining years of the American revolutionary war.[4] In what must be one of the strangest rebel-Loyalist mélanges were the 100 or so men captured from Arnold's force at Quebec who, upon being

---

[1]Petition of the officers of the de Rouville Company, Sept. 8, 1783 (NAC: MG21/B215/56-57); see also, Petition de Les Officers Canadiens des Compagnies des Captaines Monin et Boucherville, Oct. 23, 1781 (NAC: HP, MG21/B214/I/270-71); Louis Turcotte, **Le Canada sous l'union, 1841-67** (Quebec 1871), 187.

[2]McCord Museum, John Shank letterbook; Captain Shank to Government, July 11, 1784 (NAC: HP, MG21/B166); see also, Haldimand to Captain Shank, Aug. 11, 1778 (**ibid.**, B143); Register of Military Commissions, 1778-1782 (**ibid.**, B859/4-5).

[3]**Blockade of Quebec in 1775-76** (1905), 53-54.

[4]G. Murray Logan, **Scottish Highlanders and the American Revolution** (Halifax 1976), see muster roll of 1st battalion, 84th Regiment, Royal Highland Emigrants, 90-95.

discovered to be mostly of Irish birth, were given the option of enlisting in the Royal Highland Emigrants or being sent back to Great Britain to face charges of treason.[1] Some of these men were likely among those who secured Loyalist lands in Upper Canada when the regiment was disbanded in 1784.

Some Canadian officers were listed on the United Empire Loyalist rolls prepared when Sir Guy Carleton, now Lord Dorchester, determined that "those Loyalists who have adhered to the Unity of the Empire, and joined the Royal Standard before the Treaty of Separation in the year 1783, and all their children and their Descendants by either Sex, are to be distinguished by the following Capitals, affixed to their names: U.E. Alluding to their great principle the Unity of the Empire."[2] Such a one was Commodore Jean-Baptiste Bouchette of the Provincial Marine whose status as a United Empire Loyalist was unchallenged until 1798 when a memorandum was drawn up for the Executive Council pointing out that "many persons ... having no claims to the Privileges of United Empire Loyalists ought to be expunged from the lists, both to avoid offence to the real U.E.s...and to prevent...any improper expense to Government." Discharged German and British soldiers and seamen were to be excluded from the U.E. lists as they were entitled "only to receive their military lands free of expense without any land privilege being extended to their children."[3]

However, Canadian-born military men and volunteers were in a special category. Like the other colonies, the Province had been subjected to propaganda, invasion and fifth column

---

[1]Ibid., 22.

[2]Lord Dorchester's Order-in-Council, Nov. 9, 1789 (NAC: C.O. 42/67/202-204).

[3]Memorandum initialled P.R. [Peter Russell] dated Montreal, May 23, 1798 (RG1/E3/91/15-18).

infiltration from the south. Therefore those of its citizens who took up arms in its defence were identical to those Loyalists of the southern Colonies, the only difference being that the Crown forces of Quebec ultimately defeated the American revolutionaries. Yet under the new ruling with regard to U.E. status, Bouchette's name was struck off.[1]

The government had a more difficult time in the case of Canadians who volunteered for service in the early corps of Loyalists, such as Anthony (Antoine) Chennette and Peter (Pierre) La Grass. They were both designated as "Canadian Gentlemen" when they enlisted in Robert Leake's corps, one of the first Loyalist military units that eventually merged into the 1st Battalion of the King's Royal Regt. of New York under Sir John Johnson.[2] How many French or British Quebecers volunteered in these early Loyalist corps is unknown, but the presence of Chennette and La Grass in Leake's corps indicates that there were some. They, like Capts. Samuel Mackay and Picoté de Belestre, Chevalier de Lorimier, Major John Campbell, Commodore Jean-Baptiste Bouchette, and others, whether of French, British, Indian or other background, who took their place under the Royal Standard before 1783, adhered to the Unity of Empire.

---

[1]Ibid.
[2]NAC: HP., MG21/B166/189.

CHAPTER 2

The Loyalists in Quebec: A Study in Diversity

by Hereward Senior

The Loyalists who came to Quebec, or to that part of it which became Lower Canada, found that the issues of the American Revolution were overshadowed by those of the Seven Years War. In Upper Canada the influx of post-Loyalist Americans, whom Simcoe welcomed and Strachan feared, kept the issues of the Revolution alive; but in Lower Canada the memories of the Revolution faded as the Loyalists tried to come to terms with the French fact.

The refugees who sought shelter with their French-Canadian hosts shared with them the experience of military defeat. They were now exiles who, having lost their homes, hoped to keep their laws and way of life in their adopted land. The French Canadians, who sought to preserve their culture, and the Loyalists, who wished to maintain their allegiance to the Crown, were natural allies with a common interest in preserving the British presence in North America. Loyalist settlers might secure the flanks of French Canada on the western frontier and in the Maritimes, but in the heart of the Province they appeared as an unwelcome addition to the anglophone community.

As early as 1768, Sir Guy Carleton had written that "barring a catastrophe shocking to think of, this country must, to the end of time, be peopled by the Canadian race."[1] As though to confirm Carleton's prophecy, Isaac Weld, visiting Montreal in 1795, wrote, "By far the greater number of the inhabitants of Montreal are of French extraction." He noted that the merchants and principal people were English, Scots, or Irish, and that "the French retain, in a great measure, the manners and customs of their ancestors; they have an unconquerable aversion to learn English, and it is very rare to meet with any person amongst them that can speak it in any tolerable manner; but the English inhabitants are for the most part well acquainted with the French language."[2]

Apart from a sprinkling of anglophone merchants and seigneurs, and a few hundred Fraser Highlanders on the road to assimilation, there was no anglophone rural population in the province of Quebec. In the towns, anglophone merchants and professionals served francophone customers and clients and employed francophone labour. The only section of society where the anglophones were in full control was the government, but it was necessary for the officials to speak the language of the majority. Until the coming of the Loyalists, the anglophone minority was destined for assimilation.

Carleton's view of the Province was shared by the French speaking Swiss Governor, Sir Frederick Haldimand, who governed Quebec throughout most of the revolutionary war period. Haldimand supported the "French party," a group of civil servants and members of the appointed Legislative and

---

[1] Carleton to Shelburne, Nov. 25, 1767, in **Documents relating to the Constitutional History of Canada**, 1759-1791, ed. Adam Shortt and A.G. Doughty (Ottawa 1918), 254-59.

[2] Isaac Weld, "Travels Through the States of North America," in G.M. Craig, ed. **Early Travellers in the Canadas** (Toronto 1955).

Executive Councils, headed by the Scots physician, Adam Mabane.[3] Until the end of the war it was assumed that the Loyalist refugees in Quebec would return to their homes when hostilities ceased. When this became impossible, Haldimand had to balance his sympathy for the Loyalists against his conviction that Quebec must remain French. His first difficulties arose less from the Loyalists themselves than from their champions in the "British party." William Grant, speaking in the Legislative Council in the spring of 1784, argued that the presence of the Loyalists in the Province was an economic necessity, and urged that a committee be appointed to recommend constitutional changes that would make Quebec fit for their habitation. Grant wanted changes in the civil code that would abolish the substance of the Quebec Act of 1774, and called for an elected Assembly.[4]

These demands were rejected on the initiative of Saint Luc de la Corne of the "French party," and Haldimand saw in them the spirit of the revolution that had led to the separation of the old Colonies.[5] Haldimand also had difficulties with Lord North who was prepared to permit Loyalist refugees concentrated along the Richelieu River to settle in the region of Missisquoi Bay. Haldimand felt that these lands should remain a reserve for future settlement by French Canadians. As Lord North was unlikely to share his views, Haldimand pressed on him other

---

[3]Elizabeth Arthur, "The French Party of Adam Mabane 1760-1791," unpublished MA thesis (McGill University 1947).

[4]Grant's motion, Minutes Legislative Council, April 22, 1784 (NAC: RG1/E1/203); Grant's speech in favour of an elected Assembly, Minutes Legislative Council, April 29, 1784 (NAC: RG1/E1/223).

[5]Haldimand to Lord Sydney, June 29, 1784 (NAC: MG11/Q23/171); see also, Haldimand to Lords Privy Council for Plantation Affairs, May 6, 1784 (NAC: MG11/Q23/322-23).

arguments: an unsettled wilderness was the most effective barrier to invasion; border settlements would be a source of tension with the new republic; and they would, of course, become centres of smuggling.[6] North was soon converted; but such arguments could have no force with the Loyalists. Yet as virtual wards of the Crown, dependent on its bounty for future titles to lands, rations and the tools needed for resettlement, the Loyalists were not in a position to argue.

It was the Loyalists' fear of a loss of their claims on the Crown more than a xenophobic distaste for the seigneurial system of land-holding that defeated the efforts of seigneurs to attract what one of them referred to as "industrious Americans" to their estates. Charles de Lanaudière, who owned land on the Maskinonge River west of Three Rivers, offered land rent-free for three years, free use of his gristmill for four years and use of the seigneurial sawmill to turn logs into boards.[7] Seigneurs like de Lanaudière hoped that the Loyalists would increase the productivity of their estates by teaching the more advanced methods of New England farmers to the habitants. Few, if any, such offers were accepted by the Loyalists; thus their influence on the agricultural methods used in the Province was delayed and indirect. Loyalists and post-Loyalist Americans who followed taught new methods to the Scots who began to appear in Quebec in 1817 and they, in turn, taught the French Canadians.

---

[6]Lord North to Haldimand, July 24, 1783 (NAC: Haldimand Papers (henceforth HP), MG21/B50/133); same to same, Nov. 27, 1783 (**ibid.**, B56/201); Instructions to Haldimand, July 16, 1783, in **Documents relating to the Constitutional History of Canada**, 721-22.

[7]See de Lanaudière's advertisement in **Quebec Gazette**, May 13, 1783.

On the Island of Montreal the influence of the Loyalists was, apparently, felt earlier. Patrick Campbell, during his visit in 1792 when he noted "many spacious and fine farms, some of which are farmed by Englishmen, who cultivate and manure their land as is done in that country, and raise crops which astonish the natives, who are now beginning to follow their example."[8] The English he referred to must have included Loyalists and perhaps Hessians and other disbanded soldiers.

Had Haldimand not resisted the efforts of the Loyalists to remain in French Canada, their impact on agriculture might have spread beyond Montreal. But there were limits to the pressure that Haldimand could exert on the Loyalists. Apart from their experience of defeat and exile, many had acquired the habit of living as wards of a bureaucracy. Among most groups there were many who had mastered the art of writing letters to officials and preparing petitions. They had acquired skill in putting pressure on officials where it was likely to be effective as in many cases, they had been officials themselves.

Although land near the Upper Richelieu River had been granted in seigneury, there had been no permanent settlement there during the French regime, and the Abenaki Indians were content to use the area that became the Eastern Townships as hunting grounds. There was land ready for immediate settlement around Mississquoi Bay within easy reach of the Richelieu River. It is not surprising then that Loyalists squatted in this area on the site of present-day Clarenceville as early as 1777.[9] Between 1783 and 1792 there were about 20 petitions for land in this area, from both Loyalist and non-Loyalist

---

[8]Patrick Campbell, **Travels in North America** (Toronto 1937), 133.

[9]"Clarenceville Century Farmowner — Hawley Family," in **Missisquoi County Historical Society Report**, 1966, vi, 81.

Americans. Loyalist petitions were sponsored by officers of disbanded Provincial Corps such as Lt. Col. John Peters, Capts. John W. Myers and Thomas Sherwood.[10] One group headed by Capt. Azariah Pritchard bought a dubious title which James Robertson had acquired from the Indians.[11]

Haldimand, concerned, ordered Capt. Justus Sherwood to report on the Missisquoi Bay settlements. Sherwood reported that Loyalists, led by four former officers, were erecting huts there and marketing wheat at St. Jean.[12] Haldimand's first problem was to prevent further movement of the Loyalists in this direction from St. Jean and Sorel. He won a partial victory when Capt. Pritchard was induced to take a group of settlers to the Gaspé instead of moving them towards Missisquoi Bay.[13] As those already at Missisquoi Bay were not prepared to move, he then sent Lt. William Buckley to effect their removal.

Yet the governor seems to have been defeated by delaying tactics. In March 1974, Buckley arrived at the Missisquoi Bay settlement from where he reported that the settlers could not be removed until late spring.[14] Negotiations were renewed, but Haldimand remained firm. No Crown lands would be granted

---

[10]See Captains John W. Myers and Thomas Sherwood to Major R. Mathews, Oct. 26, 1783 (NAC: HP, MG21/B215/2/69); Lt. Col. John Peters to Haldimand, n.d. (ibid., 206-208).

[11]Wilbur Seibert, "The American Loyalists in the Eastern Seignories and Townships of Quebec," in **Transactions**, Royal Society of Canada, Section II, series 3, 1913, 35.

[12]NAC: HP, MG21/B162/210-11.

[13]Ibid., 392-97; see also, Return of Loyalists and Discharged Soldiers embarked on the Provincial Vessels for Chaleur Bay, June 9, 1784 (ibid., B168/30).

[14]B.D. Walker, "Missisquoi County — Eastern Townships, Quebec 1770s to 1867," unpublished MA thesis (McGill University 1974), 33-34.

to squatters; rations would be suspended, and the houses torn down. Yet no immediate action was taken, and with the departure of Haldimand in the summer of 1784, the 60 families in the area were secure for the moment and could survive without government rations.[15]

Haldimand's policy of keeping the frontier a wilderness had been defeated, but the Loyalist captains who had founded the settlement at Missisquoi Bay needed help at a higher level to secure legal title to their lands. They were soon rescued by men like Col. Henry Caldwell of Caldwell's Manor, who had purchased the Foucault seigneury which ran along the Richelieu near the frontier.[16] Caldwell agreed to present a petition, containing 380 signatures, to the Governor, Lord Dorchester, in 1786. This petition had been read by Thomas Dunn, a member of the Executive Council who acquired the seigneury of St. Armand in 1788. Dunn appointed Capt. Henry Ruiter, a Loyalist, as his land agent.[17] The seigneury was surveyed and land sold at £10 per 100 acres. Settlers still paid seigneurial dues at four pence per acre and could not claim the tools and rations provided for those who settled on Crown lands.

Similar arrangements were made on the neighbouring seigneuries of Christie's Manor[18] (Noyan) and Caldwell's

---

[15]Mathews to Sherwood, April 5, 1784 (NAC: HP, MG21/B63/181); Mathews to Capt. Ruiter, April 9, 1784 (**ibid.**, 263).

[16]Col. Henry Caldwell personally went to his seigniory in July 1784 to give titles to the tenants who had settled there, see **Quebec Gazette**, May 13 and 17, and June 30, 1784.

[17]Walker, "Missisquoi County," 38-39.

[18]R. Patterson, "General Gabriel Christie, Seignior of Noyan (Christie's Manor)," in **Missisquoi — a Store of Memories**, Missisquoi Historical Society, xii, 1972, 68-70.

Manor (Clarenceville) but not until 1792 were the Missisquoi Bay Loyalists in legal possession of their lands. Yet de facto possession lent substance to petitions and strengthened the hand of the land speculators who were seeking to reverse the policy of the "French party." With Haldimand, efforts to keep the border region as a preserve for future French Canadian settlement could hardly succeed.

By 1791 the alliance of Loyalists and land speculators had triumphed. Crown lands could be granted in "free and common soccage" and post-Loyalist Americans were being welcomed in what soon became the Eastern Townships in the same manner as they were being welcomed in Simcoe's new province of Upper Canada. Crown lands would be divided into townships of 10 square miles. each and granted to associates who would act under a leader or agent acceptable to the government and would take responsibility for surveying the land, opening a road through the township and securing signatures on petitions for land. The Missisquoi Bay Loyalists were ideally placed to act as such agents and the Missisquoi seigneuries served as areas of first settlement for Americans who, in some instances, came from as far away as New Jersey. Here they could pause before moving into the unsettled land in

Most Loyalists who became agents for associates had been, like Henry Ruiter, officers in the Provincial Corps. He continued to serve as an agent for the Dunn family, but took an active interest in the new township settlements. Another member of the family, John Ruiter, was appointed to a Board of Commissioners for the administration of oaths to American settlers; Jacob Ruiter settled near Cowansville, where he built a

---

[19]Cyrus Thomas, **Contributions to the History of the Eastern Townships** (Montreal 1866), 112.

sawmill and a gristmill on the Yamaska River.[20] The Ruiters[21] were a Dutch family from Albany County where they had been men of substance and must have brought with them some of their original capital as well as habits of enterprise and an ability to thrive in a pioneer society.

It was much the same with Capt. John Savage, born in Northern Ireland, who was on his way to becoming an important man in the Albany area when the Revolution changed the course of his life. After many wartime adventures, including several captures and escapes, Savage settled at Caldwell's Manor where he became a land agent for Col. Henry Caldwell. In 1792 he left the seigneurial lands to lead a company of associates to found the township of Shefford. Savage henceforth took a leading part in local affairs, becoming a lieutenant colonel of militia and commanding his battalion on the frontier in 1812 at the age of 72.[22]

Loyalist Gilbert Hyatt and his family played a leading part in Sherbrooke County; the original name of Sherbrooke was Hyatt's Mills.[23] Capt. Joshua Odell founded Odelltown; Frederick Scriver, Hemmingford; Nicholas Austin, Bolton; and Samuel Willard, Stukely. Mixed with these Loyalists were retired officers like Maj. Thomas Bray who applied for 5,000

---

[20]Address given by Dr. Cedric Cotton on Cowansville, in **Then and Now**, Missisquoi Historical Society, x, 1967, 27.

[21]Subsistence Account of Loyal Volunteers under Capt. Samuel Mackay, 1777 (NAC: HP, MG21/B167/I/109-112); Subsistence Return for Royalists attached to the King's Royal Regiment of New York, April 18, 1779 (**ibid.**, B166/4); see also, Return of King's Rangers, Oct. 6, 1784 (NAC: MG11/Q23/367).

[22]M.O. Vaudry, **Sketch of the Life of Captain John Savage** (Lennoxville 1921), 3-7.

[23]Catherine M. Day, **Pioneers of the Eastern Townships** (Montreal 1863), 37-38; Walker, "Missisquoi County," 33.

acres in Farnham, and non-Loyalist Americans like Isaac and William Coit who sought land along the Chaudière River.[24]

It is easier to trace the history of the more prominent Loyalists, but social distinctions were not great in a pioneer society. Settlers moved in groups of families who had to co-operate in order to survive. Links with the outside world were more easily secured by those of previous wealth and connections. Captains like Savage and Ruiter had raised companies at their own expense; clearly, they were more than yeomen farmers. Yet there were many Savages and Ruiters who were not captains. Previous importance was an advantage, but unless allied to great drive and energy, it was not sufficient to ensure prominence in the new settlements. Nearly all leaders of associates were the kind of men likely to become militia officers and justices of the peace, but they were more likely to achieve these distinctions if they were United Empire Loyalists.

The first concern of the Loyalists was to secure a foothold in the border area of the Province. This was accomplished by 1784. The second was to secure the abolition of seigneurial tenure in areas where they intended to settle. This was secured by 1792 after protracted petitioning.[25] Although township Loyalists had friends in the bureaucracy like Thomas Dunn and Henry Caldwell, they did not find a full place in the politics of Quebec

---

[24]Edwin P. Conklin, "Regional Quebec" in **Storied Province of Quebec**, ed. William Wood, ii, 925-26; see also, **Canada and its Provinces**, ed. Adam Shortt and A.G. Doughty, xv, 149-51.

[25]Petition of Your Majesty's Ancient and New Subjects, Inhabitants of the Province of Quebec, Oct. 24, 1784 (NAC: MG11/Q24/I/1-15); Petition of Sir John Johnson and the Loyalists, April 12, 1785, in Shortt and Doughty, **Documents Constitutional History**, 758-61.

until they secured representation in the provincial Assembly in 1829.

The Loyalists who settled in the Gaspé differed little from the settlers in the Eastern Townships, but they had among them disbanded soldiers of the 84th Loyal Highland Emigrant Regiment and a leaven of war refugees who had been driven from the Gaspé by revolutionary privateers. The disbanded Highland soldiers included some American Loyalists but for the most part they had been recruited in the loyal provinces and in Scotland.[26] These Loyalists and disbanded soldiers came to a sparsely settled land which was, nevertheless, already an area of conflict. Micmac Indians protested that Acadians were grazing cattle on their hunting grounds. Before the Revolution, New Englanders opposed the presence of Jersey-based fishermen on the Gaspé coast. These French-speaking protestant fishermen had among them the redoubtable Charles Robin who was forced to suspend fishing operations during the war, but had returned shortly before the arrival of the Loyalists. As Haldimand owned a seigneury on the Gaspé, he took a special interest in the area.[27]

The Gaspé already had some governmental machinery in the person of Lt. Gov. Maj. Nicholas Cox. Because of the rigors of the Gaspésian winters, Cox had made his headquarters in Quebec City until ordered to take up residence in the peninsula in 1778. At the end of the American revolutionary war, Cox was visited by Justus Sherwood who was investigating the possibilities of a Loyalist settlement at the Gaspé. Sherwood

---

[26]G. Murray Logan, **Scottish Highlanders and the American Revolution** (Halifax 1976), 15-17, 49.

[27]Blodwen Davies, **Gaspé: Land of History and Romance** (Toronto 1949) 176-89.

reported to Haldimand that the region was suitable for settlement[28] and by June 1784 a fleet of four small brigs and four whaleboats were carrying 315 Loyalists to the Gaspé.[29] In the course of the summer they were joined by 60 men of the 84th Regiment, for a total of 375.[30] These settlers, who had spent the latter years of the war at a refugee camp near Three Rivers and enjoyed the special favour of Haldimand, proved difficult to please.[31] Lt. Gov. Cox chose a site for them 54 miles west of the headquarters of Robin's fishing empire at Paspébiac. Here Loyalists of all ranks drew lots for land[32] and the town of New Carlisle, the birthplace of Premier René Levesque, was founded. Placed between Robin's Jerseymen and the Acadians, the Loyalists soon quarrelled with both. Loyalist petitions demanding land already held by Acadians were put aside by Haldimand.[33] So too, were Robin's protests that land given to Loyalists had been previously granted to him.[34]

Haldimand was aware of Robin's efforts to establish a fishing monopoly and he sought to protect Loyalist fishing rights by granting to individual settlers the right to use the beach during summer months. The Governor's intervention

---

[28]Sherwood to Haldimand, Aug. 23, 1783 (NAC: HP, MG21/B169/5); see also Wilbur Seibert, "The Loyalist Settlements on the Gaspé Peninsula," in **Transactions**, Royal Society of Canada, Section II, viii, 1915, 399-405.

[29]NAC: HP, MG21/B168/30-32; B138/364a; Barnes to Mathews, May 17, 1784 (**ibid.**, B138/358); see also **Quebec Gazette**, May 6 and 13, and June 3, 1784.

[30]Return of Loyalists and Discharged Soldiers Embarked on board Provincial Vessels for Chaleur Bay, Quebec, June 9, 1784 (NAC: HP, MG21/B168/30).

[31]Cox to Haldimand, July 3, 1784, cited in A.D. Flowers, **Loyalists of Bay Chaleur** (Victoria 1973), 60-62.

[32]Petition of Loyalists, Aug. 19, 1784 (**ibid.**, 68).

[33]Cox to Haldimand, Aug. 20, 1784 (**ibid.**, 81).

[34]Davies, **Gaspé**, 199.

on behalf of the Loyalists was apparently justified as reports of the customs collector in October 1784 showed that the new settlers "exported this year from Gaspé and Chaleur Bay 25,500 Quintals of dryed Codfish."[35]

In 1785 when Cox moved the seat of his government to New Carlisle, it was clear that the Loyalists were firmly established. Among them was the Welsh-born Capt. Azariah Pritchard who had diverted the contingent of Loyalists from settling in Missisquoi Bay. Like Sherwood, Pritchard had been employed in intelligence work during the revolutionary war.[36] Although he held a rank of captain in the King's Rangers, he must have lived in a Maritime environment as he had owned a ship before the revolution. Pritchard also had owned a gristmill and used the £450 paid as compensation for his losses to establish a mill in the Gaspé. He was an enterprising man who, after the interruption of an eight-year war, resumed his role as a man of means in the new environment.

On a slightly higher plane, Col. Isaac Man, formerly of Stillwater, New York, claimed £4,595 compensation for losses in the old Colonies and received £285; his son and partner of the same name received £78. Col. Man, who had also been given a pension of £30 a year, was made sheriff of the Gaspé district[37] where he would play a role similar to that of local representatives of the Family Compact in Upper Canada.

---

[35]Report of Customs Collector Thomas Ainslie, Oct. 1, 1784 (NAC: MG11/Q24/I/62).

[36]See Pritchard to Major Carleton, Sept. 16, 1780 (NAC: HP, MG21/B205/79).

[37]Flowers, **Loyalists of Bay Chaleur**, 69; Davies, **Gaspé**, 204.

The Seigneury of Sorel[38] was originally purchased by the Crown because of its strategic importance at the juncture of the Richelieu and the St. Lawrence Rivers. It was thus selected as a military rather than a Loyalist settlement, but most of the disbanded soldiers came from Loyalist units. Sorel was also selected as a site for a Chelsea-type hospital where military invalids and their dependents were under the care of Dr. Christopher Carter.[39]

By 1784 there were 316 Loyalists at Sorel[40] and some land had been cleared. When land was distributed, grants were kept down to 60 acres to ensure compact settlement. Town lots were provided for each settler and, as grants were for 100 acres or more, the balance of a settler's grant was allotted in Upper Canada.[41] Haldimand's intention was to found in Sorel a small colony of industrious, subsidized veterans who would presumably live in harmony; but by 1787 a report described them as "slothfully awaiting for the government to feed them." Personal jealousies, the report noted, "tempts them to falsely accuse the officers of government."[42] This situation had arisen in Sorel inspite of a clerical presence there in the person of Rev.

---

[38]For a description of Sorel prior to the arrival of the Loyalists, see Captain Shank's letterbook, 1778-1780 (McCord Museum: M7112).

[39]Walter S. White, "The Loyalists at Sorel," unpublished paper, March 1974 (Montreal Military and Maritime Museum); see also, Abbé Ivanhoe Caron, La colonisation de la Province de Québec débuts du régime anglais 1760-1791 (Quebec 1923, 3 vols.), i, 125.

[40]Return of Settlers at Sorel, Sept. 12, 1784 (NAC: HP, MG21/B168/44-46 and 111).

[41]Haldimand to Capt. Barnes, May 17, 1784 (ibid., B63/298); see NAC: RG8/C634a/96 and 102 for list of persons' names, present possessors of lots in Sorel drawn by refugee Loyalists in 1787.

[42]White, "The Loyalists of Sorel," 8.

John Doty, a Loyalist Anglican priest who had arrived July 4, 1784.[43] There was no Anglican clerical presence at the Gaspé, and the first cleric to appear on the frontier area of the Province was William Marsh of Caldwell's Manor, a Loyalist who was ordained a Baptist minister in 1796.[44]

Doty had been an S.P.G. missionary in Schenectady who, after his flight to Canada in 1777, became chaplain to the King's Royal Regiment of New York.[45] He visited St. Armand seigneury in 1798, making the first gesture of the established church toward the border settlements. Yet these settlements remained a religious dependency of American missions throughout the first decades of their existence.[46]

The well-known Loyalist Jessups family was represented at Sorel by Maj. Edward Jessup, formerly of New York. Like Col. Man in the Gaspé, he had been and continued to be a man of substance in his adopted Province, becoming a large landholder and judge of the Court of Appeals.[47] Less prominent but equally respectable was William Nelson, a distant cousin of Horatio.[48]

---

[43]Mathews to Rev. John Doty, July 5, 1784 (NAC: HP, MG21/B64/21).

[44]Subsistence Return for Royalists attached to the King's Royal Regiment of New York, April 18, 1779 (ibid., B166/5); Mathews to Marsh, July 5, 1784 (ibid., B64/28); see also, Françoise-Noël Smith, "The Establishment of Religious Communities in the Eastern Townships of Lower Canada 1799-1851," unpublished MA thesis (McGill University 1976), 39-40.

[45]Return of Officers of the late 1st battalion King's Royal Regiment of New York, encl. Haldimand to Sydney, Oct. 6, 1784 (NAC: HP, MG21/B167/Part 2/404); also listed in Ontario Historical Society Papers and Records, vol. 27, 1931, app.A, 320.

[46]John I. Cooper, The Blessed Communion (Montreal 1960), 110-111.

[47]White, "The Loyalists of Sorel," 16.

[48]For the Nelsons of Sorel see, L.-O. David, Biographies et Portraits (Montreal 1876), 276-77, 290; Wolfred Nelson, Wolfred Nelson et son Temps (Montreal 1946), 1; Charles Abrahall, "History of the diocese of

He first tried to establish an academy for young men at Three Rivers in 1783[49] but eventually settled with other Loyalists at Sorel, becoming a school master, an Anglican church warden, and father of the Patriote leaders Wolfred and Robert Nelson. Wolfred Nelson was elected to the Provincial Assembly in 1827, although living at St. Denis, from where he commanded the Patriote force in 1837. His younger brother, Robert, took the lead in Chasseur raids across the frontier in 1838.

What did these Patriote leaders owe to their Loyalist origins? Certainly not a conservative outlook, but perhaps a want of deference to members of the bureaucratic Anglophone establishment whom they regarded as social equals. They came to terms with the French fact by joining the majority party in Quebec.

For a time Sorel became an anglophone pocket at the mouth of the Richelieu River. Isaac Weld reported in 1795 that it was the only town between Montreal and Quebec where "the English language is dominant," and that the "inhabitants are largely Loyalists from the United States."[50] A small contingent of Loyalists, consisting of the Albrights, Jones, Hydes and Leroys, settled at St. Andrew's East; the Van Kleeks at Van Kleek Hill; and the Cushings at Lachute, providing a nucleus for anglophone settlement in the Ottawa Valley. Yet, as in the Eastern Townships, they merely served to open the door to the flood of post-Loyalist Americans who came after 1792.[51] Small

---

Montreal," (unpublished manuscript, 2 vols., at the Anglican Archives, Montreal), i, 71.

[49] Quebec Gazette, Dec. 11, 1783, see William Nelson's advertisement.

[50] Isaac Weld, "Travels Through the States of North America," in Craig, **Early Travellers in the Canadas**, 19.

[51] Benjamin Wales, **Memoirs of Old St. Andrew's**, (Montreal 1934), 8, 22-23.

groups of Loyalists remained at St. Jean, Chambly and Three Rivers, the latter town being represented in the Assembly by Charles Richard Ogden during the 1830s.[52]

Beauharnois was not an area of Loyalist settlement, but the Ellice family which acquired the seigneury owned property in the Mohawk Valley from whence they were driven during the course of the revolution. Their family and business connections on both sides of the Atlantic let them into the inner circles of British politics. Thus it was Edward Ellice, seigneur of Beauharnois, who acted as agent of the anglophone party in the British parliament in the 1820s.[53]

At Quebec City the Loyalists were to influence the destinies of the Province by displacing the power of the Adam Mabane party in the Executive and Legislative Councils. This triumph over the "French party" was largely the work of William Smith, former Chief Justice of New York, and of his son-in-law, the younger Jonathan Sewell. Smith's influence had begun in New York where he had won the confidence of Sir Guy Carleton. When Carleton was raised to the peerage as Lord Dorchester and returned to Canada in 1786 to resume the role of governor, William Smith came with him as chief justice, bringing imaginative plans for the improvement of the Province.

Before Smith arrived in Quebec, Mabane's authority had been challenged first by Chief Justice Peter Livius and then by Attorney General James Monk, both American-educated civil servants, but not Loyalists. Livius and Monk had attacked the

---

[52]Return of Settlers at Sorel, Chambly, St. Johns...Sept. 12, 1784 (NAC: HP, MG21/B168/44-46).

[53]Dorothy E.T. Long, "The Elusive Mr. Ellice," in **Canadian Historical Review**," (March 1942), xxiii, no. 1, 44-46, 55-56.

policy of preserving French civil law and had made much of
the inconsistencies and anomalies of the existing legal system.
Because of these attacks, Livius had been dismissed from office
before Smith arrived[54] and Monk shortly afterwards.[55] In
debates concerning law, Mabane, a self-educated amateur, was
certainly no match for the new Chief Justice, William Smith.
Yet beneath the arguments about the technicalities of the law
was the cultural conflict which had been resolved in favour of
French Canada in 1774. The coming of the Loyalists meant that
the policy of the Quebec Act would be challenged, and the
program of the anglophone community restated in more
attractive language by the Loyalist intellectuals, Smith and
Sewell.

The substance of this program was the cultural
Americanization of Quebec. Smith shared with most Loyalists
and Montreal merchants as well as with the victorious in the
old Colonies, assumptions about North American society
which were never challenged by the revolution. All assumed
that the continent was ordained by nature to be English-
speaking, and Protestant or secular. The assimilation of cultural
minorities was necessary to enable them to compete on terms
of equality with the continental majority, and anachronistic
laws and customs must be removed. Applied to Quebec society,
this meant that the seigneurial system, French civil law, the
special position of the Roman Catholic church and, ultimately,
the French language, must go.

Smith did not believe that Americans were natural
republicans and anglophobes. He saw, consequently, no

---

[54]**Diary and Selected Papers of Chief Justice William Smith, 1784-1793,**
ed. L.F.T. Upton (Toronto 1963 and 1965, 2 vols.), i, 107-109.
[55]Sydney to Monk, April 3, 1789 (NAC: MG11/Q40/108).

danger in the Americanization of the Province. Removal of what he considered to be cultural and institutional anachronisms would help realize his ideal of making Canada a model of good government which would include a federation of the remaining British provinces and a system of universal education, crowned by a university.[56] His plans, similar to those which John Graves Simcoe hoped to introduce into Upper Canada, would attract American settlers and, by force of example, lead the old Colonies back to the Empire.

Loyalists of all classes were more inclined to dismiss the egalitarian principles enunciated in the Declaration of Independence as a joke in bad taste than they were to argue about their implications. They could see no necessary connection between the natural rights of man and the diffused reign of terror to which they had been subjected by the excesses of the revolution. As Professor George Rawlyk has pointed out, both "loyalism" and "federalism" were reactions to the revolution.[57]

Misunderstanding still exists about the Loyalists and post-revolutionary America. Professor Carol Berkin in her admirable biography of the elder Jonathan Sewell, Chief Justice of Massachusetts, found him to be a man at odds with his times for whom there was no room in the "Country Massachusetts and her sister Colonies hoped to become."[58] In 1777, Sewell had been at odds with his times, but by 1790 the times had changed.

---

[56]**Report of the Committee on the subject of promoting the Means of Education** (Quebec 1790).

[57]George Rawlyk, "The Federalist-Loyalist Alliance in New Brunswick, 1784-1815," in **Humanities Association Review**, xxvii, no.1 (spring 1976), 142-60.

[58]Carol Berkin, **Jonathan Sewell: Odyssey of an American Loyalist** (New York 1974), 160-161.

There was considerable harmony between the thoughts of Sewell reflecting on the causes of his exile and those of the American Federalists who were beginning to fear that if the revolution was not brought to a halt, they would suffer the same fate as that of the Loyalists. The new enemy was the Jeffersonian left. Loyalists, now no longer feared, would be welcomed back but their property would not be restored. Of those responsible for Sewell's exile, James Otis was living in seclusion, while Samuel Adams and John Hancock were excluded from influence. The Boston of the Cabots and the Lodges was taking shape; the tea party was over.[59]

Post-Loyalist Americans in the Eastern Townships and the Ottawa Valley undoubtedly reflected the climate of opinion in Federalist New England. Lt. Gov. Henry Hamilton noted in April, 1785, that there were three classes of refugees: those who had fought against the revolution; those who opposed it but had been unable to resist; and a third class. This third class, he said, were "people who do not pretend to have been sufferers in defence of British Laws and Government, but are Actual Sufferers under the ruinous and arbitrary Laws and Constitutions of the States."[60] In Kenneth Roberts' novel, *Lydia Bailey*, a Loyalist judge returning from exile finds himself to the left of the ruling Federalist party.[61] As Jeffersonians and Federalists turned the intolerant spirit once directed against the Loyalists against one another, many of the post-Loyalists who came to Canada were fleeing from the over-politicized

---

[59]Harold and James Kirker, **Bulfinch's Boston 1787-1817** (New York 1964), 16-24.
[60]Lt. Gov. Henry Hamilton to Lord Sydney, April 5, 1785 (NAC: MG11/Q24/I/244).
[61]Kenneth Roberts, **Lydia Bailey** (Garden City, New York 1942), 1-15.

atmosphere of the new republic. When war came in 1812, the loyalty crisis was not in the Eastern Townships, but in New England.

During the post-revolutionary years, there was more Utopian idealism in the plans of William Smith and Simcoe than in those of Alexander Hamilton and Washington. In the pioneer society of Upper Canada this made little difference, but in French and Catholic Canada, Utopian idealism had its dangers. Smith could only hope to succeed in the role of benevolent despot. Like utilitarian-imperialists of the last century and revolutionaries today, he had a reluctance to share power with "unenlightened majorities." Smith's first task was to neutralize the influence of Mabane's party in the appointed Councils. This was achieved by 1789.[62] His second task was to persuade Dorchester and ultimately London of the wisdom of his plans. Though impressed by Smith's vision, Dorchester hesitated to reverse his own policy. Initiative was consequently left to London where efforts to reconcile the policy of the Quebec Act and the interests of the Loyalists resulted in the Constitutional Act of 1791. Under the new system, the Quebec anglophones, deprived of Loyalist ballast on the upper St. Lawrence, would face a permanent French majority in the Assembly. Smith's victory over Mabane mattered little because now the issues of the Plains of Abraham would be contested in the elected Assembly. Yet there was consolation to be found in the opening of the Eastern Townships to American settlement.

Smith died at the end of 1793, leaving the contest in the new arena to his very able son-in-law, the younger Jonathan Sewell. Sewell, who had come to Quebec as solicitor-general, wrote

---

[62]L.F.S. Upton, **The Loyal Whig: William Smith of New York and Quebec** (Toronto 1969), 198.

books on French law as it applied to Quebec; he wrote, too, about the commercial possibilities of the St. Lawrence; and, like Smith, he offered a plan for federation.[63] From 1796 until 1808 he represented Sorel, and then became chief justice. Fluent in French, he played a violin and was even complimented by Garrick's friend, Mrs. Siddons, on his talent for amateur dramatics. Sewell was, perhaps, the most able among those who made up what became known as the Chateau Clique and the British party. With his help, the program of the anglophones was restated to include reunion of the provinces and more encouragement of American immigration. London still had to be converted and it was not until 1807 that Governor Sir James Craig was willing to press the claims of Sewell and his friends on the Colonial Office.

As it was wartime, the obvious course of the British party was to insist that an unassimilated French population, with its own customs and institutions, was a security risk. No convincing evidence could be found to support this honestly-held belief. Yet the fact that such charges had been made and repeated inspired French Canadians to make a counter-charge that the Americanization policy of the anglophones constituted the real danger to the British connection. Pierre Bédard and his fellow proprietors of Le Canadien denounced the Eastern Township settlements as a barbarian invasion. Anticipating Etienne-Pascal Taché's "last cannon shot," they declared that French Canadians provided the real defence against the "idée

---

[63]Jonathan Sewell, **On the Advantages of Opening up the River St. Lawrence to the Commerce of the World** (London 1814); An Essay on the **Judicial History of France...Quebec** (Quebec 1824); **Plan for a Federation of British North America** (Quebec 1824).

republicain" and "la race Yankee."[64] Bédard was an independent thinker who had made a study of the British Constitution. He found able allies in the second generation Loyalists, James and Andrew Stuart, sons of the Chaplain of the second battalion of the King's Royal Regiment of New York.[65] Like the Nelson brothers in the 1830s, the Stuarts, temporarily at least, joined the francophone party. In 1809, James Stuart had been dismissed as solicitor general by Governor Craig. It was his dismissal rather than his sympathy with French culture that influenced his politics. Nevertheless, he was a formidable adversary. It was on his initiative that the Assembly instituted impeachment proceedings against Jonathan Sewell. For a time Stuart became leader of the francophone party[66] and thus the issues of the Seven Years War were contested on the floor of the Assembly with Loyalist champions on both sides.

The Loyalists in Quebec were a cross section of society in the northern Colonies. The majority were yeomen farmers who founded a pioneer society in the Eastern Townships or became fishermen on the Gaspé coast. Few, it seems, could transform themselves into artisans at Sorel. Prominent among them were captains like the Dutch Ruiters, the Ulster Savages, the Pritchards and the Sherwoods, who raised companies during the war and later founded settlements. They were perhaps the social equals of school masters like William Nelson, Anglican clergy like John Doty and William Marsh the Loyalist Baptist

---

[64]Le Canadien, Quebec, Nov. 22, 1806, Dec. 24, 1808.

[65]For Rev. John Stuart, see Petition of Rev. John Stuart to Haldimand, Dec. 31, 1783 (NAC: HP, MG21/B215/2); MG11/Q24/I/66); see also The Report of the Bureau of Archives for the Province of Ontario (Toronto 1905), cxxxiv.

[66]Fernand Ouellet, Le Bas Canada 1781-1840 (Ottawa 1976), 303-309.

minister. On a higher plane were the Jessups who raised regiments and became extensive landowners in the Province. Still higher were the Ellices who enjoyed a place in trans-Atlantic commerce and the Johnsons who transferred their financial empire from the Mohawk Valley to Montreal. The achievement of these Loyalists was to found small isolated settlements in the Gaspé and to open the door to American settlers in the Eastern Townships.

More interesting were their intellectuals like the Smiths, Sewells and Ogdens who became senior civil servants, and the Stuart brothers who for a while led the opposition in the Assembly. Smith and Sewell gave the program of the anglophone party an intellectual depth which the Grants and the Monks had been unable to provide. As advocates of an assimilation policy, they acted as Americans rather than Loyalists, which the opposition, assisted by the Stuart brothers, would point out. There were no British or monarchial reasons for imposing cultural uniformity on the province. By rejecting the revolution, the Loyalist intellectuals had rejected the ideology and zeal which could have given an assimilation policy the appearance of a crusade. They were strong enough to revive the hopes of the anglophone party in Quebec, but not strong enough to pose a serious threat to French culture.

CHAPTER 3

The Loyalists in the Montreal Area, 1775-1784

by Earle Thomas

The circumstances of the Loyalists' arrival in Quebec were quite different from those who fled to Nova Scotia. First, most of the Quebec Loyalists were refugees from the frontier regions, the northern reaches of New York, Pennsylvania and Vermont. Many of the able-bodied men from these areas had fought under Burgoyne on his ill-fated march to Saratoga, enlisted in provincial regiments like Butler's, Jessup's and the King's Royal Regiment of New York, which eventually served out of Canada. Refugees from the northern regions trekked into Montreal, mostly along the Hudson-Champlain-Richelieu route, others by way of Niagara or Oswego.

These refugees became the Loyalist settlers of Canada, an estimated seven or eight thousand of them, who trickled into the Province throughout the duration of the Revolutionary War, and even for 10 or 15 years after, making it most difficult for the authorities to distinguish between true Loyalists and mere land-seeking American frontiersmen. Only a few, like the companies led by Michael Grass and Peter Van Alstine, made the trip from New York to Quebec by sea. The overland stream of Americans into Quebec began even before the outbreak of fighting in the Thirteen Colonies. As early as June 2, 1774, Col. Christie at St. Johns had complained of the "unreasonable expectations" of the immigrants who had already arrived. In the early summer of 1775 Lt.Col. Allan Maclean fled from Schenectady to Quebec with, according to W. H. Siebert, a party of 80 fighting men and Sir John Johnson arrived the next summer. The tide continued to flow after Burgoyne's defeat at Saratoga in 1777, reaching spring proportions at the close of the war in 1783, ebbing slightly as the years rolled by and subsiding only with the outbreak of the war of 1812. The authorities were challenged by the gigantic task of providing these American immigrants with land and assistance.

Although there had been stragglers ever since 1774, the first organized group to arrive in Quebec was the Royal Highland Emigrants led by Lt.Col.Allan Maclean from Schenectady via the Oswego route in the summer of 1775, consisting of 80 men. Maclean and his troops were dispatched from Quebec to St. Johns in September to push back the American invaders, but they only got as far as Sorel. Left in a precarious position by the desertion of many of the local militia, he and his troops returned to Quebec where they later played an important part in defeating Gen. Montgomery and Benedict Arnold in the fight for the City.

The activities of Maclean and his men led them only to the periphery of Montreal. The first notable influx of Loyalists into the City itself was led by Sir John Johnson in the spring of 1776. In January Gen. Schuyler had sent Gen. Herkimer with a force of 3,000 militia to Johnstown to bring Sir John to terms. They met near Johnson Hall, where Sir John was disarmed and placed on parole. Towards the end of May, his arrest imminent, Sir John escaped with almost 200 followers, finally reaching the St. Lawrence near modern Cornwall. They arrived in Montreal on June 19, the day after the Americans had fled. Sir John was immediately commissioned by Gov. Carleton to raise the King's Royal Regiment of New York with his followers as the nucleus. The first additions on record to the Corps were refugees who joined at Crown Point in November, the same month the regiment went into winter quarters at Pointe Claire.

They were joined later in the month by the Jessup brothers and their troops, who, the following June, became the King's Loyal Americans. Ebenezer and Edward Jessup had fled from Albany in October, 1776 with a party of 60 men; they reached Crown Point in time to join with Carleton and his force before they returned to Canada for the winter. Organized by Carleton into three companies, and led by the Jessups and Jonathan Jones, once north they were temporarily attached to Johnson's regiment at Pointe Claire for convenience in drawing rations.

John Peters had arrived in Quebec in March, 1776, and was in Montreal in June with the warning that the Americans were planning another attack on the City. Peters had been a judge in Gloucester County, New York, and in 1774 had been driven from his home by a mob. Dr. Samuel Adams of Arlington arrived soon after the Jessups with four officers and 26 privates, according to the muster roll of Aug. 9, 1777.

The McDonells of Johnstown with approximately 200 recruits were the next to arrive. Alexander and John McDonell, tenants on Johnson's estate on the Mohawk, had been imprisoned for their Loyalist activities in January, 1776. Having received permission to visit their families, they escaped into Canada in the spring of 1777, bringing with them a group of Scottish and German Loyalists, all of whom enlisted in either Johnson's or Maclean's regiment.[1] The McDonells and their men no doubt proceeded straight to Sir John's encampment in Pointe Claire, since the latter was in charge of all American refugees. It is reasonable to suppose that the other refugees

---

[1]Siebert, The American Loyalists in the Eastern Seignories and Townships of Quebec."

previously mentioned spent the winter of 1776-77 in Pointe Claire as well.

The fall of 1777 saw a large influx of Loyalists in Quebec. Burgoyne returned to Quebec from England in the spring of 1777 with a commission placing him in command of the British army in the province, superseding Gov. Carleton. Large numbers of Loyalists joined him as he struck out for Lake Champlain and the upper Hudson. Others joined the force of Col. Barry St. Leger on his progress down the Mohawk, at the end of which he expected to join forces with Burgoyne at Albany. The Loyalists attached themselves to the British army in upper New York either singly or in groups. Dr. James Stuart of Ulster County joined St. Leger with 52 men and Jacob Miller with 50. Large numbers flocked to Burgoyne's colours at various points on his march: Edward Carscallen of Camden with 39 men; Samuel Perry of Saratoga with 47, Isaac Man Jr. of Still Water with 57; Daniel Jones with 30; John Howard with 100; Hugh Munro with enough to form the nucleus of a company; Francis Pfister and Robert Leake with a group of 80 which soon increased to 200; William and Thomas Fraser of Tryon County who had escaped imprisonment in Albany with 100; Gershom French with 94; Capt. Daniel McAlpin with 60; Peter Van Alstine of Kinderhook with 30; and Alexander Cruikshank who had escaped from Esopus prison with six others. Col. Peters was not long in recruiting 164 more.[2] Thus there were over 1,000 Loyalists in Burgoyne's forces that are actually accounted for. It is certain that there were a great many more, as proved to a degree by a return in the War Office Records showing 800 Provincials alive at the end of the campaign.

---

[2]Ibid., 7-8.

The date at which the Loyalists fled into Canada in the autumn of 1777 after Burgoyne's defeat is uncertain. Some were taken prisoner and managed to escape; the less fortunate did not get to Canada until they were released at the close of the war. Many decided that it was prudent to take their departure during the interval between the surrender and the signing of the convention. Col. Peters was one who set out from Burgoyne's camp, apparently with the general's blessing, on the night of Oct. 16, while others left whenever the opportunity presented itself, and set out on the risky flight to Canada and safety.

Sir John Johnson's "Royal Greens" had left immediately after St. Leger's disaster at Fort Stanwix and stationed themselves at Lachine. The corps of the other leaders, MacKay, McAlpin, Peters, Jessup, Leake and Adams had also made their way into Quebec and by the close of 1777 most had returned, along with other numerous supporters of the King's cause. By this time the many Loyalists could not be ignored by the Government. Carleton on Jan. 12, 1778, ordered that all refugees, regardless of what corps they were connected with, were to be attached for quarters and rations to Sir John Johnson's regiment. Those present at Burgoyne's signing of the terms of surrender were consequently on parole not to fight against the Americans were to do no duty. The leaders of the various corps tried to collect pay for their men and themselves for services in the 1777 campaign and recruiting excursions into the American colonies. Meanwhile destitute refugees from the south continued to pour into Quebec and join the Loyalist corps and by the summer of 1778 there were 600 Loyalist soldiers in the provinces and by the close of the war there were about 50 companies, comprising 3,000 or more men.[3]

Candidates for the Loyalist regiments were not only American refugees — there were countless women and children, dependents of the Loyalist soldiers, and the widows and orphans of men who had died in the King's service. There were loyal men who could or would not volunteer for military service and found other means of earning a livelihood, and there were those who had no means of subsistence other than the bounty of the King.

They left their homes because life had become untenable for them in the Thirteen Colonies. The lack of stability frightened them, the vision of a state controlled by certain revolutionary leaders appalled them. In addition the community had deteriorated. No longer were they regarded as respected citizens, but objects of scorn, derision and persecution, and finally their property was confiscated, leaving them homeless and bereft of the means of earning a living. Finally, they fled for their lives, often only taking with them the clothes on their backs.

A few lived near enough to the border that they were able to make their way into Canada on their own. Others were led on foot by scouts who knew the old trails through the forest, scouts who sometimes were the man of the family, who had permission from the government to return for them or who had already brought his family with him. Some, no doubt, travelled part way by means of water conveyance, as Lake Champlain was still in the hands of the British.

Many Loyalists came down Lake Champlain in British vessels under flags of truce, then down the Richelieu to St.

---

[3]A.L. Burt, **The Old Province oi Quebec** (Toronto: Ryerson Press 1913; reprint ed. 2 vols. McClelland & Stewart Limited 1968), 2:4.

Johns, and from there they were dispersed to the various Loyalist camps. By this route, for most of the war, American prisoners were exchanged for the families of Loyalist soldiers. The system was advantageous to the Americans; they got their men back and, although in accordance with the parole convention of the day, they were not to participate again in military operations against the British, there were many other ways in which they could be gainfully employed. As well the Americans were also glad to be rid of the families of their traitorous brethren. Vessels picked up refugees at a number of points along Lake Champlain, like Mill Bay, Pointe au Fer, and Crown Point. Campbell and Stevens arrived at St. Johns in September 1778 with a party of 18, mainly their own families, and a few days later another group arrived from Albany and the Connecticut River area. A third group came in the following July and another a month later, and so it continued for the duration of the war.

Other Loyalists found it more difficult to get away. Aware of their plight, Frederick Haldimand, Carleton's successor as governor in June 1778, sent out expeditions to assist them. In response to the Loyalists pleas from Johnstown on March 17, 1780, Haldimand dispatched Sir John Johnson with a force of 528 men to their rescue. They left St. Johns by boat on May 3 and landed eight days later at West Bay on Lake Champlain, reaching Johnstown after a march of 10 days.[4] Sir John's attack on May 21 surprised everyone except the local Loyalists. Gov. Clinton assembled the militia and attempted unsuccessfully to intercept the invaders at Ticonderoga, but they made it safely to

---

[4]Siebert, "The American Loyalists in the Eastern Seignories and Townships of Quebec," 20-21.

their boats at Crown Point and fled.[5] They reached St. Johns on June 5 with 40 prisoners and 150 Loyalists. They were only one of several expeditions of varying success, and refugee families continued to flood into the province. Considerable numbers arrived in the autumn of 1780 by bateau via Lake Champlain and the Richelieu to St. Johns, due to the activities of officers and men from different Loyalist corps.

It has been claimed by at least one historian that small scouting and recruiting parties were the most successful agents in bringing refugees into Canada.[6] While most of the able-bodied men enlisted or pursued a profession or a trade, there were many destitute who were forced to rely on government to keep them from perishing from hunger and cold, which strained the financial resources of the government.

As early as July, 1779, there were 855 Loyalists receiving government allowances in Quebec. Of these, Montreal, along with the villages of Lachine and Pointe Claire, attracted the largest number of refugees. Montreal, as the metropolis, provided amenities not found at the posts along the Richelieu, which, because of the lower cost of living, were favoured by Haldimand as refugee centres. Few Loyalists located at the first of these posts, Ile aux Noix, as it was too close to the border for safety. Rather, Loyalists were housed at St. Johns, Chambly, St. Ours and Sorel, with provincial soldiers stationed at each fort, often accompanied by their families. Widows and wives of absent Loyalists were usually sent to Machiche, a village established across Lac St. Pierre from Sorel on the seigneurie of Conrad Gugy. The 853 ration-receiving Loyalists in the summer of 1779 were located as follows: 209 at St. Johns, 27 at Chambly,

---

[5]Ward, **The War of Revolution**, 2:647.

[6]Siebert, "The American Loyalists...in the Eastern Townships," 23.

87 at Sorel, 196 at Machiche, 126 at Pointe Claire, and 208 at Montreal.[7] These were the figures stated in Daniel McAlpin's report of his first muster.

In spring of 1779 the number of Loyalists in Quebec increased so rapidly that Sir John Johnson was put in charge of the refugees by Gov. Haldimand. The Governor also appointed Capt. Daniel McAlpin as Inspector of the Loyalists, who was sent to Sorel with 40 men on May 27, 1779, to officially assume command of the unofficial Loyalists in Quebec on June 1.[8]

Capt. McAlpin soon discovered that his new position was not an easy one. Not only were insufficient provisions and living quarters common, but the Loyalists were often troublesome and impossible to please. McAlpin reported in one of his many letters to Haldimand's secretary, Capt. Robert Mathews, that he found "great difficulty in managing" the Loyalists,[9] and in another "The truth is there is no such thing as satisfying those people; if you give them provision they would have you put (it) in their mouths."[10]

Every attempt was made to provide Loyalists not in the army or trade with gainful employment. There was much to be done: buildings to be constructed in which to house the Loyalists, trees to be felled for firewood and lumber, fortifications to be erected or repaired, bateaux to be manned. It was quite easy to persuade a recalcitrant man to work by simply cutting him off the provision list if he refused. Women and

---

[7]Queen's University Archives (henceforth QUA), Haldimand Papers (henceforth HP), 84/21826/12, Daniel McAlpin's Report to Haldimand, July 1, 1779.

[8]QUA: HP, 81/21821/15, McAlpin to Mathews, June 3, 1779.

[9]QUA: HP, 81/21821/46, McAlpin to Mathews, Jan. 28, 1780.

[10]QUA: HP, 81/21821/63, McAlpin to Mathews, May 30, 1780.

older children were expected to make their contribution; women who found nothing else were set to work laundering for the non-commissioned officers and soldiers. But there were many, the old, the young, the sick, the wounded, who were entirely dependent on the government for their subsistence.

Before any definite plans were established for their maintenance, it was mandatory that the numbers, conditions and locations of the refugees be known with some degree of accuracy. To take such a survey McAlpin at first thought to call all Loyalists together at Sorel in order to register them. In his letter to Haldimand on June 3, 1779, he suggested that the governor get in touch with Brig.Gen. Powell, the officer commanding in the Montreal area, "where a great number of Loyalists were quartered in a straggling Manner that I must see them here on this spot before I can make a satisfactory Return to Your Excellency," and willing to except "old men, sick Women and Children" and would send an "Intelligent Officer" to see them.[11]

But the Loyalists did not come to McAlpin, who reported less than a month later "Agreeable to Your Excellency's orders in your letter of June 7 I have taken a tour of St. Johns, Montreal, Lachine, Mashies (Machiche) and I have seen every individual mentioned in the Return of Loyalists as also those annexed to Corps."[12] From this time on McAlpin kept abreast of the situation and submitted periodic returns of the Loyalists entitled to draw rations. In the fall of 1779 he reported that many were in want of clothing with the weather turning colder,

---

[11]QUA: HP, 81/21821/15, McAlpin to Haldimand, June 3, 1779.
[12]QUA: HP, 81/21821/23, McAlpin to Haldimand, July 1, 1779.

especially those from the "upper country." "I am daily pestered with petitions from distressed Loyalists," he wrote.[13]

These distressed refugees were to be cared for in areas where the cost of living was less than that in Montreal, and in concentrated groups rather than scattered among the Canadians for more reasons than one. First, Haldimand was aware that the habitants might be corrupted by American agents posing as Loyalists living amongst them. Second, he believed that the Loyalists could be administered and controlled more easily if living in homogeneous groups removed from outside influences which might prove undesirable. St. Ours on the Richelieu was Haldimand's choice as their ideal settlement, far enough from the border for safety and near enough to the stronghold of Sorel for supplies and military protection.

Consequently, Mathews sent McAlpin orders in late November to move Montreal Loyalists to St. Ours, the only exception to be those "who from infirmities or some peculiar circumstances must remain in Montreal."[14] McAlpin agreed, although he noted winter was now upon them, the river was frozen over, and the march by land would pose some difficulty. Montreal Loyalists agreed with McAlpin, who in January was forced to report from St. Ours: "The Families from Montreal is not yet arrived here and I have been so indisposed for a cold I got with a pain in my ear that I could not go for them myself."[15] Brig.Gen. Allan Maclean, commanding officer of the district, and Montreal's military governor, was so incensed with those Loyalists who refused to leave the City that he cut off their rations and firewood. At first they pleaded inability to pay for

---

[13]QUA: HP, 84/21826/23, McAlpin to Mathews, Oct. 20, 1779.
[14]QUA: HP, 83/21823/17, Mathews to McAlpin, Nov. 19, 1779.
[15]QUA: HP, 81/21821/39, McAlpin to Mathews, Jan. 3, 1780.

the conveyances required to transport them to St. Ours; Maclean countered by offering free transportation, and ordered 30 sled trains from Varennes stayed a day in town with no move from the Loyalists. Finally, the exasperated officer called their bluff by sending the trains to their doors; 36 of the Loyalist men with their wives and children refused to come out of their houses.[16]

The contumacious Loyalists were not to draw any more provisions or firewood until Captain McAlpin arrived in the City to look into the situation. He was in Montreal on January 31, and wrote to Mathews four days later: "I have taken upon me to strike off all able-bodied men who refuse to comply with His Excellency's orders in going to St. Ours." Others whom he considered quite able to support themselves without aid were also cut off as well. Those unable to leave town for whatever reason, and others in dire need had their names placed on the list.[17]

What finally transpired in the St. Ours situation is not clear. In a letter to Mathews dated on the same day as McAlpin's. Brig.Gen. Maclean wrote: "Some people have put it into McAlpin's head that it were best to leave the Loyalists here as they are until the beginning of May, that the carriages they will want now will be more expensive than water carriage in the month of May next, and that this is a severe season for moving them."[18] A few more Loyalists probably did move to St. Ours, but not the number anticipated. And it is certain that many ordered to St. Ours remained in Montreal for the duration of the war.

---

[16]QUA: HP, 59/21789/89, Maclean to Mathews, Jan. 6, 1780.
[17]QUA: HP, 81/21821/48, McAlpin to Mathews, Feb. 3, 1780.
[18]QUA: HP, 59/21789/104, Maclean to Mathews, Feb. 3, 1780.

McAlpin sympathized with the Loyalists' hardships and problems, but with malingerers and imposters he had no scruples about removing their names from the provision list. A Scot by birth, he had entered the British army as an ensign ca:1745, and was active in the capture of Quebec in 1759. He remained in the army until 1772, at which time he sold his captain's commission and settled with his family in the Albany area. At the outbreak of the Revolution he owned several thousand acres near Saratoga and a comparable tract near modern White River, Vermont. Steadfastly loyal, he was finally forced to flee from his home, raised a company of men, and finally arrived in Quebec after Burgoyne's defeat.

When McAlpin arrived in Montreal at the end of January 1780 he still suffered from an illness. By the middle of February he had composed a new list of Loyalists living in or near Montreal, with his recommendations for their rations and disposition, which was submitted to Gov.Haldimand. McAlpin continued to work. On March 27 he wrote to Mathews that he intended to settle all families from the "upper country" somewhere in the Montreal area where they would be able to learn news of their friends and relatives back home. He found it inconvenient to have them strung out at St. Johns, Montreal, St. Ours and Sorel and recommended that Gov. Haldimand settle on a place "convenient to wood and water." There they could build homes, be company for one another, and be looked after with relative ease. "It is impossible for me," he wrote, "to know their situation or their circumstances in the Straggling Manner they are at present. Besides the people require some person of authority to keep them within bounds, and make them in some degree useful to government, at least as many of them as are fit to be employed."[19]

The health of Maj.McAlpin (he had received a long overdue promotion) continued to deteriorate, but by mid-May he fancied that he had picked up a little and proposed returning to St. Ours to be near his duty, but Dr. Blake advised against it. He submitted his subsistence returns of June 22, requested a commission for his only son on the 29th, carried on into July, and died on July 21 after a military career of 35 years.

With McAlpin gone, many Loyalists remained in Montreal, which, in 1779, had between five and six thousand people. A large proportion were French Canadians, but now there were many whose mother tongue was English. Many veterans of Wolfe's army, particularly Scots, had remained, some of them marrying French women. Scottish and American merchants then began to move in, maintaining commercial ties with Boston, Albany and New York. At the beginning of the Revolution there were some 200 English-speaking families in Montreal, causing American refugees to feel more at home. They were also attracted by the churches, shops, taverns and business establishments which Montreal had to offer. For the men there were business and trade opportunities. For widows and wives of those enlisted there was the companionship of other Americans.

The Loyalists kept life interesting in Montreal. In the autumn of 1779, Brig.Gen Maclean wrote to Mathews: "I am so plagued with these Royalists real and pretended that I wish to God the General would be so good as to order some officer of McAlpin's corps here to get them all down to Machiche or

---

[19]QUA: HP, 81/21821/65, McAlpin to Mathews, March 27, 1780.

Pointe du Lac, for they are doing no good Here."[20] Maclean, first and foremost a British soldier, the possessor of a quick temper and military impatience, was not always able to understand the plight of the Loyalists. His efforts to pass the buck, however, were fruitless; the Loyalists remained in Montreal to plague him.

The maintenance of the Loyalists outside Montreal was easier on the purse but harder on the officials' nerves. Some refugees, like those in Machiche in particular, were chronic complainers. In January 1780 McAlpin was forced to deal with Jeremiah French, the officer in charge of Machiche Loyalists, and seven others who were leaders in promoting discontent. "It will be a reflection on me." McAlpin wrote to French, "for appointing a man who does all he can to Create Disorder in place of quailing it which was your duty to do."[21] The troublemakers were punished by being issued "Salt beef instead of Pork or Fresh Beef."[22] McAlpin found those not attached to a regiment very difficult to handle and whenever he could he organized them into groups to be paid as privates for work assigned to them.[23]

As the number of Loyalists increased, so did the problems, as his successor, Maj. John Nairne, soon learned. Refugees arrived in such profusion that their maintenance became an intolerable drain on the public purse. "The subsistence of loyalists," wrote Mathews on Nov. 30, 1780, "is swelling to such an amount that it must be curtailed."[24] Seventy three refugees,

---

[20]QUA: HP, 59/21789/55, Maclean to Mathews, Nov. 8, 1779.

[21]QUA: HP, 81/21821/45, McAlpin to Jeremiah French, Jan. 14, 1780.

[22]QUA: HP, 83/21823/25, Mathews to Hugh Munro, Jan. 20, 1780.

[23]QUA: HP, 81/21821/46, McAlpin to Mathews, Jan. 28, 1780.

[24]QUA: HP, 83/21823/93, Mathews to Nairne, Nov. 30, 1780.

mainly women and children, arrived at St. Johns on Oct. 9. [25] A group of women and children from Johnstown arrived at Lachine on Nov. 29.[26] Early in December a hundred or so more hungry and ragged women and children arrived at St. Johns.3[27]and so it went on. The Government was compelled to provide food and shelter, but with limited resources. Consequently, it was up to the Inspector of the Loyalists to ensure that none were being fed and housed at public expense who were able to provide for themselves. McAlpin's successor, was John Nairne, who was granted the Seigneurie of Murray Bay in 1762. In 1775 he became a major in Maclean's Royal Highland Emigrants and played a part in the defence of Quebec in the same year.[28]

Haldimand had written Nairne about the arrival of the 38 women and 77 children at St. Johns in early December, and instructed Nairne that: "You will have them supplied with such necessaries as their most pressing needs require, and direct that they may join their Connections, where they must in their different situations fall upon means to secure a livelihood, their number multiplying so fast that it will be impossible to feed them from the Provision Store."[29] To ascertain that the limited provisions and funds went where most needed it was necessary for Nairne to move about among the Loyalists in their various communities to keep his eyes and ears open. The subsistence lists were continually changing: names were added

---

[25]QUA: HP, 81/21821/148, William Marsh to Haldimand, Oct. 11, 1780.

[26]QUA: HP, 81/21821/189, Munro to Mathews, Nov. 30, 1780.

[27]QUA: HP, 83/21823/96, Haldimand to Nairne, Dec. 4, 1780.

[28]For further details, see Strome Galloway, "Death of a Family — The End of the Nairnes of Murray Bay," Families 19 (1980), 66-78.

[29]QUA: HP, 83/21823/96, Haldimand to Nairne, Dec. 4, 1780.

or removed, individual rations were augmented or decreased as circumstances altered. Nairne's returns resembled those of other incumbents in their comments about individuals: the widow Crothers was described as "a genteel sort of woman, has four children, the youngest only four months old, and is destitute of funds and relations in this part of the world." William Fraser was "a good, careful looking man," and Capt. Hermanus Flaake "a decent looking man."[30] At the same time Nairne struck Samuel Adams off the list, since Adams had discharged all the men in his Corps and was deemed quite capable of supporting himself in his capacity as a doctor. Adams seems not to have been very highly regarded, Sir John Johnson described him as a "Canting Cunning fellow" with a "very indifferent character,"[31] The Inspectors of the Loyalists were no doubt influenced in making character assessments of their charges by the amount of trouble they caused.

Nairne, like his predecessor, found the Machiche Loyalists fractious and demanding, and soon discovered that turmoil could be expected when provincial soldiers were allowed to visit with their families. Given the opportunity, they could usually be depended on to stir up some sort of trouble. Sgts William England and Henry Clow performed a magnificent service in managing "that disorderly set" and were highly praised for the success of their peace-keeping efforts by the seigneur, Conrad Gugy. In an attempt to maintain some semblance of order in the community, Gugy was to cut off the rations of any whose conduct he felt merited such treatment.[32]

---

[30]QUA: HP, 81/21821/150, Nairne to Mathews, Oct. 25, 1780.

[31]QUA: HP, 84/21826/5-7, Sir John Johnson's Subsistence List, April 18, 1779.

[32]QUA: HP, 83/21823/96, Mathews to Nairne, Jan. 22, 1781.

Even so, it appears that Conrad Gugy had "a great deal of trouble with the people at Machiche."[33]

Most likely some Loyalists were guilty of stirring up trouble just for its own sake; certainly most had by this time seen enough hardship and violence to make them bitter and resentful of authority. Many as well expected far greater reward than they received for their sacrifice and suffering, and were determined to exact recompense from the King for whose cause they had sunk to such a level of misery and degradation. At the same time, the vast majority had problems not of their own making, and presented demands which were neither frivolous nor unreasonable.

Although Haldimand often refused to grant requests that may have appeared quite legitimate, he simply realized that the funds in the treasury were not without limits. His budget did not increase in proportion to the influx of the greater numbers of homeless refugees, and the Royal Bounty had to be spread thinner and all who could possibly support themselves must be forced to do so. New arrivals were sent where they were most likely to find employment. Sick and infirm women with young children and those who could not serve were lodged together in as few houses as would hold them to save rent and fuel and to make it easier for the garrison surgeon to visit them and for an officer to inspect them frequently in order to get the sick out to service the minute they recovered. Those who were well enough were to be employed at making blankets, coats and leggings at a rate less than that which the government was forced to pay the Canadians for performing this service. All

---

[33]QUA: HP, 81/21821/200, Nairne to Mathews, Jan. 28, 1781.

Loyalists, male and female, were to be mustered once a month.[34]

Edward Jessup, who took over as Inspector of the Loyalists in the winter of 1782, was described by Sir John Johnson as "a justice of the peace, a loyal subject, and a plain honest countryman."[35] He was one of three Loyalist brothers who came to Canada from Albany. Ebenezer, the eldest, a loyal subject, lived by land jobbing and owned mostly uncultivated lands. Joseph, the youngest, Sir John regarded with apprehension: "a silly creature that lived like a common farmer by hard labour."[36] On arrival in Quebec late in 1777, the two older brothers had continued their efforts to expand their corps into a regiment to be known as the King's Loyal Americans with Ebenezer as the colonel and Edward as the major.

Competition was keen among Loyalist leaders searching for soldiers to complete their corps, with some of the more unscrupulous resorting occasionally to dubious methods. In December 1780, Haldimand wrote to Nairne complaining of the "very unwarrantable means" used by recruiters, such as "engaging Boys unfit to carry arms and handing in Papers thro' Prison Gates to be indiscriminately signed by Men of all Characters."[37] The Jessups were amongst the competitors; Maj. McAlpin was just dead when Ebenezer Jessup laid claim to his men.[38] Soon after, Jessup was in Quebec with a plan for raising

---

[34]QUA: HP, 84/21825/5, Instructions to Edward Jessup, March 6, 1782.

[35]QUA: HP, 84/21826/5, Subsistence List submitted by Sir John Johnson, April 18, 1779.

[36]Ibid.

[37]QUA: HP, 83/21823/96, Haldimand to Nairne, Dec. 4, 1780.

[38]QUA: HP, 81/21821/99, Ebenezer Jessup to Brigadier-General Powell, July 22, 1780.

a new regiment, which three months later numbered only
about 60 men.[39] The Jessups nevertheless met with considerable
success, especially when the Loyalist troops in the region were
reorganized in November, 1781, and placed either in Sir John
Johnson's Royal Rangers (the second battalion was formed by
this time) or Jessup's Loyal Rangers with Maj. Edward Jessup in
command. Incorporated into the Loyal Rangers was what
remained of the corps of Daniel McAlpin, Robert Leake and
Samuel Mackay, as well as that of Lt.Col.Peters, who, to his great
chagrin, found himself a captain under Maj. Jessup.[40] Justus
Sherwood had already brought his company into Jessup's
regiment. After this reorganization the Provincial Corps was
able to function with considerably more efficiency and
economy.

When Edward Jessup became the Inspector of the Loyalists
in February 1782, he was already in command of the revitalized
Loyal Rangers. During his brief sojourn in the Inspector's office,
Jessup was not unduly beset by problems. By this time the
system had become better organized; experience had enabled the
authorities to anticipate more readily the wants and complaints.

Abraham Cuyler, Jessup's successor, and his family arrived
in Montreal in October 1782 and soon settled themselves in a
house near the Recollets. On the twentieth of the month Cuyler
wrote to Mathews asking for rations and fuel which would, he
said, "lighten the expense attending a large family almost
destitute of everything." As a suffering refugee in New York he

---

[39]Siebert, "The American Loyalists in...the Eastern Townships," 13.

[40]For further details, see E. Rae Stuart, "Jessup's Rangers as a Factor in
Loyalist Settlement," **Three History Theses** (Toronto: Ontario Department of
Public Records and Archives, 1961).

had been "indulged...with the same allowance as a field officer" and hoped something could be done for him now that he was in Montreal.[41] Haldimand replied through his secretary that "the perilous Situation of Circumstances in this Province prevented his fulfilling his Inclinations in many Instances with respect to suffering Loyalists," but he was able to allow Cuyler fuel "in the proportion of a Captain" and provisions to the extent of "two Rations per day."[42]

Abraham Cuyler was not long in receiving his instructions on economy. On Nov. ll, Mathews wrote to Decoigne, the commissary in Montreal, expressing the Governor's approval of the renting of a house for the use of Loyalist families "in absolute want of Lodging at Montreal."[43] Mathews wrote to Cuyler the same day, commenting on the renting of the house and authorizing the purchase of clothing for the destitute and added that His Excellency "was pleased to grant a certain Latitude" regarding the families of men in the Provincial Regiments as the result of the representation of Sir John Johnson on their behalf. Some of the larger families, who had formerly lived in affluence, found it impossible to survive on the rations of a soldier. Cuyler was cautioned that "this Indulgence is only to extend to those Objects whose necessities *absolutely* require it, and where there is a possibility of *diminishing* that allowance by any favourable Change in the Circumstances of the Parties," he was not to fail to take immediate action. Further, he was ordered to keep an eye on young people and to exclude from rations "those of both sexes who are able and have been used to labour. There is no doubt,"

[41]QUA: HP, 84/21825/13, Cuyler to Mathews, Oct. 20, 1782.

[42]QUA: HP, 84/21825/17, Mathews to Cuyler, Oct. 31, 1782.

[43]QUA: HP, 84/21825/23, Mathews to Decoigne, Nov. 18, 1782.

Mathews continued, "that the allowance of provisions while it alleviates the Distress of many Loyalists in this Province is the Cause of Indolence in many who would otherwise live better and become useful Members of Society."[44] The welfare society did not exist in eighteenth-century Quebec.

Cuyler had discovered that his refusal to fight against his King did not guarantee him immunity from freezing and starving. Because of his loyalty, Cuyler had been obliged to abandon his estate in Albany in December 1776 and flee to New York, where he remained with his family for nearly six years and now found himself more than £2,000 in debt as the result of moneys borrowed to support his family, as well as advances to other Loyalists in distress. He had expected to repay this sum out of money owed him before the outbreak of war by a Mr. Greveret of Detroit, but his "plans for collecting had miscarried." In January 1783 he requested permission to proceed to Detroit to recover some of the money due him.[45] He made the trip in the spring and succeeded in collecting enough of the debt to almost pay back what he had borrowed.[46]

Back in Montreal early in July, Cuyler's presence was greatly needed, for 1783 was a busy year for the Inspector. The formal conclusion of the war opened the gates to another flood of American refugees into Quebec. The return of March 1783 showed a total of 1,716 Loyalists receiving government help, as well as those who were supporting themselves.[47]

A fleet of nine transports from New York arrived in Quebec during the month of August, bringing a total of about 700 men,

---

[44]QUA: HP, 84/21825/25, Mathews to Cuyler, Nov. 18, 1782.

[45]QUA: HP, 84/21825/34, Cuyler to Haldimand, Jan. 11, 1783.

[46]QUA: HP, 84/21825/103, Cuyler to Mathews, July 14, 1783.

[47]Siebert, "The American Loyalists in the ...Eastern Townships," 18.

women and children, all of whom were housed temporarily at Sorel.[48] There was considerable alarm when it was learned that a number of Capt. Michael Grass' party of 95, who arrived on the *Carmel* on Aug. 12, were stricken with "the small pox & Malignant fever." A physician was sent post haste to Sorel to care for them, and they were "furnished...some fresh Beef and Vegetables."[49] Cuyler reported after his visit to Sorel on Aug. 28 that 18 smallpox victims were in hospital and six had died. In mid-October, Capt. Peter Van Alstine arrived by vessel from New York with his party of 182 and proceeded to Sorel, where Cuyler had given orders for their provisioning.[50]

The refugees from New York City had to be fed and housed at government expense as it was unreasonable to suppose that so many, arriving so late in the season, would be able to find means to support themselves. Haldimand ordered Cuyler to take them under his command, "considering them in every respect and Victualling them upon the same footing with those in the Province" and suggested "And as the Regulations for that purpose were made with a View, not only to prevent Abuses and discourage Indolence, but to enable me to dispense His Majesty's gracious Bounty more generally to distressed Loyalists until such time as they can either return to their Homes or provide for themselves by settling in this Province, I require that You will continue implicitly to observe and fulfill them."[51]

Haldimand's views on indolence and economy were not shared by the majority of the American refugees. Cuyler observed that "the Loyalists in general are rather clamorous

---

[48]Ibid., 19.

[49]QUA: HP, 84/21825/48, Cuyler to Mathews, Aug. 13, 1783.

[50]QUA: HP, 84/21825/163, Cuyler to Mathews, Oct. 16, 1783.

[51]QUA: HP, 84/21825/120, Haldimand to Cuyler, Aug. 17, 1783.

and expect all to be victualled until they are properly settled." Moreover, he expected that the clamour would increase with the discharge of the Provincial soldiers later in the fall unless they were provided for.[52] To make matters worse, the new arrivals were not satisfied with the King's Bounty as it was interpreted in Quebec, and they saw no reason why they should receive less in Sorel than they had received in New York. Their petitions, strong and effective, persuaded Haldimand to rescind his former order and grant them their former allowance, since there was little chance of employment with winter fast approaching. At the same time His Excellency pointed out that the Loyalists who previously had come to the Province did not suffer from the same disadvantages, and "on that account would not be so unreasonable as to expect an augmentation of their Provisions."[53]

The influx of Loyalists across the New York and Vermont lines continued, but never reached the proportions of refugees into the Atlantic provinces in 1783. Moreover, the flood ceased abruptly in Nova Scotia with the close of the war, but it continued in Canada for many more years. The Rev. John Stuart, with his family, had taken up residence there in 1781 and remained until his removal to Cataraqui in 1785. John Platt, a valuable and trusty secret service agent, moved to Lachine from St. Johns in the spring of 1783 and later opened up a hardware business in Montreal. Dr. Charles Blake, an army surgeon in the City during much of the war, practised medicine there after his retirement from the military until his death in 1810. Isaac Winslow Clark, a deputy commissary general in the army, lived in Montreal from about 1780 until he died in 1822.

---

[52]QUA: HP, 84/21825/140, Cuyler to Mathews, Sept. 17, 1783.
[53]QUA: HP, 84/21825/144, Mathews to Cuyler, Sept. 19, 1783.

Many other Loyalists were to be found living in the City in 1783; a fair proportion of them spent the remainder of their lives there.

There were thousands of others in Montreal who were there on a temporary basis, and in addition to the throngs of homeless refugees, there were countless soldiers, many of them celebrating their liberation from military discipline. Orders for the disbanding of the Provincials were issued on Dec. 2, 1783: the soldiers were, because of the lateness of the season, "to continue...in the enjoyment of Quarters and Provisions during the Winter.[54] Both Johnson's and Jessup's regiments were disbanded on Dec. 24, and, although both commanders had received orders as well "for the regulating of the men's conduct during the winter," rowdiness and disorder were rampant on the streets of Montreal.[55] Maj. Gray reported early in January that Maj. Jessup's men "behave very insolently in the Town."[56] Col. Barry St. Leger, who had succeeded Maclean as commander of the forces in the Montreal area, was inclined to lay the blame for the misconduct on the Germans. "Frequent robberies and disturbances," he wrote to Mathews on Dec. 8, "had happened in the town, suburbs and adjoining neighbourhood, and upon some detection it was found that the disbanded German troops were the sole authors."[57]

As St. Leger put it, "The timid part of the inhabitants began to be terrified." It appeared that the braver portion of the population did not relish the situation either, and it was generally agreed that steps must be taken to render the streets of

---

[54]QUA: HP, 83/21823/312, Mathews to Capt. Herkimer, Dec. 2, 1783.

[55]QUA: HP, 60/21790/153, St. Leger to Mathews, Dec. 25, 1783.

[56]QUA: HP, 82/21822/149, Major Gray to Mathews, Jan. 8, 1784.

[57]QUA: HP, 60/21790/149, St. Leger to Mathews, Dec. 8, 1783.

Montreal safe to walk upon once more. The city magistrates sent James McGill and Joseph de Longueuil to wait upon Col. St. Leger and request his help.[58] The result of this meeting was the inauguration of a "Patroling Guard," consisting of a corporal and six soldiers and a number of civilian citizens, to patrol the streets from dusk to dawn, its object "to prevent the frequent robberies as well as the riots that have lately happened in this City." They were to take in any soldiers outside of quarters after hours and to apprehend "that Class of People who shall be suspected by the Citizens."[59]

Crime was not the only problem in Montreal during the winter of 1783-84; disease plagued the inhabitants as well. In the autumn of 1783, Dr. Blake set up a clinic for those who wished to be inoculated against small pox.[60] Late in November a little money "to procure them some necessaries" was issued to "a number of Poor Women & Children Loyalists...many of them ill with Small Pox & Measles."[61] The discharge of the soldiers seemed at first to obviate the need for keeping the General Garrison Hospital in existence, but the question of the disposal of those patients whose lives might be endangered seemed quite unanswerable. Dr. Blake promised to continue his presence there,[62] and presumably the Hospital remained for the time being.

And, of course, there was the customary bickering over rations. Some were managing to draw provisions they were not

[58]Ibid.

[59]QUA: HP, 60/21790/142, St. Leger's Garrison Orders in Montreal, Oct. 30, 1783.

[60]QUA: HP, 84/21825/55, Cuyler to Mathews, Oct. 6, 1783.

[61]QUA: HP, 84/21825/181, De Lancey to Mathews, Nov. 27, 1783.

[62]QUA: HP, 60/21790/153, St. Leger to Mathews, Dec. 25, 1783.

entitled to, some were getting less than they believed to be their fair share, while others without doubt were suffering because they were being issued with less than their needs required. Abraham Cuyler had resigned his post around the end of October and his successor, Stephen De Lancey, received the usual instructions from Haldimand concerning vigilance and economy. "While you do every justice," the Governor wrote the new Inspector of the Loyalists, "to these unfortunate people, you will at the same time carefully watch over the interest of the Crown and prevent any abuse being made of a bounty so humanely intended and so generously bestowed." The area was divided into two districts under De Lancey, with a lieutenant directly responsible to him in each. The first included Montreal and "its dependencies upwards to Coteau du Lac" under Louis Decoigne; the second, that of Lt. Gershom French, comprised Machiche, Sorel, St. Johns and the outposts.[63]

The new Inspector was well qualified for the job. A member of the illustrious New York family, he practised law in New York. In 1765 he became clerk of the city and county of Albany. After a brief period of imprisonment in Connecticut he became active as the Lt.Col. of the second battalion of his father's regiment, the New York Loyalists, better known as De Lancey's Brigade. After the disbandment of the regiment he was appointed to his Quebec position. He did not settle in Quebec; he went first to Nova Scotia, then became Chief Justice of the Bahamas, and finally Governor of Tobago.

De Lancey's job in Quebec was challenging enough; he had to try to reconcile the demands of the Loyalists with the Governor's penchant for economy. There were probably 7,000

---

[63]QUA: HP, 84/21825/173, Haldimand to De Lancey, Nov. 29, 1783.

Loyalists in Quebec in the winter of 1783-84[64] but no exact figures exist. The officers in the Provincial Regiments had asked for aid in supporting their families; they complained that they had learned from experience that the regulations of 1783 depriving those above the rank of subaltern of rations had posed a real hardship and a family could not be supported on an officer's pay.[65] On the first day of 1784, De Lancey informed Mathews that Maj. Gray and the other officers of the King's Royal Regt. of New York were very persistent in their requests to have their families put back on the provision list.[66] There was genuine concern in Montreal in December when the barrack master and the commissary announced that the issue of firewood and provisions ended on the 24th of the month.[67]Great must have been their relief to learn that this was merely the date when the present schedule terminated, and that Decoigne had received from the Governor "a substantial arrangement" to commence on the 25th.[68]

Food and firewood were not the only wants of the destitute refugees. Clothing enough at least to keep them from freezing has to be provided for a large number of them. Again the Governor cautioned "that Clothing be not indiscriminately given according to numbers, or without a knowledge of the necessities of the parties to be relieved."[69] The commissaries agreed to do their best to provide clothing and blankets for the truly needy, stretching their largesse as far as possible to do the

---

[64]Wallace, **The United Empire Loyalists**, 93.

[65]QUA: HP, 84/21825/48, Mathews to Cuyler, Feb. 26, 1783.

[66]QUA: HP, 84/21825/215, De Lancey to Mathews, Jan. 1, 1784.

[67]QUA: HP, 84/21825/199, De Lancey to Mathews, Dec. 15, 1783.

[68]QUA: HP, 84/21825/201, Mathews to Decoigne, Dec. 18, 1783.

[69]QUA: HP, 84/21825/185, Mathews to Gershom French, Dec. 1, 1783.

most good, for, as Lt. French of Sorel wrote to Mathews, "they certainly are more in distress than they were, owing, I apprehend, to the cessation of the public works."[70] In addition, special grants were made to purchase vegetables, sugar, milk, oatmeal for "Water Gruel" and the like for the sick and the aged, to be of course distributed "with the utmost Oeconomy (sic) to such as are in that disorder & destitute of the little Comforts necessary for them."[71]

During the winter of 1783-84, the Quebec Loyalists waited for the final decisions on the location of their grants and to implement their resettlement. They found waiting extremely tedious and became anxious and impatient, presenting Haldimand and his officers with a raft of ideas and schemes which seldom met with official approval. Cuyler reported as early as July 1783 that he had had many inquiries from the Loyalists concerning the lands to be allotted for their resettlement,[72] and a month later Edward Jessup observed that they seemed "to be filled with anxious care for the future welfare of themselves and their families."[73]

Haldimand was concerned about the suitability of certain areas for Loyalist settlement. He approved only of the Gaspé peninsula or the upper St. Lawrence and the Lake Ontario region. The area later known as the Eastern Townships he wanted kept free, due to the chance that the French Canadians might have need of it, but he also wanted an unoccupied corridor between Canada and the revolted Colonies. If they

---

[70]QUA: HP, 84/21825/195, Gershom French to Mathews, Dec. 11, 1783.

[71]QUA: HP, 84/21825/210, Mathews to Decoigne, Dec. 18, 1783.

[72]QUA: HP, 84/21825/111, Cuyler to Mathews, July 21, 1783.

[73]QUA: HP, 82/21822/79, Edward Jessup to Mathews, Aug. 11, 1783.

were too close to each other, there was always the danger of border skirmishes between Loyalists and rebels.[74]

But the Loyalists had their own ideas about where they should settle, and to some the notion of taking up vacant land on a nearby seigneurie had great appeal. To Haldimand's embarrassment, two seigneurs who were members of the Legislative Council advertised in the Quebec *Gazette* for American settlers on their seigneuries, offering inviting terms. One of them, Charles de Lanaudière, offered freedom of rent for 10 years among other things. Col. Henry Caldwell of Caldwell's Manor wanted several thousand families to settle on 100-acre lots which he proposed "to let out forever on the most reasonable terms."[75] Other owners made extravagant promises in their efforts to lure Loyalists to their lands. Many Loyalists, for their part, were quite willing to accept the terms offered by the seigneurs, having had all they wanted of travel in wilderness conditions and complained that the upper St. Lawrence and Lake Ontario were too far away and that travel there would consume too much of the "most convenient season for labour," and that they had received no material "Incouragement" to go to the Cataraqui region.[76] The authorities in the spring of 1784 were presented with a "List of Loyalists and Families who Refuse to Settle at Chaleur Bay or on the River St. Lawrence above Long Sew But Wish to Settle at Machiche." The list bore 42 signatures and, counting wives and

---

[74]See Hilda Neatby, **Quebec: The Revolutionary Age, 1760-1791** (Toronto, McClelland & Stewart Limited, 1966); Gerald M. Craig, **Upper Canada: The Formative Years, 1784-1841** (Toronto: McClelland & Stewart Limited, 1963).

[75]Stuart, "Jessup's Rangers as a Factor in Loyalist Settlement," 80.

[76]QUA: HP, 84/21822/174, Josiah Cass to Justus Sherwood, Jan. 23, 1784.

and children, represented a total of approximately 300 persons.[77]

Another group, led by Alexander White, wanted to settle at Sorel and were granted permission[78] but Governor Haldimand was adamant in his refusal to permit William Marsh and about 120 families to settle at Lake Memphramagog.[79] Those who wished to go to Mississquoi Bay were somewhat more persistent; they disregarded the Governor's orders and went anyway. Led by Capts Azariah Pritchard and John W. Meyers, Lts. John Ruiter and Christian Wehr and Ens. Conrad Best, they settled at Mississquoi, declaring that "nothing but superior force would drive them off the land."[80]

Haldimand, appalled that a group of his officers would have the temerity to flout his orders in such an open and deliberate manner, nevertheless managed to keep his countenance. His ultimatum issued on April 3, 1784, stated that all Loyalists wishing to receive free land grants were to be at Lachine with their families and possessions by April 10 for transportation up the St. Lawrence to the lands reserved for them. When Haldimand's order reached Mississquoi Bay some capitulated and set out immediately for the place of rendezvous. Meyers was not to be intimidated; he and many others determined to remain where they were despite the Governor's order. When Haldimand learned that Meyers' land was not, as he had hoped, on the south side of the boundary, he summoned the

---

[77]QUA: HP, 83/21824/135, List of Loyalists and Families Who Refuse to Settle at Chaleur Bay or on the River St. Lawrence above Long Saw But Wish to Settle at Machiche, May 1, 1784.

[78]QUA: HP, 82/21822/245, Alexander White to Mathews, April 21, 1784.

[79]QUA: HP, 84/21825/149, Mathews to Cuyler, Oct. 2, 1783.

[80]QUA: HP, 82/21822/183, Sherwood to Mathews, March 1, 1784.

recalcitrant officer to Quebec to render an account of his conduct.[81] The upshot of the meeting was that the group were allowed to remain on their land, all except Meyers, who was commanded to leave as soon as he had harvested his crops.

Some Loyalists wanted to return to their old homes in the American States. Capt. Barnes of Sorel believed that a fair number were "soliciting leave to return to their former Possessions in the States."[82] It is reasonable to suppose that at least a few of them succeeded, which is more than can be said for the group from Machiche who were interested in establishing themselves on the Miramichi.

Somewhat more successful was Abraham Cuyler's plan to settle a band of Loyalists on Cape Breton Island. In the fall of 1783, Cuyler sent Capt. Jones on a reconnoitring expedition and prepared an association proposal for those Loyalists interested. In October he requested Haldimand's consent to proceed with his plan to settle about 3,000 Loyalists in Cape Breton.[83] He embarked, with a letter of introduction from Haldimand to Lord North, for England in November 1783, to seek a land grant. It was spring before Cuyler's business was completed and by this time many of the prospective settlers had given up hope and accepted grants elsewhere. Cuyler had written to his wife, in Montreal, to inform her that the Secretary of State had written to Haldimand on May 21 regarding the Cape Breton plans and that he himself expected to sail for the Island on June 10. He hoped to see Mrs. Cuyler there in August.[84] Mrs. Cuyler,

---

[81]For further details see: Mary Beacock Fryer, Loyalist Spy (Brockville 1974); Jane Bennett Goddard, Hans Waltemeyer (1980).

[82]QUA: HP, 82/21822/339, Capt. Barnes to Mathews, Aug. 30, 1784.

[83]QUA: HP, 84/21825/159, Cuyler to Mathews, Oct. 13, 1783.

[84]QUA: HP, 82/21822/341, Jacob Glen to Mathews, Sept. 6, 1784.

however, was still in Montreal on Sept. 13, holding herself, in accordance with Maj. Mathews' request, "prepared to leave at the shortest notice given."[85] Jane Cuyler and her family finally reached Cape Breton with only about 100 associates.[86] Abraham Cuyler did not spend the rest of his life on Cape Breton Island; he returned to Montreal.

The majority of the Loyalists who came to Quebec in the decade from 1775 to 1785 remained in the Province and settled on tracts of land approved by Haldimand. The Governor had sent Capt. Justus Sherwood to the Gaspé peninsula in May, 1783, to seek out a location for some of the Loyalists on the Bay of Chaleur. Arriving with his family at Gaspé on June 7, Sherwood spent the next six weeks selecting suitable sites and writing reports on them. In February and May 1784, information on the Gaspé was published in Quebec and distributed to the Loyalist camps. But in spite of all the work and publicity, only about 400 went there in the spring.[87]

The largest group of Quebec Loyalists finally settled on lands reserved for them on the upper St. Lawrence and the Bay of Quinté. A few, like John Meyers, required a little more than gentle persuasion, but the majority were willing to comply with Haldimand's wishes. Some, like Capt. Michael Grass' company, had intended from the first to make their new life upriver. "I find by the papers of these people," Cuyler had written in August 1783, "they emigrated here with the intention to settle

---

[85]QUA: HP, 82/21822/345, Jacob Glen to Mathews, Sept. 13, 1784.

[86]Burt, **The Old Province of Quebec**, 2:85.

[87]W.H. Seibert, "The Loyalist Settlement in the Gaspé Peninsula," **Transactions of the Royal Society of Canada**, 3rd Series, Section 2, 8 (1914), 399-405.

at Cataraqui,"[88] as the Rev. John Stuart had done.[89] Capt. Peter Van Alstine's party likewise made no argument against the lands allotted in the Township of Adolphustown, and the same is true of most of the leaders of companies or groups.

The new home of the Loyalists, the Royal Townships, had been laid out in 14 townships, nine on the St. Lawrence and five beginning at Cataraqui and extending along the shore of the Bay of Quinté. Proceeding up river above Montreal, Township No.1 was at present-day Charlottenburg and was settled by the Roman Catholics in the first battalion of the King's Royal Regt. of New York. The Presbyterians settled on No.2, modern Cornwall. Here a little town, called New Johnstown, sprang up early in 1784 on a site chosen by Sir John Johnson. Above the Scots in Townships Nos. 3, 4 and 5 were the German Calvinists, the German Lutherans and the Anglicans. Nos 6, 7 and 8 received the majority of the men from Jessup's Regiment and their families. What probably should have been called Township No.1, the area around modern Lancaster, was considered generally too low and wet for cultivation; nevertheless, there were about 90 living there in October.

The second group, known as the Cataraqui Townships, began at Cataraqui (Kingston) where Township No.1 was settled by Michael Grass and his people from New York. No.2, Ernestown, became the home of the remainder of Jessup's Corps and some of Allan Maclean's 84th Regt. (originally known as Maclean's Royal Highland Emigrants). Next was Fredericksburg, Township No.3, with part of Sir John Johnson's second battalion and Maj. Rogers' King's Rangers.

---

[88]QUA: HP, 84/21825/124, Cuyler to Mathews, Aug. 28, 1783.

[89]QUA: HP, 82/21822/321, Rev. John Stuart To Mathews, July 14, 1784.

Adolphustown, Township No.4, was settled by Peter Van Alstine's following and the remainder of Sir John's second battalion. Township No.5, Marysburg, across the water from Adolphustown, was taken up mainly by disbanded regular soldiers, among whom were some Germans under Baron Reitzenstein. By the autumn of 1785 there were some 1,800 families in the Royal and Cataraqui Townships.[90]

The exodus of Loyalists from St. Johns, Montreal, Sorel, Machiche and other temporary refugee posts in Quebec took place during the summer of 1784 under the general direction of Sir John Johnson. A notice on May 6, 1784, informed the "Refugee Loyalists residing at Quebec who propose settling upon the lands which His Majesty has been pleased to allot for them at the Bay of Chaleurs and in the neighbourhood of Cataraqui" that they were to "hold themselves in readiness to embark for the said places on the shortest notice." A notice in the Quebec *Gazette* on May 13 advised that the vessels for Chaleur could not be ready before the 24th and that those for Cataraqui would leave Quebec on the 17th.[91]

The first embarkation for the Bay of Chaleur took place on June 9 on which date 315 men, women and children boarded vessels at Quebec. Less than 100 more left for the Gaspé later that summer.[92] Those for the Royal and Cataraqui Townships gathered at Lachine in the latter half of May and were transported by bateau to their new homes. Despite the organizing ability, energy and dedication of Johnson, and workers such as Justus Sherwood and Edward Jessup, there was a confusion. One observer wrote to Maj. Mathews from Lachine

---

[90]Burt, **The Old Province of Quebec**, 2:89-90.

[91]Quebec **Gazette**, May 13, 1784.

[92]Siebert, "The Loyalist Settlement in the Gaspé Peninsula," 401.

early in June. "The confusion here is unaccountable," he commented, "every Person pretends to a Superior Command, some of the first battn of the Yorkers who have received their Batteau & Pilots since last Thursday were at the upper end of La Chine last night, and the Canadians came back to receive more provisions, which the Commissary refused. These men in genl. move without any officers or even Sergt to conduct them which created great delay and confusion."[93] Disorder notwithstanding, Sir John Johnson succeeded admirable in the performance of his task; in July he reported that 1,568 men, 626 women. 1,492 children and 90 servants had been transported to their new homes.[94]

Not all American refugees in Quebec reached one of the new Loyalist settlements during that summer. Many remained behind. Some men were worried about taking their wives and children with them while they cleared enough land and erected the first rude shelter. De Lancey sympathized and wrote to Mathews on the subject on May 29. "There is several People in the district of Montreal," he informed his superior, "who are unable to go on the lands allotted for them...& must suffer if they are stop't their provision." Some elderly were unable to go at the present as well as "some few cripples some widows and orphans."[95] The infirm Loyalists who remained behind had mixed feelings over Mathews' reply on June 3 to De Lancey's letter. They were to be allowed provisions "untill they shall be able to Join their Connections, which must be done as soon as possible." This they liked, but the next condition was less to their taste. "All in that Predicament are ordered to repair to

---

[93]QUA: HP 82/21822/288, Capt. Maurer to Mathews, June 7, 1784.
[94]See Craig, **Upper Canada: The Formative Years, 1784-1841**, 6.
[95]QUA: HP, 84/21825/248, De Lancey to Mathews, May 27, 1784.

Sorel, where there were Vacant Barracks & where being under the Eye of one Person, issues will be attended with less trouble and impositions."[96] The Loyalists informed the Governor through De Lancey and Mathews that they would rather lose their lands and "thrust themselves at the mercy of the Rebels" than go to Sorel, where they had heard that their fellow sufferers were so cruelly treated.[97] In the end some went, while others found ways to evade the order. The Invalid Asylum at Sorel, founded at this time, continued to function until the middle of the nineteenth century.[98]

Only a few remaining behind were actually candidates for the Invalid Asylum. Capt. Barnes' abstract of the October muster of 1784 showed that there were 2,065 Loyalists in the Royal and 1,755 in the Cataraqui Townships. In the Montreal area there was a total of 1,521, broken down by community in the following manner: 316 at Sorel, 315 at St. Johns, 66 at Chambly, 207 at Lachine and 617 at Montreal.[99] Most were still on government rations in the autumn of 1784, necessitating the muster conducted by Capt. Barnes. Gov. Haldimand, aware of the irregularities which persisted in the dispensation of the Royal Bounty, informed Barnes that he "would find Montreal and neighbourhood a large Field for abuse."[100]

More than 1,500 Loyalists remained in the Montreal area after the great exodus in 1784. Their influence was a valuable factor in the development of the region. Many of their

---

[96]QUA: HP, 83/21823/231, Mathews to Sir John Johnson, June 10, 1784.

[97]QUA: HP, 84/21825/251, De Lancey to Mathews, June 10, 1784.

[98]For information on the Invalid Asylum of Sorel, consult Volume 634a, RG8, Military "C" Series, National Archives of Canada (henceforth NAC).

[99]QUA: HP, 85/21828/155, Major Barnes' Abstract of Musters

[100]NAC: HP, B65/49-51, Mathews to Barnes, Sept. 13, 1784.

descendants live there today, some bearing the original English, Scottish, German or Dutch Loyalist names, others completely integrated into the French milieu. This important group, along with its contribution to the Canadian scene, has been largely overlooked by historians, who have been mainly concerned with the Loyalist fact in Nova Scotia, New Brunswick, and Ontario.

CHAPTER 4
Provincial Troops in the Montreal Area 1775-1784

by Mary Beacock Fryer

That British regular troops were stationed in and around Montreal during the American Revolution is well known. Not as well known was the presence of regular regiments from German states which Britain employed for service in North America. Nor has much attention been given to soldiers serving in Provincial Corps of the British Army, better known as Loyalist regiments. Provincial Corps were units raised by Britain in North America for service against the rebels of the Thirteen Colonies, which were attached to each zone where the British regular army was in firm control.

To cope with the troubled Colonies, Britain organized four military departments: East and West Florida formed the Southern Department; Nova Scotia the Eastern, or Northeastern; the New York City area the Central and the old Province of Canada (now Quebec and Ontario) the Northern Department. Three provincial regiments, and a number from two others, were attached to the Northern Department stationed in and around Montreal. These were, in sequence: the first battalion Royal Highland Emigrants 1775, the King's Royal

Regt. of New York 1776, Butler's Rangers 1777, the Loyal Rangers 1781 and three companies of King's Rangers 1783.[1]

For those serving with the provincial corps, Montreal provided a place to shop and to enjoy some social life. Many officers belonged to the Freemason's Lodge, and those who could afford the extra expense housed their wives and children in the City. When the war ended, many were reluctant to leave to settle lands purchased for them along the upper St. Lawrence River and the Bay of Quinte.[2] Provincial troops formed part of the Montreal garrison, and after the rebel occupation of 1775-76 many were employed on construction to improve the city's defences, and to seal off invasion routes.

A barracks stood on Notre Dame Street, but most of the troops were quartered outside the City in widely dispersed communities, for two reasons. First to guard access points, especially from Lake Champlain and the Richelieu River, by which the rebels had invaded the Province. Second, the troops were scattered as they were provisioned from local supplies in the various areas. The first Census of Canada, ordered by Gov. Frederick Haldimand, estimated that the total population in the province might be 120,000.[3] Canadian farmers could not produce a sufficient surplus to feed the influx of soldiers, refugee Loyalists and destitute Indians.

Both governors-in-chief, first Sir Guy Carleton, then Gen. Haldimand, were hampered in their military efforts until

---

[1]Fryer, Mary Beacock, **King's Men: The Soldier Founders of Ontario** (Toronto 1980), 26-7, 31.

[2]NAC: Haldimand Papers (henceforth HP), B162/190.

[3]McIlwraith, J.N., **Sir Frederick Haldimand** (Toronto 1926), 190.

adequate provisions were received on a regular basis from Britain, and that was not until 1781.[4]

To best guard the access points, provincial troops were stationed at Fort Chambly, Fort St Johns (St. Jean), Ile aux Noix, the Loyal Blockhouse on North Hero Island in Lake Champlain, Pointe au Fer, Rivière du Chêne, Sorel and Yamaska. Due to limited provisions others were sent to Berthier, the Cedars, Châteauguay, Côteau du Lac, Ile Jésus, La Chénage, Lachine, Longueuil, Machiche, Mascouche de Terre Bonne, Pointe Claire, St. Anne's, Terre Bonne, Trois Rivières and Verchères. Some were employed in the bateau service, to move supplies from Montreal that were required by the western garrisons — Oswegatchie, Carleton Island, Niagara, Detroit, Michilimackinac, and in 1782 Oswego.

The need for an adequate defence force in Canada became apparent in the spring of 1775. On May 20 a spy informed Gov. Carleton that the rebels were planning their invasion from Lake Champlain as a means of forcing the Province to join the Continental Congress in its struggle with the mother country.[5] Carleton hurried from Quebec City to Montreal, where he set up military headquarters, but a few months later the Continentals captured Montreal, taking many prisoners of war, while Carleton barely escaped to Quebec City.

Following the rebels withdrawal in June 1776, when Carleton received reinforcements of regulars, Montreal was ruled by a military governor. The first was Lt.Col. Allan Maclean of the Royal Highland Emigrants, who was given the rank of Brigadier of Provincials. He remained in office until the

---

[4]Bowler, R.Arthur, **Logistics and the Failure of the British Army in America 1775-1783** (Princeton, N.J. 1975), 230-35.

[5]Stanley, George F.G., **Canada Invaded 1775-1776** (Toronto 1973), 28-9.

autumn of 1781, when he was succeeded by Brig. Ernst von Speth, a German officer. In the autumn of 1782, Brig. Barry St. Leger, the Lt.Col. of the 34th Regiment, superceded von Speth until after the war.

The military governor who commanded all forces was subordinate only to the governor-in-chief, and was responsible for security, prisoners and refugees. Prisoners deemed a security risk were sent to compounds around Montreal, while others were billeted in homes and placed on parole. Refugee families in the area also had to be provisioned and housed if they were unable to fend for themselves.

The Provincial Corps

The Royal Highland Emigrants

This corps, the first to be attached to the Northern Department, had a small component of American Loyalists. Only the first battalion was stationed in Canada, where many of the men were recruited, while some were from Newfoundland. A second battalion was based in Nova Scotia. The regiment was placed on the regular establishment in December 1778 as the 84th Regt. of Foot, the only Corps in Canada so raised.[6] The corps was supposed to consist of Highlanders settled in North America, but a list of the first battalion 84th Regt. dated Jan.1, 1783, at Rivière du Chêne states that of 520 officers and men, 94 were English, 119 Scotch, 174 Irish, 114 were Foreign.[7] The foreigners included American Loyalists and one company of French-speaking Canadians.[8] The men were uniformed as were

---

[6]Harper, J.R., **The Fraser Highlanders** (Montreal 1979), 153.

[7]NAC War Office Records 28/10/4/486.

[8]NAC: HP, B118/13.

other Highland regiments: the coat was red, faced with dark blue that denoted a Royal regiment, the kilt and plaid of Black Watch tartan.[9]

Lt.Col. Allan Maclean, a native of the Isle of Mull, Scotland, was a veteran soldier. He had fought under Prince Charles at Culloden, and spent some years in exile in the Netherlands, serving in the Scots Brigade. He served in North America during the Seven Years' War, and in London in the spring of 1775 he received a warrant to raise the Royal Highland Emigrants.[10] He commanded the first battalion in Canada directly, while the second battalion was in the charge of a major.

Maclean sailed to New York City and tried to recruit in the Mohawk Valley. Finding the Loyalists there had been disarmed, he left for Canada with very few recruits, as any unarmed would be easy prey for the rebels. With a small party of officers he went to Oswego and descended the St. Lawrence to Montreal, arriving in August 1775. Leaving the officers to recruit, Maclean sailed to Quebec City to meet Gov. Carleton, who put him in command of that fortress. Carleton then set out for Montreal as the rebels were known to be moving down Lake Champlain. With the garrison in Montreal were about 100 Royal Highland Emigrants, while an officer and 19 men were at Fort St. Johns, all of whom were captured during the enemy's advance along the Richelieu and into Montreal. Most were eventually exchanged.

The garrison at Quebec City had 200 Royal Highland Emigrants, who helped repel the rebels from December 1775 until May 1776.[11] About 300 officers and men of the Corps

---

[9]Harper, 158.

[10]NAC: W.O. 28/4/212.

[11]NAC: Colonial Office Records, Q/12/344.

accompanied Maclean as part of Carleton's army that forced the enemy to evacuate Montreal in June. Later, about 100 recruits left the Mohawk Valley for Canada and joined the Regiment. Following the liberation of Montreal in 1776, the Regiment was quartered in the City until the following winter, when some of him men were sent to La Chénage, Terre Bonne and Rivière du Chêne, where provisions were more plentiful.

When Gen. John Burgoyne was planning his expedition into New York State in 1777, he decided to leave the Royal Highland Emigrants in the Montreal area. Some of them were Americans, captured at Quebec City, who had enlisted rather than remain prisoners of war, and Burgoyne feared desertions if he took such men into the rebelling colonies.[12] Another reason for rejecting Maclean's corps could have been because the commander was a former Jacobite. As Burgoyne headed south, one company of Highland Emigrants was on duty at Fort St. Johns and small detachments were at other forward posts. In October, after a series of setbacks, Burgoyne was attempting to retreat to Canada. Maclean took his regiment to Chimney Point, on Lake Champlain, to assist the battered force, but when he learned that Burgoyne had surrendered at Saratoga, Maclean withdrew to Montreal.[13]

In the fall of 1778, by which time Gen. Haldimand had superseded Carleton as the governor-in-chief, the Royal Highland Emigrants moved to Sorel where the new governor established the headquarters for all his provincial troops stationed along the lower St. Lawrence. Maclean himself remained in Montreal as the military governor. Later, most of

---

[12]Lt.Gen. John Burgoyne, **A State of the Expedition from Canada** (London 1780), Appendix iii.
[13]NAC: C.O. Q/14/310.

the Royal Highland Emigrants were moved from Sorel to guard the western forts, although one company went on a raid to destroy enemy outposts along Lake Champlain in 1780,[14] and another on an expedition to the Mohawk Valley in 1781.[15]

In November of 1783, two months after the peace treaty was signed, Haldimand was ordered by Prime Minister Lord North to disband all his provincial troops by December 24.[16] Because most of the Royal Highland Emigrants were then on duty in the west, they were not disbanded until June 1784, due to orders arriving too late in the season to be carried out. The Regiment's main contribution in the Montreal area was the liberation of the city in June 1776, and in the administrative duties Brig.Maclean performed in the five years that followed. When the regiment was disbanded, most of the men returned home. Those who were Loyalists from the Colonies were resettled among the first battalion, King's Royal Regt. of New York, or near the outposts where they had served.

The King's Royal Regiment of New York

This provincial corps was the one most strongly identified with Montreal. The corps' name implied that it was based somewhere in New York State when it was headquartered in Montreal. Because the King's Royal Regiment of New York had such a cumbersome title, it was often shortened to the Royal Yorkers. Comprised of mostly American Loyalists from New York State, it was the second corps to be raised for service in the

---

[14]Enys,Lt. John, **The American Journals of Lt. John Enys**, Elizabeth Cometti ed. (Syracuse, N.Y. 1976), 35.

[15]Stone, William Leete, **Life of Joseph Brant** (Cooperstown, N.Y. 1845), II, 186.

[16]NAC: HP, B45/115.

Northern Department, and was also the largest, with two battalions in this Department, although the second was never completed.

The regiment made three excursions into New York State to lay waste to large stretches of the Mohawk Valley, but most of their time was spent building fortifications and other works for the defence of Canada. Gov.Haldimand once wrote to Sir Henry Clinton, the commander of the Central Department at New York City: "Sir John Johnson's Regiment tho' a usefull Corps with the Ax are not altogether to be depended upon with the Firelock."[17]

This was most unfair. On occasions when the Governor let the Royal Yorkers enter rebel territory on raids, they proved themselves as capable with the firelock as with the axe. The Regiment was underused, partly due to the difficulty of supplying expeditions, and partly owing to Haldimand's low opinion of colonials as soldiers. Even though the Regiment was not allowed many opportunities, with the help of Butler's Rangers, Britain's Indian allies, and detachments of regular troops, the men achieved military control throughout the northern colonies. They won their war in the north, but Britain gave away their gains at the peace table.

The Corps was commanded by Sir John Johnson, the Second Baronet of New York, heir to Sir William Johnson, the Superintendent of Indian Affairs, Northern District until his death in 1774.

Sir John had fled to Canada and reached Montreal on June 18. Carleton received him at his headquarters, and gave him permission to raise a regiment from among his tenants and

---

[17]Cruikshank, E.A., **The King's Royal Regiment of New York,** Ontario Historical Society Papers and Records, vol. 27, 1931, 219.

friends in New York State. Johnson was the Lt.Col. commandant, and Carleton signed the warrant at Fort Chambly on June 19, 1776. The men were uniformed in green coats, faced with dark blue, white small clothes of linen for summer, wool for winter, and lace and accoutrements of silver. When a second battalion was authorized in 1780, the corps switched to red coats faced with blue, gold lace and accoutrements. Later the first battalion received red coats when their original uniforms wore out.[18]

Comprised mainly of those who had come to Montreal with Johnson, the Royal Yorkers accompanied Carleton's expedition along Lake Champlain in the autumn of 1776. After returning to the Island of Montreal they were quartered at Pointe Claire, Ste. Anne's and Lachine,[19] and employed for fatigue duty, working on the defences surrounding Montreal. In June 1777, Gen. Burgoyne decided to send a diversionary force from Oswego via the Mohawk Valley to meet his main army at Albany. Col. St. Leger, 34th Regiment, would lead the expedition, and Sir John's regiment would accompany him.

At Lachine, 48 bateaux were assigned the Royal Yorkers, with felling and broad axes, fishing lines and hooks, 440 barrels of provisions of which the rum was to ride in the officers' boats for security. St. Leger got as far as Fort Stanwix (Rome, N.Y.), where his force of 500 regulars and provincials and 1,000 Indians was halted because his artillery was not heavy enough to reduce the fort's walls. Retiring to Oswego to await heavier guns from Fort Niagara, Burgoyne ordered St. Leger to abandon

---

[18]The coat of Lt. Jeremiah French, 2nd battalion, is in the Hamilton Military Museum, Dundurn Castle. It is red, faced with blue, with gold lace and buttons.

[19]Johnson, Sir John, **Orderly Book of Sir John Johnson During his Campaign Against Fort Stanwix** (New York 1881), 3-62.

the Mohawk Valley and to reinforce the main army on the Hudson River. Returning to Montreal, the Royal Yorkers were sent to reinforce Fort St. Johns, while St. Leger took his regulars south hoping to reach Burgoyne. When St. Leger arrived at Lake George he learned that Burgoyne had surrendered, and returned to Fort St. Johns. The Royal Yorkers spent the winter of 1777-78 again quartered at Lachine, Pointe Claire and Ste. Anne's, working on fortifications.

In June 1778, when Haldimand superseded Carleton, he set out to strengthen his western defences. While a detachment of Sir John Johnson's men went to Fort Oswegatchie to work on fortifications, two companies posted to Carleton Island, with three companies of the 47th Regiment, constructed Fort Haldimand, which was added to the existing chain of posts.[20] In the autumn the provincials returned to Montreal as Haldimand wanted all his provincials at Sorel for inspection, but beforehand one lieutenant and 30 members of the regiment accompanied an expedition to destroy rebel posts along Lake Champlain.[21] Following this raid the King's Royal Regt. of New York marched to Sorel, where Haldimand ordered a large detachment to remain, building defences to help seal off the Richelieu used by enemy reinforcements to penetrate Canada through Sorel in 1776.

In September 1779, Johnson left Montreal with 12 officers and 201 other ranks for Fort Niagara, to assist Butler's Rangers and the Iroquois against a rebel army that was destroying the Indians' lands. By the time he arrived, the rebels were withdrawing. Sir John and John Butler, the Ranger's commander, went to Oswego, hoping to raid the settlements of

---

[20] NAC: C.O. Q/15/261.
[21] Enys, **Journals**, 23.

the Oneida Indians, who had sided with the enemy. This plan was abandoned when it was learned that a Cayuga Indian who had been at Niagara had warned the Oneidas. Sir John and his men returned to Montreal, Butler to Niagara.

Meanwhile, Johnson had asked Haldimand to raise his regiment to the British regular establishment,[22] but the Governor refused, as he considered Johnson's amateurs unfit to serve in a regular regiment. Throughout the winter of 1779-80 most of the Royal Yorkers worked on defences at Sorel, others were at Côteau du Lac, the site of a prisoner of war compound, and where a canal was planned to bypass the Cedars Rapids.

In May and June 1780, Johnson led a force consisting of his own regiment, Capt. Robert Leake's independent company, regulars and Indians, in all 600 men, to the eastern end of the Mohawk Valley to assist Loyalists. Any Loyalist in the Valley who refused to join a ranger company was taken to Albany in irons, his home burnt, his property confiscated.[23] Johnson's expedition travelled to Crown Point, on Lake Champlain, in Provincial Marine vessels, and then marched to the vicinity of Johnstown, destroying rebel property as they went. They returned to Crown Point where the ships awaited them with 134 men, some women and children. Vast quantities of flour, bread, Indian corn and other provisions had been seized or burnt, and they had captured arms, cash, killed many cattle and taken 70 horses.[24]

Most of the Loyalists from the Mohawk Valley enlisted, and Sir John's first battalion was almost completed. On July 13, 1780,

---

[22]HP, British Museum, Add. Mssm 21819/47.
[23]Ibid., 52-3.
[24]Cruikshank, King's Royal Regiment, 263.

Haldimand authorized Johnson to raise his second battalion. Capt. John Ross, of the 34th Regt. was the major, with Robert Leake as senior captain, and his independent company was incorporated into the battalion. In August, Maj. Ross took the second battalion to Côteau du Lac to work on the canal around the Cedars Rapids. Sir John and the first battalion remained quartered around Montreal while a second raid was planned into the Mohawk Valley, this time from Oswego. The crop had been good, and Haldimand wanted it destroyed before it could be moved from the valley to feed the Continental Army, the rebels' regular troops.

In September, Johnson's force travelled in bateaux to Carleton Island, and the Provincial Marine ships carried them on to Oswego. The combined force of provincials, regulars and Indians, numbering some 800 men, destroyed all the grain for 50 miles. While Sir John was in the western end of the Mohawk Valley, Capt. John Munro, of his regiment, led 100 men from Lake Champlain to Ballstown, north of Schenectady, as a diversion. The tour of destruction completed, both forces returned to Montreal to the various billets around the city.

At Sir John's suggestion, Haldimand appointed Maj. Ross the commandant at Fort Haldimand, on Carleton Island, where members of the second battalion would join the garrison. In November Ross left Côteau du Lac with 100 men.[25]

A list of the first battalion, compiled in March 1781, showed that 379 rank and file were fit for duty, 23 were sick in quarters, 58 were at Côteau du Lac, 5 were sick in hospital, 20 were on furlough, and 31 had been taken prisoner. In June, while Sir John was in Quebec City and Maj. James Gray of the first battalion was on leave, Capt. John Munro was in command of

---

[25]NAC: HP, B127/212-214; HP, Br. Mus. Add. Mss. 21819/155.

the detachment at Côteau du Lac. Munro failed to report the escape of some prisoners to Brig. Maclean, the military governor. Maclean reprimanded Munro and heaped scorn on the entire regiment. On his return, Sir John complained to Haldimand, who chided Maclean for being too hasty: "Young Corps stand in need of admonition & indulgence and naturally commit many errors which in old ones could be faults."[26]

That autumn of 1781 the Rev John Stuart, Anglican missionary to the Mohawks in their valley before most fled to Canada, arrived at Fort St. Johns.[27] Stuart was appointed chaplain to the second battalion, and received a grant to open a classical academy for boys in Montreal. Not long after Stuart reached Montreal, Sir John Johnson took a leave of absence and with his family sailed for England.

Maj. John Ross, with four companies of his second battalion then at Carleton Island, three companies of Butler's Rangers from Niagara, some regulars and Indians, in all some 700 men, led an expedition from Oswego through the Mohawk Valley. There they repeated the destruction of the previous autumn, but, pursued by the enemy, they were forced into a battle near Johnstown. His rearguard skirmished at West Canada Creek, and the entire force jogged 30 miles to escape the rebels, even though they had been subsisting on only half a pound of horse meat per man per day, before they stopped to rest.[28]

The winter of 1781-82 saw most of the second battalion was at Carleton Island, and only those who were not properly equipped or ill remained near Montreal with the first battalion.

---

[26]Cruikshank, King's Royal Regiment, 233.

[27]NAC: HP, B176/299-300; see also Talman, J.J., Loyalist Narratives from Upper Canada (Toronto 1966), 341-44.

[28]Hastings, Hugh, ed., George Clinton Papers (Albany 1900-14), VII, 472-75.

In the spring of 1782 the last of the second battalion went to
Carleton Island. In March Ross left Fort Haldimand with 170 of
his battalion and some regulars to occupy the forts at Oswego
that had lain empty since the Seven Years' War, to fulfil a
promise Haldimand had made to the Indians.[29] A detachment
of the first battalion was reinforcing the garrison at Côteau du
Lac on rumours that prisoners might attempt to break out.

While in England Sir John was appointed Superintendent
of Indian Affairs, a post formerly held by his cousin, Guy
Johnson. Sir John returned to Quebec City on July 14, 1782,[30] but
his active command of the King's Royal Regt. of New York had
ended. Peace negotiations were under way, and the Indian
allies, many of whom had been left inside the United States,
feared reprisals. Soothing them required Johnson's full
attention, and the command of his corps fell to the two majors,
James Gray and John Ross.

By that time the war was nearly over. The first battalion
remained on duty around Montreal, the second at Oswego with
Maj. Ross. A cessation of hostilities was proclaimed in June,
1782, but the following winter the second battalion was alarmed
when the rebels made a last, unsuccessful attempt to seize
Oswego.[31] Despite the momentary excitement, the men in both
battalions were weary of soldiering and longed to return to
civilian life.

Maj. Ross reported that his men's spirits were low, and that
British regulars were more suitable for his garrison at Oswego
following the announcement of the cessation of hostilities. In
Montreal, Maj. Gray ordered a court martial at which two

---

[29]NAC: HP, B127/299-300.
[30]Ibid., B55/201-3.
[31]Cruikshank, King's Royal Regiment, 263.

privates were sentenced to be flogged. One was suspected of attempting to desert, while the other had been drunk and impertinent.[32] Men who had willingly endured the hardships of the campaign were bored and restless in their billets, with little meaningful work to do.

In the summer of 1783, the second battalion moved with Maj.Ross to Cataraqui, (Kingston, Ont.), to build a new military base, as Carleton Island might be ceded to the United States once the peace treaty was signed. On December 25, Brig. St. Leger, then the military governor of Montreal, reported that he had disbanded the first battalion, King's Royal Regt. of New York.[33] Because the second battalion was at Cataraqui, it was not disbanded until June 1784, at the same time as the Royal Highland Emigrants.

Members of the first battalion were expected to remain in their quarters through the winter of 1783-84, until they could be resettled. Most wanted to remain in Montreal, and St. Leger recommended that Capt. Munro, whose children were attending Stuart's school, be in command of them. In the spring, the migration of the disbanded provincials and their families up the St. Lawrence began. The first battalion was assigned five townships along the upper St. Lawrence, the second battalion two townships at Cataraqui.

Records show that in 1784, 1,462 people had settled in the five townships assigned to the first battalion — 549 men, 275 women, 631 children and 25 servants. Of the second battalion, 310 people were at Cataraqui — 199 men, 32 women, 69

---

[32]Ontario Archives, uncatalogued document from a descendant of Capt. Archibald MacDonell.

[33]NAC: HP, B63/104-6.

children and 10 servants.[34] These records suggest that the whole of the first battalion migrated from Montreal, and imply that part of the second battalion was not included, for it numbered 450 officers and men. A comparison of muster rolls and land board records shows that a number from the second battalion had settled in the five townships assigned to the first. Furthermore, not all the first battalion moved up the St. Lawrence that season. Exactly how many disbanded Royal Yorkers remained around Montreal is difficult to establish.

Most who left for the new settlements were farmers from the frontiers of New York, or in some cases accepted enducements offered by seigneurs to rent land closer to the city. Probably most of those who remained in the Montreal area were skilled in some trade and did not need the free grants offered by the government in order to survive. Of the men who led the regiment more is known. Sir John Johnson made his home at Lachine and was a prominent figure in Montreal until his death in 1830. Maj. John Ross returned to Britain and Maj. James Gray settled among the men of the first battalion.

Butler's Rangers

This provincial corps was quartered at Fort Niagara, the headquarters of the Indian Dept., while Montreal served as their base of supply. John Butler, the corps' commandant, did not receive his warrant until September, 1777, and some of the men who joined the regiment were at Montreal before the rebels captured it.

In July 1775, Guy Johnson, then Superintendent of Indian Affairs, learned that the enemy was inciting the Indians against him and plotting to have him kidnapped. Guy left his home

---

[34]Ibid., B168/42.

near Johnstown and marched up the Mohawk, accompanied by several of his officers from the Indian Dept., among them John Butler and his son Walter. From Oswego, where Guy held a meeting with the Indians, the officers descended the St. Lawrence, arriving in Montreal in August. At a conference with Gov. Carleton, Guy Johnson recommended sending large numbers of warriors against the rebels, then massing on Lake Champlain. Carleton refused, and an affronted Johnson went on a leave of absence to England, accompanied by his brother-in-law, Daniel Claus.

With his departure, Carleton dispatched John Butler to Fort Niagara to take command of the Indian Dept., while Walter remained with the defence force in Montreal. Walter, a lieutenant in the Indian Dept., went to Fort St. Johns with a large party of warriors who were to track rebel movements. In mid-September, Walter was with the Indians when they dispersed a force of rebels who attempted to capture the fort.[35]

On Sept. 23, 1775, Walter was with the troops that marched from Montreal to deal with Ethan Allen, the famed chieftain from Vermont's Green Mountains, who arrived in Montreal's east end with some 200 volunteers and a rash plan to storm the city. After a brief skirmish, in which many from both sides fled, Lt. Peter Johnson of the Indian Department and Sir John's half-brother, captured Allen.[36] Before the capitulation of Montreal, Walter departed for Fort Niagara to assist his father.

The Battle of the Cedars, above Montreal, in May 1776, was the first setback for the Continentals which led to the

---

[35]Cruikshank, E.A., **Butler's Rangers**, Lundy's Lane Historical Society, (Welland, Ont. 1893), 26.

[36]Graymont, Barbara, **The Iroquois and the American Revolution** (Syracuse, N.Y. 1972), 79.

evacuation of the city that June. John Butler played a crucial role in this success. In March, at Fort Niagara, he received orders to send some native warriors to Fort Oswegatchie, on the upper St. Lawrence (Ogdensburg, N.Y.). Butler persuaded 100 Senecas and Cayugas to join the commandant, Capt. George Forster of the 8th Regiment, at the fort. They were to reinforce the garrison at Oswegatchie, which consisted of a detachment from Forster's regiment. Guy Johnson was expected back from England, and the warriors agreed to "open a path" so that he could reach his headquarters at Fort Niagara. This implied removing the Americans holding Montreal so that Johnson could get through.

Capt. Forster found the arrival of the Senecas and Cayugas at Oswegatchie timely, and he was able to persuade a large body of Mississauga Indians to follow their example. With most of his garrison and the warriors, Forster set out in bateaux and canoes for the lower St. Lawrence, where he was joined by more Indians at St. Regis.[37] Forster routed the rebels at the Cedars, and John Butler expressed pride at the part he had played in Forster's success as the Senecas and Cayugas he dispatched were the catalyst that brought other warriors to Forster's side.

Not long after John and Walter Butler left the Mohawk Valley with Guy Johnson in 1775, John's wife, Catherine, and their three youngest children were taken to Albany as hostages. After long negotiations, Catherine Butler and the children were exchanged in March 1780, and escorted to Skenesborough (Whitehall, N.Y.) under a flag of truce, where they were handed over to Haldimand's representatives.[38] Catherine stayed in Montreal until late in July. Meanwhile John went to Quebec

---

[37]Stanley, 119-121; see also Cruikshank, Butler's, 27.
[38]NAC: HP, B96-1/251-53; B175/4.

City to confer with Haldimand on the difficulties of supplying Fort Niagara's garrison and the distressed Indians and Loyalist refugees gathered there. On his return journey John stopped at Montreal for Catherine and the children, and they reached Fort Niagara aboard the sloop *Ontario* on August 6. [39]

Butler's Rangers, the most active and effective provincial corps in the Northern Department, used guerrilla tactics. They set the frontiers of New York and Pennsylvania aflame, as well as rebel settlements in the Ohio country and the Kentucky Valley, where they defeated a force under Daniel Boone.[40] To alleviate the supply problem, when on raids the rangers lived off the country, receiving food from loyalists still in their homes, at friendly Indian villages, and by robbing rebel farms. Large detachments of rangers went with the King's Royal Regiment of New York on its expedition of the autumn of 1780 and again in 1781.

Burgoyne's Provincials

When Gen. John Burgoyne led his campaign into New York State in June 1777, his force, some 9,000 strong, included provincial troops. Some were men who had fled to Canada in 1776 and were placed under the command of Sir. John Johnson. Their leaders objected, and insisted on their right to raise their own battalions, as Gov. William Tryon of New York had promised. Carleton insisted that they be quartered with Johnson's regiment, for convenience, so that they could be provisioned and paid. The Jessup brothers, from northern New York, and a party of 80 men they had brought with them, were

---

[39]Ibid., B100/447.

[40]Elliot, Lawrence, **The Long Hunter: A New Life of Daniel Boone** (New York 1976), 162-7; see also Cruikshank, Butler's, 108-09.

quartered at Châteauguay to ease the supply situation on the Island of Montreal where the rest of Johnson's men were billeted.

Other Loyalist volunteers joined Burgoyne as his expedition moved southward. These were organized into three fledgling battalions that never reached full strength, in part owing to losses during the campaign. One was the King's Loyal Americans, under Lt.Col. Ebenezer Jessup, the second, the Queen's Loyal Rangers, led by Lt.Col. John Peters, the third the Loyal Volunteers under Lt.Col. Francis Pfister. Two other units, led by Capt. Daniel McAlpin and Dr. Samuel Adams, consisted of a few companies. On July 4, the night before Burgoyne captured Fort Ticonderoga, on Lake Champlain, Samuel Mackay, a resident of St. Johns, reached the British army as a volunteer, where he was asked by Loyalists arriving there to be their commander.[41]

Burgoyne was to fight his way to Albany, where he would then be subordinate to Gen. Sir William Howe, the commander of the Central Department at New York City.[42] These orders were to have serious consequences for the provincials in Burgoyne's army who were considered part of the Central Department, which meant that they had no status in the Northern Department. In issuing warrants to Jessup, Peters and Pfister, Carleton was complying with the wishes of Gov. Tryon of New York, while some of the officers' commissions had been approved by Gen. Howe before they joined Burgoyne.

Gentleman Johnny Burgoyne's only success was the capture of Fort Ticonderoga. Then one disaster followed another. At the Battle of Bennington on August 16, John Peters had about 300 of

---

[41]NAC: MG 23/B43, Samuel Mackay to General Allan Maclean.

[42]Lunt, John, **John Burgoyne of Saratoga** (London 1957), 121-32.

his Queen's Loyal Rangers, and Francis Pfister some 200 Loyal Volunteers. Both corps were badly mauled, with many casualties. Peters later claimed that in the course of the campaign he had enlisted 643 men, more than enough for a full strength regiment — but they were lost almost as fast as they joined up.[43] With Pfister mortally wounded, Burgoyne gave the command of the Loyal Volunteers to Capt. Samuel Mackay. By October, at Saratoga, Burgoyne was forced to ask for terms — he abhorred words like capitulation and surrender, thus the document he signed was known as the Saratoga Convention.

Prior to the surrender, Burgoyne suggested his provincial troops escape in small groups, and try to reach the British garrison he had left to secure Fort Ticonderoga. Burgoyne feared that he might be unable to protect them as provincials from the Thirteen Colonies — the self-proclaimed United States of America — would be regarded as subjects of the Continental Congress and treated as traitors. Many, however, did not leave, some on a matter of principle, others due to wounds or illness. When the Saratoga Convention was signed, Burgoyne's provincials were protected after all. Under Article 8, all captured personnel were to be regarded as British subjects, and therefore prisoners, to be treated according to the rules of war.[44] All signed paroles to take no further part in the hostilities as a condition of being released. On muster rolls kept in subsequent months, these prisoners of war were referred to as Convention troops.

The provincials captured at Saratoga were escorted under a flag of truce to Fort Ticonderoga, and handed over to the British garrison. When the garrison evacuated the fort and withdrew

---

[43]**Toronto Globe**, July 16, 1877, A Narrative of John Peters.
[44]Lunt, Burgoyne, 208-210, Terms of the Saratoga Convention.

up the Richelieu River, the provincials, both those who had escaped and the paroled prisoners of war, went into winter quarters around Montreal. Their officers might have been held until they could be exchanged, but Burgoyne had never signed any of their commissions as their units were never brought to full strength. Thus all were officially privates, and eligible for parole.

A report on the several detachments of "Royalists" who had returned from Saratoga stated that Capt. Daniel McAlpin had 2 lieutenants, 3 sergeants, and 26 rank and file on duty in Canada, while 1 lieutenant, 2 ensigns, 1 surgeon, 4 sergeants and 38 rank and file were under the Saratoga Convention. Serving with Capt. Samuel Mackay were 1 other captain, 8 lieutenants, 4 ensigns, 1 adjutant, 1 quartermaster, 15 sergeants and 88 rank and file. Under Convention were 2 of Mackay's captains, 1 sergeant and 20 rank and file. Ebenezer Jessup had 1 captain, 1 lieutenant, 1 ensign, 1 sergeant and 25 rank and file, with 16 others shown as prisoners of the rebels. Under Convention were 4 captains, 5 lieutenants, 2 ensigns, 1 adjutant, 1 quartermaster, 10 sergeants and 60 rank and file. Another 16 privates were shown as remaining with Gen. Burgoyne. John Peters had 5 captains, 4 lieutenants, 3 ensigns, 1 adjutant, 1 quartermaster, 1 surgeon's mate and 9 sergeants, with 53 rank and file available for duty. Under Convention were Capt. Justus Sherwood and 10 privates, while 79 others were prisoners of the rebels. Dr. Samuel Adams had no active officers and only 13 privates ready for duty. Under Convention were Adams, 1 other captain, 2 lieutenants and 1 ensign, with 28 rank and file.

All told, the list showed 9 captains, 15 lieutenants, 9 ensigns, 5 staff officers, 29 sergeants and 205 rank and file able to be active. Under the Saratoga Convention were 9 captains, 8 lieutenants, 5 ensigns, 3 staff officers, 15 sergeants and 156 rank and file. Another 16 were with Burgoyne and 303 privates and 9 commissioned officers were prisoners of the rebels. The remnants of Burgoyne's provincial force — all ranks — was 796 men, of these 468 were safe in Canada, and 196 of them were under the Saratoga Convention.[45]

These records are revealing. Although Burgoyne later blamed his failure on a lack of support from Loyalists, many more joined him than secondary sources admit. If 796 provincials were known to have been alive at the close of the campaign, a conservative estimate of the total numbers who joined him was at least 1,000 men.

When these provincial troops reached Canada late in the autumn of 1777, they were treated as refugees. Since they were not attached to the Northern Department, Gov. Carleton had records compiled which he called his temporary list. The men were entitled to subsistence and pay for whatever work they did, but they were not to be encouraged to build up the ranks of regiments that might be removed to the Central Department, depriving officers of Carleton's own provincial corps of valuable recruits. Carleton ordered that the provincials from Burgoyne's army be supervised by Sir John Johnson, which satisfied no one. Sir John felt imposed on as he had enough to do in connection with his own regiment, and small corps leaders wanted to preserve their identities and complete their battalions. One exception was Robert Leake, who had served with the Loyal Volunteers, who attached his company to the King's Royal Regiment of New York after returning to Canada.

On June 1, 1778, orders from headquarters in Quebec City declared the Saratoga Convention no longer binding because the Americans had broken its terms. The British promised to

---

[45]NAC: W.O. 28/4/266.

send Burgoyne's regulars to England as these troops had signed paroles and were not eligible for service in North America, but they could be used to relieve soldiers on duty elsewhere, who could then be sent against the rebels. The only men who had returned home on parole were Burgoyne and some of his staff. All those who were prisoners of war on parole in Canada were returned to duty, but not as part of the Northern Department.[46]

After Carleton removed the paroles, the King's Loyal Americans were employed for a time at Quebec City, working on fortifications. The Queen's Loyal Rangers were on duty at Fort St. Johns, used as scouts. In the fall of 1778, after Gov. Haldimand had taken over from Carleton, the provincials were posted to Sorel, which Haldimand intended as the main base for all his provincial troops. Edward Jessup, Ebenezer's elder brother and the major of the King's Loyal Americans, kept a receipt book, and all entries until August 1780 were made at Sorel.[47] The remnants of Peter's Queen's Loyal Rangers and the Loyal Volunteers under Samuel Mackay, as well as Dr. Samuel Adams' men and Capt. Daniel McAlpin's, were also quartered at Sorel.

For a time Haldimand continued Carleton's policy of regarding Burgoyne's provincials as only temporarily in Canada. Planning to place them in a second battalion, King's Royal Regt. of New York, Haldimand changed his mind, fearing dissent among the leaders, and investing public money on troops that might be detached from his command. He discouraged recruiting to fill the depleted ranks, because neither the first battalion, King's Royal Regt. of New York nor the Royal Highland Emigrants were close to full strength. Like

---

[46]NAC: HP, B83/97.
[47]Ontario Archives, Jessup Papers.

Carleton, Haldimand did not want Jessup, Peters, Mackay, McAlpin and Adams competing for recruits that might fill his own regiments.[48]

On May 17, 1779, Haldimand informed Sir John Johnson that he planned to consider Burgoyne's provincials as one corps, to be commanded by Capt. Daniel McAlpin, who would hold the rank of major of provincials.[49] Haldimand had more faith in McAlpin than in other leaders, as he had been a lieutenant in the 60th Regt., Haldimand's own, during the Seven Years' War. Johnson was to go to Sorel to ensure a smooth takeover for McAlpin.

By the fall, Haldimand was encouraging recruiting. The first battalion, Royal Yorkers, was close to full strength, as was Maclean's battalion of Royal Highland Emigrants. The governor gave Ebenezer Jessup and John Peters permission to raise battalions.[50] Soon he had to establish a Board of Officers to deal with disputes that arose over the few recruits found among refugee Loyalists in Canada or brought in by recruiting agents who operated in the rebelling colonies.[51] Probably, too, although his surviving correspondence does not specify, Haldimand had received reassurances that Burgoyne's provincials would not be removed to New York City and that they could be taken into his department.

The Governor thought he had solved the problem of the below strength corps from Burgoyne's army, but on July 22, 1780, Maj. McAlpin died after a lengthy illness. Again the Governor asked Sir John Johnson to take charge, but Sir John,

---

[48]NAC: HP, B83/97.

[49]HP, Br. Mus. Add. Mss. 21819/17.

[50]NAC: HP, B54/266-69.

[51]Ontario Archives, Jessup Papers, Military Order Book, Jan. 29, 1780.

who was busy raising his own second battalion, King's Royal Regt. of New York, was not happy with this arrangement. By September, Haldimand was offering enducements to recruiting officers working for Jessup and Peters, by allowing recruits a bounty of 22 shillings and 6 pence. Officers whose corps were completed to ten companies of 56 rank and file and 3 contingent men would have their ranks made permanent in America, entitling them to half-pay when their regiments were reduced.[52]

Apart from garrison duty, Burgoyne's provincials occasionally went on raids. John Peters took some of his Queen's Loyal Rangers to destroy a blockhouse in the autumn of 1780. Afterward Haldimand ordered the King's Loyal Americans to Verchères, where they were quartered for a year, although some were on duty at other posts. In October 1781, while Maj. John Ross' force was marching through the Mohawk Valley, Maj. Edward Jessup led a large party to make a feint towards Saratoga, to prevent rebel troops stationed in that area from gong in pursuit of Ross.[53]

In December, 1780, Maj. John Nairne, Royal Highland Emigrants, took command of Maj. McAlpin's provincials, again considered as one corps, although Jessup and Peters were still trying to complete their battalions. Haldimand decided that all his provincials, except the King's Royal Regt. of New York and the Royal Highland Emigrants, would be uniformed in green coats with red facings.[54] The following November he finally tidied up the below-strength corps by forming a new regiment, the Loyal Rangers, which absorbed the King's Loyal Americans

---

[52]NAC: HP, B83/140.

[53]Ibid., B134/171.

[54]Ontario Archives, Jessup Papers, Military Order Book.

and the Queen's Loyal Rangers. Haldimand chose Maj. Edward Jessup as the commanding officer while John Peters and Ebenezer Jessup, neither of whom had impressed the Governor, were demoted to the rank of captain, the first in command of a company of invalids, the second a company of pensioners.[55]

When Samuel Mackay died in 1781, Robert Leake took charge of his men. Leake's company, and the men who had served with Dr. Samuel Adams, who had retired, were taken into the second battalion, King's Royal Regt. of New York. Maj. John Nairne transferred to the 53rd Regiment, and spent the last two years of the war as the commandant of Ile aux Noix. Once the reorganization was completed, Haldimand had three full strength regiments of men from the colonies attached to the Northern Department — the Royal Yorkers, Butler's Rangers and the Loyal Rangers. The Royal Highland Emigrants were also at full strength, one battalion in Canada, the other attached to Nova Scotia.

The Loyal Rangers, which included many of Burgoyne's provincials, were based at Verchères, with detachments at: Pointe au Fer, the Loyal Blockhouse, Ile aux Noix, Yamaska where there were two blockhouses, and at Rivière du Chêne. After the Corps was disbanded on Dec. 24, 1783, the men were assigned the three upper townships beside the St. Lawrence, to the west of the townships assigned the first battalion, King's Royal Regt. of New York, and also the second township at Cataraqui that overlooked the Bay of Quinte. Some Loyal Rangers elected. to remain in Montreal, and some, despite Haldimand's desire not to resettle any Loyalists close to the borders of the United States, managed to settle at Mississquoi Bay.

---

[55]NAC: HP, B83/108.

The King's Rangers.

Raised in 1779, the Corp never amounted to much, and for nearly four years was not part of the Northern Dept. Its history provided a chapter in the life of Robert Rogers, folk hero of the Seven Years' War, that should never have been written. By the time the King's Rangers were being recruited, Robert Rogers was an alcoholic, and probably senile, an embarrassment to his elder brother James, and a laughing stock in three military departments.

Robert first raised the Queen's Rangers, of the Central Department, but lost this command in 1777.[56] In October 1778, he visited Quebec City and asked Gov. Haldimand to let him raise a corps of provincials along the frontiers of Canada. Haldimand declined, as it would interfere with completing his other regiments of provincials. Robert then went to New York City and received a warrant to raise a regiment from Sir Henry Clinton, the commander there.[57]

On July 17, 1779, Robert wrote Haldimand from New York City, informing him that he was sending his elder brother James, the major of the King's Rangers, to Canada with some officers to obtain recruits. Haldimand was furious. Having turned down the old warhorse once, he was being presented with an accomplished fact. The governor wrote to Robert ordering him to recall his officers at once, but James Rogers arrived at Fort St. Johns, having travelled overland along the

---

[56]Hough, Franklin B. Ed., **Journals of Robert Rogers** (Albany N.Y., 1883), Appendix E, 275-78,

[57]HP, Br. Mus. Add. Mss, 21820/1-220. This bundle consists of the letters that passed between James Rogers and Haldimand's secretary, Robert Mathews, from 1779-1783.

Hudson and Lake Champlain route. He promptly applied to Haldimand for subsistence and pay for his officers, and the disputes over recruits that were a plague to the governor became even more intense. Haldimand agreed to allow James to keep his recruits brought from the frontiers, but he was not to seek any among the refugees already being provisioned in Canada. Men who were living off the King's bounty were to be assigned to Haldimand's own provincial corps.

Robert then arrived in Quebec City, boasting that he had recruited 700 men in Nova Scotia. Haldimand ordered him to take his officers and repair there at once as so many recruits would need their officers. But Robert was not telling the truth, for he had scarcely raised 60 men in Nova Scotia. He lingered for a while in Canada, then left for Halifax after Haldimand advanced him money for his travel expenses. James remained, and continued his recruiting efforts, causing more quarrels. From Nova Scotia, Robert sent bills which he expected to have paid from the regiment's non-existent funds, and became such an embarrassment that James asked Haldimand for permission to resign from the King's Rangers and be under the governor's protection. Haldimand refused. Robert's warrant was from the Central Department, to which the King's Rangers belonged, and he had no authority to accept such resignations.

Meanwhile, the few recruits who had arrived needed shelter, and Haldimand arranged for them to be quartered at Fort St. Johns. in a new barracks that housed a military hospital. Some of the officers and ranks were employed as agents in the secret service, probably the most useful work they performed.[58] As time passed, Haldimand came to accept the presence of James Rogers and his King's Rangers and they continued to be

---

[58]Ibid., 83, a muster roll showing which men were on secret service.

quartered at Fort St. Johns. In 1780 Robert went off to England and his affiliation with the corps ceased.

Detachments of King's Rangers were part of the expeditions along Lake Champlain in 1780 and again in 1781 — the only actions in which the regiment was involved. James Rogers succeeded in completing only three companies in Canada. The rest of the regiment apparently consisted of some 60 men attached to the Central Department, who were used as guides and pioneers. In 1782 Sir Guy Carleton succeeded Sir Henry Clinton as the commander of that department, and in December he recommended that the King's Rangers be attached to the Northern Department. Haldimand acquiesced, and for the final year of the war the King's Rangers, small as the corps was, belonged to Haldimand's command. Like other corps or battalions that were in the lower part of the province, the King's Rangers were disbanded on Dec. 24, 1783. They were assigned the third township at Cataraqui.

The British Secret Service, Northern Department

Provincials made better spies than regular soldiers. They knew the country, and were fed and concealed in the homes of Loyalists still in the rebel-controlled territory. Secret agents travelled on foot, keeping lines of communication by land open, their messages often on thin paper, written in lime juice.

The secret service evolved gradually, with commanders assigning men to go on scouting parties or recommending reliable men to the British officers who commanded at the various outposts. The commanders in all four military departments were also dependent on networks of resident agents, Loyalists in the rebelling colonies who supplied information to visiting scouts.

Early on, Carleton, and later Haldimand, depended on Sir John Johnson's sources of information, but as time passed Haldimand placed more and more confidence in Capt. Justus Sherwood of the Queen's Loyal Rangers and later the Loyal Rangers. In 1779 he appointed Sherwood Commissioner of Prisoners and Refugees to arrange exchanges and safe conducts. Further, in October 1780, he sent Sherwood to Vermont to arrange a truce with the Vermont leaders.[59] For the remaining years of the war Vermont was neutral, and Sherwood conducted delicate negotiations which, he hoped, would lead to Vermont's becoming a British province. He failed, but neutrality was a useful end in itself, for Haldimand felt that Canada was more secure.

In December 1780, Sherwood was put in charge of all scouting parties that left Ile aux Noix. Talk was loose at most of the outposts and Sherwood wanted a private headquarters. In July 1781, with Haldimand's consent, he began building his Loyal Blockhouse on North Hero Island, in Lake Champlain.[60]

Sherwood's deputy was Dr. George Smyth, long a resident agent in Albany, code name "Hudibras." Smyth escaped from Albany a warrant for his arrest was issued, reaching Fort St. Johns in June 1781.[61] Sherwood's relationship with Smyth was not a happy one. The doctor tried to pretend that Sherwood, a much younger man, was his assistant, which caused friction. In fact, the doctor was a difficult, vindictive man who alienated many people. His health was poor, and he often left the Loyal Blockhouse for the comforts of Fort St. Johns. To ensure him a

---

[59]NAC: HP, B180/42-58, Sherwood's journal.
[60]Ibid., 183.
[61]Ibid., B176/131.

pension, Haldimand appointed Smyth a surgeon in the Loyal Rangers.

The Loyal Blockhouse garrison consisted of men from the Loyal Rangers and King's Rangers, usually from 30 to 50 at a time. These troops maintained the post, working on its defences, cutting firewood, and establishing a farm so that the post could be self-sufficient in food. The secret agents were a separate group, generally officers from below-strength provincial corps, although Sherwood sent members of his garrison in support of agents going into rebel territory to gather intelligence.

Describing the secret service of the Southern Department, John Bakeless decided that the rebels and the British were equally served by their intelligence "and quite as badly served by their counter intelligence."[62] The same could be said of Sherwood's operation. The secret service, Northern Department, wound down as the winter of 1783 approached, and the provincials were replaced by British regulars at the Loyal Blockhouse. In 1796, under the terms of Jay's Treaty, the Loyal Blockhouse was among the posts handed to the Americans. In the spring of 1784 Sherwood had helped superintend the migration of the Loyalists, and later settled with his family in the seventh township beside the St. Lawrence with other Loyal Rangers. Smyth, too old to pioneer, spent his remaining years at Sorel.

When the war ended in 1783, 50 companies — some 3,000 men — had been raised in the North American colonies and attached to the Northern Department. Since Haldimand's garrison of British and German regulars amounted to between 6,000 and 7,000 troops, his provincials constituted one third of

---

[62]Bakeless, John, **Turncoats, Traitors and Heros** (Philadelphia 1959), 28.

his defence force, apart from his militia. Of his provincials, 23 companies — about 1,400 officers and men — were in the Montreal area when they were disbanded in December 1783. Counting their dependents and other civilian refugees, about 6,000 people were gathered along the lower St. Lawrence and the Richelieu awaiting resettlement in the spring of 1784.

CHAPTER 5

Loyalists in the Inspectorate and the Commissary

by John Ruch

Regular inspection in every government department was the responsibility of each senior official. In some services there was a specific office of inspector while other arms of the Crown gave the authority of inspector to an officer who performed several tasks, of which inspection was one. The groups of Loyalists which found asylum in Quebec tended to be treated as military units at the very outset when there were few of them. Their leaders were entrusted with their supervision, and their knowledge of each other was often already intimate. However, when their numbers swelled the tasks of administration and supply also became proportionately larger. The situation of their care verged on the chaotic. At this time the Governor created a new, temporary office within the Loyalist department — the inspectorate. A new official, the inspector, was appointed, and by altering the existing structure, subordinate officers were placed under him. Subsequently a much higher degree of order was achieved in handling the refugees by the new rule of channelling all demands upon government through the new official.

The succession of officers who were charged with supervision of the Loyalists began with Sir John Johnson, and to a certain extent could be said to have ended with him many years later. As the highest-ranking American refugee in the Province, he was naturally looked to for leadership of his fellow fugitives. Also commissioned to raise a Provincial regiment, of which he was to be the commander, by mid-1779, at a time when Johnson was becoming increasingly occupied with his soldiers, numbers of newly-arrived refugees added to his burden. Gov. Haldimand thereupon separated Johnson's tasks and turned the refugees over to a veteran officer, Capt. Daniel McAlpin, who was appointed Officer Commanding, the Unincorporated Loyalists, which included all the miscellaneous groups, whether in town or country, in camp or in billets. McAlpin was not a well man, already prematurely aged by his hardships as a hunted Loyalist during the months preceding Burgoyne's invasion of New York. He lasted barely a year in his new post, dying in mid-1780.

Inspection of the Loyalists was an implicit task, and followed the military method of procedure in handling groups of people. Some Loyalist leaders, such as Samuel Adams, lacked the discipline and objectivity of veteran soldiers like McAlpin and his successor in the post, Maj. John Nairne, who over a period of some 32 months put order into a mass of people with conflicting aims and objectives. Through rigourous compilation of lists, personal inspection of claimants, and revision of the rolls, the two officers helped the Governor to achieve one of his objectives: regulating the issue of different kinds of relief to refugees. After McAlpin had formed the miscellaneous units into a large corps, Nairne continued toward Haldimand's end of training and organizing these men into respectable, large, regimental formations.

The Governor's aims became clear with this re-organization, when the Loyalist regiment, the Loyal Rangers, under Loyalist commanders, Jessup and Peters, now existed alongside the other Provincial regiments of longer standing. Nairne, who had his own military responsibilities as a company commander in the 84th Regt. (Royal Highland Emigrants), was now able to turn over the formation to its officers and leave the area. The general duty of supervision now fell to Maj. Edward Jessup, an unassuming but capable man who displayed greater leadership qualities than his prospective rivals. His duty as ordered by the Governor was to

management of the several corps of Loyalists."[1] Jessup carried the combined burden from February to October, 1782. In that time it became obvious to well-informed authorities that a major event was impending that would have extraordinary effects on Canada and the Loyalists — the separation of the American Colonies from the Empire.

The final wartime phase in the handling of the refugees in the Province was now reached. Haldimand anticipated massive problems when shiploads of Loyalists would arrive from south of the border. For the most part destitute and bereft of all possessions, they would need everything on which their survival and future livelihood depended. He knew that the budget for Loyalist assistance was unlikely to be greatly increased, and that frugality must be maintained. Experienced men who were capable of dealing with administration and supply must be appointed whose sole responsibility would be to cope with the dispossessed Americans. The man for the senior post in this new formation was Lt.Col. Abraham Cuyler who proved to be the solution to a number of problems. Cuyler, a former mayor of Albany, a victimized Loyalist, the energetic leader of a volunteer corps, was looking for both government support and an opportunity to restore his lost prosperity. He was a good representative for the Loyalists who had already won the approval of the home government through services in politics and war. Several officers already occupied with supplying the Loyalists' needs and the review of their circumstances were placed in subordinate positions under Cuyler's direction. Nevertheless, such competent and

---

[1]Mathews to Nairne, Oct. 25, 1781 (NAC: Haldimand Papers (henceforth HP), B163/196). McAlpin's charge was "to have the command and direction of the several Corps of Loyalists including both those who are paid and those who are not," Haldimand to Johnson, May 17, 1779, **Ibid.**, B159.10, pub. in Mary B. Fryer, **King's Men** (Toronto 1980), 198-199.

experienced people were so scarce that they still continued to function under orders from other commanders as the necessity arose. Useful men, jacks-of-all-trades, became the governor's trouble-shooters, including the French-Canadian civilian Louis Decoigne at Montreal, and Lt. Gershom French of the Loyal Rangers at Sorel.

Cuyler was appointed specifically as Inspector of the Refugee Loyalists, which title was shortened to Inspector of Loyalists in later usage.[2] Through past experience and a series of "ad hoc" measures taken to remedy particular difficulties, the duties of a supervisor of civilian and military Loyalists was already established. He worked under the instructions in his original commission and the special orders received directly from Haldimand. In some measure his early duties did not differ greatly from those of the former "inspectors," however the job of inspection was his sole responsibility, and he no longer had command of a military unit. The size of the task was steadily increasing as the total of refugees mounted. In mid-1783 shiploads of exiles began to arrive in the St. Lawrence from New York City. Cuyler was charged with the documentation of these people and the assessment of their immediate requirements, and was often on the move from camp to camp. At the same time he was a Loyalist whose predicament was not that different from other refugees. He had a future to plan. To pursue his ideas in a direction that would assist the government as well as himself. To achieve both goals, he needed a leave of absence, thus he resigned and headed for England.

There was no great consternation about replacing Cuyler as a suitable candidate had already arrived on one of the ships by late summer. Stephen De Lancey, a former associate of

---

[2]Cuyler to Mathews, Oct. 28, 1782 (NAC: HP, B165/13), he has arrived in Montreal and is ready for duty.

Cuyler's in the municipal government at Albany had many of the same qualifications, except that he seems to have had no military service during the Revolution. To him fell perhaps the heaviest burden of the whole period of the inspectorate, to carry on the unfinished work of Cuyler, subject to bouts of poor health, deal with the many new problems of transporting Loyalists onto lands for settlement, and settle their disputes and numerous demands for assistance.

With the dispersal of Loyalists from the Montreal district, the authority of the inspector needed to be divided among a few more officers who enjoyed the respect of their particular groups, and in settlements far from Quebec and Montreal they had to represent the inspector on the spot. Lt. Neil Maclean and Capt. George Law(e) were appointed deputy inspectors of Loyalists at allowances of pay commensurate with their responsibilities. Both were officers of the 84th Regt. and had served faithfully in various posts. Maclean was given supervision of the majority of the settlers along the upper St. Lawrence and received £100 a year, the same as Cuyler.[3] Law, who had been a barrack master from late 1777 to mid-1782 at Montreal,[4] was charged with directing the settlers of Chaleurs Bay.

The communications between government and the refugees should theoretically have all funnelled through the Inspector in Montreal. In this way the Governor hoped to reduce the number of demands pouring into his headquarters,

---

[3]His salary for six months was £50 (NAC: RG1, E15a/33, June 19, 1787).

[4]A paper by Kenneth Annett, "The Life and Times of Capt. George Law," in the series "Gaspé of Yesterday" (Quebec City 1979) was well researched in federal and provincial archives, but is unfortunately not referenced. There is a biographical sketch in James M. Hadden, (Horatio Rogers ed.) **Hadden's Journal and Orderly Books** (Albany 1884, reprint Boston 1972) 137-139nn.

and eliminate the trivial ones which would fall into the laps of subordinates in the inspectorate. It was much easier to deal with petitioners and complainers at their settlements where the circumstances were common knowledge. Nevertheless, Haldimand was not inflexible, and some Loyalists were far from being intimidated by the formalities at the outset. Letters and petitions on a variety of subjects still reached the Governor's office, and orders were issued directly to specific authorities in response. By sending copies of bothersome correspondence to the officer previously by-passed, Haldimand kept his men informed. And by insisting on the observance of procedures he had already laid down in orders, he discouraged most of the petitioners from approaching him directly.

The Governor could foresee many problems that would plague settlements in the upper country and planned to provide an authority of stature and influence to manage them. There were at least three major areas of administration which were of increasing importance the government of the district west of the seignories and the Ottawa River, the supervision of the Indians, and the Loyalist Department. As usual he wanted to assign several tasks to one person. He proposed that Sir John Johnson be appointed lieutenant-governor, and commandant of that district, as well as "Superintendent General of all the Loyalists therein."[5] Simcoe, however, was eventually selected over Johnson.

The last inspector was De Lancey, who continued in charge until 1791. Of necessity he was in close collaboration with Johnson, to whom he was related by marriage. As the later 1780s passed, and the settlers became more self-sufficient, the

---

[5]Haldimand to Johnson, May 17, 1784 (NAC: HP, B65/29-30) pub. in E. Cruikshank, **The Settlement of the United Emptire Loyalists**, Ontario Historical Soc. (Toronto 1934, reprint 1966), 99-100.

need for inspection of the old kind became less. People who could feed, clothe and house themselves by working their own land had no need for government hand-outs. Only the sick and elderly pensioners in the "asylum" at Sorel remained as a charge upon government, which they continued to be for many years.[6]

The inspectorate and its employee included the officers Nairne, Johnson and Jessup, while others are almost completely forgotten. Indeed De Lancey's identity has long been confused with his namesake cousin. That the deeds of these people be brought back into the pages of Quebec's history, the following biographical sketches are given, not omitting some reference to the others.

Daniel McAlpin and John Nairne were both veteran Scottish officers who had served in Canada under Wolfe, and had distinguished themselves at the taking of Quebec City in 1759. Both settled in the new world subsequently, Nairne in 1763 on a seigniory at Murray Bay (la Malbaie),[7] and McAlpin nine years later near Saratoga, N.Y., after having served in the interim with the 60th Regt. (Royal American). They considered themselves as loyal servants of the Crown and were ready to serve again on the outbreak of the Revolution. Nairne was in the thick of the action during the siege of Quebec in 1775-1776, with a group from the 84th Regt. McAlpin's role was quite different for he had to play a waiting game with the local rebels. The two men could see themselves objectively and with

---

[6]George A. Neville, "Returns of the asylum at William Henry for Loyalist Invalids," Families, vol. 16, no.3, Ontario Genealogical Soc. (Toronto 1977) 103-121.

[7]George M. Wrong, A Canadian Manor and its Seigneurs (Toronto 1908) and Strome Galloway, "Death of a Family, the End of the Nairnes of Murray Bay," Families.

humour. McAlpin pictured himself in his command of the refugees as "an old gray-headed fellow at the head of a parcel of raw undisciplined people with bad arms in their hands."[8] Replying to an old army friend, Nairne teased him about referring to their early wartime experience a generation before when they were attending social gatherings nowadays. It made them appear too old, particularly in front of the young ladies.[9] Both McAlpin and Nairne married Scottish ladies on return visits to their homeland, but returned to raise their families in the new world. McAlpin died in harness as commander of the refugees, Nairne many years later at a ripe old age.

The life of Daniel McAlpin is representative of a number of Scottish soldiers who fought and later settled in the American Colonies. He joined the British Army about 1745, and purchased an ensigncy. Not much is known of his career until he achieved some prominence at the fall of Quebec,[10] later serving as a lieutenant in the same regiment, the 60th, as Haldimand. About 1772 he sold his captain's commission and retired to the Albany area. By then he had been married about a decade and had by his wife Mary three children: Isabella, the eldest (later wed to Lt. Thomas Hill, 29th Regt.), James Murray born about 1765, and Mary Jr. four years younger. The family settled on a tract of several thousand acres Daniel had purchased near Lake Saratoga. He owned a similar acreage near the junction of the White and Connecticut rivers, now in Vermont. For a few years he occupied himself in clearing and developing his lands.

---

[8]McAlpin to Mathews, July 26, 1779 (NAC: HP, B161, 29).

[9]Nairne to Maj. Dundas, Dec.5, 1780 (NAC: Nairne Papers (henceforth NP), MG23/GIII/23 vol.3/255.

[10]Mary McAlpin's Memorial to Haldimand (NAC: HP, B215/258); another is dated March 5, 1781 (ibid., B214/200).

Several times the rebel authorities in the Albany area ordered him to report with his two dozen employees and servants for militia training. He ignored these summonses in 1775-1776, for which he was finally imprisoned. Six weeks later he was released on parole, and returned home only to suffer continual harassment from bands of rebels. Meanwhile Gen. Howe sent him a commission and secret instructions to raise a company of men for the King's service.[11] During that winter, after a friend had warned him that he was to be arrested again, he fled into the woods. He had recruited over 40 men at Ballston, but lost many of them shortly afterward when they were caught by surprise in a rebel raid. Again he escaped into the frigid forest, occasionally hiding in a hollow tree which protected him from view. When the greatest danger was passed sympathetic people took him in but by then his health had suffered permanent damage. Only in midsummer when Burgoyne's invading army reached Fort Edward was it possible for Daniel to come out of hiding with his remaining men and newer recruits to join the main army. They served variously during the short months prior to the debacle at Saratoga, when he and others fled north to Canada. Here, serving under Carleton, McAlpin was posted with his unit to several stations — Sorel, Vercheres and Nouvelle Beauce in succession.

Haldimand, Carleton's replacement as Governor, knew McAlpin, and when a commander was needed to organize the refugee Loyalists in 1779, he appointed Daniel. This task eventually took him from St. Ours and Sorel to Montreal early in 1780, but ill health impeded his progress, and he was at last confined to the town on doctor's orders. He continued to do the best he could as his condition deteriorated, writing his will and

---

[11]NAC: HP, B214/200.

a final letter to the governor on 20th July. The next day this "faithful old servant" of the Crown died.[12]

After Nairne completed the work begun by McAlpin, he passed on responsibility for the Loyalists to Jessup. Maj. Edward Jessup (1736-1816), born in Connecticut, was the eldest of three brothers of English descent who moved to the Hudson Valley in the 1760s and there became prosperous and prominent. They owned, developed and speculated in large tracts of land on both sides of the river near Albany.[13] So influential were they that the area was called Jessupsborough. They were the first timber men in the district, the present site of Luzerne, where they built mills. Edward lived at Jessup's Little Falls, and served in the previous war as a militia captain, later becoming a justice of the peace well acquainted with the governors of the Colony. Both he and brother Ebenezer were said to have been surrounded by taste and culture in their homes, a fact masked by the rough exteriors of their log houses. Edward, while shrewder, was less pretentious and imaginative than the other, but both lived in a style which strongly contrasted with the simplicity in which their youngest brother Joseph lived.

After the Jessups had raised a regiment to fight under Burgoyne, been captured, and released, they made their way to Canada. Here they were permitted to raise their own regiment known as the Loyal Rangers with Lt.Col. Ebenezer as the promoter and Maj. Edward as the effective leader.

Edward also served as the commander of the civilian Loyalists in mid-1782 until relieved of this duty by Cuyler. He

---

[12]Mary McAlpin's Losses Claim, 1785-1786 (NAC: A.O. 12/21, 51-65); see also articles by John E. Ruch in **Loyalist Gazette** (Toronto) Autumn 1979, 4-5, Spring 1980, 10-11, and Autumn 1980, 18.

[13]Fryer, **King's Men**, 180-182; see also Hazel C. Mathews, **Frontier Spies** (Fort Myers, Fla., 1971), 6-7; see also Hadden op. cit. 67-74nn.

suffered from poor health, remaining in Sorel over the winter of 1783-1784. He was appointed justice of the peace again, this time on Nov. 27, 1783,[14] and although charged with some of the duties of settling the refugees upriver, he finally managed to obtain permission to visit England, staying there 1784-1786. He returned to Canada and to work, but left again for England in 1789 to plead his case before the commissioners who were deciding upon compensation for the dispossessed Americans. It wasn't long before he was back on his land grant in Augusta (no.6) Township plotting the foundation of several villages such as Johnstown, with little success. He continued to be active in the Brockville-Cornwall area, and was appointed Lt.-col. of a battalion of militia raised in his own township of Edwardsburg and Elizabethtown, by Dorchester's order in 1788.[15] In 1810 he laid out the town of Prescott on his own land, where he died in 1816.

To a certain extent Cuyler and the Jessups were self-made men of the merchant class, verging on the status of local landed gentry. De Lancey belonged to the class of professionals, but stemmed from a well-established noble Huguenot family. They were all associates of Sir John Johnson before the Revolution, thus the leadership of Loyalists had some degree of continuity and similarity in character.

Lt.Col. Abraham Cornelius Cuyler (1742-1810) descended from a family of early Dutch immigrants who arrived in New Amsterdam (New York City) in the 17th century. He became a successful businessman and was engaged in trade with the Indians. In 1770 Gov. Tryon appointed him mayor of Albany, and in 1772 commissioned him as major of the local militia.[16] The rebels were suspicious of him because of these posts, and

---

[14]Mary B. Fryer, **Buckskin Pimpernal** (Toronto 1981), 219.

[15]Ibid., 235.

[16]Losses Claim (NAC: A.O. 12/19, 90-95v. and A.O. 13/54, 281-).

his membership in the ruling Anglican party.[17] During the war he demonstrated his loyalty to the Crown beyond doubt.

During the revolutionary ferment in 1775 he was spied on and stopped when he set off by boat for Montreal,[18] but, unable to find incriminating documents, his captors released him to continue his "trade" journey. The next year he was arrested for drinking a toast to the King's health on the royal birthday.[19] Other Loyalists, seized on this occasion by the rebels for the same offense, committed at Cartwright's tavern, included his brother Henry, Stephen De Lancey, and four prominent citizens. Accused of being "notoriously disaffected," they were imprisoned at Albany, then transferred to another jail at Hartford, Conn.,[20] from which Abraham escaped several months later, arriving in New York City in Nov. 1776.[21] Next year his wife and family were expelled from Albany and joined him.

On entering the British-occupied city of New York, he found employment in government service, providing senior officers with intelligence about the Albany region gleaned from his own experience and from the numerous fellow refugees who sought him out for assistance. Gov. Tryon, Gen. Vaughan, and Sir James Wallace made use of him and his contacts throughout the Hudson Valley. He forwarded information to the commandant at Niagara of some rebel plans to attack that

---

[17]Alice P. Kennedy, "The Albany Dutch: Loyalists and Patriots," **New York History,** XLII, 4 (New York Historical Association Oct. 1961), 331-360.

[18]Maryly B. Penrose, **Mohawk Valley in the Revolution** (Franklin Park, N.J. 1978), 21.

[19]J. Sullivan ed. **Minutes of the Albany Committee of Correspondance,** I (Albany 1923), 402.

[20]**Ibid.,** 434.

[21]Losses Claim; family permitted to join him, Sullivan **Minutes,** 854-855.

outpost should Quebec fall to them first. In 1776 he was requested to provide a courier to carry dispatches from Tryon to Carleton in Quebec City, which was highly dangerous given that Quebec was still under siege. The message, however, was urgent for it informed Carleton that help would be on the way as soon as the ice broke up in the St. Lawrence.

Like many other Loyalist leaders, Cuyler recruited a company of men to march in support of Burgoyne, forming part of the forces that would strike north up the Hudson. However, Gen. Clinton's indecision and refusal to move as far north as would really help relieve the beleaguered General coming south met with considerable opposition. Cuyler and his colleagues urged an immediate advance. During the six-week delay, once he had managed the general landing of troops at Esopus, Cuyler and his 27 men were kept as idle as the rest. He was repeatedly consulted by Vaughan and Wallace about local conditions, and in spite of all arguments to the contrary, Clinton dallied until the opportunity was lost forever, then withdrew to the city. The same Loyalist leaders were pleading with the commander-in-chief again in 1778 to return to the offensive up the Hudson. They kept him informed of the state of the enemy-held territory and public opinion there, all to no avail.

In the next two years Cuyler was occupied with raising Loyalist forces, and received a commission as lieutenant-colonel in October 1779, and by August 1780 he was promoted to colonel of voluntary militia. On his own initiative, and with the dubious approval of authorities, he launched an operation on the mainland in Bergen, N.J. opposite Bloomingdale. At his own expense he had his men, the Loyal Refugee Volunteers, build and man a blockhouse, protecting about 200 woodcutters employed to fell trees. Enemy activity in the area had been slack until news of this leaked out, causing Gen. "Mad Anthony" Wayne to lead an unsuccessful attack against them, allowing

Cuyler to complete the project, which had been to fill a government contract for 3,000 cords of firewood.[22] On the whole the British were too slow to exploit enemy weakness such as Cuyler and his Provincials had just done, who returned in high spirits to their post at Smith's Town, Long Island.

Cuyler was continually short of funds in spite of occasional payments he received for the supply of wood, which forced him to sail for England with his family in 1781 to seek government help. The Treasury relaxed sufficiently to pay him £500 for expenses, and an annual pension, plus an allowance to support his elder son at school in England, but the rest of the family returned to New York to face the bleak prospect of an unjust war settlement. Abraham began planning to emigrate. In close touch with the Loyalists Chief Justice William Smith and Lt.Col. Beverley Robinson, when Cuyler spoke of his plan to Smith he was talked out of leaving. The Judge considered himself a spokesman for official policy-makers, and told Cuyler he would be setting a bad example for other Loyalists. To have him desert the stronghold of New York would be a blow to the morale of many. Cornwallis' surrender at Yorktown that autumn put a permanent end to whatever optimism Cuyler's presence might have encouraged.

Abraham Cuyler re-applied for permission to leave for Canada and received it in August 1782.[23] He presented his credentials to Gov. Haldimand along with Carleton's recommendation that his Loyalist pension of £100 per year be continued in Quebec.[24] Cuyler was obviously an energetic,

---

[22]Losses Claim; W.h.w. Sabine ed. **Historical Memoirs of William Smith** III (New York 1971), 249-291.

[23]Sabine, **Smith**, 499; see also Losses Claim (NAC: A.O. 13/54, 281v.

[24]Carleton to Haldimand, Aug. 25, 1782 (NAC: HP, B146/1/7 endorsed "received Oct. 7th").

capable and enterprising officer, who Haldimand had no intention of putting on relief when too many were already idle. He continued Cuyler's pension on the condition that Cuyler take on the duties of an inspector in charge of administering for his fellow refugees.[25] During the summer of 1783, while still employed in this manner, he continued to work at restoring his former prosperity, and, with partial success, he tried to recover money from his debtors and pay off his own debts. Realizing the potential size of the Loyalist migration to Quebec, he planned to organize his own settlement of refugees destined for Cape Breton Island, but he needed a large grant of land from the British government to begin. Resigning his post, he went to London to solicit for such a land grant.

The inevitable delays encountered in the bureaucracy and in trans-Atlantic communication meant that news of his success did not reach Quebec until the most opportune moment had passed. His wife, her relatives and friends were in charge of the group which was to migrate, but as settlements began to open upriver, many people who had planned to go with them impatiently set off for Cataraqui and other areas. Late in the year a small party of 100 Loyalists left for Cape Breton. They became an important element on the Island until early in the next century, when they began to be submerged in the fresh floods of emigrants arriving from overseas.[26]

Cuyler returned with his family to Montreal by the 1790s. His colony in Cape Breton had not been the success he

---

[25]He reported that he was ready for duty in Montreal, 1. to Mathews, Oct. 28, 1782 (NAC: HP, B165/13).

[26]Settlement of the island in this period has been studied by Robert J. Morgan who wrote and outline of it in "The Loyalists of Cape Breton," **Dalhousie Review**, vol. 55, no.1 (Spring 1975) 5-22, and a doctoral thesis "Orphan Outpost: Cape Breton Colony, 1784-1820," (Ottawa 1975).

had hoped it would be. He then began the last and most frustrating period of his life. Land papers devoted to his petitions for land for himself, his wife and three of his four children, and related documents extend from Sept. 22, 1794, to 1810.[27] As his own entitlement was large, the total for his family was 20,000 acres, but specific grants could not be given until townships had been surveyed, and other Loyalist applicants had been taken into consideration. There were lengthy delays and even after revisiting England to plead with the government, he still had not received anything near his allowance. His elder son, Capt. Cornelius Cuyler, now returned from service in the 69th Regt., assisted him with the paperwork, and also petitioned for land on his own behalf, and for his cousins James, William Howe and Burton Cuyler — sons of former commissary Henry Cuyler of Green Bush near Albany.

The Cuylers were related to another prominent Albany family by marriage. Abraham's wife was Jannet (Jane) Glen by whom he had four children: Cornelius, Jacob Glen, Cathalyna and Elizabeth. The Glens, although not loudly proclaimed to be Loyalists, definitely sympathized with the Crown. While Abraham Cuyler's siblings Cornelius and Margarita (Mrs. Isaac Low) definitely were exiled Loyalists, Henry remained in the U.S. until later notwithstanding having once been jailed as a Loyalist.[28] On the other hand, Jane Cuyler's brothers Cornelius and John Glen took the rebel oath of association and escaped persecution. Yet John's son Jacob left home to join Sir John

---

[27]Lower Canada Papers (NAC: RG1/L3L/69, 34617-34926); he was also granted land in Upper Canada; see also Capt. Cornelius Cuyler's petition for himself, **ibid.**, 39432, 34940-1, for cousins, 34936.

[28]Kennedy, 32-33.

Johnson's regiment as an ensign.[29] The elder Glens' loyal feelings were masked for the most part, but in June 1783 they journeyed north from Schenectady to Montreal on a special mission. Ostensibly they were carrying the Cuylers' abandoned possessions to Abraham's family, however it is clear that they had business in mind, and something else beside, from their private talks with the joint-chief of intelligence Dr. Smyth.[30] At least one of them agreed to become what would now be described as a "mole", a non-active agent who could be used on special occasions to perform intelligence work,[31] although his subsequent work in this line is not known. It is ironic that Wing's Falls on the Hudson was renamed because Abraham Wing, the Quaker miller who had owned the property, was a Loyalist spy. The location became Glen's Falls thereafter.[32] Abraham Cuyler died Feb. 5, 1810, still attempting to obtain the balance of his land. In 1798 he had been granted five lots near Sorel which he sold seven years later for £60,[33] leaving him far from affluent. Sir John Johnson, after attending the funeral, wrote a touching tribute in a letter to the governor:

> ...one of my oldest friends and acquaintances, one of His
> Majesty's most faithful, brave and loyal
> subjects....expended the whole of whatever he might
> have received as compensation in the support of

---

[29] Mary B. Fryer & William A. Smy, **Rolls of Provincial Corps.** (Toronto 1981), 23; for his later life see Thomas A. Ramsey, "La famille Glen de Chambly," **Les Cahiers de la Seigneurie de Chambly,** no.7 (Feb. 1982), Société d'Histoire de la Seigneurie de Chambly, 31-36.

[30] bis. Smyth to Mathews, June 20, 1783 (NAC: HP, B.178/185-185).

[31] Smyth to Mathews, Aug. 1, 1783, **ibid.,** 197-198.

[32] Mathews, **Frontier Spies,** 178.

[33] Memorial of Abraham Cuyler (NAC: RG8/C279/192); deed of sale to Allen Morison, Aug. 20, 1805, **ibid.,** 193.

himself and family, in building ...in the pursuit of a
further grant, he vainly hoped to obtain in lieu of losses
uncompensated.[34]
Cuyler was buried in the Protestant cemetery near his
home in Ste. Therese on the Richelieu.

After Cuyler resigned, Haldimand appointed Stephen
De Lancey to the post, who was already in Montreal by Nov. 10,
1783, as Inspector of the Loyalists.[35] He was one of three
Stephen De Lanceys in the same generation, all of them
grandsons of their first namesake in America, Etienne De Lancy
(sic) a noble Huguenot refugee who came to New York via
London from France in 1686,[36] and founded the family which
held political and economic power during the next century. Of
the three Stephens, the best know was the lieutenant-colonel
serving in De Lancey's Brigade, a formation raised and
commanded by his father, Gen. Oliver. Later this Stephen was
transferred to the New Jersey Volunteers.[37] After the

---

[34]NAC: RG8/C256/59-60.

[35]Haldimand to De Lancey, Nov. 10, 1783 (NAC: HP, B165/173); Memorial of
De Lancey, nov. 27, 1783, ibid., 181.

[36]The most useful work on the De Lanceys is a typescript by George De
Lancey Hanger of Roanoake, Va, "Those Later Years," based on research in
NAC by Mrs. John Coderre of Ottawa. See esp. pages 200, 252-255, 280-282, 534-
540. Confusion between the two brighter Stephens exists in almost all earlier
works beginning with Lorenzo Sabine who admitted he could not reconcile
some of his findings with other facts, **Loyalists of the American Revolution,**
I (reprint 1979), 371-372. On genealogy of family see Thomas Jones, **History of
New York,** I (New York 1879, reprint 1979), 649-655; and D.A. Story, **The De
Lanceys: A Romance of a Great Family** (1931).

[37]Murtie J. Clark, **Loyalists in the Southern Campaign,** III (Baltimore
1981), 351, Lt.Col. Stephen De Lancey, reduced April 22, 1782, from 2nd De

Revolution he established his unit in Nova Scotia and New Brunswick, and accepted official posts abroad,[38] dying in 1798 shortly after being appointed Governor of Tobago.

The least mentioned of the Stephens was the second son of New York's lieutenant-governor, James De Lancey. He was not of the same calibre as his other namesakes, and after leading a quiet life in Westchester County, N.Y., died there in 1795.[39]

Inspector De Lancey (1738-1809) was the oldest of the three Stephens, the first son of Peter De Lancey. Trained as a lawyer, he obtained appointments as clerk to the city and county of Albany, and became a master in Chancery.[40] As an outspoken Loyalist, a close associate of Cuyler, and a member of the Anglican party, he was watched closely by the rebels from the beginning of hostilities, who finally used the excuse of his having participated in public celebrations of the King's birthday to arrest and imprison him along with Cuyler and others.[41] Released many months later, he joined his exiled wife and

---

Lancey's Brigade, now in 2nd New Jersey Volunteers, and later page 346 in 1st N.J. Vols.

[38]There are references to his work in the Maritimes settlements in the Winslow Papers, and in the Carleton Papers which demonstrate his presence there during late 1783 and 1784, e.g. De Lancey at Annapolis to Winslow, March 28, 1784 (PAC: Winslow Papers, III, 19); for appointments see L. Sabine loc. cit. and **Dictionary of National Biography**, V, 754-755, under Sir William Howe De Lancey.

[39]Jones, **New York**, I, 657-658.

[40]Of numerous references in **Losses Claims** the more important are his Memorial May 30, 1783 (NAC: A.O. 12/99/289) and Memorial July 5, 1787 (**ibid.**, 27/22-25). Two other memorials are dated June 1, 1980 (NAC: A.O. 13/113/1/316) and March 19, 1784 (**ibid.**, 39-40).

[41]Sullivan, **Minutes** I, 455, 457, 459, 510.

children in New York City, and, without means of support, he
petitioned the military governor, Gen. Robertson, for aid. His
loyalty was rewarded with the grant of a farm, formerly the
property of a rebel, on Long Island, and the family managed to
survive by farming until the mass evacuation of the area in late
1783. They migrated to Canada, where his friend Cuyler was
about to leave his post, an office which Stephen was very
suitably qualified for. It is possible, but unlikely, that he knew
beforehand of the inspector's intention to leave, and therefore
decided to come to Quebec rather than Nova Scotia where his
brother and namesake cousin migrated.

Stephen's choice of Quebec as a place of permanent
settlement was probably determined by the presence of a
number of other relatives with whom his family would feel at
home. Sir John Johnson's uncle Peter Warren had married
Stephen's aunt Susanna De Lancey, Lady Johnson was the
daughter of his other aunt, Anna De Lancey Watts. Maj. Robert
Leake's wife was a sister of Lady Johnson and Stephen's wife
Esther Rynderts was a Cuyler descendant. About the time the
family embarked at New York his wife gave birth to a son who
survived the journey along with three other children. In May
1784, Peter was 20 years old, Elizabeth eight, Cadwallader six and
the infant (Balthus) ten months.[42] The De Lanceys were
unlucky with their children. Four children succumbed in 1773
to the "cruel throat distemper" (diptheria). Peter was a problem
child who was slightly deranged by an accidental blow at an
early age, and in adult years was aggravated by another blow on
the head during a fight with his Caughnawaga Indian wife,

---

[42]Wife's name, L. Sabine, op. cit. Children's ages, De Lancey to Mathews, May
17, 1784 (NAC: HP B165/242) pub. Cruikshank, 102. Their names in Hanger,
534-535.

when in self-defense she hit him with a billet of wood.[43] He was in the 60th Regt. (2nd Battalion) in the 1790s and twice went absent without leave, and was arrested and punished with 1,000 lashes the first time. On the second arrest he faced "serious" punishment, wrote Joseph Chew euphemistically, but the Indians pleaded on his behalf for his discharge from the army.

The De Lanceys moved upriver from Quebec to Montreal early in November, 1783,[44] where they discovered that the necessities of life were "so very extravagant" in price. He was first paid $1 per day until the next year when it was changed to £100 per year,[45] at which time he was also allowed a house.

His term of office began inauspiciously, for he was immobilized by an attack of gout through most of December. On recovery, he and De Coigne were dispatched on a mission to take the rolls of Loyalist refugees in several camps.[46]

By April he had moved to Lachine, where he leased a farm to help support his family,[47] and which was closer to the refugee camps at the head of the inland river transport system. Haldimand permitted him, during the early summer, to devote some time to his farming, which so absorbed him that he did not get back to his office until a jarring letter arrived from the

---

[43]Correspondence between Jospeh Chew and several officials, Feb. 18-24, 1794 (NAC: RG 8/ C930/113-119), wrongly indexed in Reference Room as "Delaney, Peter."

[44]High cost of living, De Lancey to Mathews, Nov. 27, 1783 (NAC: HP B165/181).

[45]**Losses Claim** (NAC: A.O.12/26/25).

[46]Mathews to De Lancey, Jan. 22, 1784, ibid., B63/50-51, (pub. Cruikshank, 43).

[47]Moved to Lachine, De Lancey to Mathews, April 18, 1784 (NAC: HP, B165/231v); had "hired" a farm, De Lancey to Haldimand, Aug. 26, 17844, **ibid,** 266.

Governor in August. A number of disputes had broken out among the refugees, said the latter, and continued:

> "The nature of your office, your Authority as a
> Magistrate, your knowledge of and influence with
> the greatest part of these people, if residing with
> Them, could not fail to prevent in a great measure,
> the misunderstandings and discontents which have
> occurred..."[48]

De Lancey has long been considered a nonentity in Canada, or at best a place-holder, a man who got credit for other people's work. However, the scattered correspondence and references to him indicate that he was relied on a good deal by both government and settlers. All Loyalists' payments were made through the Inspector's office, rather than through the Quarter Master General of Loyalists' office.[49] Apart from deciding on the eligibility of refugees for aid, the Inspector now had to determine the amounts of supplies to be issued them.

Stephen was inclined to be lenient when authorizing issues of stores, as he had travelled with many of the newcomers and knew of their losses. Some Loyalists now well-established in the Province resented loosing subsistence and other aid to those who had only just arrived and would seem to have merited it less. Haldimand had always been sparing in the matter of government relief to the destitute, and had indoctrinated his officers with the principle of careful husbanding of their limited resources. Thus De Lancey's subordinates exercised greater strictness in evaluating the

---

[48]Haldimand to De Lancey, Aug. 23, 1784, ibid., B64, 179-180, (pub. Cruikshank, 156).

[49]Haldimand to De Lancey, Dec. 20, 1783, ibid., B165/207v.

immediate conditions of refugees, consequently coming into conflict with those who demanded too much.

In April 1784, tempers were on edge, De Coigne argued bitterly with one of the senior McDonnells[50] and French, who had a sharp tongue at the best of times, gave it free play on the complainers at Machiche.[51] The former dispute was smoothed out by De Lancey, but the latter reverberated through Sorel, Quebec City and Montreal. There had been some grounds for objection to French's parsimoniousness, but longterm grudges against him and a propensity to find fault gave the Machiche veterans a chance to get even. De Lancey reprimanded him for his behaviour and French, in an outburst of anger, handed in his resignation to the Governor. But being too valuable to lose, attempts were made to keep him in the service, and before long he was entrusted with other important commissions.[52]

During the summer of 1784, the direction of the Inspector's efforts changed. In the previous year major problems were receiving, housing and generally caring for the incoming refugees. Now transportation of these same people to permanent settlements far from their camps had to be arranged. Acting in close co-operation with the quarter master, the commissary and other services, the Inspector had to help organize the transport of supplies as well as settlers. Moving a European army was a small problem, but transporting hundreds of Loyalist civilians strained all available resources. De Lancey was required to publicize the Governor's plans for movements and settlements, and to take rolls of those who

---

[50]De Lancey to Mathews, April 18, 1784, **ibid.**, B165/231v.

[51]De Lancey to Mathews, May 27, 1784, **ibid.**, B165/248 (pub. Cruikshank, 238-241).

[52]Mathews to De Lancey, May 24, 1784, **ibid.**, B63/342 (pub. Cruikshank, 112-113).

wanted to go to particular locations — upriver to New
Oswegatchie, New Johnstown or Cataraqui, downriver to Gaspé
and Cape Breton. The Inspector and also his team had to gather
the various groups at departure points where fleets of small
vessels would take them to their destinations. Those for the
Gaspé and Chaleurs Bay were marshalled at Quebec, those for
the upper St. Lawrence at Sorel or Lachine, and later, those
destined for Cape Breton at Quebec. Before they embarked, the
Inspector ensured that the people were properly prepared for
the journey according to the Governor's orders.

After the massive movements of 1784, the Inspector was
largely concerned with work in two spheres. The first may be
referred to as social welfare, providing for the aged, the sick, the
invalid, the orphaned, the weak — many of whom stayed
behind when the boats sailed for the new settlements. The
second concern was with the settlers. De Lancey had to cope
with disputes, and misunderstandings. In the autumn of 1784
he went to the Cataraqui area to look into problems of settling
the third and fourth townships (Adolphustown and
Fredericksburgh), and reported back to the Governor on Sept.
26, Oct. 2 and 16.[53] John Collins, the Deputy Surveyor-General,
and Capt. John Barnes, Deputy Quarter Master General, were
also among those attempting to disentangle the snares in way of
settlement. Sir John Johnson, in charge of the whole operation
under Haldimand's instructions, with De Lancey and other
officers were appointed as commissioners of the peace so that
the voluminous paperwork involved in administering oaths,
certifications and the taking of evidence could be shared.

After Haldimand's departure for England late that year,
the record of the Inspector's services becomes less continuous
and fragmentary. However he retained the important role of
informing the settlers of the Governor's instructions. In reply to

---

[53]De Lancey to Haldimand, Oct. 16, 1784, **ibid.**, B162/379 (Cruikshank, 172).

to their petition that other military units receive the same generous land grants as had been promised to the 84th Regt., De Lancey quoted the words of Gov. Dorchester to him:

> "These people engaged in His Majesty's Service as early and are in every respect as deserving as those of the 84th...I shall put them all on an equal footing."[54]

He further quoted Lt.Gov. Hope:
> "Be assured I shall at all times cheerfully do everything in my power to promote their interest and prosperity."

Johnson and De Lancey, both in positions of authority over the Loyalists, were close friends and relatives, co-operated closely in the management of the settlers' affairs. Thus in the eyes of the Loyalists they were joint guardians of their interests. The high-handed and autocratic behaviour of some of their local leaders, as in the elections of representatives early in 1787, caused a great deal of apprehension. The Inspector had a circular letter read to the electors in each of the new townships informing them of their freedom of choice and its relevance to forthcoming decision-making, "On the choice you are now to make your's and your Posterity's future happiness will much depend."[55]

In this and other matters it is clear that De Lancey was acting on the advice and with the guidance of Dorchester and Johnson. Patrick McNiff, surveyor, was very much involved both as a courier and as a counsellor to the settlers, and the would-be local magnates looked on him as "a Seditious &

---

[54]De Lancey to W. Faulkner, W. Sutherland et al., Dec. 24, 1786 (NAC: RG4/A1/31/10073-74).

[55]Unsigned circular letter, Dec. 26, 1786, **ibid.**, 10075-76.

Dangerous Incendiary."[56] It was McNiff who later told the settlers in a letter, "if it had not been for Sir John Johnson & Stephen De Lancey Esq." the officers would have had a distinct advantage over them in future.[57]

De Lancey continued to operate a farm to make ends meet. Haldimand granted him 1,000 acres in his own right, holding status equivalent to a field officer, and 50 acres for his wife and each child, all on Riviere Raisin,[58] and he also received town lots at Sorel in 1787. He petitioned to be allowed to harvest hay on Ile Ronde at Montreal, but this was found to be already reserved for the Commissary.[59]

Stephen became the vehicle of the new settlers' messages to those in authority beyond their townships, forwarding their letters of special significance which were later published in the Quebec *Gazette*. In this way the general public was made aware of the Loyalists' gratitude to John Collins for having dealt justly in surveying land at Quinte, thus settling their disputes.[60] About 100 men signed this letter, including De Lancey. A loyal address of greeting and thanks was later presented to Lord Dorchester on his arrival as Haldimand's successor, consisting of three separate messages, one from each

---

[56]Settlers of New Johnstown to De Lancey, Jan. 18, 1787, ibid., 10219-22, enclosing McNiff's letter, 10221-22.

[57]Settlers of the townships , Jan. 31, 1787, **ibid.,** 10258.

[58]Land grant of 1,200 acres on Riviere Raisin by Haldimand's warrant, sold to Sir John Johnson, Sept. 19, 1792 (NAC: CP, MG19/F1/15/65) and Hangar, 539, 86. Town lots in Sorel, Hanger loc. cit. received 1787, sold later (NAC: Lower Canada Land Papers, RG1, L3L.

[59]Register of Memorials, no. 291, minute July 30, 1789 (NAC: RG4/A3/2 (n.p.)); see also 155 for continuation of his pay.

[60]**Gazette** (Quebec) no.1065, Jan. 19, 1786, the letters of thanks dated Oct. 7 and 8 preceding, De Lancey's covering letter, Jan. 1, 1786.

of the areas of New Johnstown, New Oswegatchie and Cataraqui.[61] Dorchester's reply to these was addressed care of De Lancey and published at the same time.

In the late 1780s, De Lancey was appointed to the Legislative Council[62] while he continued to serve as a magistrate for Montreal, and later for Sorel.[63] The style of his official title became Inspector General of Loyalists.[64] With the visit to Montreal in 1787-88 of the British commissioners enquiring into war losses, Stephen finally had an opportunity to lay his claims for compensation. His outright losses amounted to £2,350 and expenses involved thereafter totalled £2,166.8s.

His move to Sorel was precipitated by the situation which had arisen there during the first three post-war years. This settlement was to be developed into an industrial centre, one of many projects left in suspense when Gov. Haldimand left Canada in 1784. The population of Loyalists was composed of artisans, craftsmen and destitute people. As the years passed without constructive action being taken on the plan, discontent mounted to fever pitch and the place seethed with petty grievances. Finally, after the new governor arrived, a commission of enquiry was set up to investigate complaints emanating from that quarter. The initial finding was something of a surprise. Those pleas for redress which had reached Quebec City, and which had resulted in the establishment of the fact-

---

[61]Ibid., no.1114, Dec. 21, 1786.

[62]Ibid., no. 1089, June 29, 1786, appointments as commissioners of the peace, and members of the legislative council include no. 19 Stephen De Lancey, no.20 John Barnes, no.21 Neil McLean, and no.22 Justus Sherwood.

[63]Commissioners of Peace for Montreal District, Stephen De Lancey at Sorel, July 18, 1788 (NAC: RG4/A1/40/13019A).

[64]Hanger, 535, 539/12 cites Ontario Archives **Report** 19.

finding team, represented only the tip of the iceberg. They reported to headquarters that there were about 20 times more real grievances than had previously been disclosed. The evidence of this fills scores of pages in official records, a veritable mine of information of the residents of Sorel in the mid-1780s.[65] De Lancey's role was to assist the commissioners by explaining the circumstances under which relief had been authorized for various individuals, and by vouching for those he was acquainted with and whose merits he was certain of. After the enquiry was completed, the report of July 12, 1787, recommended that any further relief decided on by the Governor be administered by the Inspector: "the Humanity and tender attention of Mr. De Lancy (sic) to those objects of his care render him the properest person to be entrusted."[66]

Early in 1791 Stephen decided to move to Annapolis, N.S., to be nearer to his brother Maj. James De Lancey, former leader of the famed Loyalist cavalry unit nicknamed "De Lancey's Cowboys." On his retirement from the post of inspector his salary ceased, but he received a pension of £150 p.a. until his death.[67] In Nova Scotia, having received several appointments and a grant of land, he died on May 20, 1809,

---

[65]The Sorel papers begin with Alexander White's petition, April 21, 1786, 29/9634-9636 and continue, e.g. the three-man report on number of complaints ibid., 9646; five-man commission dossier, ibid., 32/10494-10622, 33/10656-10675, and 10714-10754.

[66]Ibid., 33/10668/7. De Lancey's name occurs numerous times in the evidence, e.g. 32/10506 and 10590.

[67]Records of his allowance of £100 p.a. as inspector from 1788 on are in Treasury records (NAC: T50/331-41). His office ceased June 24, 1791, from which time he was paid a pension of £150 p.a., ibid., 32/27 and 33/6v. A few earlier payments are recorded in the old "S" Series (NAC: RG1/E15/28: account of Loyalists, July 14, 1785 and 33: Account, July 19, 1787).

leaving as his sole heir his daughter Elizabeth (1774-1856).[68] She had married William De Lancey three years earlier, the son of her uncle James, thus uniting the families of the "inspector" and the "outlaw."

Without some mention of the subordinates who served the inspectors and superintendents of Loyalists the story would be incomplete. The names which merit attention are those of Neil Robertson, Louis Decoigne, Neil Maclean, George Law and Gershom French. Of the group, only Decoigne did not hold a commission in a military unit. He was actually on the staff of the Commissary, but late in the war he came into close contact with the inspectors. Probably related to the schoolmaster R. Mathieu De Coine (fl.1766), he appears to have enjoyed several official posts after the Revolution.[69]

Neil Robertson had been the right-hand man of both McAlpin and Nairne when they served as officers commanding the Unincorporated Loyalists.[70] He had arrived in this province as an ensign in Jessup's corps in 1776. Later under the command of McAlpin, as a lieutenant, with his knowledge of the people and his ability as an administrator, he became adjutant for the combined groups. Nairne found him equally

---

[68]Died May 20, 1809 (NAC: T50/41/6) which agrees with the entry in Stephen's family **Bible** in the Fort Anne Museum, Annapolis Royal, N.S> Elizabeth's marriage, Story, 176, and W.A. Calnek (A.W. Savary ed.) **History of the County of Annapolis** (Toronto 1897, reprint Belleville 1972), 343. She died Nov. 15, 1856, aged 82, **Bible**.

[69]Mathieu De Coine (De Couagne) advertised his change of address, **Gazette** (Quebec) in Oct.-Nov. 1766, nos.92, 95, 96, and 99. One Louis Decoigne signed several public addresses, and was appointed a notary, **ibid.**, no. 2193, May 7, 1807, and J.P. no.3162, Oct. 25, 1821.

[70]Fryer, **King's Men,** 183.

useful and left him in this position,[71] which was detrimental to his military career, for while other potential leaders were recruiting their own units, he was kept occupied in an office with routine matters.[72] He eventually transferred to the King's Royal Regt. of New York. finally settling in Upper Canada.[73]

Lt. Neil Maclean, on the other hand, served throughout the latter part of the war with the 84th Regt. Like De Lancey, he is one of three namesakes frequently confused in historical writings. The others were a captain in the same regiment, and a commissary, later a judge at Kingston.[74] If the identification is correct, Lt. Maclean lived from 1757 to 1832, and was the last surviving officer of the old Royal Highland Emigrants.[75] He was much involved with administration in Cataraqui at the time of the first settlements, later serving in official posts and as a senior militia officer in the Cornwall area during the 1812 war.[76]

Capt. George Law (Lawe(s), Lowe) was a veteran officer, probably born in Ireland about 1730, who joined the British Army prior to the Seven Years War, and served until 1764.[77] He emigrated to America, and settled on a land grant near Lake George, N.Y. An early Loyalist volunteer, he was present at the siege of Quebec City in which he executed a daring manoeuvre

---

[71]Nairne to Mathews, July 5, 1781 (NAC: HP, B161/282).

[72]Officers Names (NAC: HP, B166/142).

[73]He became a lieutenant in 2nd K.R.R.N.Y., Johnson to Haldimand, July 22, 1780, **ibid.**, B158/137, and is found on the **Old United Empire Loyalists' List** (Toronto 1885), 243; see also Fryer and Smy, 25.

[74]The commissary, **Dict. Can. Biog.**, IV.

[75]J.F. Pringle, **Lunenburgh or the Old Eastern District** (Cornwall 1890, reprint Belleville 1972), 225.

[76]**Ibid.**, 200, 225, 259.

[77]See above n.4, Hadden, 137, Annett,1.

that gained him the governor's commendation. Practical knowledge of field constructions and his ability as an intelligence agent made him particularly valuable. He had four sons, three of which were lost on military duty, and a daughter by his first wife. His second wife, whom he married in 1778, was Rachel Franks, believed to have been the daughter of the Montreal merchant John Franks. Evidently financial problems forced him to sell his commission in the 84th Regt. in late 1782, having been Barrack Master at Montreal for several years,[78] after which he was given several important missions by the governors. As superintendent he headed the party of Loyalists that migrated from the St. Lawrence region to settle at Chaleurs Bay.[79] Later he took up residence at Quebec City until about 1790 when his new post, and the prospect of land grants, drew him to the newly-created province of Upper Canada. Lt.Gov. Simcoe made him Overseer of Works at the then capital, Newark (Niagara-on-the-Lake), and in 1793 gave him dispatches to carry to England. Accompanied by a daughter and two sons he made the voyage and visited Ireland on family business as well. He returned to Niagara where he died about 1800.

Lt. Gershom French, the last to be mentioned as an aide to and associate of the inspectors, is one of those ubiquitous characters of the early and mid-1780s who turns up in numerous documents identified only as Lt. or Mr. French.

Gershom and his elder brother Jeremiah were from Connecticut originally, and had large landholdings in Manchester (Vermont). They were active Loyalists during the Burgoyne campaign in 1777 with Peter's corps. Gershom first held a commission from a Colonial Governor dated October 26,

---

[78]Annett, 2, some correspondance in NAC: HP, B183/B184.

[79]Paid as superintendant of Loyalists, Chaleurs Bay, £63.18s., Nov. 1, 1784 to April 30, 1785, Accounts of Deputy Receiver General (NAC: RG1/E15a/28).

1776,[80] and became a hunted man in New York with a price of £100 on his head "dead or alive."[81]

In mid-August he joined Peter's regiment with 90 men and three officers at Fort Miller,[82] and was later captured and expelled together with his family to Quebec.[83] The brothers were aggressive, energetic and enterprising — characteristics which several times led them into trouble with the military authorities. When in 1781 Nairne's efforts at re-organization of Loyalist units were completed, the Frenchs were split up. Jeremiah went into the K.R.R.N.Y. and Gershom joined the Loyal Rangers, and from then on it becomes somewhat easier to separate the various records which refer, ambiguously, to Lt. French.

At Sorel and its dependent camps, Gershom French was regularly engaged in the problems of supervising issues of necessities to the refugees. He tended to be strict in controlling the supplies shipped in for their use. Scolded by De Lancey for his miserliness and injudicious language, French tendered his resignation, but Mathews, the Governor's secretary, wrote to

---

[80]His commission from Gov. of Bahamas, Montfort Brown, dated Long Island, Oct. 26, 1776 (NAC: HP, B167/1); commission from Gen. Howe, Oct. 26, 1776, Fryer, **King's Men**, 209. In earlier histories the Frenchs were sometimes confused with the town major of Montreal, Maj. French, e.g. Hadden, **Journal**. Appendix 19, 545-546.

[81]An armed party was sent to Rensselaerwyck to capture or kill him and Andrew Palmetier and break up their group, Aug. 7, 1777, Sullivan, **Minutes I**, 823.

[82]His statement of services in Burgoyne's campaign (NAC: HP, B161/1-3); Fryer, **Buckskin Pimpernel**, 65; **King's Men**, 209.

[83]Sullivan, **Minutes**, I, 839, 17 men and their families were to be sent to the "enemy," French's included, Sept. 3, 1777.

the Inspector, advising him to try persuasion rather than harsh words on his subordinate.

> His temper may not be the smoothest in the world, but believe me he is possessed of more cleverness and activity than one half of the people employed, & that if you loose him, you will severely feel the want of him, besides that from his approved Assiduity and Integrity in different Lines, he has proved himself a very useful Man & is much protected by the General (Haldimand).[84]

French continued in government service.

His most important tasks during the period 1783-84 were related to the settlement of the refugees. In the late summer of 1783 he led one of several survey parties sent into the upper country to look for suitable land for farmers. They left Montreal on Sept. 20 and ascended the Ottawa River, making field trips along the way from above Carillon to the mouth of the Rideau River, where they struck southward following the river to its source, crossing the portage, and descending the Gananoque River to Cataraqui, where they arrived Oct. 13. French's journal of the trip is still preserved,[85] being the first survey of the route. Over 40 years later it was of considerable use to those who surveyed and planned the Rideau Canal. When in 1784 the great movements of Loyalists from the refugee camps to their new homes were dispatched, French performed yeoman service at the posts in and around Sorel, where he worked closely with Capt. John Barnes, Quartermaster. Released from service on half-pay, Gershom settled at Coteau du Lac on property which

---

[84]Mathews to De Lancey, May 24, 1784 (NAC: B63/342 (Cruikshank, 112-113).

[85]Journal of Lieutenant Gershom French (NAC: HP, B31/31-41), Cruikshank, 14-18.

remained in the possession of his descendants into recent times.[86] He died there on June 23, 1831.[87]

The inspectorate existed as a distinct office directly under the governor's command for nearly nine years, 1782-91. It had been created in anticipation of a massive influx of destitute Loyalists for which no single existing department was prepared or responsible. Haldimand chose as inspectors educated and intelligent men, impoverished American Loyalists of administrative experience, social status and proven fidelity. The office was far from a sinecure, particularly in the hectic period of immigration 1783-84, but they did their work well although beset by their own personal problems. When peacetime conditions returned to Quebec, the focus of the inspector's work changed as the role of the Loyalists altered from being dependents of the Crown to independent, pioneer settlers. The need for supervision of distressed Loyalists decreased steadily as the numbers of "refugees" diminished, and by 1791 two events influenced the governor to terminate the office. Early that year the long-serving and most experienced inspector resigned and left for Nova Scotia. Political division of the Province of Quebec into two entities removed the greater part of the Loyalists from the jurisdiction of Quebec. The governor at Quebec and Lt.Gov. of Upper Canada vied with each other as champions of the Loyalists, but for a generation after they had left Canada forever, the legendary mantle of the Loyalists' chief leader rested on Sir John Johnson's shoulders in Lower Canada.

---

[86] Genealogical notes in William Wood ed., **The Storied Province of Quebec**.

[87] List of American Officers (NAC: RG8/634a/108).

The Commissary

For survival, Loyalists were usually completely dependent on various government departments ordinarily concerned with the prosecution of the war. In emergencies, such as the evacuation of refugees from enemy territory, and later their settlement in what became Upper Canada required transportation.

Food for both man and beast was the responsibility of the Commissary. The bulk of supplies throughout the Revolution was shipped from Britain on orders from the Treasury Department.[1] In Canada the Commissary stored and distributed provisions under instructions from the Governor, and procured other supplies locally when required. The staff was largely composed of civilians, about half of whom were Loyalists, the remainder included veteran soldiers, both British and French-Canadians. They were paid according to rank within the Department: Commissary General, Deputy Commissary General, Assistant Commissary General, Deputy Commissary, Assistant Commissary, and Issuer. A number of coopers and ordinary labourers, usually unnamed in returns, were also employed.

The size of the Commissary establishment grew larger during the Revolution, yet it varied in numbers during that time. Twice it increased, and each time had to be reduced subsequently. The first growth was experienced in the early phase of the War to support Burgoyne's large army in 1777.

---

[1]Edward E. Curtis, **The Organization of the British Army in the American Revolution** (New Haven 1926, reprint New York 1969), esp. Chap IV "Provisioning the Army." His information concerning the Province of Quebec is largely based upon correspondence between Secretary Robinson and Commissary General Day in Treasury records, T64/102-104.

When the army was captured a few commissaries were imprisoned, while others escaped and returned to Quebec, where the department now found itself over-staffed. Several were released, including Daniel Bliss, Thomas Scott and Landrieve.[2] The second major increase in staff was forced by the rapid increase in the numbers of refugees flooding into the province, especially in 1782-3. In 1779 there were 43 compared to 52 staff members in late 1782,[3] with the number of commissary posts increased to 34

These posts varied in size, depending upon the numbers of tthose they served. Quebec City and Montreal were major depots and thus required the largest staffs, with Montreal in 1782 being the larger of the two: 11 officials and several other workers were stationed in the area — four officers at Montreal, two at Lachine, and one each at Verchères, Lachenage, Laprairie, the Cedars and Coteau du Lac. The smaller posts were run by an Assistant Commissary and/or an Issuer with perhaps a labourer or two and a cooper. The Montreal district extended west to Michilimackinak, and included another nine officers, while the Richelieu Valley from Sorel to Lake Champlain was staffed by 10 officials.

Following the flight of the American invaders from Quebec in 1776, a new regime began in the Commissary. A new Commissary General, Nathaniel Day, arrived with two

---

[2]Nathaniel Day to Gov. Haldimand, Jan. 4, 1779 (NAC: Haldimand Papers (henceforth HP), B191. This volume contains the Commissary correspondence, while its accounts are in B194 and 195.

[3]Contingent Accounts for Commissarys and Issuers, Dec. 25, 1777 to June 24, 1778 (NAC: HP, B191/62-63) cf..Return of Officers and their Assistants, Dec. 25, 1782, ibid., 219r and v.

assistants, the Clarke brothers, Isaac and Jonathan.[4] Day chose his officers carefully, informing Carleton that he wanted only "active, sober, honest (men with)...the good of the service at Heart."[5] Isaac would serve the department from then on for 46 years while Jonathan carried out his duties under great hardship. With his health ruined he was later released, and returned to Quebec, only to die a few months later.[6] The kind of men available for responsible employment is indicated by the case of Daniel Bliss of Concord, Mas. who had been banished by the rebels. A Harvard-educated lawyer, he worked as a commissary until the branch was reduced after Burgoyne's 1777 fiasco at Saratoga. In late 1778 he was rehired to take the place of a commissary who had resigned at Niagara.[7]

The officials employed in 1782 included other Loyalists. In the immediate area of Montreal were: James Blakeley, Jeremiah Daly, John Davey, Joseph Johnson, Ephraiam Jones, Thomas Dennis, Alexander Robertson and Levi Willard. John Coffin was hired to substitute for the deputy commissary at Chambly by Parkhurst. The salaries ranged from five shillings per day for

---

[4]Curtis p.107/91, based on T64/104 containing Day's commission with instructions, March 20, 1776. The appointment of the Clarkes was announced 29th following. (NAC: **HP**, B38/41); see also E.A. Jones. **Loyalists of Massachussets**, 90-91. John Craigie succeeded Day in late 1784.

[5]Day to Robinson, June 20, 1777, T64/102, quoted by Curtis, 110.

[6]Jonathan Clarke's appointment as Extra Deputy Commissary, Treasury to Haldimand, April 26, 1862 (NAC: HP, B51/61); his arrival in Quebec in Quebec **Gazette**, June 27 following.

[7]Day to Haldimand, Dec. 7, 1778 (NAC: **HP**, B191/38) Bliss "a deserving good man;" Day had suggested Cartwright first, **ibid.**, Nov. 30, 30 as he thought Bliss and family would not want to leave Quebec City.

an assistant commissary down to two shillings and six pence p.d. for lesser jobs.

The commissaries were concerned with the issue of general provisions to the military. Thus at some posts such as Machiche, where Loyalists were numerous, they were served by their own commissary. Donald Munro, who was assistant commissary "to the Royalists," Louis Decoigne (Decoigne Mars or Decouagne)[8] who held such a position, probably was the longest serving in this capacity in Montreal. He was an "Inhabitant" rather than a refugee, and as a partial reward for his services received subsistence rations as did the Loyalists. When their numbers soared, his work became increasingly difficult. He performed his tasks faithfully and successive commanders recommended him highly.[9] Other French-Canadians employed in this area were: Louis Bouthillier, Francis Galien, Gamelin Gaucher Sr., and Jr.

In preparation for the arrival of the refugees in Quebec toward the end of the war Gov. Haldimand rationalized services so that the large numbers of Loyalists could be handled more efficiently. Until October 1782 supplies were from the separate departments, causing the situation to become chaotic with limited supplies, numerous conflicting orders, scales of issue, and demands. A new post was created specifically to regulate the Loyalist administrative problems. As often happened, the frugal Governor was able to kill two birds with one stone. A Loyalist field officer from New York had just

---

[8]Memorial of Loúys Decoigne (NAC: HP B218/89); he is listed on various subsistence returns, e.g. return of those Royalists entitled to house rent and fire wood, Montreal Jan. 1, 1782, **ibid.**, B165/3.

[9]Cuyler to Mathews, March 27, 1783, **ibid,** 68. Nairne to Mathews, March 30, 1782, **ibid.**, B161/425.

arrived in Quebec to explore the possibilities of settlement here for himself, his men and other New Yorkers. This was Abraham Cuyler. Gov. Carleton expected Haldimand to place Cuyler on his Province's payroll, while Haldimand needed a senior Loyalist administrator. By creating an Inspectorate of Loyalist Refugees Haldimand satisfied himself, Cuyler, Carleton and the immigrants.

Necessity caused the Inspector to work closely with the Commissary, as demands on the latter from Loyalist civilians were now ordered to be made through the inspector's office. The work of identifying the individual refugees and evaluating their needs was henceforth shared between their leaders and the inspectorate. Cuyler and his successor were given the responsibility of compiling and reviewing refugee lists, and after mustering them in person were given the authority to order necessary supplies for them from the Commissary.

The assistant commissaries and issuers were in direct contact with the refugees, many of whom had unreasonable demands and expectations. Leaders of individual units knew their own people and tended to be more lenient than the more objective officials. Most of the arrivals in 1783 were in need of clothing, but officers interpreted the order too liberally and often ordered clothing for those who were not in dire need. Commissaries charged with issuing to the newcomers could see the inequality of needs, and complained anonymously to higher authorities. Decoigne informed Capt. Maurer and the governor's secretary of abuses of the regulations of a "most indiscriminate, irregular & profuse manner."[10] As in an

---

[10]Mathews to Barnes, Sept. 13, 1784 (NAC: HP, B65/49-51). pub. by E.A. Cruikshank, **Early Settlement of the Upper St. Lawrence** (Toronto 1934, reprint 1966), 165.

affluent welfare state, Sir John Johnson and Stephen De Lancey
had ordered issues according to what the scale of allowances
permitted, not according to the actual immediate needs of
individuals. Such open-handedness was anathema to "poor
Decouagne whose circumstances are miserably circumscribed."

The Quebec Commissary was beset by a number of other
problems. Day and his subordinates could not foresee or
prevent all the troubles which occurred. Departments such as
the Commissary which kept large quantities of supplies were
peculiarly susceptible to bungling, neglect or chicanery on the
part of employees. The warehouses were at the mercy of thieves
and winter storms.

Buildings used to store these supplies were inspected to
ensure that they were in good repair. On several occasions in
the Montreal area officers were sent to investigate reports of
damaged goods in stores. Isaac Clarke and Gamelin Gaucher
were occupied with such work in 1778 and again in 1780.[11] The
warehouses were in need of repair, and Joseph Perrau was hired
to restore these buildings. In the first case both Montreal and
Lachine stocks had suffered, in the second Lachine only, and on
a third occasion, five months later, Montreal was again
involved.[12]

Sharp practices of some warehouse keepers and their
associates caused the commissaries a good deal of difficulty. In
checking into complaints that rancid flour was in stock it was
discovered that quantities of privately owned flour in a
deteriorated state had been substituted for good government
property, the latter had been removed and sold for personal

---

[11]NAC: HP B191/22, 23-24 and 77; Perrau's estimate, 78.

[12]Ibid., B194/105, Clarke's return of damaged provisions, July 1780.

profit.[13] Complaints were also received in 1779 that some flour
was very old, having been stocked in 1776, hauled to
Ticonderoga and back in 1777. A defective stock-taking
procedure did not distinguish between goods fit or unfit for
human consumption. Thus a false impression was given of
available resources in keepers' returns.[14] Even after goods left
the warehouses destined for Loyalist camps they were still
subject to depredation. Some of the men hired to transport
them were skillful thieves, who stole butter from barrels, and
buried stones in what they left to make up for the loss in
weight.[15]

Commissary supplies were doled out to the refugees at their
camps, or at storehouses in the settlements. A daily ration for a
Loyalist adult was the same as for a soldier, and fractions of
rations were issued for children according to age-groups. In
times of scarcity the size of the whole ration could be reduced
on orders from headquarters, where careful note was kept of
stock on hand. When food of one kind was not available a
substitute was made, such as one type of meat for another. The
government had good intentions as far as contemporary
nutritional theory was understood.

A typical daily ration was prescribed as:
Flour or bread 11/2 lbs
Beef 1 lb
or Pork 1/2 lb
Pease 1/4 pint
Butter 1 oz

---

[13]Governor's Orders, signed by Day, Dec. 17, 1778, B191/44-45.
[14]Clarke to Day, Nov. 25, 1778, **ibid.**, 28.
[15]Curtis, 97-98, based on T64/102, Day to Robinson, June 20, 1777.

Rice 1 oz [16]

It was will known that during the winter or other prolonged periods of deprivation of certain fresh foods people were apt to suffer from scurvy. Consequently particular items were supplied to the Commissary specifically aimed at the prevention of this disease. These anti-scorbutics included such foods as sauerkraut and onions,[17] as well as porter, claret and spruce beer. Quebec brewed spruce beer was contracted by James Grant. Three to four pints per person were issued daily when it was in stock.[18] The full range of foods stocked by the Commissary could vary from dried or fresh fruits and vegetables to fish and meats to cereals and dairy products. Sago, raisins and molasses were also stocked, but not on a regular basis. Special, bland diets were prescribed for patients in hospitals.[19]

Once the provisions reached their destination intact there were still difficulties to deal with. The Commissary had to try to satisfy the tastes and prejudices of different nationalities. Neither the Indians nor the French-Canadians employed at the upper posts would accept salt beef that had been supplied for them.[20] The French-Canadians also objected to the type of biscuit issued, and Commissary General Day went to considerable pains to replace this English type with the French

---

[16]Curtis, 88.

[17]Ibid., One account for spruce beer supplied to Royalists and refugees Dec. 25, 1780 to 24th June 1781 totals 32,241 gallons at 3d. each, B194/138 cf. ibid., 162-163.

[18]Curtis, 93.

[19]Ibid., 111.

[20]Ibid.

sort they preferred.[21] The English on the other hand sometimes refused to take oatmeal as part of their issue.[22]

It might have been assumed that the Loyalists who arrived in Quebec destitute would have been content to receive any rations to keep from starving. Most were, but others with little to occupy their imaginations began to find fault with their rations. Early in 1780 a group at Machiche was stirred up by a few trouble-makers to protest the supposed inferior quality of beef supplied to them. Maj.McAlpin, a fair man who was then in command of the Unincorporated Loyalists, sampled the meat and found it palatable. Nevertheless for an independent opinion he called in butchers who examined the supply and reported it to be wholesome.[23] The Governor had a simple remedy for such unfounded complaints, he issued orders that the rations for the leading complainers be stopped, and that their followers receive less-desirable rations, i.e. salt meat instead of fresh beef or pork This was a salutary lesson for one of the ringleaders who had a large family and was left without means of supporting them. Within a short while his family was restored to the subsistence list, while he was back in favour doing constructive work for the Loyalists. The responsibilities of the Commissary were often complex. Problems of procurement, storage, transportation and distribution of essential food stuffs were its daily concern. The military forces and civilian population together could not have survived on the Province's own resources at the time. This Department was the western terminus of a lifeline which extended across the Atlantic from producers in Great Britain. The maintenance of

---

[21]Ibid., 111-112n.

[22]NAC: HP, B161/43, McAlpin to J. French, Jan. 14, 1780.

[23]Ibid., B163/25, Mathews to D. Munro, Jan. 20, 1780.

this main artery and of its network of smaller channels called for close co-operation among the various government departments involved and careful co-ordination with the military. Consequently, neglect of important details or lack of vigilance anywhere along the route could cause break-downs in the system.

After the Revolution the Commissary continued to be an important government service in Canada well into the 19th century. It was helpful in times of civil emergency as during the famine of 1788-89. However, as Loyalists became more independent, the need for civilian assistance lessened and by the end of 1783 in the region from Montreal eastward to the Gaspé at least six men had been discharged and fifteen were retired on half-pay. A few of these were later re-hired when the post-war situation became clearer. Isaac Clarke was one of the fortunate few. The continuing major role which the Department played can be gauged from the fact that in 1819 it occupied 32 buildings in the Montreal district alone - five being in the town and fourteen at Lachine.[24]

---

[24]Return of Buildings, Oct. 1, 1819 (NAC: RG 8 (Military "C" Ser.) C407/33).

CHAPTER 6

Minority Groups Among the Loyalists

Mission Indians in Peace and War
by Gerry Rogers

For many years following the Revolutionary War, old stone chimneys, standing on a bluff overlooking the water, marked the head of Carleton Island and all that remained of the military and naval fortifications that guarded the entrance to the river St. Lawrence. It was the most important post above Montreal. Merchants dealing with the Indians had long used the Island as a gathering place. As early as 1775 the British had located a supply depot there, and by 1778 established a shipyard and a small fort for the protection of vessels and stores.

Correspondence of Francis Goring, a trader at Niagara, states that in June of 1778 "there are upwards of forty canoes of Indians on the ground at present. Two small parties are now singing the war song to go on a scouting party to Fort Stanwix." In December the garrison was alarmed by the arrival of Onondaga Indians with information that a body of Americans from Fort Stanwix was about to attack the Island. In May, 1779, Hawton, Johnston and Lamothe, officers of the Indian Department, marched for Fort Stanwix at the head of 140 warriors. That fall, detachments of the 34th Regiment, Hanover Jaegers and the Kings Royal Regt. of New York, assembled under Sir John Johnson in preparation for an expedition to the

Mohawk Valley. They were joined by over 200 Canadian Indians commanded by Capt. Alexander Fraser. On one of the last raids from Carleton Island, Maj. John Ross sailed for Oswego on Oct. 4, 1781, with 250 troops and 60 Indians, where he was joined by Capt. John Butler from Niagara with 150 Rangers and about 100 Indians.

Who were these Indians, some from Canada but many more from New York State, whose paths of war crossed on Carleton Island? During Jacques Cartier's first visit to the Gaspé in 1534, he met the Iroquois who occupied the land on the south shore of the Lower St. Lawrence River. When he returned the next year, he met members of the same nation at Stadacona (Quebec) and Hochelaga (Montreal), who had inhabited these sites for several generations, travelling as far as the Atlantic Ocean to catch salt water fish during the summer months.

A few years after Cartier's last visit in 1541, the Iroquois were driven from the Valley and Hochelaga destroyed, probably displaced by Algonquins. In 1603 Champlain confirmed that none remained except for a few remnants above Montreal along the St. Lawrence and the Ottawa Rivers. In 1609 Champlain met with them on Lake Champlain, where they had moved to inhabit the country from the Mohawk Valley to Lake Ontario and the Niagara River.

Until the British occupation of Quebec, there was an Indian-controlled zone in Upper New York State. On the French side there were Indians converted by Jesuit missionaries, with a large settlement at Caughnawaga. To the south were the Six Nations of the Iroquois, under the influence of Protestant missionaries, who mostly sided with the British. When hostilities threatened, the Caughnawaga Indians, like the French Canadians, adopted a policy of neutrality. Of the Six

Nations, the Mohawks, Onondagas, Cayugas and Senecas were Loyalists, while the Oneidas and Tuscaroras aided the Continental Congress.

Sir William Johnson, commissioned as Superintendent of Indian Affairs (Northern Department) in 1755, had long recognized the advantage of Indian military power and had watched the growth of the American dispute with great apprehension. On his death in 1774, his son, who became Sir John Johnson, inherited Sir William's vast estates in Tryon County, the Baronetcy and the leadership of more than 600 Scottish Catholic Highlanders, who settled on his estates and were loyal to the Crown. In 1775 Sir John promised the New York Congress that he and his men would remain neutral if not harassed. However he was forced to arm Johnson Hall and his tenants. In May of 1776, Molly Brant warned him that an arrest warrant in his name had been issued. He fled to Montreal on May 19 with 250 followers. After three weeks in the woods the St. Regis Indians paddled up the Racquette River with food and clothing, and guided them to their village. This incident strengthened the friendship between the Canadian Iroquois and Sir John Johnson's Royal Greens and other regiments in the Montreal area.

While Sir John had inherited the estates, Sir William's nephew and son-in-law, Guy Johnson, took over his Commission and the task of managing the Indians, and was hard pressed to calm the Indian anxieties on the outbreak of war. He knew the attitude of the Indians would have an important influence on the outcome of the struggle. He was assisted by Joseph Brant, brother of Molly Brant, last wife of Sir William Johnson. Brant, closely associated with the British since boyhood, persuaded the majority of the Six Nations to join the British cause and remain with the Crown. In 1775 he accompanied Guy Johnson, John Butler, Daniel Claus, Gilbert Tice and a few loyal Tory and Indian friends, to Oswego and on to Montreal. Sailing with Johnson for England, he was presented to George III and ably argued his point that only by active participation could the Indians hold their traditional lands.

Meanwhile the American campaign to take Canada began in May 1775, after Ticonderoga and Crown Point were captured by Ethan Allen and Benedict Arnold. Days later Arnold and a small force of about 30 men sailed down the Richelieu and took St. Jean. Col. Templer, in Montreal, alerted by Moses Hazen, a retired officer living near St. Jean, immediately dispatched a force of about 150 men, but by the time they arrived, Arnold, with a captured sloop and a few prisoners, had escaped up the Richelieu.

Col. Templer, acting for Maj. John Campbell who was now in charge of Indian Affairs, ordered the local Indians to prepare to take up arms, but they refused, claiming neutrality, influenced by Father Huguet, the Jesuit priest at Caughnawaga, who was later castigated by Bishop Briand. The Americans had already contacted the Indians and were aware that many sympathized with their cause, perhaps in part because numerous Caughnawaga families were of New England ancestry. Another reason may have been due to Carleton's decision to utilize them only in a defensive role.

At an Indian Congress in July at Lachine, the several hundred North American Indians in attendance reluctantly gave their support to Carleton and agreed to take up arms if necessary. They were disappointed with his decision to use them mainly on scouting parties and restrict them the use of arms except in a defensive role. During August a small party from Caughnawaga, led by Chevalier de Lorimier, was active along the frontier and assisted in defending the fort at St. Jean. In the same month a band of Caughnawaga Indians, acting on their own initiative, sent a deputation to see Gen. Washington, then stationed at Cambridge. They informed the General of their willingness to aid the American cause, a position which Carleton was aware of. Following the capitulation of Montreal, Gen. Wooster was assured of Caughnawaga's neutrality, while Sieur la Corne St. Luc, a French officer of the old regime, sent 10 or 12 warriors to St Jean to assure Montgomery that they would not war against Americans.

In September Richard Montgomery took possession of Ile-aux-Noix while an advance party of Continentals heading for St. Jean was repulsed by Gilbert Tice with a small band of Indians. Later that month Ethan Allen attempted to take Montreal but was forced to surrender, making a deep impression on both the French habitants and the Mission Indians. Over the next six weeks, Carleton, with Indians from Caughnawaga, St. Regis and Oka, made several attempts to drive the Americans from along the St. Lawrence, opposite Montreal, but failed. On Nov. 13, 1775, Richard Montgomery took possession of the city.

During the occupation of Montreal, the western Indians still supported the Crown, and from their base on the upper St. Lawrence joined with the Canadiens in harassing the invaders from the rear. In June, when the Continental forces were about to withdraw from Montreal in face of a British reinforcement which landed at Quebec City, Sir John Johnson arrived with a party of Loyalist Americans and Mohawk Indians. With these reinforcements, a combined force of Loyalists, Indians and French Canadians liberated Montreal, before the arrival of British regulars.

After the invaders were driven from Quebec, Guy Johnson and Joseph Brant returned from England and Carleton was made Governor of New York, then under British occupation. Carleton persuaded them to rally the Indians in an attempt to end the war that year in a combined movement of three separate armies: Burgoyne through the Champlain Valley, St. Leger down the Mohawk River from Oswego and Sir William Howe along the Hudson from New York. The campaign ended in disaster as St. Leger, following the bloody engagement at Oriskany, withdrew to Oswego and Burgoyne surrendered over 6,000 men to Gen. Gates on Oct.17. Few if any Six Nations or American Indians served under Burgoyne, rather they were mostly Mohawks from Caughnawaga, St. Regis and Oka, and Abenakis from St. Francis. Col. John Butler of Butler's Rangers from Niagara and Joseph Brant with a large contingent of American Indians had joined St. Leger at Oswego for the Mohawk Valley campaign. During the siege of Fort Stanwix Butler, Sir John Johnson and Brant with over 800 Indians took part in the Oriskany ambush of Gen. Nicholas Herkimer's force, but were forced to retreat with heavy losses.

After the failure of Burgoyne's invasion, the Iroquois were subject to reprisals by the Continentals, who forced 2,700 Iroquois to take refuge in Niagara. The question then arose as to how these forces were to be employed. As the war was being fought with greater bitterness, it was decided to raid the American frontier settlements. Sir Frederick Haldimand, now Governor of Quebec, was in charge of operations.

Typical of the raids involving the Indians were the following:

May 30, 1779: letter from Crofts at St. Francis to Haldimand: "An Indian came to St. Francis to say that 600 men set of from Cohoes under Whitcomb, a British regular officer, for

Mississquoi, to be followed in 4 days by a 100 more. About 300 to 400 men at Cohoes. Many animals slaughtered and other preparations. Joseph Louis and his son Traversie and Gamelin are returned from Boston."

June 3, 1779: letter from Haldimand to Crofts: "Lt. Davis of 31st regiment to accompany 25 to 30 Indians to strike the rebels and have ordered 8 to 10 men from the 34th regiment to St. Francis to accompany the scout and to take prisoners on the Connecticut River and scout troop movements. Crofts to remain at St. Francis and to inform Lt. Col. Campbell of the scout. Also Capt. Schmidt of Yamaska to supply 10 good Canadians to go along. The whole under the command of de Fleurimont. Also that Joseph Louis and Traversie, if met, should be brought to St. Francis."

June 30, 1779: a letter from Crofts to Haldimand: "Party returned from Connecticut with 2 prisoners from Upper Cohoes. Sent to Quebec with de Fleurimont and Belisle. One was from Upper Stratford and says that the rebels have abandoned any idea of a large raid this summer. Maj. Whitcomb has been employed most of the spring scouting toward Lake Champlain. Talked with Schmidt and to send out a combined scout and keep them near the carrying place of Nicolet and to make 6 or 8 canoes and not borrow from the Indians."

July 1, 1779: from John Campbell at Caughnawaga to Haldimand: "I have to inform your Excellency that the party of Indians under the direction of Lorimier set out yesterday and that they are about 200 in number. Have left it to Capt. Fraser to give what orders he may judge proper. I beg leave to observe to you that the parties are very experienced. I would propose if your Excellency intends to continue parties toward Fort Stanwix that Capt. Fraser's post should be at Carleton Island with a larger proportion of officers, interpreters of the Indian

Department and supplied with goods for presents. I am sorry to inform you that Father Gordan died here last night of the bad fever that killed so many Caughnawagas. He is a great loss to Government."

July 31, 1779: from John Campbell to Haldimand: "Mister Lorimier is returned late yesterday from his scout and brought in one officer, 30 privates and 4 scalps of the garrison of Fort Stanwix."

September 27, 1779: from John Campbell to Mathews (Haldimand's secretary): "You will please inform his Excellency, the commander in chief, that there is about 270 Indians from Caughnawaga, the Lake of Two Mountains and St. Regis, gone to the assistance of the Five Nations, the last of which passed St. Regis the 23rd instant, that the whole were conducted by LaMothe and La Brière."

October 28, 1779: letter from Mathews to Crofts: "Col. Campbell issued orders to prepare 2 scouting parties and Crofts to engage necessary Indians. Lorimier returned 2 days ago. His Indians behaved very well and brought in a Lt. Colonel and a French Captain with despatches. The Indians were recompensed by Haldimand but still asked Crofts for new equipment claiming that theirs had worn out — blankets, shirts, leggings and breech cloths,"

April 3, 1780: from Lt. Houghton to Haldimand: "The scouts sent out from Oswegatchie by Capt. Robertson are returned. The first left Oswegatchie the 12th of February and the other the 21st. Owing to the hardship of the weather the last overtook the first near the settlements and was joined there by a scout of Mohawks sent out by Col. Claus. The 3 parties proceeded together and fell in with 6 Oneidas who proved friendly. The joint scouts struck the settlements below Fort Herkimer on the Mohawk and took 5 prisoners and 1 scalp. There is a scout out

from Carleton Island consisting of 14 soldiers and 54 Indians. Mr. Crawford of the Indian Department is out with this scout. They have orders to strike at Canojaharie."
October 7, 1780: "Crofts ordered by Capt. Fraser, Deputy Superintendent of Indian Affairs, to meet Col. Campbell with 30 Indians augmented to 50 by scouts returning. Crofts sprained ankle on uneven ground. Houghton left with about 270 Indians and without any British officers to assist him. Crofts to return in 2 days to St. Francis and put out Indians against rebels and spies."

With the war over it was evident that the American Indians who had taken refuge in Canada during the rebellion would have to remain there. In Haldimand's opinion, the Ottawa was the realm of the French Canadians, while further west was Indian territory. Further, he wanted to move the Loyalist refugees in Quebec to the Maritimes. But on learning that western Indians would welcome the Loyalists he changed his mind, and sent them west, ordering that the Loyalist Indians move with them too, of whom there were 125 including 40 warriors.

Prior to their departure westward, these Loyalists lived in barracks near Lachine, mostly on government rations. They had their own school and had erected a modest chapel at their encampment, the first Church of England in the province. Rev. John Stuart, formerly a missionary in the Mohawk Valley, had come to Montreal to be near his former Indian followers. These Indians were settled in and, like other Loyalists, were reluctant to move. But Haldimand, perhaps anxious to separate them from the Caughnawagas, who had an indifferent notion of loyalty, was firm. Their three chiefs, John Deseronto, Isaac and Aaron Hill were ordered to move to the Bay of Quinté area where their descendants live to this day. As one chief commented, "you tell us to go with the earliest opening in the River, and not to leave a soul behind. This is our intention as soon as the ice is broken."

Blacks Among the Loyalists
by John Ruch

"There are black people that have been of great service..."
William Parker 1782

During the Revolution, there were about as many black refugees as there were whites.[1] Estimates of their numbers vary, but the figure for each group ranges between 80,000 and 100,000 souls. They left the American Colonies as civilians, soldiers, free or enslaved, with few arriving in Quebec. The majority chose the Maritimes, which received over 3,300 from New York alone. Of those who chose to live in the Lower Province few have been identified, but much can be said about these people and their circumstances.

Blacks had served both as soldiers or labourers in various army services during the war. Among the military units were the Black Guides and Pioneers, and several other groups, such as the Black Brigade.[2] A great many of these Loyalists who emigrated to Nova Scotia soon joined a scheme which allowed them to re-emigrate to Sierra Leone in Africa.[3] The 300 men strong Black Carolina Corps, which included artificers, dragoons and pioneers, were sent to the island of Grenada and was still

---

[1]Ellen G. Wilson, **The Loyal Blacks** (New York 1976) cites various figures, e.g. 6,000 from Charleston, 5,000 from Savannah, 4,000 from New York, pages 3, 100, 27; see also Robin W. Winks, **The Blacks in Canada: A History** (Montreal 1971), chapter 2; see also James W.St.G. Walker, **The Black Loyalists: The Search for a Promised Land in Nova Scotia and Sierra Leone 1783-1870** (Dalhousie 1976), chapter 1.

[2]Wilson, 34; Winks, 31.

[3]Walker op. cit.

serving years after the war; it was probably the longest
surviving Loyalist regiment.[4]

Several British military leaders had issued proclamations to
slaves during the Revolution, offering them freedom if they
would desert their rebel masters and join Loyalist forces. The
response was great, but the measure was really one-sided. The
same opportunity was not so freely accorded to the slaves of
Loyalists. Slaves were brought behind British lines by other
methods too. It was a common practice among the less
principled rangers and roving Indian scouts to abduct Blacks on
the pretended assumption that they were all slaves. Brought in
as prisoners, these unfortunates could be, and often were, sold
as slaves. The malefactors looked on the game as an easy way of
making money. Gov. Haldimand objected strenuously to this
trade.[5] Regardless of his personal sense of justice and humanity,
he was in an invidious position concerning some of the Blacks,
as will soon be made clear.

At Quebec Haldimand received many complaints from
Blacks, from former slave-owners, and from concerned citizens.
Private William Parker wrote to him on the subject of
mistreated black people in 1782, but he was not the first to object
to the enslaving of refugees whether or not they had been
slaves in the Colonies. In 1778 and 1780 these abuses led to
enquiries. On the first occasion, Jonathan King and Rastas
Coffee petitioned at Quebec to be freed. King stated that he had
been twice captured by the rebels, and both times sold.[6] On each

---

[4]Roger N. Buckley, **Slaves in Redcoats** (New Haven 1979), 4. I thank Elinor K.
Senior for this reference.

[5]Daneil G. Hill, **The Freedom Seekers: Blacks in Early Canada** (Agincourt,
Ont. 1981), 13.

[6]Memorial (NAC: Haldiman Papers (henceforth HP), B217/19).

occasion he escaped to Canada bringing two white men with him. During the winter of 1777-78 he was a "servant" for Capt. McCoy at Montreal. He states:

> Your petitioner has gone through many perils and danger
> of his life in making his escape ...He hopes that your
> Excellency ... will grant him his liberty..."

Clearly his "servant" status was not that of a free man. Indeed the word "servant" was often a euphemism at the time for "slave." Some "servants" were regarded as Loyalists while others were not. Thus it is impossible to say with precision what the status of a particular servant was, unless there is definite additional evidence. Nor does "slave" necessarily mean a black person in contemporary documents. During the French regime in Canada, Indian slaves outnumbered Blacks as the French preferred to have the former, whom they called "panis."

In mid-1780 Haldimand learned that Blacks were again being brought into Canada, and some were sold in Montreal by Indians.[7] This time the official enquiry that he had set up listed 43 blacks and stated that there were others at Niagara.[8] Those who had been slaves of rebel masters were distinguished from those owned by Loyalists for a special reason. Haldimand had to consider the possibility that his superiors would order the slaves returned to their rebel masters, as well as the likelihood

---

[7]Mathews to Campbell, July 24, 1780, **ibid.**, B113/97 contains order to compile a return of these blacks.

[8]Return of Negroes and Negro Wenches Brought into the Province, **ibid.**, B103/369.

of rebel reprisal attacks on Canada led by infuriated slave-owners.

Those listed in the Return of 1780 were known only by Christian names. However, many acquired surnames shortly thereafter. Some enlisted in the Bateau Company under Capt. Hanyost Herkimer, one of whom was his "servant" Mark, who adopted the surname Herkimer. Since official procedure required family names, the Blacks took, or were given, their former masters' names. Frank, Quack, Terry and William became Johnsons as Sir John's former servants. There were two other Johnsons in the company who could have been either Sir John's or Col. Guy's men. One "wench" unnamed on the later roll might have been any one of the five mentioned on the Return — Betty, Hager, Phillis and two Janes. Of the people known from the Return, about one-third had been part of Sir John's household and four had belonged to Col. Claus. Among rebel owners were the Fondas, Adam and Dow.[9]

Negroes accompanied numerous Loyalists to Canada. William Parker told the governor:

> ...it is from a sensible feeling I have for my fellow
> creatures that urges me to petition you. I have for a
> series of times past, scouting and reconitring (sic) in the
> country, I have several times conveyd Subjects (into
> Canada)...but there are black people that has been of great

[9]Names of Bateau Company men are scattered through the Subsistence List, Oct. 25 to Nov. 24, 1780, ibid., B166/33-38v. Another of the captain's men, Fenalus Harkimer, protested to the governor in 1786 or '87 that rebels had captured him from Hanyost and sold him. He had subsequently escaped and served in the military only to be re-enslaved by his first owner (NAC: RG4 (formerly "S" Ser.), A1/29/9450).

service to his Majesty's scouts has this late Summer came in Voluntarily with me in hopes of gaining their freedom...but for their loyalty they are now rendered Slaves in Montreal. I was out 3 times last summer and brought in 16. If your Excell(enc)y would be so kind as to order the poor people their freedom, as they are dayly complaining to me to petition for them. I desire nothing for my trouble for bringing them in, and the ensuing Summer I could have the General part of Schanactady in with me.[10]

Indeed, at times there was near panic in the Albany-Schenectady area among the rebels who feared an imminent uprising by Negro slaves led by Loyalist agents.[11] Draconian measures were taken to restrict the movement of slaves within the community.

In the Province of Quebec, Black refugees fared the same as destitute white people. They received rations, clothing and accommodation from the government, but when they were in easier circumstances and had support from employers or owners, strict economy dictated that the official assistance be withdrawn. The same treatment was accorded whites, for it had been found that a number of people who had an income now were disposing of their rations, etc. to others for a profit.[12] Since the amounts of supplies and facilities were severely limited, the

---

[10]Memorial, Feb. 16, 1782 (NAC: HP, B214/241.).

[11]On Indians and Negroes see J.A. Crowley, **The Old Albany County,** chapter 7.

[12]Mathews to De Coigne, Dec. 11, 1783 and Haldimand to De Lancey, Dec. 20, 1783 (NAC: HP, B165/193v and 207).

Governor impressed the new Inspector of Loyalists, Stephen De Lancey, with the need for economizing. Among the first orders issued to the latter in December, 1783, was for an examination of the condition of Loyalists' needs and removal from subsistence lists the names of those who no longer required relief. Many needier refugees had recently arrived from New York City who had to be cared for.

Until mid-1783 most refugees had arrived in Quebec by inland routes. On the mass evacuation of New York City in the later part of that year, a number of ships carried people who wanted to settle inland by the sea route past the Maritimes and up the St. Lawrence. The vessel *Blacket*, which carried Capt. Alexander White's Company, arrived at Quebec in mid-August and included, in addition to two "servants," four free Negroes from Carolina.[13] As usual, they were known only by given names: Richard, Nancy, Seely (Sally?) and Nelly. There is not much doubt that they were Loyalists, for the Inspector Abraham Cuyler, who was responsible for taking the particulars of the people on board, noted that some passengers were not Loyalists among the "Europeans." Elias Smith and Moses Sherwood arrived in their schooner *Industry* in September with a total of 40 passengers, among whom five were "servants."[14] These were almost certainly black people, for next year he sold a woman named Meg at Montreal before returning to New York temporarily with his family and three servants.[15] The fifth servant arriving with them in 1783 had belonged to Sherwood.

---

[13] Passenger List, Aug. 17, 1783 (Quebec), **ibid.**, B148/177-178.

[14] Passenger List. Aug. 25, 1783 (New York), **ibid.**, 173.

[15] **Gazette** (Montreal), May 1784 advertisement brought to our attention by Mrs. Sue Jackson, Glen Ellyn, Ill. Smith applied for a travel pass, May 25, 1784 (NAC: HP, B165/244), transcript was sent to us by Earle Thomas, Kingston.

At the time of the emigration from New York, the greatest protector of the black people was Sir Guy Carleton, then Commander-in-Chief of the British forces. Yet even he could not offer them complete security from the rebels. Article 7 of the Peace Treaty forbade all Negroes to leave the new United States. According to George Washington this meant all, but Carleton, adamant that no Loyalists, black or white, should be surrendered to the enemy, stated:

> "Prior engagements binding the National Honor ...must
> be kept with all Colours..."[16]

The British government was committed to paying former slave owners emancipated by Britain, if they could prove the bond had once existed.

Very little is known about the adventures of the black Loyalists who came to Quebec during the Revolution. Perhaps the most touching stories recorded of their personal services are those connected with Sir John Johnson's family, but of their own lives not much has been documented. Johnson was accompanied to Montreal in early 1776 by a large group of Loyalists including Indians and some of his slaves. Other of his slaves remained with Lady Johnson and her young family.[17] She was already advanced in her fourth pregnancy when the rebels arrested her and took the family into custody. They were transported first to Albany, and then after some period there, to

---

[16]William H.W. Sabine ed., **Historical Memoirs of William Smith**, III (New York 1971), 586.

[17](Sir) John Johnson, **The North American Johnsons** (London, Eng. 1963), 56, 66-67; see also Thomas Jones, **The History of New York**, appendix on Johnson family.

Fishkill where she was confined in the house of a friend. With her she had a sister, a nurse and two servants — one black, one white. Shortly after the birth of her child she planned an escape. The small party set forth in the middle of a winter's night. Long, her Black servant, guided the Johnsons along the banks of the thawing Hudson River while carrying one of the older children in his arms. Finding a boat, he ferried them across open water and to safety behind the British lines.

Before leaving his Mohawk manor house, Johnson had the family treasures and documents buried secretly by his slave, Charles, who was captured and sold by the rebels to a local officer.[18] Charles kept his secret for four long years and, in late 1780 when Sir John returned on a raid, among the Loyalists his men liberated was Charles. The Negro led Johnson to the hiding place and the treasures were unearthed. Although the important paper records had perished, the family silver was still in good condition and was taken back to Montreal. Charles remained in service with the Johnson family long after the complete emancipation of slaves, dying in Montreal in 1820.[19]

Slavery had existed in Quebec both before and after the change of regimes in 1763, however, the effect of the Revolution was to hasten its decline.[20] It was a time that saw a great influx of Negroes.

---

[18]Ibid.

[19]Johnson, op.cit. A number of black Johnsons appear in church registers of the time in this province, e.g. at Quebec (Anglican) William and Elizabeth had a daughter Catherine baptized May 27, 1782. A woman named Catherine Johnson, slave of Pierce Ryan, received the same sacrament on Aug. 14, 1796 and Henry Johnson, "a man of colour," was baptized aged 36 years on Sept. 17, 1826.

[20]Winks, chapter 2.

Apart from those brought in as Loyalists' "servants," a number owned by people in the Vermont area were hurriedly transported over the border and sold in Canada when the nascent state outlawed slavery in 1777. Mention has been made of the free blacks, the runaway slaves who came here to join armed forces, and the captives brought in by scouts or raiders. The presence of such a variety of Negroes, including free people and craftsmen, began to alter the "image" of the blacks — the conception of the permanent status of slavery was changing. Until this time black slaves were mainly used in an urban setting, greatly outnumbered by Indian slaves or "panis." Now the balance changed. Blacks helped clear the Eastern Townships, and farmed for their owners, while those who had U.E. status were entitled to land grants.

The Loyalist slave-owners were in the minority. Ellen Wilson found that the idea of slavery was associated in their minds with the rebels and the United States.[21] Thus the Revolution had turned many who had previously been either indifferent or mildly opposed to slavery into abolitionists. By the mid-1790s, advertisements in newspapers for runaways and sales of slaves were no longer common.[22]

Before agitation for reform had become strong enough to affect legislation, the already changing attitudes of the slaves encouraged rebelliousness among them. Old law prevented judges from sentencing slaves to jails or prisons, but they could be sent to "houses of correction." Yet these facilities were already inadequate and crowded. In 1799 a slave-owners' lobby joined local merchants and concerned citizens to petition the government for new buildings. Several Loyalists signed the

---

[21]Wilson, 21.

[22]NAC: Index to **Gazette** (Quebec) under "Negro."

document, of which Elias Smith was one of the authors.[23] It was approved, and money was allotted for the erection of buildings in both Montreal and Quebec.[24]

The governors and the law courts tended to be hostile toward the practice of slavery. However, neither Carleton nor Haldimand was able to attack it outright because of the political problems involved. In cases of the enslavement of formerly free Negroes, they could and did release them. Toward 1800 the judges were more lenient toward slaves, even when on technical grounds the owners had superior legal right. Monk reversed the sentence imposed by P-A Panet and Isaac Ogden on one Robin (or Robert), a runaway.[25] Winks remarked on cases such as this that slavery had become "virtually untenable in Lower Canada."[26]

Although it had yet to gain its greatest strength, the anti-slavery movement was already underway in Quebec in 1790. Although several bills were brought to the provincial legislature after Lower Canada became separate in 1791, none became law before Upper Canada's Act of 1793. This was not as complete a denunciation of slavery as Lt.Gov. Simcoe had hoped for, but it was certainly a progressive measure in the strictest sense of the term. The evil was to be eliminated in three stages, so that the child of a slave would be freed at the age of 25 years, and his or her child would be born free. In Lower Canada, Chief Justice Osgoode, recently promoted from the

---

[23]Elias Smith, **Letterbook 1799-1800**, Baker Library, Harvard School of Business (NAC: Microfilm (HH 13), MG23).

[24]Winks, 101.

[25]**Ibid.**, 102, based on NAC: Miscellaneous Documents 16/121/King's Bench, Feb. 1800.

[26]Winks, 102.

Upper Canada bench, dealt the critical blow in 1803 when he ruled that slavery was inconsistent with British law. This resulted in the liberation of 300 slaves in the Province.[27]

Thereafter opposition to slavery was re-directed toward the offending United States, with the Loyalists and their descendants taking an active interest in the cause. Samuel Gale's son Samuel Jr., as a judge, took up the plight of American slaves as special subject.[28]

> He could not speak with patience of any compromise with slavery, and waxed indignant in denunciation of all who in any way aided, abetted, or even countenanced it...he was one of the most active among those who aroused agitation here.

The spirit was not lost later in the 19th century in pursuing other problems of the black people. Chief Justice Jonathan Sewell's grandson, William G. G. Sewell (1829-1862) wrote a book called *The Ordeal of Free Labour in the British West Indies*, which was published in New York a year before his death and contemporary with the struggle over slavery in the United States. Thus the voice of a fourth generation Loyalist was raised in the eternal battle of man's exploitation of man.[29]

---

[27]Hill, 18.

[28]William Atherton, **History of Montreal**, III (Montreal 1914), 57. Gale's deepest interest in emancipation was shown during his retirement 1849-1865.

[29]"William George Grant Sewell," **Macmillan Dictionary of Canadian Biography**.

Return of Negroes and Negro Wenchs brought into the Province by Parties under the Command and Direction of Lieut. Colo. Sir John Johnson Bart.

*= property of Loyalist or Rebel

Names	Former Master	*	By whom brought in	to whom sold	price sold for	where they are at present, remarks
Tom	Conyne	L	Canadian Indians	Jacob Jordan Esqr.	£12.10	Montreal with Mr. Gordon
Charles	Smyth	R		Revd. Mr. DeLisle	20	Montreal with Mr. DeLisle
Nero	Col. Gordon	R	Mohawk Indians	John Mittleberger	60	Montreal in the Provost Taken at Balls Town making his escape out of a Window in Col. Gordon's House — Runed away some time ago from his late Master.

Jacob	"	R	Mohawk Rangers	Samuel Judah	24	Quebec taken at the same place endeavouring to make his escape — also runed away rom his late Master
A Negro Judah — Wench Johnson in Wench & Property which exchanged for	"	R			60	Montreal with Mr. sold by Sir John lieu of a Negro Child of his Colo. Gordon the Wench.
Betty	Capt. Collins	R	Mohawk Indians	John Gregory	45	Montreal with Mr. Gregory
Tom	Colo. Fisher	R	"	Captn. Thomson	25	Montreal with Mr. Langan— Sold by Capt. Thomson of Colo. Bulter's Rangers, to Sir John Johnson who gave him to Mr. Langan.
Jack	Barny Wemple	R	Royal Rt. N.Y.			Montreal Captn. Anderson Since Dead
Diana	Adam Fonda	R	"			"
Willm	Major Fonda	R	Mohawk Indians	Mr. McDonell	30	Quebec—taken at his Master's house by Captn. John the Mohawk, with a Waggon & Horses which he got ready to convey his Mistress to Schenectady.
Comb-wood	I. Wemple	R	"	Capt. Sherwood	12.10	St. Johns wood with Capt. Sherwood
Cath-arine	Dow Fonda	R	Canada Indians	John Grant	12.10	St. Genevieve with Capt. A. McDonell—sold by John

Name	Master	L/R	Place	Comment
				Grant to Captn. Alexander McDonell
Simon				Niagara with Mr. Wemple— A Free Negro who formerly lived with Captn. Fisher.
Boat swain	Lewis Clement	L	Canada Indians	Niagara with his former Master
Jane	"	L	"	"
Dick	Colo. Butler	L	Mohawk Rangers	Niagara with his former Master
Jack	Wm. Bowen	L	Royal Rt.N.Y.	Niagara with Captn. McDonell—Sold by Wm. Bowen his Former Master to Captn. John McDonell of Butler's Rangers.
Colo.				
Peggy	Mr. Young	L	"	Niagara with her Former Master
Mark	Capt. Harkemer	L	"	Coteau du Lac with his former Master
Tanse	Adam Fonda	R		came in with Sir John Johnson and are now employed in Capttn. Herkamer's Com(pan)y of Batteau Men (Tanse through Jack)
Cato	Pruyme	R		
Jack	Major Fonda	R		
Jack	"	R		
Willm	Sir. J. Johnson	L	Rl. Rt.N.Y.	with his Master
Frank	"	L	"	"
Farry	"	L	"	"
Qack	"	L	"	"
Abra- ham	"	L	"	"

Tom	"	L	"	"
Sam	"	L	"	Since Dead — all these
Jacob	"	L	"	marked for Sir John Johnso
a boy				Joyned him in the Mohawk
Tanae	"	L	"	River
a Boy				
Phillis	"	L	"	with her Master
Betty	"	L	"	"
Betty	"	L	"	"
Jude	"	L	"	"
Jane	"	L	"	"
Hager	"	L	"	"
Nicho- las	Colo. Claus	L	Mohawk Rangers	with his Master
Tom	"	L	"	"
Peter	"	L	"	"
Maria	"	L	"	"

A Negro Man name unknown   by a Soldr 8th Ret—Sold by a
Soldier of the 8th Regt. to
Lieut. Herkamer of the Corps
of Rangers, who sold him to
Ensign Suthurland of the
R..Rt.N.Y.

N.B. Several others carried to Niagara by Indians & White Men

| Chars. Grandison | R | Mohawk Indns | Sent a Prisoner to Fort |
| Colo. Warner | | | Chambly — the Indians still |

claim the allowance
promised them by ye.
Commandr. in Chief
John Johnson
Lieut.Col.Comm.

Religions: The Quakers
by John Ruch

The best known of the minor Protestant religious sects, the Friends or "Quakers," were neutral as a group. Loyalty to the established state authority was a fundamental rule of their conduct. However, their most basic authority was their own conscience, and since they believed in non-violent methods, they were opposed to any active participation in the revolution. They disowned members of their Society who either took up arms or helped the armed services, but this did not prevent many, especially the younger men, from taking sides. A number who can be reckoned as Loyalists settled in Canada, and many relatives, friends and associates formed part of this migration. A few came to the province of Quebec, followed some years later by other Quaker families who eventually formed a congregation in Farnham Township.[1]

Some Quakers supported the King. It is believed that most of their leading members in New York and Philadelphia were secretly Loyalists.[2] The rebels expelled many from the latter city when the British left in 1778. There was a tendency to persecute such neutrals on the grounds that if they were not on one side, they must favour the other. Part of this group was among the Loyalists evacuated from New York in 1783, who settled at Pennfield, Beaver Harbour on Passamaquody Bay, N.B.[3]

1Arthur G. Dorland, **A History of the Society of Friends (Quakers) in Canada** (Toronto 1927), 40.
2**Ibid.,** 47.
3**Ibid.**

Nevertheless, the integrity of many Quakers in maintaining their pacific lives won the respect of military authorities and civilian administrations. Some were chosen by various powers to undertake different missions between two opposing forces. They also ministered to the needy, the sick and the imprisoned, and it is in this latter effort that we encounter a Loyalist, a militant Quaker , who later settled in Quebec.

Abraham Wing (born 1757) was early suspected of being a Loyalist.[4] He was imprisoned at Rockingham (now in Vermont) and later, when released on parole, promptly joined Burgoyne's invading army. After the General's defeat Wing seems to have retired to his somewhat isolated farm and continued life there. However, by late 1780 he was in touch with Dr. George Smyth, the head of Loyalist intelligence gathering in the Albany area.[5] While Smyth was in prison, Wing, as a Quaker, was permitted access to the jail, and was able to smuggle messages in and out. John Platt, a courier between St. John, Que. and the Hudson Valley, formed a line of communication between the north and New York City by linking with Wing, who was also free to visit that port. Wing's farm served as a location for secret messages to be transmitted from one carrier to another. By his own admission he was "the only friend at large to execute the plan."[6] Unfortunately, his property was among those stripped by rebels in mid-1777, and devastated by Carleton's raid in 1780, Wing

---

4Hazel C. Mathews, **Frontier Spies** (Fort Myers, Fla. 1971), 11-12, 21, 60, 68.
5St. Leger to Haldimand, Nov. 29, 1780 (NAC: Haldimand Papers (henceforth HP), B133/374-375, on Platt's report).
6**Ibid.**, 374v.

brought his family to Canada and applied to the Governor for aid.[7]

Wing's relative, Gershom Wing, son of Jedediah of Duchess Co., N.Y., settled in Elizabethtown Township, Upper Canada.[8] Abraham was the son of Abraham Sr. of Queensbury Township, who had built a saw and grist mill on the upper Hudson River at a place known as Wing's Falls (now Glen's Falls) in 1770. Gershom was a cooper, and it was in his shop in Elizabethtown that the first regular gatherings of the Quakers from the townships of Leeds, Yonge and Elizabethtown were held from 1804 on.[9]

There were few members of the Society of Friends in the Montreal area. Their contacts with each other were mainly of a social or business nature, and only rarely do we find reference to a gathering for religious observance. During the Revolution some came to Canada either as refugees, soldiers or emissaries on behalf of rebel prisoners in the Province. In late 1780 Hannah "Matilda" Lawrence and her new husband Lt. Jacob Schieffellin of the Detroit Volunteers travelled by ship from New York City to Quebec and then by boat and overland to Niagara.[10] The daughter of a prominent New York Quaker

---

7Rebel depredations, Mathews, 22; other statements (NAC: HP, losses Sept. 14, 1777: B160/4; Carleton's raid: St. Leger to Haldimand, Nov. 29, 1780, B133/375v; cert. of loyalty, June 3, 1781: B161/274; memorial for relief, Sept. 17, 1781: **Ibid.**, 331).

8William D. Reid, **Loyalists in Ontario** (Lambertville, N.J. 1973), 343.

9Dorland, 89.

10"Hannah Lawrence Schieffelin's Letter" to John Lawrence, Dec. 4, 1780, **New York Genealogical and Biographical Record**, vol. 72, 1941, 120-123, photocopy sent to us by Sue Jackson, Glen

merchant, John Lawrence, she had eloped with the young Loyalist officer. Although she was disowned by the Society for marrying a soldier, she nevertheless found a warm welcome from another disowned Quaker family at Coteau du Lac. Capt. Thomas Gummersall, 2nd Battalion King's Royal Regt. of New York, was an English-born merchant who had become acquainted with her father when he himself had been in business in New York.[11]

The Schieffelin family had come from Philadelphia to Montreal after the British Conquest. Jacob (1757-1835) had engaged in trade with the upper posts, and served in the militia. He was for some time a secretary in the Indian Department, was captured and imprisoned along with Lt. Gov. Hamilton, then escaped together with Philip de Rocheblave to New York.[12] No doubt the daring adventure impressed the young lady as much as his ardent personality. After the war they stayed in Montreal until 1793, when Schieffelin went to New York City where he built an empire on the pharmaceutical trade.

In the later stages of the war, some Quakers visited this province to arrange the release of those taken prisoner on raids

---

Ellyn, Ill., along with a number of references to the Schieffelin family.

11From Yorkshire, he joined the New York Monthly Meeting in 1771. He served eight years with Loyalist forces, Mary Fryer and William A. Smy, **Muster Rolls of the Provincial Regiments** (Toronto 1981), 22.

12Schieffelin's Losses Claim, March 9, 1786, Montreal (NAC: Audit Office Records, A.O. 13/81/358-365); Memorial to Haldimand, Oct. 21, 1780 (NAC: HP, B216, 24); there are numerous references to him in B115 (Indian lands, 1783) and B122 (his experiences to 1780).

in the Colonies by British and provincial forces.[13] After the peace treaty had been signed, representatives of the Society from New York and Philadelphia journeyed through Canada to restore or make links between their older established centres and the infant communities. They took a keen interest in their brethren north of the border and were especially concerned for their welfare and the preservation of their Association.

Although there were several locations in which the Quakers settled, the first group to show strength was that in the Niagara peninsula. In Lower Canada two men arrived on a visit in 1795 to raise the interest of local Friends and sympathizers. Joshua Evans, a prominent minister from Newtown, N.J. and his travelling companion Timothy Rogers held a public meeting in St. Gabriel Street Presbyterian Church in 1795 "the first of the kind ever held there (Montreal)."[14] A thousand people attended, mainly out of curiosity, and many were disappointed being unfamiliar with the Quaker style of meeting in which members remain silent unless "moved by the spirit" to speak. The visiting Quakers, however, were surprised to find so many kind-hearted people in the Town, and more "openness" than they had expected, but the directness of expression that extended to the use of much profanity shocked the Minister, especially since women indulged in it as well as the men.

13Benjamin Gilbert **le trembleur** came in July 1782 for two people, Mr. Loyd and Abigail Dobson (NAC: HP, B137 and B139 corresp. between Riedesel and Haldimand); see also De Speth to Haldimand, July 18, 1782, **ibid.**, B129, 16-17.
14Dorland, 38-39, both men left journals of their trip which continued to Nova Scotia.

A number of Montrealers had more than a passing interest in this first meeting of the Society of Friends. These were the few who had been born into faiths of similar pacific natures, as well as Abraham Pastorius who was a Quaker. Descended from the leader of the first colony of German immigrants to settle in America, he had been raised in Germantown, Penn., between the Quakers of Philadelphia on one hand and Mennonite neighbours on the other. His great-grandfather Francis Daniel Pastorius was a Pietist through personal conviction in the late 17th century, which he continued in the New World, joining neither of the two locally influential religious bodies.[15] Abraham was a saddler who served the British as a guide in eastern Pennsylvania during the 1777-8 campaign, was attainted of treason by the rebels, and eventually came to Canada. He and his family were prominent in social welfare activities, such as relief for the needy, and the creation of the Montreal General Hospital.[16]

Most Quakers who had come to Quebec as Loyalists had by this time dispersed. Several came with the emigrants from New York City in mid-1783, but after spending the winter in the Montreal area moved upriver to settle in what was soon to be Upper Canada. This included Capt. Joseph Allen and Capt. Thomas Dorland and their relatives.[17] It was probably just as well that the Society was not well organized in Canada at the time, as when meetings were later established on a regular basis

15Cornelius Krahn, et al. ed. **The Mennonite Encyclopedia** (Scottdale, Penn 1955-1959, 4 vols.), "Pastorius." The Pietists form the sect most closely related to the Mennonites.
16Abraham was involved with church committees in Montreal, and his daughter Eleanor, Mrs. Benaiah Gibb, was a leading member of the Female Benevolent Society.
17Dorland, 50-51.

the disciplinary authority of the community could act contrary
to the personal interests of the Loyalist Quakers. As a religious
group, the Friends took a strong stand against the acceptance of
land grants to Quakers as "U.E. Loyalists"[18] To them this
implied that the recipient had performed military services, or at
least been partisan during the war. And it was held that the two
terms "Quaker" and "Loyalist" (or "Patriot" for that matter)
were incompatible. A Quaker who had become a Loyalist
should in principle be "read out of" membership.

Quakers did eventually settle in a few locations in the
Eastern Townships. Nicholas Austin, who early performed
loyally for the British government, was unpopular with the
local rebel authorities in New Hampshire. Nevertheless, he
remained in the State after the war, and not until 1787, when he
was a member of the House of Representatives did he choose to
settle in Canada.[19] Shortly thereafter he other Loyalists applied
for land near Lake Memphramagog. On March 26, 1792, they
were granted part of Bolton Township.

The Quaker community which really took root in this
Province was formed in the first quarter of the next century in
East Farnham. Aaron Bull came from Vermont with his
father's family in 1801[20] and became a convert to the faith after
experiencing a religious revelation during a time of stress.
However it was not until his marriage to the Quakeress,
Philadelphia Knowles, in 1814 that he built a home for newly-

18Ibid., 308-309, re. the Pelham Preparative Meeting's decision
that Jeremiah Moore's grant was "inconsistent with our profession,"
Aug. 30, 1809.
19Harry B. Shufelt, **Nicholas Austin the Quaker, and the
Township of Bolton** (Knowlton 1971), 25-27, 56.
20Dorland, 38-41.

arriving Quakers from the border states. By 1826 enough people were interested to be considered as a congregation, and within another decade substantial moves had been made to establish regular observances and land purchased for a cemetery and a meeting house.

CHAPTER 7

Portraits of Some Loyalists

Sir John Johnson: Loyal American Knight

by Earle Thomas

When Sir John Johnson, hungry, tired and emaciated, arrived in Montreal on June 19, 1776, he would not have believed he was there for the rest of his life. He expected to return one day to his beloved Johnson Hall, in the Mohawk valley, when he reasoned the American rebels were put in their place, for he could not see how untrained, inexperienced colonials could withstand for long the might of King George's redcoats.

Warned by a friend that his enemies were on their way to Johnson Hall to arrest him, Sir John left home hastily on May 19. Taking time only to bury his silver and most valuable papers in the basement, to gather together a few necessities for his trip, and to bid farewell to his pregnant wife and two children, he departed with more than 200 of his friends and tenants. To confuse his pursuers, Lady Johnson made believe that the group were on their way to Niagara, when actually they were heading towards Montreal, then held by the Americans. Instead of taking the usual route via Lake Champlain, they travelled north along the River Sacandaga and the St. Regis over rough, trackless Adirondack terrain. Practically all of the men had surrendered their arms the previous January so they were unable to hunt for game. Soon out of provisions, they found little food in the wilderness, only berries, roots, wild onions, and leaves, and an occasional animal or bird. The 19-day march through the wilds with insufficient food and inadequate shelter was a nightmare. Nevertheless, about 200 survived the trip and reached the St. Lawrence at St. Regis (near modern Cornwall).[1]

The party reached Montreal the day after the American invaders left and re-crossed the river to Laprairie in hopes of cutting off the Rebels' retreat. They met Guy Carleton, the governor, who warmly welcomed Sir John and at once granted him a commission to raise the King's Royal Regiment of New York, with Sir John as the new Regiment's colonel.[2] The officers and men were to wear green coats with dark blue facings, white "small clothes," and silver lace and accoutrements. Sir John, a well-proportioned man, with large blue eyes, blonde hair and a clear complexion, looked handsome in his new uniform, once he had rrecovered from his privation in the Adirondacks. Described by his contemporaries as shy and reserved, and by nineteenth century Whig historians as arrogant and antagonistic, he displayed none of these characteristics as the commander of the Royal Yorkers, as his Regiment was nicknamed. He was a highly competent and respected leader.

Sir John had been toying with the idea of raising a Loyalist regiment in Tryon County for some time, and that is in part how he got on the wrong side of the Tryon and Albany Committee of Safety and of Gen. Philip Schuyler, with all the

---

[1]Sir John Johnson to Daniel Claus, Jan. 20, 1777 (NAC: Claus Papers (henceforth CP) MG19/F1/1/230-233, M/f C-1478).
[2]Ibid.

repercussions that followed. News of his request to Gov. Tryon for permission to raise a regiment leaked out, and Gen. Schuyler was dispatched up the Mohawk with a force of 3,000 or more men to reason with him. It was not as if this were the only complaint against Johnson. Ever since his return from Britain in 1767 he had vehemently opposed the American attempts at redress of grievances, believing that most of the complaints were quite unjustified and that British military strength would crush momentarily any feeble American attempt at force. He steadfastly refused to sign the "association" or any other "rebel" document; he announced that he would rather have his head cut off than oppose his King. He refused to turn over to the Committee the Gaol and Courthouse in Johnstown, both of which his father had built at his own expense. It was believed that Sir John had 600 or 700 men under arms and that they were even provided with cannon. Rumours and reports of his alleged subversive activities spread like wildfire through the Valley and were constant topics of discussion at the meetings of the local Committee, who wrote the Provincial Congress that they were "Daily scandalized, provoked, and threatened." Sir John's letter to Gov. Tryon was but the last straw.

Schuyler commenced his march in the middle of January, 1776. He wrote to Sir John from Schenectady on January 16, requesting the meeting which took place at Guy Park on the 17th. Sir John found Schuyler's terms so harsh and rigid that he asked for time, which was granted, to ponder them. At the last possible moment Sir John sent his counter-proposals, which did not please the General, now a few miles closer to Johnstown. "What you have sent me," he replied in a curt note, "is very imperfect, and, also, unsatisfactory." He gave Sir John until midnight to reconsider, at which time Sir John acceded to the General's demands — he had no choice. Accordingly, the troops marched into Johnstown and Sir John, allowed to retain one set of arms and some powder for his own personal use, delivered up the remaining arms and military stores in his possession. The Highlanders, Sir John's tenants, marched before the troops and surrendered their arms. Schuyler took six hostages from the Scottish tenants and six from the others as a guarantee that the Johnstown men would keep their promise not to fight against the Continental Congress. Sir John was required to post a bond of £1,000 not to aid the King's supporters or to go beyond a certain distance from his home. General Schuyler returned to Albany, greatly pleased with his success.

By March Sir John was in trouble again. Accused of trying to provoke an Indian attack on the back settlements, he was summoned to appear before Schuyler. Although he was able to exonerate himself on this count, the Albany Committee, aware that he kept in touch with active Loyalists, regarded him as a serious threat to the Cause and kept a constant pressure on Schuyler to do something about him. Realizing that his position was worsening daily, and, perhaps, by this time clutching at straws, Sir John stated in a letter to Jelles Fonda on April 4 that he was not hostile to the American Cause.[3] Nobody believed him, least of all Schuyler, who early in May was ready to act. Col. Elias Dayton, sent with a detachment to arrest the baronet, arrived at Johnson Hall on May 19 — too late. Sir John, warned by Daniel Campbell of Schenectady, had already departed. Lady Johnson was arrested a week later and taken, with her two children and her sister, to Albany. Sir John's two sisters, with their husbands and families, had gone the year

---

[3]New York State Library Archives, Rep. No. 12365.

before.[4] Although none of them realized it at the time, the Johnsons had left the Mohawk Valley forever

Sir John Johnson had lived his first 34 years in the Mohawk Valley. Born at Mount Johnson on the north bank of the river on Nov. 5, 1742, the son of Sir William Johnson and Catherine Weisenberg, a runaway indentured servant, who may or may not have been Sir William's legal wife (no marriage record has been found and the children were baptized under the name of Weisenberg). Young John lived at Mount Johnson with his parents and his two sisters, Ann (Nancy), later Mrs. Daniel Claus, and Mary (Polly), later Mrs. Guy Johnson, until they moved a mile or so upstream into the beautiful new Georgian stone Mount Johnson at the junction of Kayaderosseros Creek and the Mohawk River in 1749. This mansion, fortified during the Seven Years' War, became known as Fort Johnson.

Little is known of young John's mother, a pretty Palatine German, who died in 1759. John's father, son of a small land-owner in County Meath, Ireland, had come to America in 1738 to manage the 13,000 acre Mohawk valley estate of his uncle Peter Warren, who had married into the rich and powerful De Lancey family and later became a rear admiral and baronet. A courageous, enterprising, and strongwilled young man, Johnson soon branched out on his own and eventually became a baronet, the Superintendent General of Indian Affairs, a high-ranking army officer, and one of the largest land-owners in the colony of New York.

John Johnson grew up at Fort Johnson in the shadow of his illustrious father, but always loved, and directed by him. John

---

[4]Sir John Johnson's sister Mary (Polly), wife of Col. Guy Johnson, got only as far as Oswego, where she died in childbirth.

loved his father too, revered him almost, and continually strove to please him. It was really not until the death of Sir William in July, 1774, that Sir John was his own man.

Sir William showed great concern that his son would acquire the proper education and training to equip him suitably for life both on the Mohawk Valley frontier and among the aristocracy of the colony of New York. Accordingly, he sent him off to the Academy in Philadelphia in October, 1757. John remained there until July 17, 1760, although his attendance was somewhat sporadic. He learned to read, write and cipher; the rest of his education, the more practical side, he got from his father. When John was only 13 years old, William Johnson, with the rank of general, commanded an expedition against the French at Lake George. John went along, too, as did young Joseph Brant. For his success in the 1755 campaign, Johnson was given a baronetcy, a cash grant of £5,000, and the promise that young John would be knighted at the age of 21. Again, in 1759, John accompanied his father on a four-month military expedition to Niagara, and on another in 1761 to Detroit. On excursions such as these John learned the art of frontier warfare, of travel by canoe and bateau, of survival in the wilderness.

John learned early about the qualities, customs and habits of the native people. All his life he had been accustomed to seeing Indians in and about his home; they had come to trade at his father's store and later to consult the Superintendent General of Indian Affairs on all sorts of topics. After Molly Brant came to live with Sir William at Fort Johnson, there were always children about the house, children who were partly Indian, John's half-brothers and half-sisters. When he grew older he accompanied his father to most of the Indian conferences, sometimes as an observer, sometimes playing a minor part, but always watching the proceedings attentively. In 1764, Sir William had sufficient confidence in his son to send him in charge of an expedition of Indians and whites against the Delawares on the Ohio.

Sir William was still not satisfied. A man with John's future required the opportunity to develop as a man of the world, to find a wife from a family with status, and acquire some sophistication, or, as Sir William phrased it, "to wear off the rusticity of a country education."[5] A grand tour of the British Isles, it seemed to Sir William, would solve the problem admirably. John arrived in London, with Lord Adam Gordon, son of the Duke of Gordon, who was to be his companion and mentor, on November 18, 1765. Four days later he was presented at Court and knighted by King George. Immediately he was caught up in the whirl of social life in the metropolis. In the spring he went to visit his relatives in Ireland and enjoyed himself so much that he stayed much longer than he had planned. The result was that his tour of Scotland was so brief that it was likened by Lord Gordon to a "Wood Cock's flight."[6] Sir John was back in October for another winter's social activity in London, the anticipation of which did not please him at all. "I must content myself," he wrote to his brother-in-law, Daniel Claus, "as well as I can this winter in London, but be assured I shan't think myself happy until my return."[7] He had hoped to leave for home long before this, but his father had bade him

---

[5]Milton W. Hamilton, **Sir William Johnson: Colonial American, 1715-1763** (Port Washington, New York 1976), 309-310.

[6]**The Papers of Sir William Johnson** (University of the State of New York, 1921-1965), 15: 250.

[7]Sir John Johnson to Daniel Claus, June 4, 1766 (NAC: CP, MG19/F1/14/100, M/f C-1481).

stay another winter, and much as he loathed London and homesick as he was, he could never bring himself to defy his father. As a matter of fact, he had not wanted the tour in the first place. "You can't imagine the grief I was in at leaving home," he had written to Daniel, "parting with all I esteemed dear to me in this world."[8] Sir William had not intended that his son's tour should be entirely social; there were a few business matters that required his attention. Among other things he was to seek for his father official title to the 80,000 acres on the Mohawk given to Sir William by the Indians; he was, as well, to procure a clergyman for the new church at Johnstown. Although he was successful in neither, the fault was not Sir John's. Nor did he succeed in finding a wife; in this task he seems not to have tried very hard. In response to his friend George Croghan's admonition to beware of the wiles of the many London ladies who would spread their nets for him,[9] he stated that he had the same opinion as his friend of "the London Dames" and thought his "own Country women as Handsome."[10]

Sir John arrived back in New York on September 27, 1767, and made his way to the Mohawk Valley as soon as possible, outwardly suave and affable but still retaining some of the shyness of his youth. He had, as one would expect, absorbed the ideas of the British Tory gentry with whom he had associated for the last two years. He visited his father at Johnson Hall (Sir William, Molly, and their children had moved into the newly-constructed mansion in 1763) and obtained permission to live

---

[8]Same to Same, Dec. 14, 1765 (NAC: CP, MG19/F1/14/75, M/f 1481).

[9]George Croghan to John Johnson, Nov. 9, 1765, **Papers of Sir William Johnson**, 11: 964.

[10]Sir John Johnson to George Croghan, Dec. 14, 1765, **ibid.**, 11:979.

at Fort Johnson. He had the big house all to himself, for his sisters had moved with their families into their new homes, Polly at Guy Park and Nancy at Williamspark, during his absence.

Soon after his return the young knight fell in love with the lovely young Clarissa Putman of nearby Tribe's Hill. He took her to live with him at Fort Johnson, where she bore him two children, William and Margaret (Peggy). Sir John wanted desperately to make Clarissa his wife, but Sir William would not consent to the marriage, insisting that his son marry into one of the aristocratic families. Finally, Sir John gave in to his father. Clarissa and the children moved out, and Sir John brought his new wife, Mary (Polly) Watts of New York, to Fort Johnson. There he lived like a country gentleman until his father's death on July 11, 1774, after which he moved his wife and infant daughter to Johnson Hall and Molly Brant took her children to live at Fort Johnson. Sir John succeeded to his father's baronetcy and inherited one of the largest estates in America. He had never displayed any indications of overwhelming ambition, nor did he now. Long ago he had turned down the offer of a commission in the army; now he declined the invitation to assume his late father's position as Superintendent General of Indian Affairs, which then went to his cousin and brother-in-law, Guy Johnson. The new baronet seemed quite content to ride, hunt and fish, to manage his huge estate, and to act as laird to his numerous tenants. He enjoyed the peace and quiet of his idyllic life at Johnson Hall for but a brief period. It came to an abrupt end in May 1776.

The King's Royal Regt. of New York spent the winter of 1776-1777 quartered in Lachine, Pointe Claire and St. Anne's and occupied their time working on the defenses surrounding

Montreal.[11] Sir John had hoped to engage his regiment in an expedition to the Mohawk Valley, but, this not coming to pass, threw himself into an attempt to rescue Lady Johnson and the children from the Rebels.

Lady Johnson had been confined in Albany as a hostage for her husband's behaviour. Her pleas to be permitted to go to New York fell on deaf ears. After her third child, a son John, was born at Albany on October 7, 1776,[12] she was allowed to go to Coldenham near Fishkill to live, where, she was told, she could apply for a permit to go to New York. She arrived at Coldenham in December, and in January the courageous lady took a bold plunge for freedom. She and her party succeeded in escaping in disguise to New York, where she was reunited with her husband. The Johnsons made their way from New York to Quebec by sea.

Johnson and his regiment contributed more to the war effort than the mere garrisoning of posts and the building and repairing of fortifications and works; they participated in several important expeditions in the Mohawk valley, considered the breadbasket of America. They had been humiliated and driven from their homes by their Rebel neighbours and were eager to strike back; in addition, they were zealous supporters of the King. In 1777 they got their first chance. The British military strategists had formed a plan to take control of Lake Champlain and the Hudson River, thereby weakening the Rebels by dividing them into two parts. Gen. John Burgoyne, sent to replace Carleton as the commander-in-chief in Canada, was to lead a force by way of Lake Champlain to

---

[11]Sir John Johnson's Orderly Book, 3-62.

[12]Sir John and Lady Polly Johnson's first child, Ann (Nancy) was born at Fort Johnson on July 5, 1774; William was born at Johnson Hall Aug. 21, 1775.

the Hudson where he would meet an army led by Gen. Clinton coming up the river from New York. Brig. Gen. Barry St. Leger, with Sir John as his second in command, was to cross Lake Ontario to Oswego and take Fort Stanwix, which guarded the portage between Wood Creek and the Mohawk, and proceed down that river. The three forces were to meet at Albany, having conquered all before them. The strategy looked excellent on the drawing-board; its execution was a dismal failure.

St. Leger's detachment, numbering about 875 white men, was joined at Oswego by Joseph Brant with between 800 and 1,000 Indians. Although the force left Oswego on July 26, they did not reach Fort Stanwix until Aug. 2, so effectively had the obstructions placed by the enemy impeded their progress up Wood Creek. The Indian Loyalists immediately attacked the fort, but the garrison within held firm. After three days St. Leger received intelligence that Col. Nicholas Herkimer was on his way with a large force to relieve the Fort. St. Leger sent a detachment led by Sir John, John Butler, and Joseph Brant to ambush them from the cover of the heavy woods on the banks of a marshy ravine at Oriskany. Herkimer and his men walked into the trap and the tiny stream ran red with blood. Oriskany has been called the goriest battle of the war; more than 300 lost their lives.[13] Herkimer, although mortally wounded, continued to direct his men, propped up with his back against a large beech tree.

The British and Loyalists failed to capture Fort Stanwix. During the Battle of Oriskany, Marinus Willett with 250 men left the fort and systematically looted the camps of the British, Loyalists and Indians. Willett got all of Sir John's papers. He stripped the Indians' tents of everything movable. The Indians'

---

[13]Christopher Ward, **The War of the Revolution** (New York 1952), 2:491.

rage, coupled with the rumours of the approach of thousands of the enemy, caused great numbers of them to desert their colleagues. Fort Stanwix looked like a lost cause, and St. Leger withdrew, fully expecting to return once they had obtained more artillery. The other two prongs of the triple thrust met with no greater success. Burgoyne surrendered to the enemy at Saratoga on October 17, 1777, and, as the result of a foul-up in communications, Clinton's march did not materialize. For the British, Saratoga was the beginning of the end.

Those of the Regiment who had not accompanied Sir John on the Mohawk expedition were variously employed. A detachment went in June to Oswegatchie to work on fortifications, others as part of an expedition intended to make raids on Lake Champlain, and two companies were on Carleton Island. In the autumn all returned to Montreal island and went into winter quarters at Lachine, Pointe Claire, and St. Anne's. Along with his own men, Sir John was responsible for all provincials who had been engaged with Burgoyne on his expedition. Since they were actually attached to the Central, rather than the Northern Department, Carleton put them on what he called his temporary list. Nevertheless, they were entitled to subsistence and pay for whatever work they did. Sir John, in charge of their supervision, was no happier than their officers, who were afraid of losing them from the already depleted ranks of the regiments they hoped to build. Sir John, unhappy over the Saratoga defeat and even unhappier over the entrance of France into the war on the side of the Americans, felt he had enough to do without the responsibility of these refugees. Certain up to this point of the imminent defeat of the Continentals, he now began to feel a few twinges of doubt. The birth of his fourth child, a son Warren, in Montreal on the day before Christmas, 1777, gave him some cause for rejoicing, but the thought that this beautiful new baby might never see his lovely Valley was enough to plunge him into despair.

1778 found Sir John still in charge of the Loyalist refugees. Carleton again found it necessary to "have recourse" to Sir John's "good assistance and great zeal for the Service," and on May 11, 1778, ordered him to send the Royal Yorkers, with all the Royalists attached to it, to Quebec to improve the defenses of that city. On June 1, all those who had fought at Saratoga were released from their parole, the Americans having broken their word to send Burgoyne's men home. In the same month Maj. Gen. Frederick Haldimand replaced Carleton as Governor General. Still in charge of the Loyalists who were not in his regiment, and with a large part of that regiment in Sorel, Sir John was back in Montreal in August. There was trouble at home. On Aug. 17 he wrote to Daniel Claus: "We are all well except poor little John who seems to be declining fast. I believe it is with worms. We are trying everything we can to relieve him."[14] On Sept. 14, about three weeks before his second birthday, little John died.

Sir John occupied himself with plans to form the various bodies of Loyalists into a battalion, a plan frustrated by the commanders of those bodies, "through the misrepresentations and trifling claims of a set of men" who had often told Johnson they considered it a good idea.[15] The "trifling claims" he referred to represented the ambitions of the officers in the Province who wished to complete their own regiments. Overworked, frustrated and grief-stricken, in October Sir John

---

[14]Sir John Johnson to Daniel Claus, Aug. 18, 1778 (NAC: CP, MG19/F1/2/47, M/f C-1478).

[15]Sir John Johnson to Frederick Haldimand, Oct. 29, 1778, (NAC: Haldimand Papers (henceforth HP), M/f 1018, 79, Queen's University Archives.)

dispatched Capts. Crawford and Byrne with a detachment of his regiment to Johnson Hall. After they returned he wrote to Haldimand, "they brought off the ruins of my papers, none of which are legible." He computed his loss at £20,000.[16]

In the spring of 1779, Johnson was relieved of the responsibility for the Loyalists in the Province. Haldimand, thinking Sir John "should employ his whole attention in forming his Regiment," appointed Capt. Daniel McAlpin to the command of the Loyalists. Sir John devoted his attention to bringing his regiment up to strength and attempting to have it placed on the British regular establishment.[17] In May he wrote Haldimand that he "would leave nothing undone...to prepare the Regt for any service they might be thought fit to be employed in."[18] Although he considered the Regiment "a useful Corps with the Axe, not altogether to be depended on with the Firelock,"[19] Haldimand decided to give them a trial on combat duty. He sent Sir John off with 12 officers and 201 men to join Butler's Rangers and some Iroquois in an attempt to aid the Six Nations in western New York against the rebels. He admonished Sir John that although the Butlers, father and son, were "Characters that require...much Patience to do Business with," he was to employ his "understanding and address in the Management of them."[20] It was well into October before

---

[16]Same to Same, Nov. 24, 1778 (NAC: HP, M/f 1018, 79, Queen's University Archives).

[17]His request was forwarded to Lord George Germain, but the latter required a recommendation from Haldimand before anything could be done.

[18]Frederick Haldimand to Sir John Johnson, May 20, 1779 (NAC: HP, M/f 1018, 79, Queen's University Archives).

[19]Haldimand to Sir Henry Clinton, May 26, 1779 (NAC: C05/98/190).

[20]Haldimand to Johnson, Sept. 9, 1779 (NAC: HP, M/f 1019, 80, Queen's University Archives).

Johnson, Butler and their men reached Oswego to raid the Oneida villages. Finding that the rebel Oneidas had been warned, and aware that it was too late in the season to venture far in search of the rebel army under Sullivan, Sir John and his men returned to Montreal. They had accomplished nothing, but the fault was Haldimand's — he had waited too long.

The majority of the King's Royal Regt. of New York passed the winter of 1779-1780 at Sorel working on the fortifications. Some were at Coteau du Lac, guarding the prisoners of war compound. Sir John Johnson himself was in Montreal where on Feb. 17 Lady Johnson gave birth to their fifth child, a daughter whom they named Catherine. Haldimand was invited to act as sponsor at the baby's christening and graciously accepted, writing on Feb. 24 that he would "with great chearfulness comply with (Lady Johnson's) desire."[21]

In the winter of 1780, Sir John's regiment was very nearly up to strength; on July 13, Haldimand granted him permission to raise a second battalion. The Governor appointed Capt. John Ross of the 34th Regiment as major, and Robert Leake, married to Lady Johnson's sister, brought in his own company and became senior captain. From a military point of view this was Sir John's greatest year; in addition to starting the recruitment of his second battalion, he led his men into the Mohawk valley in two very successful campaigns.

In May and June Sir John led an expedition of some 600 men, consisting of soldiers from his own Regiment, Capt. Leake's company, some Indians and some regulars, into his Valley to rescue a number of the Loyalists who remained. One half of the force attacked Caughnawaga (now Fonda) on May 21,

---

[21]Same to Same, Feb. 24, 1980 (NAC: HP, M/f 1019, 80, Queen's University Archives).

burning the buildings and killing all the men capable of bearing arms. The other half burned Johnstown and laid waste several miles of the valley. They returned to Montreal early in June with 40 prisoners and about 150 Loyalists.[22]

The rescued Loyalist men enlisted in Sir John's first battalion, bringing it near enough to full strength that the second one was permitted to begin formation. In August Maj. Ross took it to Coteau du Lac, where it commenced work on the new canal circumventing the rapids at The Cedars.

Early in September Sir John was off on another raid. He took the detachment from his regiment to Carleton Island, thence to Oswego. The force increased to about 800 when it was joined by Brant and Butler with their Indian and white warriors. In the month of October they scoured the Mohawk and Schoharie valleys for about 50 miles, spreading terror and burning crops and buildings. At the same time Capt. John Munro created a diversion by leading about 100 men via Lake Champlain to Stillwater, Ballston and the adjoining area. Sir John was eminently satisfied with the excursion. "We destroyed every grain before us for near fifty miles," he reported to Haldimand. He estimated the loss to "be at least 600,000 bushels."[23] Haldimand who complimented him on the success of his campaign; Sir John, on his part, made use of the favour he was in to request officers for his second battalion, to ask again for a place for his regiment on the Establishment, and to beg leave to go to England.

Officers were appointed as needed, Sir John was granted permission to go to England, and the establishment of his

---

[22]Earle Thomas, "Loyalists in the Montreal Area."

[23]Johnson to Haldimand, Nov. 2, 1780 (NAC: HP, M/f 1018, 79, Queen's University Archives).

regiment was under discussion. There were no more excursions to the Mohawk valley for Sir John, although he kept in touch with Johnstown through scouts. He and Lady Johnson and their three oldest children sailed for England on October 25, 1781, leaving little Catherine and infant Adam Gordon (born May 6, 1781) in the care of Nancy and Daniel Claus. After a short visit with relatives in Ireland, they reached London on Jan. 3. Although the passage was "boisterous" and Nancy and William, as a result, were so sick "we were near to loosing them both at sea," the Johnsons had a very profitable winter. Nancy and William were put in school and left there when their parents returned home. Sir John was appointed Superintendent General and Inspector General of Indian Affairs, replacing Guy, whose performance in the post had left much to be desired. In addition, Sir John was appointed Colonel Commandant, with the rank of Brigadier General of his first Battalion on the American Establishment. There was good news in the family, too, for when the Hero docked in Quebec on Aug. 14, 1782, there was another Johnson, a second John having been born on board on Aug. 8.

Sir John no sooner had his feet on the shores of Quebec than he was confronted with problems relative to his new position as head of the Indian Department. Cornwallis had been defeated at Yorktown on Oct. 19, 1781, in the battle which to all intents and purposes was the conclusion of the war. In England the old Government had fallen, and the new one wanted peace. The Indians' homes had been looted and destroyed; they feared that the Americans would not honour the Stanwix agreement of 1768; and suspecting they would not be included in the peace negotiations, wanted to go to war. All summer they had been coming in groups of 500 or so to Oswego, where Maj. Ross was now stationed with the second battalion of the Royal Yorkers, but by early fall all had returned to their villages after failing to obtain permission to go to war. Ross had received instructions to tell them they might "rest assured that they will never be forgotten. The King will always consider and reward them as his faithful Children who have Manfully supported His and their own Right."

This was in general the message Sir John carried to the Indians as he made his rounds among them. A few days after his return to Montreal he embarked by canoe at Lachine with Joseph Brant, James Stanley Goddard, and Lt. Col. Henry Hope on a tour of the forts at Michillimackinac, Detroit and Niagara. Away nearly two months, he spoke to group after group of Indians, persuasive, placating, placid, a credit to his father's image, and succeeded in mollifying them, at least for the time being. Almost immediately upon his return to Montreal, Haldimand appointed him Brigadier General of the provincial troops in the Province.

His duties as Brigadier General were not onerous in 1783, for the war was officially over. His first battalion, under Maj. James Gray, was stationed in the Montreal area. His second battalion, after staving off a rebel attempt to capture Oswego during the winter, moved to Cataraqui in the summer and commenced the construction of a new military base. The first battalion was disbanded, with quarters and rations continued for a time, on Dec. 24, 1783, and the second not until the following June.

If Sir John's military duties at the time were light, those in the Indian Department were quite the opposite. In the autumn of 1782 he placated the Six Nations by assuring them that, when it came time to negotiate and sign the peace treaty, neither King nor Congress would disregard them. Now the treaty had been signed, the Indians had not been consulted, and they were angry and anxious. Sir John sympathized with them; nevertheless, he tried to avoid going to Niagara to discuss the precarious situation. Butler was there, Johnson wrote to Haldimand, and possessed every requisite to meet with them. Besides, his own presence was required at home at this critical moment to promote the interests of his own family, to attend to any opportunity that might arise for the recovery of his property, "too great to be totally unattended to."[24] Haldimand viewed it in a different light. If ever there was a time when the superintendent ought to be with the Indians, this was it. The Indians had respected and trusted no white man like Sir William Johnson; Sir John was his son, and highly regarded by them too. Sir John must go.

There were 1,600 Indians present at the conference in Niagara from July 23 to 31. Sir John spent a total of 15 days there, talking with the leaders from various tribes, those he "thought had most weight." On July 23, he addressed the whole council. Although he and the Indians knew the British Government had betrayed them, he had to try to persuade them to the contrary. He trod very lightly over the question of what would happen if the Americans failed to honour the Indian boundary line established at Fort Stanwix in 1768; he felt sure the Americans would respect it, he said. Actually, Sir John fed his listeners with false hopes, but there was nothing else he could do. Any other course would have helped to foment an Indian uprising against the Americans in which the Indians could only have been the losers. Sir John was satisfied with his success and he wrote to Haldimand, "as well pleased as ever

---

[24]Same to Same, May 20, 1783 (NAC: HP, M/f 992, 52, Queen's University Archives).

they were seen to be, and as well reconciled to their present uncertain, painfull situation as could be wished."[25]

Sir John was as anxious as the Indians about the future. What he wanted most was to be able to return to his Valley, but failing that, he hoped for a reasonable settlement for his mansions and thousands of acres. As usual he was concerned about providing for his large family. Their eighth child, a son Christopher, was born in Montreal on Dec. 13, 1783; he died the following spring. Little Catherine had died not very long before.

As the shouting and the tumult died, at last it became obvious to the governments of Quebec and Great Britain, as well as to the Loyalists themselves, that they would not be allowed to return to their old homes in the new United States. Homes must be found somewhere else for thousands of displaced persons, Indian, black and white. One band of Mohawks, led by John Deserontyou, settled at Thayendenagea on the Bay of Quinte, and another larger group, under Joseph Brant, on the Grand River. Haldimand determined to settle the majority of the disbanded troops in what is today Ontario. In May, 1784, he appointed Sir John Superintendent of the refugee Loyalists, to take upon himself "the Management and Direction of Distributing to the said Loyalists and the disbanded Troops in the upper part of this Province, the Crown Lands" allotted to them. These lands had been laid out in townships along the upper St. Lawrence and the Bay of Quinte. Sir John was to supervise the settlement, with the assistance of Maj. Samuel Holland, Surveyor General, and Loyalist officers Stephen De Lancey, Maj. Edward Jessup and Capt. Justus Sherwood. Although Sir John's position was largely administrative and

---

[25]Same to Same, Aug. 7, 1783 (NAC: HP, M/f 992, 52, Queen's University Archives).

much of the work was delegated, he did considerable travelling. In June he was at New Johnstown (now Cornwall) settling his first battalion on their land. He continued up the river with Maj. Holland, allotting land along the way, and reached Cataraqui about June 27. He stayed until July 5, distributing land to his second battalion and other units. The settlement of the Loyalists on their land progressed slowly. The surveyors were slow, the bateau service was less than adequate, supplies did not arrive when expected, if at all, refugee Loyalists quarrelled over the size and location of their grants, and the officers, contrary to Haldimand's orders, demanded preference in the choice of location. Such were the problems Sir John had to solve. It was an exhausting and thankless task.

In the meantime, he had his own personal problems to consider. He too received land grants, large ones, which required attention; moreover, he was eager to petition the British Government for compensation for his immense losses in the United States. To leave the country while the Loyalist refugees were still in the process of being settled was unthinkable, but by the autumn of 1784 the gigantic task of the spring and summer was largely accomplished. Leaving Gordon and John in Montreal, Sir John and the rest of his family sailed for England in October.

The Johnsons were reunited with their two oldest children, Nancy and William, who had been in school there since their last visit. Lady Johnson gave birth to another son, James Stephen, on Jan. 30, 1785, the ninth child and seventh son of their marriage. While Lady Johnson was occupied with her new baby, Sir John engaged himself in business outside the home. He presented a petition to the King praying that the Loyalists recently settled in Canada might be relieved from the rules of the French seigneurial system and that the country from Lake

St. Francis westward might be comprehended as a district distinct from Quebec but subordinate to that province in the way Cape Breton was to Nova Scotia. He also submitted his claim for compensation for his losses in New York and left his brothers-in-law, Guy Johnson and James Watts, as attorneys to press those claims (he is said to have received £47,000 in addition to large tracts of land, a settlement which fell far short of the value of his losses). The Johnsons returned to Quebec in October.

The family was still growing; the tenth child, Catherine Maria, was born in Montreal on May 12, 1786. Sir John as well continued to support Clarissa Putman and their two children, William and Margaret (Peggy) in Schenectady. William, now 17 years old, went in March to Niagara to learn the business of the Indian Department under the tutelage of the Deputy Agent John Dease, his father's cousin. A few years later, Peggy married James Van Horne of Schenectady who Sir John offered a post in the Indian Department, which he refused. Sir John supported Clarissa the rest of her life.

Appointed to the Legislative Council in 1786, where, seeming to have lost the "diffidence and reserve" of his youth, Sir John was active in debate and forceful in presenting the Loyalist point of view. He and Lady Johnson spent the winter in Quebec. Along with his activities in the council and in the Indian Department, he expended considerable effort on behalf of his brother-in-law and dear friend, Daniel Claus, who, with his family, was in Britain. Daniel wished to sell or let his "large and commodious" house in Montreal and purchase suitable property in the country, and Sir John was continually on the look-out for him. (Daniel's death the following November in Cardiff, Wales, was to be a tremendous shock to Sir John). On Aug. 27, 1787, Lady Johnson gave birth to their eleventh child,

Robert Thomas, although Sir John was absent on the occasion. He was on an extended tour to Niagara and the Grand River, where he conferred with members of the Mohawk tribe and others of the Six Nations. He made treaty payments on Sept. 2 near Buffalo. On Sept. 23 he met the Mississaugas at Carrying Place (near modern Trenton) and made a large land purchase for the Crown. In March, 1788, his other brother-in-law, Guy Johnson, died in London. In August he and John Butler accompanied the new Governor, Lord Dorchester (Sir Guy Carleton) to Toronto, and on Oct. 29, 1789, the Johnson's twelfth child, Charles Christopher, was born.

By 1790 it was common knowledge that the new Province of Upper Canada was about to be created. Lord Dorchester sent to London a strong recommendation for what everybody seemed to expect — that Sir John would be the governor of the new province. Johnson had settled Upper Canada, had been instrumental in its creating, and was known and respected by the majority of its inhabitants. Sir John himself expected the appointment, perhaps even regarded it as his right. Great was his chagrin when Lt. Col. John Graves Simcoe instead was awarded the post. "I have not overlooked the situation and services of Sir John Johnson," Lord Grenville wrote to Lord Dorchester on June 3, 1790, "but motives of very considerable weight in my opinion induced me to think that the nomination of a person belonging to the Province, and possessing such large property in it, was not desirable, especially in the formation of the new Government."[26] It was a bitter potion for Sir John to swallow, especially since he was at the time involved in the unpleasantness of a dispute with Joel Stone over land at the mouth of the Gananoque River. But he

---

[26]E.A. Cruikshank, ed., **The Simcoe Papers** (Toronto 1931), 1:13.

had little time to wail his woes, for he had been instructed to tour the province-to-be to investigate land irregularities and Indian affairs, to look into the complaints of the former rangers who had settled opposite Detroit, and to purchase lands north of Lake Erie from the Indians. He was back in Montreal for the birth of his and Lady Johnson's thirteenth child, Marianne, on Jan. 28, 1771.

The appointment of Simcoe as Lieutenant Governor of Upper Canada did nothing towards establishing a friendship between him and Sir John, although Simcoe found in Sir John "every appearance of good Humour."[27] The organization of the Indian Department, however, served to sour the relationship between the two. The department was under the command of the commander-in-chief of the army, Lord Dorchester, and the Superintendent General was responsible to him and him alone. Sir John was not required to consult with Simcoe on any aspect of Indian Affairs in Upper Canada, a situation which alarmed Simcoe. The Lieutenant Governor visualized all sorts of events transpiring in his own domain of which he disapproved and over which he had no control. He wrote letters of complaint to his superiors. Sir John, as a result, found the Indian Department much more difficult to administer. To add to his difficulties, the British Government had still not surrendered the western posts to the United States, and there was increasing friction over the issue. His family, as it increased in size and the children grew older, became a greater burden; of the 13 children, 10 were still alive, and Lady Johnson was pregnant again. Angry at being overlooked after all he had done for King and country; he was disconsolate, discouraged with his life in

---

[27]Ibid., 1:90.

Canada. He applied to Lord Dorchester for permission to go to England for an extended period.

In June, 1792, he put his house on St. Paul Street in Montreal up for sale, and in July left with his family for England. They took up residence on Golden Square in London and placed their older children in school or university. Lady Johnson gave birth on Dec. 19, 1792, to her fourteenth and last child, a son named Archibald Kennedy. Sir John bought a house in nearby Twickenham and the family moved in, presumably to live the life of country gentry. Much of Sir John's energy and money went to seeking out and buying military commissions for his older sons. He assumed responsibility as well for his fatherless nephew, William Claus, who was by this time ready to be launched in life.

Life soon palled for Sir John; he began to realize that he was a North American, born and bred. Not finding suitable employment in London, he found the maintenance of the customary Johnson style of life extremely costly, believing that those he had left in charge of his affairs and estates in Canada were not being attentive to his interests. As early at 1795 he was making plans to return home, plans which Lady Johnson did all she could to balk. Finally Sir John prevailed, sold the house at Twickenham, and returned with most of his family to Montreal in October 1796.

This was Sir John's last trip to England, but not Lady Johnson's travels. Now liberated from the restraints of childbearing, she showed her husband that she had a mind of her own. If her husband would not accompany her on the excursions she wished to take, she would go without him. In September 1797, she travelled to Albany and New York. "She speaks in raptures of the Country," Sir John wrote to his nephew, William Claus, "and wonders how I can think of laying out Money in this Country."[28] So enthralled was Lady Johnson that she visited New York again in January 1798. Not at all contented with their huge home on St. Paul's St. or with life in Montreal in general, she tried without success to talk Sir John into returning to England. In 1801 she went without him. She was back in Montreal the following year, but left for England again in 1807 and stayed until the summer of 1809. "I hope," Sir John confided in William Claus during her first trip to New York, "she will be less prejudiced when she returns, and better disposed to Cooperate with me, instead of Opposing every Measure for the benefit and Comfort of herself and family."[29]

Sir John found considerable change in the Indian Department on his return from England and did not approve of much that had been done. The surrender by the terms of Jay's Treaty of Niagara, Detroit, Oswego, Michillimackinac, and all the western forts had necessitated a sweeping reorganization, one would prove that the Government of Upper Canada could not be ignored when dealing with Indian Affairs in that Province. Whether he agreed with them or not, Sir John implemented the new set of regulations. He remained as Superintendent General the rest of his life, aided, as he grew older, by his nephew, William Claus, who became Deputy Superintendent General in 1799, after the death of Col. Alexander McKee.[30] Sir John's sons, Archy and Charles, in turn, aided him in the Montreal office.

---

[28]Johnson to William Claus, Sept. 22, 1797 (NAC: CP, MG19/F1/15/278-288, M/f 1482).
[29]Ibid.
[30]William Claus died in 1826.

The latter part of Sir John Johnson's life were somewhat of an anticlimax. First, he was continually in debt, incurred by the extravagance of maintaining several establishments in Canada, and sometimes another in England for Lady Johnson, who was dissatisfied with life in Canada and determined not to live there. Secondly, his large family involved him in great expense. Not only did he feel that he must maintain them in a style befitting the children of a baronet, but each must be launched suitably in life, all of which involved school fees, dowries, property, commission purchases. There seemed no end to it.

Sir John's family had ceased to increase early in the 1790s; early in the 1800s it began to decrease. In 1801 Warren, a major in the 4th Regiment, died and was buried at sea in the Caribbean. The year 1812 was just one tragedy after another. In January the oldest Johnson son, William, died in Montreal, leaving a wife, the former Susan De Lancey, and three daughters. On April 1, Robert was drowned while crossing the St. Lawrence, and four days later James was killed in Spain in the siege of Badajos. In June, Catherine Maria's husband, Maj. Gen. Barnard Foord Bowes, was killed at the storming of the Forts of Salamanca, and Nancy's husband, Col. Edward Macdonnell, died in Montreal in October.[31] It is doubtful if Lady Johnson ever recovered from these continuous shocks. She herself was stricken and died in the summer of 1815. "She was only about three weeks Ill," Sir John wrote to William Claus. "Her Complaint was the Dysentery with Symptoms of Palsy."[32]

---

[31]Frank B. Risteen, "Children of Sir John Johnson and Lady Mary (Polly) Johnson, Married at New York June 30, 1773," **Ontario History** 63 (1971) 93-112.

[32]Johnson to William Claus, Aug. 27, 1815 (NAC: CP, MG19/F1/17/158, M/f 1482).

252   The Loyalists of Quebec

Marianne, too, was in critical condition with the former ailment, but she recovered and became her father's housekeeper until his death.

Sir John spent his declining years in Montreal or Lachine or travelling about among his seigneuries. He had amassed a very large amount of property in both Upper and Lower Canada, but he was never contented, constantly launching new land claims, resurrecting old ones, engaging in disputes with other land owners, and complaining about the abuses he had suffered. In retrospect it seems an almost pathetic conclusion to a life which had started out so brilliantly, a life which had in effect been ruined by the American Revolution.

Sir John Johnson, Baronet, member of the Legislative Council of Lower Canada and Superintendent General of Indian Affairs, died at the home of his daughter, Catherine Maria Bowes, in Montreal on Jan. 4th, 1830. His colourful military and Masonic funeral on Jan. 8th was one of the largest Montreal had ever seen. Several hundred Indians from St. Regis, Caughnawaga, and the Lake of Two Mountains attended; a chief gave an oration in Mohawk. As the remains crossed the St. Lawrence on its way to the family vault at Mount Johnson, the troops on the upper bank fired several volleys which were answered by a 15-gun salute from St. Helen's Island.[33]

Thus was laid to rest the most prominent of the Loyalists in the Province of Canada. Respected by the Indians, partly because of his famous father, but mainly due to his work among them, and his concern for their welfare. The leader among the

---

[33]Frank B. Risteen, "Some Highlights in the Life of Cornwall's Founder, Sir John Johnson," a paper presented to the Stormont, Dundas, and Glengarry Historical Society, Cornwall, Ontario, March 17, 1976.

Loyalists in Quebec during the revolution, he was their leader, too, as they took up their land grants west of Lake St. Francis and founded the province that was to become Ontario. It has been said that Sir John was not the man his father was; if not, he was no less for it. He was the product of a different time, of a different set of events and circumstances, to which he responded as effectively as his father had done a generation before.

Commissary Clarke: Isaac-of-All-Trades
by John Ruch

Isaac Winslow Clarke (1746-1822) represented the best of well-to-do, educated, American Loyalist families. The Clarkes' loyalty to the Crown and their stock-in-trade, however, singled them out as targets for one of the most notorious, violent acts leading up to the American Revolution. Exiled from their Boston home, Isaac and his brother Jonathan settled in Canada.

The Clarkes descended in several lines from Puritan pioneer families of the Massachussets Colony. Among the first on the Mayflower were Edward Winslow and James Chilton. Edward's brother John married James' daughter, Mary, in 1624, and their great-granddaughter, Elizabeth Winslow, became the wife of Boston merchant Richard Clarke in 1733. Among their 10 children were Isaac and Jonathan, who thus belonged to the fifth generation of native-born Bostonians.[1] Richard was a prosperous and respected citizen by 1773 when he became an agent for the East India Company's tea cargoes. Shortly thereafter, government tax on this commodity excited the passions of New England rebels, resulting in riots and forcing the Company agents to take shelter at Fort William in late 1773. Meanwhile the tea was thrown into the harbour by the rebels, an incident that became known as the famous Boston Tea Party.

The Clarkes returned to Boston from Fort William during its subsequent occupation by British troops, but departed with them when the area was finally evacuated. Richard, with some

---

[1]Mayflower Families Through Five Generations, II, 98; D.P. Hotton, John Winslow Memorial: Winslows and Descendants in America, I, 1877, 60. Additional information on the Clarke family in E.A. Jones, Loyalists of Massachussets, (London, reprint Baltimore 1969) 90-92.

of his children, went to London to join his daughter Susanna, who was residing there with her husband, John Singleton Copley. A promising artist, Copley was a protégé of Sir Joshua Reynolds and Benjamin West. One of his most popular paintings depicts Richard Clarke with Copley's young family grouped around him.[2]

Isaac and Jonathan, erstwhile consignees of part of the tea cargo, had managed to protect other goods throughout their stay at Fort William. In the spring of 1775, the brothers moved their business to Canada and scarcely were they established in Quebec City when a rebel invasion threatened them again. This time they moved the remainder of their stock to England,[3] and briefly were re-united with their father and sister. Upon receiving postings from the government as deputy commissaries with the army in Quebec, the brothers returned to Canada. Jonathan was stationed in Quebec City and in 1777 was selected to accompany Burgoyne's ill-fated expedition into New York as a commissary.[4] After Burgoyne's surrender at Saratoga, Jonathan continued to secure provisions for the imprisoned army. He undertook a number of official missions on behalf of the various prison camps, and between the British and rebel headquarters.[5] The revolutionaries treated their prisoners badly, making his task unenviable. He was forced to battle

---

[2]Reproduced in Jones, **op. cit.,** plate XIV.

[3]**Losses Claim,** Audit Office records, A.O. 13, 97, 268-69, (Public Record Office (PRO) London, England).

[4]Historical Manuscripts Commission, **Report on the American Manuscripts in the Royal Institution,** (London 1904-09, 4 vols.) esp. vols. 1 & 2, see indexes.

[5]**Ibid.** and Thomas Anburey, **Travels Through the Interior Parts of America** (reprint in 2 vols., New York 1969), vol. 2, 379.

against obdurate rebel officers for even the barest essentials of food and clothing for four years.

Jonathan was released from his duties by an exchange of prisoners, returning to England where he obtained an appointment as "Extra Deputy Commissary" in Quebec.[6] Returning to Canada, he died shortly thereafter early in 1783.[7]

In contrast to Jonathan's short but eventful life, Isaac's was long and productive. From March 1776 until his death, Isaac served in the Commissary Department for 46 years, first working under Commissary General Nathaniel Day as Deputy Assistant. His signature appeared on thousands of documents — orders, oaths, certificates, letters, judgements, etc. From mid-1777 in Montreal, Isaac was responsible for a routine of duties including the reception, storage and issuing of large quantities of supplies for the armed forces and other government departments. His duties also involved regular inspections of the materials, and of the state of the buildings which housed them, reports on which he submitted periodically.[8] It was a humdrum existence compared to that of his unlucky brother, who had occasional encounters with the commanders in chief, Clinton and Washington, and often faced danger in the line of duty.

At the end of the war, the army and its non-combatant services had to be drastically reduced in size, and Isaac was one of the many who lost his job. Reluctant to go back into private business as his brother and partner had just died, he petitioned Gov. Haldimand, citing his services and losses, for an

---

[6]Haldimand Papers (HP), B.51, 61.

[7]Protestant Church records index, Archives Nationales, Quebec City.

[8]HP, B.191, 22-24, damaged stores Nov. 1778; 194-105, buildings needing repair Feb. 1780.

appointment to the new commissariat. Failing that, he hoped to be granted half-pay according to the military system.[9]

Isaac received an appointment under the new Commissary General John Craigie, and his career took on new promise. However, before settling into his new job, he was granted leave of absence for a visit to England.[10] Apart from wanting to see his family again, he planned to appear before the Losses Claims Commission to plead his case. By his own calculations, he and his brother's losses due to enemy action totalled just over £933.[11]

At this time, Richard Clarke was residing with the Copley family on fashionable George Street, Hanover Square, London. Some distance away lived two of Isaac's friends, Benjamin Hallowel and Charles Paxton, both formerly from Boston where Paxton had been a commissioner of customs. Richard and Charles, colleagues of the former governor Thomas Hutchison (d.1780), attended weekly meetings of Bostonians in a local coffee house.[12] In London, Isaac participated in such gatherings, and must have met many old acquaintances around Westminster where New Englanders congregated, particularly if he patronized the New England Coffee House, or frequented St. James Park.[13]

Back in Montreal were he resided, Isaac included among his close friends William Dummer Powell and his young family, also former Bostonians. Powell had arrived in Montreal in

---

[9]Ibid., B.230, 196-197.

[10]Ibid., B.130, 127-130, late 1784.

[11]Losses Claim.

[12]Mary B. Norton, The British American, (London 1974), 73-76.

[13]Loss and Losses Claim.

1779, fresh from completing law studies in England.[14] His
abilities were soon recognized and he began to receive
important commissions. He proved himself most useful to the
government in the enquiry into legal practice in Quebec, and in
arbitrating disputes among the Loyalists, notably in 1787. The
next year, Gov. Dorchester appointed him judge of the newly-
created district of Hesse (western Ontario). He received the
exceptional salary of £500 per annum. Isaac Clarke, three
decades later after a lifetime of service, was earning only £440
per year.[15]

Clarke and the Powells got on well together, Isaac becoming
particularly fond of his friend's young sister Ann. When
William packed up and moved his family west, Isaac
accompanied them and made use of the opportunity to check
on commissary arrangements and properties in the upper
country. Ann kept a journal of the trip beginning on May 11,
1789,[16] recording many interesting incidents along the way
including a stop at Niagara Falls, a "magnificent view" which
she left with regret. At this point Isaac left then and returned to
Montreal. Ann went on with her family toward Detroit, but
later returned to Montreal to marry Isaac. Their marriage was
short-lived. Ann died in 1792.

Early in 1790, Isaac was promoted to the rank of Assistant
Commissary General in Montreal. This position was far from

---

[14]Nina M. Tiffany and Susan I. Lesley, **Letters of James Murray, Loyalist**,
(Boston 1901, reprint Boston 1972), 276.

[15]RG 8, Military "C" :Ser., C.140, 218, Isaac's pay.

[16]Mrs. Forsyth Grant, "Gleanings from the Journal of Miss Ann Powell, written
for her cousin Miss Eliz S. Quincy in 1785 (sic)," **Transactions**, The Women's
Canadian Historical Society, Toronto, no. 10, (1912), 3-7. Ann is not to be
confused with her brother William's wife Ann née Murray, for whom see
Tiffany, **op. cit.**

sinecure, rather it involved considerable responsibility with commensurate influence in the community. For over 30 years, Clarke used this power and trust for the public good.

In Audet's *Biographical Notes*,[17] Isaac is justly referred to as the government's jack-of-all-trades. Clarke was relied on implicitly to carry out innumerable odd-jobs which did not fall into the sphere of any one department, or come under the responsibility of a particular functionary. Many of these duties should have been performed by a member of the Governor's household, if there had been one in Montreal. In this capacity as a "palace official" Clarke performed services connected with vice-regal visits to the district, including preparations for Gov.Prescott's reception in Montreal in late 1798.

Montreal's Government House (Château de Ramezay) was the logical place to accommodate Prescott and his party, but it was in a neglected state. Clarke was asked not only to provide suitable quarters and services, but in addition to find horses for transportation. Pointe-aux-Trembles was chosen as an overnight stop, but its King's Inn was unsuitable, leaving Isaac to suggest Dr. Samuel Adams' house instead, for it was commodious and "they entertained there tolerably."[18] Adams was a Loyalist from Vermont who had captained a company of volunteers during Burgoyne's offensive in 1777 and for some years afterwards.[19]

Château de Ramezay had to be repaired, cleaned and appropriately furnished — a tremendous task, as well as servants procured. Clarke first approached local hotel keepers to cater the visit, but both Tisdale and Dillon declined, for as Dillon said, it took away staff and attention from his own

---

[17]**Audet's Biographical Notes**, (NAC: mss. MG 30/D1/12/4-8).

[18]RG 8/C.223, 47-49, Clarke to Green, July 5, 1798.

[19]See chapter on medicine.

business to its detriment.[20] Dillon had had unhappy experiences in having done such work for Dorchester earlier. Clarke ended up hiring his own staff and began with Mrs. Manson, a housekeeper, to advise him. One of her first observations was that "all the bedsteads are in a crazy condition and require repair."[21] Red cedar and curly maple planks were purchased for furniture while drapery and bedding materials along with kitchen and dining utensils were bought from local merchants, some of whom were Loyalists. James Dunlop supplied rose-coloured wool blankets. According to one list, £62 were spent on such furnishings.[22]

Since there was not enough room in these quarters for the entire party, Clarke offered space in his own residence for two of the officers. One was his friend, the Governor's military secretary Major James Green, the other was the aide-de-camp, Col. Mann.[23] Isaac was also responsible for securing seven horses that would be reliable as the Governor needed a "steady" mount, and a pair was required for his landau, another for his calèche, and a third to assist with the servants and baggage.

Late in 1801, the British government decided to try to foster the cultivation of hemp in Canada. Russia was the principal source of supply of the large quantities of the material used by the Royal Navy in the form of canvas and rope. Due to the Napoleonic blockade that put a halt to the importation of products from the Baltic to England, including forest products and hemp, England needed to find another source, and quickly. If Quebec could produce hemp, it would benefit both economies

---

[20]RG 8, C.223, 42-46.

[21]RG 8, C.223, 52-53.

[22]Ibid., wood, 54-55; list of purchases, 59.

[23]Ibid., 48.

as well as reduce Canada's financial dependence on Britain. The history of the project demonstrates the on-going chronic lack of co-ordination and communication between the governments on both sides of the Atlantic.

Clarke was chosen by Gov. Milnes to set up a committee for the Montreal District, parallel to another in the Quebec City area, to promote the introduction of hemp as a staple crop.[24] Lord Portland's instructions had arrived from England too late to allow adequate preparation for the current year, and prevented the presentation of a bill to the legislature for the necessary funds. Milnes acted promptly, however, to ensure that another growing season would not be lost. He authorized funds for the purchase of seed, and chose two administrators who were assured that the government would provide for inspection and purchase of the crops. Clarke was chosen "on account of his knowledge of the subject of agriculture and the well-known integrity of his character."[25]

Isaac acted hastily to profit from the first harvest, while agents were dispatched to the United States to purchase seed. Members of his committee were also representatives of societies sympathetic to the project, through which it was publicized by offering prizes for growers with the best results. It was hoped that the farmers of French-speaking Canada would take advantage of this opportunity to introduce a new cash crop. Unfortunately they were reluctant to try an unfamiliar commodity with an unproven record. In addition, the clergy was opposed to the idea for economic reasons, as the tithe the Church was accustomed to receiving was confined to cereal crops, not hemp.

---

[24]Some correspondance between London and Quebec is in the Colonial Office Records, C.O. 42/121/231-240, (PRO London).

[25]Ibid., 238v.

Commissary Clarke leased land, hired labourers and rationed the hemp seed to two and a half bundles per farm, including his own. Many lessons were learned from the first season's experiments with the quality and quantity of hemp grown varying considerably from farm to farm. At the end of the year's work, however, Isaac reported the results of his committee's efforts: a ton of hemp had been sent to England for examination by authorities. Mr. Harrison, a local weaver, had purchased 800 pounds of "tow" to be turned into thread for weaving. For the next year's experiments, they had collected 40 bushels of seed from the first crop, nearly three times as much as they had started with.[26]

In a typically bureaucratic manner of settling accounts, Clarke was granted land but not reimbursed the difference between the original allowance for the project and the £560 debt.[27] He was, however, given the satisfaction of winning the gold medal awarded by the Society of Arts in 1804 for the quality of hemp which he had produced on his own farm.[28] The experiments continued for several years, while Clarke's connection with the project ceased about 1806. By 1839, it was stated that the growing of hemp had long since been neglected due to the expense and ununiform quality.[29]

---

[26]Ibid., Clarke's letter, report and accounts 231-233; expenses for hemp seed in 1801 were £51/17/9d. for 15 3/4 bushels, RG 8, C.725, 99.

[27]His first petition for land on the Chateauguay River was unsuccessful, the next for land in Barford Township was granted April 15, 1802, Lower Canada Land Papers, NAC.

[28]William H. Atherton, **Montreal**, II (Montreal 1914), 528-529; see also Newton Bosworth, **Hochelaga Depicta** (Montreal 1839, reprint Toronto 1974), 179-180.

[29]Newton Bosworth, **Hochelaga Depicta**.

Although Isaac had done his best in this undertaking, ironically the greatest achievement of the project was of a literary nature. John Lambert had left England for Canada to assist a relative participating in the hemp scheme. On his return home a few years later, Lambert published an account of his travels in North America which became one of the most popular books of its kind. *Travels through Lower Canada and the United States* went through three editions between 1810 and 1814.[30]

During this same period, Clarke had been appointed to various committees through which can be traced the outline of Montreal's civic history. In 1791, when Quebec was divided into Upper and Lower Canada and new shipping regulations and customs duties were formulated, Clarke was chosen as one of three commissioners of customs at Montreal. Eight years later, the government allocated money for the construction of a new court house in Montreal.[31] Clarke was one of the commissioners charged with carrying out this project. Scarcely had the edifice of this building been finished when the City Gaol burned in 1803, which saw Clarke on the committee to erect a new prison.

Other commissions on which he served were the Lachine turnpike and canal. The Lachine rapids, too dangerous to navigate, necessitated the forwarding of merchandise and passengers to Montreal by a land route — the Lachine road. This route was a hazard until 1805 when an Act for its improvement was passed, allocating funds for repairs and maintenance. The Act also provided a toll booth in the hope of recovering some of the costs. Clarke was chosen as a

---

[30]J.J. and Ruth Talman, "The Canadas 1763-1812," 103 on Lambert; see also Karl F. Klinck, **Literary History of Canada**, 2nd ed., I, (University of Toronto 1976), 97.

[31]**Biog. Notes,** 391 and Bosworth, 158-9.

commissioner on the project, and 16 years later, a member of the group overseeing the construction of the Lachine canal when it became financially feasible.

In peace time the work of the Commissariat went on as an essential but unglamorous routine, while during periods of emergency or warfare the services of this department were brought into the forefront. Isaac's competence and long experience in his post, part of it during the previous war, made him invaluable at such times and was recognized by the authorities in the many appointments they conferred on him. In 1812, he was appointed assistant Commissary of the British Army in Canada and a little over a year later, commissioned as a Lt.-col. and Deputy Superintendent of the Provincial Commissary for de Salaberry's Voltigeurs Regiment. This was followed by his new title of Deputy Commissary General of the army.[32]

The importance of Isaac's services during the 1812 war was underlined years later by Lt. Gen. Sir Gordon Drummond, who cited Clarke's efficient handling of the military supply services as having been essential to the successful operation of British and Canadian forces. Clarke's involvement with the veterans of the war continued for some time and in 1816, as a commissioner of oaths, he was charged with examining the claims of demobilized soldiers, evaluating the petitions of officers for retirement on half pay.

Clarke's odd jobs were generally confined to the Montreal District and included negotiating for the purchase of property on behalf of the Crown. In 1809 he became an issuer of licence to gun powder dealers, and 10 years later controller and administrator of Government House in Montreal, acting on

---

[32]Biog. Notes, 392; see also Margaret Clarke Coffin's obituary, clipping from 1898 newspaper in scrapbook M 14041, McCord Museum, Montreal, transcribed by Joyce Bradford of Toronto.

behalf of the Governor of domestic affairs. At least on one occasion, he arranged transport for Sir John Johnson, and organized special relief for the noble refugees from the French Revolution.[33]

Isaac was in a very good position to support various charitable societies, which he did freely and unstintingly. Montreal's rapidly increasing population presented the community with ever-growing numbers of poor, needy and sick. The churches tried to assist through facilities, such as the Hôtel Dieu Hospital, that too often became overburdened. Meanwhile, a group of English-speaking ladies banded together to help orphans, single mothers, and ailing immigrants. A few years later, their vigorous activity resulted in the founding of the Lying In Hospital, which later evolved into the Montreal General Hospital. In the records of these organizations as well as the Emigrant Society, Commissary Clarke's name appears as an ardent supporter.

Occasional inspections of government-owned supplies revealed damaged or obsolete goods. It was Clarke's sharp eye which noted what could be of use to the benevolent organizations. Ordinarily, the "condemned" stores would have been sold at auction, but Clarke was able to persuade the authorities that the gain by auction would be negligible, and that the need of the impoverished was greater than the government's. The supplies would then be diverted to the hospitals and societies. An example of Clarke's timely intervention is noted in 1819, when bedding and clothing were sent to both Hôtel Dieu and the Montreal General, the latter, just opened, was in dire need of supplies. The next July, a check of the quartermaster's stores revealed that 450 pairs of trousers had been damaged by moths. Clarke suggested to the Governor that these would better serve needy immigrants in the cold

---

[33]Biog. Notes; see also RG 8, card index.

weather to come. The garments were divided between Dr. Blackwood of the Montreal General, the Female Benevolent Society and the Emigrant Society. On October 10, Clarke, on behalf of the recipients, formally thanked the Governor for the clothing.[34]

Clarke enjoyed the confidence and trust of both government and community, which is evident from his being entrusted to public money. Couriers sent to the United States to obtain large shipments of cash occasionally absconded with the funds. In 1811, Isaac was sent south to bring back the required specie for the government's treasury. It was not until a few years later in 1817 that the Montreal Bank, (Bank of Montreal) was founded, followed by the Montreal Savings Bank, of which he became the President. The Bank's objectives were:

> to open to the lower orders a place of deposit for their
> small savings, with the allowance of a reasonable
> monthly interest...to encourage industry, economy and
> sobriety among them.[35]

This financial institution was absorbed by the Bank of Montreal in 1856.

Isaac remarried in middle age to Jane Desmond Sutherland (1770-1836), who was much younger than her husband. Their three surviving children were Richard, Susan and Margaret,[36] who through their marriages united three of the most prominent Loyalist families in the Province. Susan was the second wife of Charles R. Ogden, son of Isaac, in 1829. Margaret

---

[34]Blackwood 113 (C127, 85-86, Clarke's thanks).

[35]Merrill Denison, **Canada's First Bank**, II (Montreal 1967), 80.

[36]Jones op. cit. for refs. to children and their pensions, Margaret's obit. 1898, Susan's wedding 1829 clipping in scrapbook M14041, McCord Museum.

married William E. Coffin (later Lieut. Col). Isaac kept close contact with his daughters by correspondence, and occasional visits.

In spite of the fact that Isaac's brother-in-law was one of the leading portrait painters of his time in Britain, Copley's only known surviving work of Clarke, in Montreal, is a silhouette preserved in the McGill University Archives.[37] Comparing Isaac's facial structure with that of his father's (Richard) in Copley's earlier work, the resemblance is easily seen through the same high-bridged nose and protruding chin. Isaac was depicted in the 1790s fashion wearing a high-collared coat, with this hair fashioned in a queue.

The latter part of Clarke's life was spent assisting the Female Benevolent Society in their quest to build a new hospital. Isaac was conscripted by his peers to lead the project, which was completed in 1821. In mid-1822 Isaac set sail for London to obtain a Royal Charter for the Montreal Hospital, as its fifth president. His ship had not gone far down river from Quebec City when he died suddenly near Cape Chat at 74 years of age.[38] His body was taken back to Montreal for burial in the City's Protestant Burying Ground.

The noted archivist, Audet, wrote of Isaac Clarke:

> Le Gouvernement avait toujours foi en lui, et avec raison, car it etait digne d'éloges. Ce devait être, en effet, un bie brave homme...pendant plus de trente-cinq ans, jamais une plainte ne fut préferé contre lui..."[39]

---

[37]Donated by Clarke's granddaughter Miss Paulin M. Carrière to the hospital in 1930, it is illustrated in Edward H. Bensely, "Issac Winslow Clarke," **M.G.H. News,** Fall 1977, Montreal General Hospital, 9.

[38]Jones **op. cit.,** 90.

[39]**Biog, Notes.,** 391.

James "Demon" Dunlop: Loyalist Magnate

by John Ruch

"I defy you. I run all risk, and take it upon myself."[1]

Rash words in the mouth of a lesser man, the defiant stance of James Dunlop was the style upon which he built his commercial empire, unrivalled in Canada. A Scot of extraordinary ambition, energy, daring and ability, he was a man who invites description in superlatives. Dunlop had the vision and imagination to develop and expand upon principles of commercial practice which most of his contemporaries did not share. He has been called "archetype" of later business giants such as Aitken (Beaverbrook), Dunn, Taylor and Weston.

A portrait of Dunlop dated from ca.1800, which is in possession of his descendants, shows a fashionably-dressed gentleman in his 50s, of stocky build with cleancut features. The tall forehead, eyes deep-set beside a prominent aquiline nose over a firm mouth and chin stand out well in this profile.

Virginia

James Dunlop (1757-1815) was the youngest son of David Dunlop, a Glasgow merchant and textile manufacturer. As a young man he was sent to work for William and John May's

---

[1] I am grateful to A.J.H. Richardson for correcting a serious error in the identification of Dunlop, and for several observations. See the **Dictionary of Canadian Biography**, V, by David S. Macmilland and Richardson; **Court Martial Proceedings**, Dec. 10-14, 1813, RG 4, A 1, vol. 132, pp 42411-42450.

firm which was then trading in the Virginia area to which he would eventually emigrate.

During James' early years in America, just prior to the American Revolution, his Dunlop kin of Garnkirk acquired land and buildings in Virginia and Maryland, several of which were in the vicinity of present day Washington D.C. In time, the Dunlops had made improvements to their properties thereby enhancing their value considerably.[2]

James' letters of the early 1770s tell a good deal of his life and times.[3] An impression emerges of an educated, optimistic and vigorous young man suddenly confronted with many business opportunities, and, later, an ominous political situation. "I love the country well," he wrote from Gray's Creek on June 28, 1773,[4] although his taste was not for buckskin and homespun clothes. Rather, he donned fashionable cloth imported from Britain complete with "maccaroni" material for breeches, and silver furnishings, which he claimed were cheaper and better-made than the local product. His taste for English literature caused him to ask his brother, a bookseller, to send him new books and plays, especially "any new thing that is written which is reckoned clever." Ever a businessman, he had actually sold one of his own classics to a friend, but regretting the action ordered a replacement for this copy of Steele and Addison's *Spectator*.

Before long he experienced his first political shock. His business concerns constantly led him to new fields to exploit

---

[2]**Losses Claim**, "Colin Dunlop & Co.," Audit Office Records, A.O. 13, vol. 28, ff. 275-304, esp. f. 293, Public Record Office, London, England.

[3]**Dunlop Papers**, Scottish Record Office, H.M. General Record Office, Edinburgh, Scotland.

[4]**Ibid.**, letter no. 1.

until the Patriot rebels' activities could no longer be ignored. On July 20, 1775, in a long letter to his relatives, he described the warlike preparations in the Colony: armed men "daily growing more ungovernable accoutered themselves with uniforms, truculent slogans and badges." Everyone would have to choose sides soon.[5] British-born merchants were almost without exception loyal to the Crown, the Dunlops among them, and were hotly denounced by Virginians for their stand, although the ulterior motive for this hostility was economic rather than political.

The Colony suffered from a backward economy, landowners overspent their incomes, and were in debt to the merchants for purchases of imported luxury goods. The British government's land policy, protecting the Indians, restricted the landlords from expanding their properties to increase their income. Unfailingly they blamed the merchants for the government's actions, and in an effort to rid themselves of debts, creditors, land restrictions, and poverty at one stroke, they declared independence from Britain.[6]

Some of the revolutionaries were experienced in defamation. While accusing the merchants of perfidious conduct, they themselves were committing far greater outrages with a posture of absolute innocence. They intercepted mail and published ordinarily unexceptional business letters as evidence of the merchants' unscrupulousness. Instructions to Dunlop concerning the collection of debts appeared with a journalist's fulsomely self-righteous comments in 1775.[7] Dunlop and 10

---

[5]Ibid., letter 1, no. 5.

[6]Peter McQ. Mitchell, **Loyalist Property and the Revolution in Virgina,** (Thesis, University of Colorado 1979), 2-5.

[7]**American Archives:** Fourth Ser. Peter Force, Washington, II, Col. 975.

others at Port Royal the next year refused to take the oath of allegiance to the Rebel cause, and were named in a newspaper account and branded "monsters of ingratitude."[8]

Their properties were seized and sold in order to finance the Revolution in Virginia — an old political stratagem: denounce your opponent as a criminal, seize his wealth, and use it for self-enrichment. Dunlop, publicly damned and stripped of his assets, saw the proceeds from the sale of his company's holdings benefit the Rebels' treasury to the tune of £10,600.[9] This sum appeared to be somewhat inflated, as a decade later, when James prepared his Losses Claim, he evaluated his share as a mere £1,935, plus $2,142.10 owed to him by individual Virginians.[10]

Dunlop could have spared himself had he thrown in his lot with the rebels. When Governor Dunmore called for loyal men to rally, young James joined the militia, and "took up arms as an ardent Loyalist and participated in some of the bloody campaigns that followed."[11] When the government's efforts failed to end the troubles, Dunlop left Virginia with other refugees, sailing north in the hope of recouping his losses.

Canada

James was one of hundreds of expatriate Scots who came to Canada as a refugee from the American Revolution. After his arrival in this Country in the late 1770s, following the British removal from Virginia, his remarkable talents began to

---

[8]Op. cit. Fifth Ser. Washington, 1843, II, col. 104.

[9]Mitchell, op. cit., 211-219.

[10]Losses Claim, ff. 279, 301.

[11]David S. Macmillan & A.J.H. Richardson, Dictionary of Canadian Biography, V; also Macmillan, "Demon of the Bill Brokers," The Canadian Banker & ICB Review, XXXIV, no. 1, 1977, 14-18.

manifest themselves. Shortly thereafter, he formed a partnership with John Porteous for a brief period until 1781. While having other partners later, Dunlop always became the most dominant associate of the firms.   The development of his import business can be studied from contemporary newspaper advertisements. In 1779 his store was on the upper floor of a house in Lower Town, Quebec City. A late arrival of goods is recognized by his proclamation that the merchandise was to be sold "cheap for ready money,"[12] to help finance a buying trip to Britain before winter set in.[13] The items cited were typical of his stock: textiles, tableware, stationery, jewellery and toilet articles, as well as riding tackle.

In the 1780s, Dunlop's business expanded to include a wider variety of goods — much ready-made clothing and basic necessities for the flood of emigrating Loyalists. He also offered a wide range of yard goods, clothing patterns, dyes, shoe leather and threads,[14] as well as assorted hardware and candle-moulds.

During periods of peace, he was quick to exploit new products. His bilingual advertisement dated July 25, 1785, headed "Dry Goods — Marchandises sèches,"[15] included bottled and draught porter from Boston, wines and teas as well as Cheshire cheese, and "a variety of books by the best authors." These notices continued to appear in Quebec and Montreal newspapers over the next three decades from overseas.[16]

The import business was only one side of Dunlop's commercial endeavours. He was just as keenly engaged in

---

[12]Quebec Gazette, no. 739, Oct. 28, 1779.
[13]Ibid.
[14]Ibid.
[15]Ibid.
[16]Ibid.

exporting Canadian materials to distant ports. Details of this are found less often in the newspapers than in his letters, which have numerous references to eastbound cargoes. This area of trade, however, was almost completely monopolized by the fur traders who had established themselves in the Province before Dunlop's arrival. Like John Richardson, another late arrival in Montreal, Dunlop was able to see alternative areas of trade with vast potential...products whose importance was to eventually outstrip that of furs. Timber and potash, grain, butter, beef and pork formed the bulk of these exports, while in season he sent fruit and vegetables to favoured relatives and friends in Scotland.

Experience in the coastal trade in Virginia had given Dunlop ideas which he later applied to his Canadian ventures. Unlike Phyn & Ellice, a company that kept its ship *Eweretta* berthed for most of the year in order to make one trans-Atlantic round trip bearing a pay-load each way, Dunlop built up a triangular trade with ports in the Caribbean, Canada and Britain. Until the outbreak of the 1812 war he traded with U.S ports, purchasing a variety of goods including tobacco, and later, during the Napoleonic Wars, Dunlop rerouted his cargoes to wine-producing Portugal. His ingenuity and resourcefulness allowed him to keep the mass of accumulating materials in motion.

He capitalized on the laws of supply and demand. A practical man, he realized that in order to better control his import/export operation, he had to be able to control the ships and their destinations. This he accomplished by investing in vessels directly, while controlling shares in others. When times warranted more ships, he would simply purchase what was needed, or if the cost was too steep, he had them built by his own employees, hiring shipwrights from wherever he could find them. By implementing such control over his endeavours, his companies were almost self-sufficient.

Dunlop owned one of the largest fleets in Canada at that time: 10 outright, with vast holdings in 30 others.[17] Being his custom to name the ships after family members or famous figures, it stands that there was a *James Dunlop* — two in fact, the second replacing the first, which ran aground and broke up. Comparing the measurements of those registered between 1792 and 1815, a continual growth in the size of his vessels emerges.[18] Lengths increased from 84 ft. to 115 ft., beams from 23ft. to 32ft., and tonnages from 332 to 482, with no two vessels exactly alike.

His role in promoting ship-building in Montreal has long been overlooked. Quebec City had dominated this industry due to the shallow St. Lawrence waters which prevented passage to and from the port of Montreal. This did not discourage Dunlop, who was one of the first to found a shipyard in Montreal in the 19th century. His yard provided work for 40 men year round; the quality of their craftsmanship as well as the safety record of the yard was well known. The local tradesmen must have learned technical skills from foreign shipwrights hired by Dunlop, such as Logan and Munn, and from the other eleven whom he brought to Montreal from New York on one occasion.[19] Apart from appearance and performance, the speed of the ships was important to Dunlop for commercial advantages, and if the need arose, for purposes of war. A sound vessel which sailed well could be turned into a "privateer" to prey on enemy transports.

---

[17]Macmillan, **op. cit.**

[18]**Quebec Shipping Register**, RG 12, A1, vol. 183 (1787-1823) passim.

[19]**Dunlop Papers**, 1, no. 52, Oct. 15, 1810.

Every expansion of one sector of his business caused development or enlargement in another of his enterprises. Orders from the British Army for flour, timber and rum were paid for in government "bills." In the relatively primitive Canadian economy, hard cash was in short supply while government and personal "bills" were more common. Nearly everyone needed some ready money, but few were eager to take paper credit money in exchange, although some merchants were able to turn a tidy profit by accepting it at less than face value. Typically, Dunlop developed this market into a major part of his activity from which he reaped large gains, while performing a vital function for the growth of Canadian commerce.

The size and nature of Dunlop's business gave him a decided advantage in the purchase and sale of paper bills. He had the financial resources with which large bills could be bought for cash at discounts mounting sometimes as high as 20 per cent. As early as 1800 he purchased £21,000 worth, then in 1814 he remitted a bill of exchange for over £32,000.[20] The bills themselves were of little immediate use to him unless they could be quickly converted into cash or cargoes. The financial centres of London and New York offered bills solidly backed by the British government, and the demand was so great that the buyers were willing to pay nearly two per cent more than face value in cash, ensuring the seller a considerable profit.

Dunlop's military service was a part of his career of which he was inordinately proud. His role in the militia during the American Revolution is, however, obscure, as there were several Dunlops in the Queen's Rangers stationed in Virginia,

---

[20]Macmillan.

including a Capt. James Dunlop who was killed in 1781.[21] In the years following the war, his unquestioned loyalty, his dealings with government, and his financial success assured him a special role in military service. He was appointed agent in Lower Canada for the Queen's Rangers, and acted in this capacity from 1799 to 1804.[22]

His great opportunity for martial enterprise and glory came with the War of 1812. In 1790, Dunlop enlisted in the Montreal Incorporated Volunteers, and was commissioned a captain in 1803 in the artillery company, in which he was still serving when the news arrived on June 24, 1812, that the Americans had declared war.[23] The next year he was promoted to major and commandant of four companies of the 1st battalion, training his troops well, producing a "fine showy company."[24]

Dunlop drove himself hard to maintain the balance between his military and business careers. He was evidently the first in Montreal to get news of the War's outbreak in 1812, which he received by express post from Albany, relaying it immediately to Quebec City.[25] From that moment on, he was constantly active with his military duties. In the fevered preparations against invasion, he reported daily, sometimes twice a day, to his station. Until sufficient assistance could be mustered to share the burden, he had to drill his company twice a week and mount guard about every eighth day.[26] In July,

---

[21]Muster Rolls, RG 8, Mil. "C" Ser., vols. 1861-64, esp. "Casualty List," vol. 1864, 25.
[22]See index to RG 8, Mil. "C" Ser., National Archives of Canada (NAC), Ottawa.
[23]Dunlop Papers, 1, no. 80.
[24]Ibid., 1, no. 83, Aug. 22, 1812.
[25]Ibid., 1, no. 85, Sept. 26, 1812.
[26]Ibid., 1, no. 81, July 20, 1812.

he sped to Quebec City to secure a letter of marque for his ship *Dunlop*, making the downriver journey in about 35 hours, only to find the Governor unable to help.[27] He was to note that time did not permit meals nor sleep, the elation of being involved in such events of international importance sustaining him. The success of his "intimate friend," Gen. Isaac Brock, at Detroit, over Hull's army of "blustering insignificant people," delighted him.[28] His spirits were further lifted when his protégé, James Macnair (his sister's nephew-in-law), once a disappointing failure in Dunlop's firm, procured a commission in the light infantry, and became a model soldier.[29]

The next year, army routine was eased by the presence of additional soldiers, but even so Dunlop carried on with great zeal. As major-commandant, he was called on to drill with his troops once a week, mount guard with members of his unit once every four weeks, and sit on court-martial boards whenever required.[30] Sometimes late at night while waiting for the changing of the guard he found a few moments to write to his sister of his "great guns" which he was impatient to test on the Americans, certain that they would lay low hundreds of the enemy.[31] In August he was appointed superintendent of gunboat construction at Isle aux Noix.[32]

---

[27]Ibid., 1, no. 84, Aug. 29, 1812.

[28]Ibid.

[29]Ibid., 1, no. 85.

[30]Ibid., 1, no.87, Nov. 9, 1812.

[31]His appointment was to be made on Aug. 21, 1813, but he seems to have already been engaged in the work preparatory to construction by Aug. 12; see RG 8, mil. "C" Ser., vol. 730, 85-88, and card index under "Dunlop, James."

[32]Dunlop Papers, 1, no. 86, Nov. 6, 1812.

There were indications, however, that not everything was going well for him. As if an omen of personal disaster, the *James Dunlop* ran aground and broke up.[33] One night on a tour of inspection, he was thrown from a borrowed horse and was only a "little hurt."[34] Meanwhile, some of his ships were captured by the enemy and their valuable cargoes, uninsured, seized. By late 1813, the American forces had advanced into Canada, suffering heavily at Chateauguay. Dunlop's unit with others were ordered to Lachine to block an anticipated attack on Montreal's west flank.

During this tour of duty a junior officer played a spiteful joke on Dunlop. Under other circumstances it would have been a trivial incident, but there was already a bitter personal animosity between them and tempers quickly flared. The officer, Hart Logan, exaggerated the seriousness of Dunlop's conduct and brought military charges against him.[35] The subsequent court martial cleared Dunlop of this charge of drunkenness on duty, but found him guilty of using abusive language towards Logan, and ordered him to apologize. Dunlop became defiant, having little but contempt for Logan, and for the Governor, in whose name the order was given.

Many in the English-speaking community were disenchanted with Governor Sir George Prevost's efforts to secure support for his prosecution of the war by courting the opposition in the Legislative Assembly, and for his ineptness as an offensive commander. Dunlop compared him to Drummond, a more fortunate campaigner in the field. The

---

[33]Ibid.

[34]Court Martial, see note 1 above.

[35]General Militia Order, RG 8, Mil. "C" Ser. Vol. C1203, 1/2 J, 196, Jan. 25, 1814.

disasters at York, Niagara and Sackett's Harbour helped to lower Prevost's reputation, as well as his many missed opportunities to wage attacks. Thus an order from Prevost bore little weight with the soldier, who had lost all confidence in him. Dunlop's outright defiance gave Prevost no alternative but to dismiss him from service for disobedience.[36] Once freed from the bonds of military procedure, Dunlop wrote critical letters to the British prime minister and to the newspapers in which he attacked Prevost openly.[37]

This incident did little for Logan's nor Dunlop's credibility, although it did not lessen Dunlop's reputation with his peers, he being a very popular man in Montreal society at that time. "That court martial has given me much consequence in the Country," he wrote home,[38] which is evident by the invitation from Sir John Johnson to be toastmaster at the banquet celebrating the Prince Regent's birthday, a function he performed again at the King's birthday celebrations the next year.

Just as Dunlop's business recorded its most profitable period in 1813-14, an economic depression engulfed the Country. Large quantities of unsold goods clogged Dunlop's warehouses and his ships, already westbound on the Atlantic, soon arrived to add more goods to the glut. He doubled and redoubled his efforts to keep his affairs solvent. That July he was desperately searching for cargo to fill his outward bound ships.

On a hot, humid day illness struck, and for four weeks he slowly declined, weakened by the doctors' efforts: large doses of

---

[36]**Dunlop Papers**, 1, no. 108, Mar. 27, 1815, (re. prime minister), 1, no.101, July 12, 1814 (newspapers).

[37]Ibid., 1, no. 102, Aug. 16, 1814.

[38]Ibid., 1, no. 101.

physic, enemas, injections, and bleedings. Death came on August 28, 1815, at which time he was considered to be the wealthiest man in Canada.[39]

---

[39]Macmillan, **op. cit.**; Robert Campbell, **History of St. Gabriel Street Church**, (Montreal 1887), 97.

Ann Scott Barnet Hall: the undaunted washerwoman

by John Ruch

"an honest woman who earned her living by her labour
to support herself and three children."[1]

Few Loyalist women commanded attention in their own
right as did Ann Scott, also known as Widow Barnet and later,
Mrs. Hall. Women were mostly mentioned as daughters, wives,
mothers and widows, with thumbnail sketches of their lives
found in official records statistics. But in Ann's case, there is
more documentation which portrays a woman possessed with
common sense and determination.

There were several Scotts in the Stiillwater area on the
Hudson River just south of Saratoga, where Ann was born
ca.1750.[2] There was a Walter, and a Thomas, the latter a mason
who later relocated to South River, Lake Champlain.

In the late 1760s Ann married a veteran soldier, Conrad (or
Coenradt) Barnet, who was born in Germany in the 1730s, and
who had emigrated to America and served for 7 1/2 years with
the 47th Regt.[3] On retirement, Conrad leased 150 acres of land
from (later Gen.) Phillip Schuyler at Stillwater in 1764.

After Barnet had cleared about two-thirds of the land he
built a home to which he brought his wife and their three
young children. At the onset of the rebellion, too old for active
service, he left no doubt as to where his loyalty lay, being jailed

---

[1] NAC: A.O. 13/11/210.

[2] Walter Scott's Losses Claim, **ibid.**, 15/562-563.

[3] Ann Barnet (Mrs. Hall) Losses Claim, **ibid.**, 207-215; also pub. in Ontario
Archives, 2nd report (Toronto 1904), 931.

in the early part of 1777 for six months due to his support of the British government.

During her husband's imprisonment, Ann was the target of repeated harassments by rebels, and after their farm was pillaged, all their property was confiscated. This included their personal belongings and 62 head of livestock.[4] Conrad obtained his release only to realize that military movements in the upper Hudson Valley would soon threaten the lives of all those who remained loyal in Stillwater. Burgoyne's forces made slow progress southward from Canada while the rebel armies began to assemble north of Albany, establishing a major encampment close to Stillwater at Bemis Heights. Conrad immediately set off to inform Burgoyne, with whom his old regiment, the 47th, was serving, of this activity.

That fall two fierce battles were fought in the area between Saratoga and Stillwater — Burgoyne's disastrous defeat leaving all local Loyalists now in real jeopardy. Provincial troops were ordered withdrawn before the surrender on October 17, to escape vicious reprisals by the rebels. And while these small bands of men or troops were generally armed and able to defend themselves against rebels, many Loyalist families fled often without supplies of any kind and unarmed, as did the Barnets. With their speed of escape restricted by their children, the youngest just two years of age, and the eldest eight, Ann would later recall how they travelled through the forests for days, eluding the rebels but not the Indians. Captured by a band of unfriendly braves, fortunately they were not as badly molested as other captives had been.[5] Once freed, they eventually reached Canada, where they purchased their only material comforts with a small sum of money: one blanket for 2 shillings and 6

---

[4]Livestock, A.O. 13/11/207.

[5]Alexander Anderson was murdered by Indians, see his widow Mary's Losses Claim, Ont. Arch., 2nd. report, 387.

pence and a bundle of straw for 5 pence, that was used to make a warm bed for the nights.

They sought refuge at La Prairie near Montreal, where they lived "in the Greatest Misery and want having lived for some time on the Charity of well disposed people." After three months Conrad died on Jan. 19, 1778, leaving his family destitute. From this point on, records document the determination of his widow to provide for her children.

There were not many honourable occupations open to women in the late 18th century, especially in a frontier town, other than common drudgery. A good deal of laundering and seamstress' work needed to be done for both the troops and civilians. To prevent exploitation, Gov. Haldimand set a standard of costs for a number of items. The washing of a shirt, for example, was set at 4 pence, and it was by saving these pennies that Ann was able to ensure the survival of her young family.

According to two testimonials drawn up later for "Nancy Barnet," Ann had worked in La Prairie from the time she had arrived, by washing and sewing for local citizens,[6] who included a few influential people. A number of her noteworthy clients signed these documents and included: Richard Cartwright, Stephen De Lancey, Robert Ellice, Thomas Forsyth, Robert Leake and Thomas McCord. These men attested to her late husband's loyalty and to the devotion which she displayed in the upbringing of her children. Industry, honesty and uprightness characterized her: "She has been able to support her children (three in number) with decency."[7] She was to continue in this work for at least six years later in Montreal.

---

[6]Two certificates, A.O. 13/11/209, Nov. 8, 1783, and another 210. Certificates of Conrad's loyalty, **ibid.,** 80/32.
[7]**Ibid.,** 209.

The family was placed on the government rations list and began to receive food supplies along with other needy refugees.[8] After three years, late in 1781, Ann married Isaac Hall, a refugee shoemaker.[9] Her sons were of an age when they needed the presence and guidance of a male figure and not only could Isaac give Ann emotional support, but he could also train the boys in his craft, thereby ensuring them of a means of support when they were older.

There were numerous Halls in Montreal during the latter years of the 18th century, but their relationships are not entirely clear. Besides Isaac, a James and an Archibald are also found on refugee lists.[10] In addition, there were four brothers in the Presbyterian congregation: Joseph and Jacob, hatters; Benjamin, merchant; and John, baker. The Barnet-Hall family was early associated with the Anglican Church.

Life after her marriage to Isaac continued to be a struggle for Ann. Conrad had left her nothing but his last will, which was misplaced for many years. Only in 1783, when a government commission called for victimized Loyalists to submit statements regarding their losses in hope of compensation did the will become important. Not letting the missing document stop her, Ann made a claim supported by other papers and entrusted them to the leading young lawyer in Montreal, William

---

[8]Barnet and Scott families received subsistence, e.g. see NAC: Haldimand Papers (henceforth HP), B161/130, return dated Sept. 1780; B167/283v.-284r., List of Unincorporated Loyalists, remarks about Walter Scott, "old, infirm, suffered much." Col. Carleton aurhorized rations for the Barnets in 1779, **ibid.**, B165/3, return dated Jan. 1, 1782.

[9]Ann Barnet married Isaac Hall, Oct. 4, 1781, Anglican Church Register, Montreal.

[10]Isaac, James and Archibald on Return of Unincorporated Loyalists, Feb. 7, 1784, (NAC: HP, B168/5-6.) The four Hall brothers cited by Robert Campbell, **The History of the Scotch Presbyterian Church on St. Gabriel Street** (Montreal 1887), 234.

Dummer Powell,[11] who presented them to the Losses Claim Commission in London. However the Commission would not oblige her, due to a lack of adequate documentation.

Several years later Ann pursued the matter of compensation, when two Commissioners visited Canada to deal with outstanding claims and to hear claimants' evidence in person. Presenting her case on June 18, 1787, Ann was the tenth person, and second woman to be heard in Montreal.[12] Records of the hearing, still preserved in London, show that she retrieved her papers from Powell to lay before the Commissioners. An inventory put Conrad Barnet's possessions, seized by the enemy, at a total value of £562.7.6d.[13] The visitors were impressed by Ann, and decided in her favour.

The amount of money voted by Parliament to be applied to Loyalists' compensation was only a fraction of their actual losses. The Commissioners were bound by the limited funds at their disposal and the desire to be equitable. Thus Loyalists who had proven their cases were awarded compensation in proportion rather than in full. The sum calculated for Ann's award was £205, which she, like other recipients, was unable to collect in cash. To minimize the outlay a method of payment by installments was set up. A debenture, bearing 3 1/2 per cent interest, was issued to each successful claimant in an amount slightly less than the full award,[14] and thereafter the holder received semi-annual payments for eight years. Ann would not receive her final installment until nearly 20 years after the property had been lost!

Although the compensation received was a good deal less than losses sustained, impoverished Loyalists often felt very

---

[11]A.O.13/11/213.

[12]A.O. 12/120, claimant no. 707.

[13]A.O. 13/80/34.

[14]Mary Beth Norton, **The British Americans** (Boston 1972), 221.

fortunate to get anything at all. However, there were others who thought the settlements miserly and grudgingly slow in realization. Whatever her reactions may have been, Ann held her tongue, but only briefly. When it came to the methods used by the paying agents in liquidating the Loyalists' credits she made her opinion clear.

After the Loyalists' funds were allocated by the British government, they were set aside in the Treasury until reputable Canadian or British merchants with representatives in Canada were appointed as paying agents and the money was then placed in their London bank accounts. In Canada the firms concerned received lists of the Loyalists to whom these agents were to pay the appropriate semi-installments. But with a chronic shortage of hard cash in Canada, the twice-yearly payments of numerous claimants' installments caused an unprecedented drain on financial resources. In brief, to settle even one payment to all creditors would nearly exhaust the merchants' cash flow, leaving little for the continuance of regular business.

These merchants did find an alternative to the cash settlement — to offer merchandise from their stock to the amount of the Loyalist's credit. Dobie & Badgeley were the merchants with whom Ann dealt. And while at an earlier time she might have been happy with such an arrangement, she was now established in Montreal, and wanted cash. Dobie & Badgeley refused.

Not understanding the intricacies of high finance, but determined to get her money, Ann, being illiterate, found a friend to write a letter for her to someone in high office.[15] "Dear Friend" the letter to Commissioner Pemberton began, and was followed by two folio pages explaining her plight. At times verbose and rambling, she did make it clear that she was

---

[15]Letter to a "Friend" (Pemberton), Oct. 20, 1787, Montreal A.O. 13/11/215-216.

indignant over the iniquitous behaviour of Dobie & Badgeley, and that she wanted to know how she could receive her compensation in cash.

Repeated several times in the letter was the phrase "my Debenture." Admittedly a considerable sum of money was involved, but to a person such as Ann it represented more. The compensation was hers by right, a consolation for the lost years in Stillwater.

In the 1790s when John and William Barnet reached legal maturity, they asked their mother for their share of the estate. They were thinking of marrying, and would soon have grants of land to develop, all of which would require expense. Ann told them to expect nothing.

Her sons brought suit against her to obtain a settlement of their father's estate. By Conrad Barnet's will, which had finally been found, his wife was restricted to one-third of the estate should she remarry, with the remainder distributed among his children.[16] The boys obviously felt justified in their action, perhaps believing that their mother and stepfather were hoarding the money for themselves. Called to account for their conduct by the court, Ann and Isaac Hall presented a list of expenses incurred in caring for her three Barnet children. During their years of minority in Canada the two boys and a girl were stated to have cost the guardians £650 for "Boarding, Lodging, Schooling, Cloathing and Washing."[17] The total yield of the estate, however, was only £228, leaving their mother and stepfather out of pocket by £422. This ended an unpleasant episode in Ann's life.

---

[16]Conrad Barnet's will, Jan 10, 1778, deposited with notary Oct. 12, 1793; a certified copy of Jan. 20, 1800 is in **La Greffe** (Notarial Records) of John Gerbrand Beek, Archives Nationales de Quebec, Montreal.

[17]Administration Account of the succession of the late Coenraat Barnett, April 1, 1796, **ibid.**

The Barnet-Hall family later applied for lands which were to be granted to Loyalists and their children. Their names appear in the Lower Canada Land Records for Clifton Township in the early 1800s. Besides John, William and Mary Barnet, three Hall children received grants in the region: Isaac Livingston Hall, Mary Catharine Christy Hall and Ann Blake Hall.[18]

---

[18]John Barnet, shoemaker, married Mary McDonald of Montreal Sept. 23, 1793, Anglican Church Register. Halls appeared along with Barnets in List of Patentees for Clifton Township, (NAC: Lower Canada Land Records, RG1/L3L/4/1278).

Abraham Pastorius, the Quaker Saddler:
An Outstanding Guide"

by John Ruch

"All loyal Subjects are oblig'd not only to honour
fear, obey and pray for those in authority, but
also to pay unto them taxes..."

These words of Francis Daniel Pastorius,[1] the founder of
America's German community, are expressive of the attitude of
his great-grandson Abraham, who was prevented from joining
the King's cause until Gen. Howe's forces drew near to
Pennsylvania. Abraham then left his saddler's shop in
Germantown to serve as a guide for troops stationed in the area.
Forced into exile by the army's withdrawal, Abraham
accompanied the troops to New York, from where he left for
England. Migrating to Canada in the late 1780s, he became a
respected Montreal citizen and was a member of its first Land
Board.

Abraham Pastorius was not a man of warlike disposition.
His family's history helps us to understand his character and
his loyalty. He was descended from a long line of weavers
named Schäffer who are traceable from 1439 on in Westphalia.
Abraham's branch rose to the official class, and dignified their
common surname (meaning shepherd) by Latinizing it as

---

[1]Mary Anne Shafer, **Francis Daniel Pastorius: His Influence Outside of
Germantown.** Masters' thesis, Pennsylvania State University, 256, quoting
from passage published by Henry J. Cadbury, **Pennsylvania Magazine of
History and Biography,** 58.3 (July 1934), 255-259.

Pastorius. Francis Daniel (1651-1720) enjoyed the benefits of a good education, extensive travel in Europe and influential relatives. The door was open to him in official and professional circles, and he could no doubt have had posts in various courts. However, being serious-minded, he engaged in studies in history, law and theology. Spurning the wishes of his family to take an easy road to success and a comfortable bourgeois life, he turned his back on the courts and chanceries with their ceremonials and formality.

Francis joined an austere religious group, the Frankfurt Pietists, and became acquainted with the English Quaker, William Penn, who toured the Rhineland visiting such sects in a effort to recruit settlers for his new American Colony. Francis was chosen to lead an emigrant flock from Germany to the area of Philadelphia where they founded Germantown one year after Penn Jr. had broken the first ground at the site. Francis became the settlement's official jack-of-all-trades, using his many talents and knowledge as businessman, lawyer, clerk, notary, mayor, schoolmaster and councillor to help establish the infant colony. His biographer described him as the "most many-sided literary man in America."[2]

Although Abraham was born a quarter-century after Francis' death, the memory and literary heritage of his forefather were guarded with reverence by the family. His treasured manuscripts and relics were passed on from eldest son to eldest son, thus descending to Abraham. When he joined the King's forces, Abraham may have violated his ancestor's pacifist principles, but at the same time he was

---

[2]Ibid., 226. See also "Pastorius" in **Dict. Amer. Biog.; New Century Cyclopedia of Names;** Wheeler Preston, **American Biographies** (New York 1940).

adhering to Francis' rule of obedience. The Pietists eventually merged with the Mennonites of Germantown and the Quakers of Philadelphia, forming what was largely a neutral block. During the Revolution their religious beliefs forbade them to support either side, and for those members who got involved, they were openly ostracized.

It was not, however, until hostilities broke out in the area that many pacifists, such as Pastorius, felt compelled or were able to join the British side. He chose a non-combatant role volunteering for the Royal Guides and Pioneers, a Corps which was attached to Beverley Robinson's Loyal American Regiment.

> "When rebellion reared its hideous head, he was the
> first to abandon his valuable property, and join the
> Royal Standard under which he rendered invaluable
> services to his country."[3]

The British occupied Philadelphia in Sept. 1777, where they remained over the winter. During this time Abraham was employed without pay or reward, and was responsible for himself and his two horses.[4] Although he was not engaged in active combat, as a guide he was placed in the thick of the fighting and frequently in considerable danger as he led the way for troops on many sorties and raids into the Pennsylvania countryside.[5] Pastorius even helped small naval craft navigate

---

[3]Obituary, **Herald** (Montreal, May 20, 1815).

[4]Land Petition, July 25, 1789 (NAC: Lower Canada Land Papers, RG1/L3L/154/75662-75664.

[5]Certificate signed by J. Graves Simcoe, Dec. 1785 (NAC: RG8 (C Ser.)/190/142.

the inland waters.[6] This is verified by a number of certificates he received from senior officers such as Lt. Gen. Howe, the Commander-in-Chief, down to Lt. Col. Simcoe, who spoke of his loyalty, service, zeal and sacrifices.

The best clues to operations in which Abraham participated were given by Simcoe in his Journal; the future Lt.Gov. of Upper Canada commented on the types of military service at which the Americans excelled. Patrolling or "in their antiquated dialect 'scouting,'" was favoured by Loyalists who knew the country and the ways of the Indian.[7] Simcoe did not fancy this method of warfare, except in cases such as the occupation of Philadelphia, where the surrounding area was peopled by "well-affected" settlers. He approached scouting systematically, and tried to obtain "the most minute maps of the country and the best guides."[8] Abraham served Simcoe in this capacity frequently and accompanied him in the field, "in particular on an Expedition that I Plan(n)ed to surprise the rebel Genl. Lacy he was a most useful guide."[9] This latter statement, in a certificate, thus identifies the unnamed man who "admirably guided" Simcoe's Queen's Rangers in the raid on Crooked Billet May 1, 1778.

Simcoe, together with Brig-Gens. Balfour and Abercrombie, had made arrangements for a combined attack on the forces of the youthful rebel leader John Lacey. The enemy's strategy was to choke off the supply of farm produce to the town and

---

[6]John Graves Simcoe, **Military Journal**, 1844 (reprinted as **A Journal of the Operations of the Queen's Rangers** (New York 1968), 51).

[7]Ibid., 75.

[8]Ibid., 135.

[9]Simcoe's certificate, 1785 (NAC: RG8/190/142); for Lacey see **Dict. Amer. Biog.**

military camps. Lacey's militia was assembling at a few outlying points for a campaign of attacks on storehouses and supply trains. While other British units advanced directly by road toward the rebel groups, Simcoe's Rangers proceeded by a circuitous route to ambush the enemy from the rear. Discovered before they reached the intended position, several skirmishes took place in which a number of Rangers were wounded, and enemy casualties numbered 50 to 60 men. The King's soldiers had lost the advantage of surprise, but the raid "had its full effect of intimidating the militia, as they never afterwards appeared, but in small parties, and like robbers."[10]

Of all Pastorius' military adventures, this affected him the most as he had been seriously wounded and suffered from the injuries for the remainder of his life.[11] From this point onward he does not appear to have taken part in much activity until the army left Philadelphia. Previously he was almost constantly employed in various kinds of operations, but not always with the Queen's Rangers.[12] However, he did accompany one of Simcoe's parties sent upriver in boats manned by naval crews. The sailors miscalculated the tidal movements, delaying the operation until Simcoe's "good guides" found him an alternative landing place and an overland route to his target. The engagement which followed is knows as "the affair at Hancock's Bridge."[13]

---

[10]Simcoe, **Journal**, 56-60.

[11]Obit., **Herald**, May 20, 1815.

[12]Abercrombie certified to his essential services (NAC: RG8/190/139).

[13]Simcoe, **Journal**, 51. The incident occurred March 18, 1778. Certificate of Lt. Bogers, H.M.S. Liverpools, cited in Land Committee Report, June 18, 1789 (NAC: Lower Canada Land Papers, RG1/L3L/154/75658-75659).

Officers like Simcoe were able to get the best performance from their men by ensuring that they were well treated and used in the most efficient manner. Simcoe wanted the Queen's Rangers to be self-reliant guides, thus lessening the need to call on other units or civilians for help. Further, he kept a special record of the home counties of each of his soldiers, and of the areas with which they were especially familiar.[14] Nevertheless, Simcoe could not dispense with the services of refugee Loyalists such as Pastorius, of whom he had many. When the army, now under Gen. Clinton's command, withdrew through New Jersey toward New York, Simcoe was able to provide him with a guide who was a native of Monmouth County. Pastorius also accompanied Clinton on the march in June 1778,[15] and was present at the Battle of Monmouth. Abraham was in touch with Simcoe on at least two later occasions when he applied to Simcoe for certification of his service, which Simcoe did willingly "to so loyal and deserving a subject."[16]

Various sources verify that Pastorius was a respected citizen in comfortable circumstances at the outbreak of the Revolution. He was the owner of "landed property, which...has been in the possession of someone of the name of Pastorius ever since the year 1684."[17] Besides the two-storey stone house built by his ancestor on Germantown's main street, with a 3 1/2 acre lot, Abraham also had a wooded lot of 16 acres.[18] Samuel Shoemaker, the Loyalist ex-mayor of Philadelphia, who not only knew him but was probably related to him, later testified

---

[14]Simcoe, **Journal**, 66.

[15]Report of Land Committee, June 18, 1789, 75658.

[16]Simcoe, Certificate, 1785.

[17]Land Petition, July 25, 1789.

[18]Losses Claim, March 9, 1784 (NAC: A.O. 12/42/21-27).

that his estate was "good" and the wood lot "very valuable."[19] His estate, which also included his shop, tools and household furniture, was sacrificed when he left for New York. The rebels confiscated what they could find (although it is believed that he and his relatives had concealed a good deal of his possessions)[20] and sold at auction after he had been found guilty of treason.[21] The inventory of his assets taken on July 29,1778 had an estimated value of £263.17.9d. However, this only accounted for the contents of his house and shop while a large quantity of leather, tanned by Abraham, and the moiety of his town lot were sold two years later at inflated prices, bringing the rebels £1912.12s. and £7,000 respectively.[22] Unimpressed by such figures, the Loyalist estimated his losses at £1,191.[23] for which the British government eventually granted him £720 in compensation, and a large acreage in Lower Canada.

Pastorius' move from the town of his ancestors to an unknown destiny which forced him to make some difficult decisions. He does not seem to have taken his young family

---

[19]Certificate, signed by Samuel Shoemaker (NAC: RG8/190/14); Losses Claim, A.O.12/42/27.

[20]Edward W. .Hocker, **Germantown 1683-1933** (Germantown 1933), 121. Abraham's house was on High Street, later demolished. Germantown Hist. Soc. Scrapbook compiled on 255th Anniversary of Germantown, 8, 49.

[21]**Pennsylvania State Papers**, 6th Ser., XII, (inventory), 363-365, (bill of sale) 886-887. 22,162 (leather), 828; XIII (lot), 499. Concerning inheritance from his father in 1766 see Naaman A. Keyser et al. **History of Old Germantown** (Germantown 1907), 38, 41 and (map) 42.

[22]Ibid., (leather) 16d, 828; XIII (lot), 499. Concerning inheritance from his father in 1766 see Naaman A. Keyser et al. History of Old Germantown (Germantown, 1907), 38,441 and (map) fp.42.

[23]Losses Claim, 22; compensation awarded.

with him,[24] and the ancestral manuscripts and relics were confided to his youngest brother, Daniel.[25] He was without means of support, as were some of his fellow guides who'd also retreated to New York, and if his health had permitted, he could have been able to earn something from his craft as a saddler and tanner. Late in 1778, the Commander-in-Chief recognized their plight and commissioned ten of these men to enable them to draw pay, thus Lt. Abraham Pastorius was now entitled to an allowance of $1 pr day.[26] As the time of the final evacuation of New York approached, the guides became apprehensive, they were not on active duty and provisions announced by Gen. Carleton for the settlement of Loyalists in Canada did not make specific reference to their circumstances. Together with Nathaniel Vernon, Abraham Iredell and John Knight, Pastorius wrote to the General for clarification about the granting of lands and other entitlements.[27] Satisfied with the reply to their queries, they embarked for a new homeland via England, where Pastorius presented his evidence supporting his claim for compensation before the parliamentary commissioners on March 29, 1786.

A number of Pennsylvanians returned from Britain to Philadelphia to remain there, while others collected what was left of their possessions and headed north. Well before Samuel Shoemaker and Jacob Duche, who came home to stay in 1789 and 1790 respectively, Pastorius returned to Philadelphia to

---

[24]Eleanor Leech, his first wife, died Feb. 28-Mar.1, 1779 in childbirth, and was buried at Oxford Meeting House, Penn. Learned, **Pastorius**, 308.

[25]**Ibid.**, 242-243.

[26]As "Pistoras" in Muster Rolls of Guides and Pioneers (NAC: RG8 (C Ser.), 1888/12,19,26,38,43,50.

[27]NAC: RG1/L3L/154/75656.

gather his children and on July 12, 1787, he married again, his first wife having died during his exile in New York.[28] The family then moved to Montreal, and settled on a small farm on the Island's eastern shore at St. Mary's Current, an area which had become predominantly English-speaking with the advent of the Loyalists.

Now settled, Abraham began to concentrate on his entitlement to Crown lands, as a Loyalist veteran. It was a complicated matter as two different scales of land grants had been promised to different Loyalist regiments. The Royal Highland Emigrants (84th Regt.) and the King's Royal Regt. of New York were offered larger grants of land than other Provincial units. Authorities had tried to keep this discrepancy secret, to minimize the amount of land required for the Loyalists , but it was a futile effort. Further, land allotment in what soon became the Province of Lower Canada was impeded by Haldimand's original policy of keeping the lands bordering the United States free of settlements as a strategic measure. Even after this and other areas were approved for development, the process of surveying townships and lots proceeded slowly.

Pastorius avoided the problems which he would have encountered in the area southeast of Montreal by exploring for land to the Island's northwest. Hiring a competent boatman familiar with local waterways, and accompanied by his new bride, Hannah Mendenhall, Abraham explored the countryside west of the Ottawa River as far as Long Sault, and then north on the Assomption River. He found useable "waste" land on a western tributary of the Assomption at Lacora (liquori)[29] close to an Acadian settlement and a seigniory belonging to the

---

[28]Report, July 14, 1789, **ibid.**, 10/2953.
[29]Petition, July 25, 1789, **ibid.**, 154/75662.

Sulpician Order. Believing that he was the first Loyalist to investigate this area, he applied for a grant.

His petition for 2,000 acres was among others that reraised the question of the differing scales of land grants.[30] Gov. Dorchester worked toward bridging the gap by increasing the entitlements of the other regiments in 1787. But there was still a difference of scale. When Pastorius and others applied for grants on the scale of the 84th and the King's Royal Regt. of New York in 1788 the Governor was forced to reduce the still existing inequality as he did on Oct. 22 of that year. However, prior to this last adjustment the Land Board considered the technically ineligible petitions and sought means of justifying equal grants. As Pastorius was eligible for only 750 acres (500 for himself, the remainder for his family) on the lower scale, the committee recommended that the Governor sanction an extra grant of 1,250 acres as a special reward for his services to the King's cause.[31] Nevertheless, there was an understandable unwillingness to grant large acreages before the petitioner's intentions were clearly established. Pastorius was allowed 1,000 acres on the understanding that if he settled this land, another 1,000 would be granted in due course.[32] This compromise was reached after Dorchester's second increase of the lesser scale. Abraham's petition was in the course of consideration, thus he could not submit another based on the new regulations until a decision had been reached on the first under the old regulations. Although the law had been changed, he received approval for less than what he would now be entitled to. Now

---

[30]NAC: RG1/L3L/Land Book A/262.

[31]Ibid., Land Book B, May 1, 1791, both A and B were published in Ontario Archives Report, no. 17 (1928).

[32]Pastorius to Lt.Gov. Alured Clarke, July 9, 1793 (NAC: 154/75652).

he petitioned for the grant to be reconsidered under the new scale, but his request was temporarily shelved.[33]

Pastorius was treated in the same fashion as many others in spite of the fact that between the time of his first petition and the Committee's decision he had been appointed to the newly-created Montreal District Land Board on Feb. 17, 1789.[34] Others appointed at the same time were: Sir John Johnson, William Dummer Powell, William Rankin and a senior army officer ex officio. Johnson and Pastorius were reappointed in 1792 along with three new members: Joseph Chew, Eli Branson and Arthur Davison. Powell had left the province shortly after his appointment to take up a judgeship in Upper Canada.[35]

In compliance with the conditions of his first land grant, Pastorius recruited a number of families to settle on his thousand acres in what is now Rawdon Canton (township).[36] By 1793 enough land had been cleared and cultivated to support the settlement by growing wheat and peas. However, Abraham discovered that others were claiming lands in the same general area, which could cut off his access to the river that served as the only highway in the region. He wrote to the Lieutenant Governor, causing the latter to order the surveyor-general to report on the situation, subsequently, it was learned that there had not been an official survey of the area. Further, the grants already made had been quantitative with no specific lots clearly defined having been surveyed, assigned or drawn for, but that

---

[33]Report of Surveyor General S. Holland, July 23, 1793, **ibid.,** 12/3832.

[34]Petition, Feb. 10, 1802, ibid, 154/75669.

[35]Ibid.

[36]The committee recommended grants of 200 additional acres for Abraham, 1,200 for his wife, and 200 for each of the four children, Minutes, Sept. 4, 1802 (extract) **ibid.,** 154/75683.

the landholders, Capts. Dunbar, Grant, Sanford and Lt. Pastorius had merely been granted a number of acres each.[37] Any later settlement they had made in the region was carried out at their own risk. Sanford, on the opposite side of the river, was not a potential threat to Pastorius, but Dunbar and Grant had chosen the same side as Abraham and might at some future date block his path to the water. But the survey had to await financing and since the grantees were to pay half the cost the surveyor-general predicted it would be a long time before there were enough grantees to share the expenses.[38]

Pastorius meanwhile occupied himself with the development of his settlement, and the management of his small holding at St. Mary's. In early 1802 when he returned to the question of land grants, it was to petition for the thousand extra acres promised him conditionally in 1789.[39] The Constitutional Act of 1791 allowed for large land grants with the stipulation that for every 1,200 acres granted, a family had to be established on the land within one year. Pastorius interpreted this to mean that each family could apply for 1,200 acres, and accordingly submitted a petition for the land on behalf of his wife and each of his children.[40] They received their grants within a year, but only according to the usual scale of 200 acres each, as the wife and children of a U.E. Loyalist, as established by

---

[37]There are 17 grantees' names (including Pastorius") on the list, **ibid.,** 6/1649.
[38]Ibid, 1648.
[39]The 1802 petition was reconsidered, and two more were submitted of date Mov. 17, 1817, **ibid.,** 154/75684, 75687.
[40]Report of Committee, July 27, 1818, **ibid,** 75678.

Dorchester several years earlier.[41] These were the last names to be added to the Rawdon list of grantees in 1802.[42]

The land claims by the Pastorius family were not pursued again until after Abraham's death thirteen years later. Executors of his estate were determined to obtain a settlement from the government, and in 1817 presented three petitions on behalf of the heirs.[43] Little had been done about the 1802 grants, while others, in the meantime, had been allotted the land that Pastorius had claimed. As the only unoccupied land remaining in the Township was too rocky for farming, the heirs wanted their grants transferred to Weedon Township, only to learn that this area had been reserved for members of the militia. Further, the government refused to grant the family lands because the conditions regarding earlier grants had not been met.[44] The heirs' claims were again pressed in 1821 when Mrs. Pastorius petitioned on behalf of her family for land in Kildare Township.[45] The petition was successful and within a year land was surveyed and allotments made.[46] A patent was later applied for, but a bureaucratic error had to be rectified before it could be issued. Officials had overlooked the fact that two of Abraham's children had died, leaving their minor children as heirs. Working with the information given in the 1802 petition they were unaware of Charles' death ca.1815 and Eleanor's sometime

---

[41]Petition, Jan. 24, 1821, **ibid.**, 75702.

[42]Description of grant, **ibid.**, 75698.

[43]Dating depends on Abraham's will, May 15, 1815, and Charles' petition, Feb. 18, 1823, **ibid.**, 75673 and 75698 resp.

[44]Court order, **ibid.**, 75689.

[45]**Ibid.**, 7/2208.

[46]Patent (draft), Dec. 15, 1834, **ibid.**, 154/75724-75759.

between 1817 and 1823.[47] Special provisions had to be made for
their offspring, and representation secured through their uncle
and guardian, Daniel Pastorius.[48] The children eventually
received equal shares of their parents grant in Kildare, [49] and in
1834, nearly 50 years after Abraham's original petition, his
family's claims were finally patented.[50]

Pastorius led a quiet and unobtrusive life in Montreal but as
a Quaker he and his family were active in works of social
welfare. He served on committees established by the Protestant
English-speaking congregations, and is known to have been
involved in such charitable acts as placing an orphan as an
apprentice to a craftsman.[51] His later years were passed in great
discomfort due to his old war wound and gout, and after a
"tedious illness" he died on May 18, 1815.[52] Hannah
Mendenhall, his widow, survived into the late 1820s. Of the
four Pastorius children only the youngest, Sarah Ann, was her

---

[47]A number of documents to which Pastorius was a party are in the notarial
records (greffes) in the Archives Nationales de Quebec, Montreal, e.g. some
concerning personal engagements are in J.G. Beek papers, 587,1140,1165,1249.

[48]Wound mentioned in petition of Hannah Pastorius, Oct. 24, 1821 (NAC:
RG8/634a/62); gout referred to in his will (NAC: RG1/L3L/154/75673), copy
exists in the greffe of H. Griffin, 878, Arch. Nat. Que., Montreal. His obituary,
Herald (Montreal) May 20, 1815.

[49]Six children were baptized at the Anglican cathedral in Quebec City from
1811 to 1824, according to Protestant Registration Index, Archives Nationales
de Quebec, Quebec. John Theodore Hoyle (1788?-1851) was survived for
several years by Sarah Ann (1787?-1859).

[50]Charles' marriage, Jan. 17, 1803, Christ Church Register, Montreal.

[51]Muster Roll, Jan. 22, 1813 (NAC: RG8/C695a (formerly in C678/18-20).

[52]He and four other men received town lots at Amhersburg after the
evacuation of Detroit in 1796, their petition for clarification of legal status, April
17, 1819 (NAC: RG 8/C273/154). Concerning tenders and contracts 1819 to 1820
see ibid., C404/186/C125/62,102,116-117.

child. Sarah Ann was admired by British officers for her "good looks," but married John Theodore Hoyle, a Quebec merchant,[53] by whom she had at least six children.

Abraham's children by his first wife lived into the 19th century. Charles (b.1774-d.ca.1815) the eldest, was a farmer at Sault-aux-Recollets on the northern shore of Montreal Island. He married Eleanor Konobock (Knoblauch?) daughter of Johannes of Terrebonne, a butcher, in 1813. Daniel (1776-fl.1828) appears to have served in the militia during the war of 1812, and to have been wounded on the Battle of Frenchtown near Detroit on Jan. 22, 1813. By 1820 he was contracting to the commissary for the supply of beef and timber at Amherstburg, Upper Canada. After Charles' early death, Daniel became guardian of his brother's four minor children: Margaret, Eleanor Ann, Elizabeth and Abraham Charles.

Abraham Sr.'s first wife, Eleanor Leech died in childbirth, the surviving daughter, Eleanor Leech (1779-ca.1820) was her namesake. Eleanor later marrying Benaiah Gibb, was perhaps the most remarkable of his children, and followed him in her devotion to community work. Under her leadership the newly-formed Female Benevolent Society surged in importance in the mid 1810s. Founded to care for orphans, foundlings and single mothers, the society extended its attention later to the hordes of destitute and sick immigrants who arrived in Montreal after 1815. From soup-kitchens to clinics to the construction of a hospital, the women's work became essential to the City. By her husband Benaiah, Eleanor had two children: Eleanor Catherine (b,1813), later Mrs. James Miller, and Daniel Orkney (b. 1813)

---

[53]Charles' widow, Elizabeth married Leonard Dutelle, a Montreal innkeeper, who together with Daniel Pastorius became the children's tuteurs (legal guardians) on May 23, 1815 (NAC: RG1/L3L/154/75689.

who married Louisa Stevens. Gibb had children by a previous marriage, who were prominent in Montreal society and were patrons of the hospital which Benaiah Sr. and Eleanor Sr. had helped to found. His grandson, Benaiah, an art lover, through a large donation to the Art Association of Montreal, enabled the Institute to erect their own building on Phillips' Square in 1879-80, which was the first art gallery in Montreal. Further, his bequest of paintings and *objets d'art* provided the new gallery, which is today the Museum of Fine Arts, with the basis of a rich and important collection.

John Platt: Blacksmith and Secret Agent

by John Ruch

It was suggested in 1781 by a junior officer that Mr. John Platt's name be struck off the list of Loyalist refugees that were entitled to government support.[1] In fact, some six years earlier Platt had performed his most valuable military service, and what was, perhaps, the most important mission carried out by a civilian in the border campaign during the early stages of the American Revolution. Reviewing the young officer's suggestion, a military board under Lt. Col. St. Leger recommended, instead, that Platt's pension be continued:

"...for his steady adherence to the Government from the commencement of the Rebellion, and in that time for many essential Services rendered by him and for which he has never received the smallest pecuniary or other reward."[2]

This statement is remarkably vague, as it does not indicate the nature of Platt's services. When read in company with many other records of Loyalists' sacrifices it lacks details or general remarks which would give an idea of his "essential" contributions to the British cause. Only through a careful investigation of the Haldimand papers does the real reason for this reticence become clear. In fact, Platt was a secret service agent who settled at St. John's under the guise of a "suttler" although his career had begun before the Declaration of Independence.

---

[1]NAC: Haldimand Papers (henceforth HP), B166, 126.
[2]Ibid., B167/228, dated Feb. 24, 1781.

Accounts of Platt's civilian life are scarce. He was born between 1745 and 1750,[3] and obtained the rudiments of an education. In the late 1760s he married Ann Wragg and on the outbreak of hostilities was a blacksmith with some connection with Fort Miller just north of Saratoga. As a civilian he undertook several espionage missions, but after Burgoyne's defeat Platt fled to Canada.[4] In 1780 he became a volunteer officer, at first under Maj. Rogers, later under Jessup. After the war he returned to civilian life and by putting his experience and business ability to use he became a prosperous Montreal hardware merchant.

Like so many other secret service operatives in the 18th century, Platt was self-appointed, working in Saratoga in the summer of 1775 when rumours began about a forthcoming invasion of Canada. The rebels had already been in possession of local forts since May. The rumours and preparations spurred him into action, and in July he set out to spy on the rebels.

In 1781, Platt intended to discover the routes planned for the rebel armies' invasion,[5] and on a pretext he journeyed northward to Fort Edward, where he lingered to observe a gathering force of soldiers. He then crossed the land divide between the Hudson River and Lake George, continuing north to Ticonderoga where General Montgomery's army was assembling. He picked up information from rebel officers and at Crown Point won the confidence of a certain Maj. Elemore, who gave him a pass for a local trip. Platt hired a boatman at an

---

[3]His age is given as 35 in the 1781 report (see n.2), and as 61 on his gravestone in 1811, N.A.C. **Report** 1889.

[4]NAC: HP, B215/216, her death is mentioned, 1783?

[5]NAC: HP, B214/211-212, **Memorial**, June 17, 1781.

exorbitant rate, and made his way north to the British fort at St. John's.

Platt's intelligence was of considerable importance to the defenders of Canada, secrets he passed on to Maj. Preston, commandant at St. John's, provided the major with a current account of the rebel plans three weeks prior to the invaders arrival to lay seige to his post. With this insight, Preston was able to stave off the invaders for two weeks, thereby delaying the occupation of Montreal. With the invasion still in the offing, Preston made further use of Platt, whom he instructed to pose as a rebel "prisoner," and be confined with other rebels. The urgency of the situation brought Gov. Carleton to Montreal in haste, to hear Platt's report in person. Gov. Carleton thanked him "for the Services he had done his Majesty's Arms by his speedy and faithfull Intelligence." Promises of reimbursement for Platt's expenses and a suitable reward were made, but, in the confusion of the ensuing events, were neglected.

After the fall of St. John's and Montreal, Platt made his way back to Albany County evidently protected by his having been known to have been found imprisoned. However, as he neared his own locality he encountered those who suspected him. His unexplained absence of three months between July and October had roused rebel sympathizers against his family, who had been terrorized, and his house pillaged. Platt chanced upon Philip Lansing and a number of enemy soldiers at the home of one Mr. Jones, and later reporting to Gov. Haldimand:

"Said Lansing with an oath, God damn me if there is not Platt. Where the devil have you been all this time?
I replied, I had been taken prisoner by the Indians and carried into Canada. He replied he knew better and I had been about that, that was not good for Congress, which

I hope will be found out very soon, which has not been
in their power to prove."[6]

Platt's activities from then on for many months is obscure,
although it is assumed that he and his family sought refuge
among other Loyalists. A blacksmith's work was always in
demand, especially in time of war, thus he must have worked
perhaps at Fort Miller, biding his time. A smithy was an ideal
place for collecting intelligence, being patronized by all
travellers — a favourite haunt of those in search of gossip and
news. The next account of Platt is in 1776, when he was
approached by a Sgt. McFall, 26th Regt., carrying dispatches
destined for Gov. Carleton, accompanied by Loyalists. Platt
provided two horses and provisions, and guided them beyond
Saratoga where they were to rendezvous with another "pilot."
But the rebels had learned of this adventure and took after him,
forcing him to abandon his home and flee to Albany where he
hid for quite some time.[7]

Next, the Platt family is recorded in St. John's, and on a
provision list John is mentioned as a suttler, giving no account
in his statements of previous service, but shortly thereafter he
volunteered to Sir John Johnson during the latter's venture
into the Mohawk Valley in May 1780. Johnson passed him on
to Maj. Rogers who commissioned him as a temporary captain
with an order permitting him to recruit a company in the
Colonies. Finding it difficult to enlist sufficient Loyalists, he
lingered at Saratoga in the attempt until September, when news
reached him of an important message held up in Albany for

---

[6]NAC: HP, B27/238, Platt's statement regarding his suspicion of Lansing's
recent conversation to loyalism (July 1780?).

[7]NAC: HP, B166/10, provision list, St. John's July 1, 1779.

want of a courier. Platt sent three men separately to try to get through enemy lines to retrieve the information. John Greaves, Platt's brother-in-law succeeded. But there was more than a single message, as the local head of the intelligence network, Dr. Smyth of Albany, induced Platt to guide James Quin to Canada bringing information from the rebel inner circles.

There were pressing reasons for immediate action, so, abandoning his recruiting, Platt and Quin set off at once for Canada. Haldimand, Governor at Quebec since 1778, now became well aware of Platt's ability, the latter having given a lengthy report of his mission and arrangements for the courier service between New York and Canada.[8] Quin, at the same time, had actually been present at the most recent meeting of Congress, and was sent to report in person to Haldimand.

The Governor reacted quickly to Quin's news and that in the dispatch, by sending Platt on another mission, this time to carry a secret message to Sir Henry Clinton, Commander in Chief at New York.[9] In a month Platt had delivered the "artfully concealed" message to Albany, made plans for the future with his contact man, "abducted" John Greaves with the help of a companion, and returned to report his success at Fort St. John. This was recorded in a letter from his commander, Barry St. Leger, to the governor on November 29, 1780.[10]

The whole of this was not easily accomplished as Platt was not well. Near panic had gripped the rebels, and persons under the slightest suspicion were seized and jailed. Even the legendary "Hudibras," (the code name for Dr. Ralph Smyth),

---

[8]Capt. Monsell at St. Johns to Haldimand, Oct. 22, 1780 (NAC: HP B133/340r), enclosing Platt's report, same date, **ibid.,** B161, 152.

[9]St. Leger at St. Johns to Haldimand, Nov. 7, 1780, **ibid.,** 340v.

[10]Same to same, Nov, 29, 1780, **ibid.,** 314-315.

was imprisoned on a charge of treason, although his undercover role seems to have been unsuspected by his captors. From his cell in the Albany Prison he continued to direct intelligence operations in this area of the Colony. His wife received and sent out messengers with intelligence, partly under her husband's direction. The link to the outside was a "neutral" Quaker named Wing, who had free run of the jail and who could smuggle messages through the gates.[11]

John Platt and Abraham Wing discussed the problems presented by the round-up of Loyalists, of which some were couriers. A reliable man was needed to help Platt return to St. John's and to serve as runner between Wing and the border. They chose John Greaves, who had already worked with success in fetching Quin and the dispatch for Platt as well as showing Loyalist sympathy during Burgoyne's campaign. As a cover for his leaving, to allay suspicion, Greaves was supposedly carried off by force at dead of night. The plan was for the "prisoner" to escape later from Chambly in the company of a declared rebel, who could give him a good alibi on return to the Colony, where an apprehended person, who could not produce a suitable explanation of his presence, was liable to be summarily executed by his captors. Plans for Greaves as a "constant courier" did not become effective for some time, due to the advent of winter which suspended many operations. However, a suitable dropping-point for messages was arranged "to be on the hunting ground of Wing, to avoid jealousy or suspicion from frequent visits."[12] This appears to have been "in a safe and

---

[11]Wing's name appears a number of times in HP. He remained loyal in spite of the destruction of his property by Maj. Carleton's raiders earlier, **op.cit.,** B133/375. He is also mentioned on the old U.E.L. List.

[12]Ibid., 378, Dec. 9, 1780.

obscure corner of a mountain between Fort George and Fort Edward,"[13] where messages were left unattended, so that only one courier at a time ran risk of arrest. Platt and Wing were confident that this was the "straightest and less intricate mode they can adopt" with safety to themselves.

For the troops, winter was a period of enforced idleness as snow not only impeded travel over long distances, but also retained the telltale footprints of secret travellers and raiding parties. St. Leger kept Platt for possible news-gathering missions to the south in advance of British scouts,[14] and in the spring sent him to Saratoga with a rebel deserter to gather information,[15] travelling over dangerous stretches in a load of hay. On their return they also brought in the details of the "Articles of Union" proposed between Vermont and New York.

The expenses of Platt's largely voluntary services were now beginning to be felt. On June 6, 1781, St. Leger wrote to the Governor:

"Mr Platt having exhibited to me the deplorable state of
his finances...has obtained my leave
to prefer his suit and explain his circumstances in person
to His Excellency to whom both he and his services are
known."[16]

Platt presented his memorial of service personally to Haldimand.[17] After listing his missions, Platt wrote that he had held himself "in readiness for any secret service, and has remained in this capacity...at his own expense at St. Leger's

---

[13]Ibid., 375.
[14]NAC: HP, B13, Jan. 24, 1781.
[15]Ibid., B214/211.
[16]Ibid., B134/58.
[17]Ibid., B214/211-212, June 17, 1781.

command, St. John's. He would not apply for relief until
necessary which it now is." St. Leger replied:

> "...his pension in my opinion is proportional to his talents...
> time and some well authenticated circumstances have
> discovered to me that although he has a warm heart to
> Government and a bold one to attempt said service, he
> wants two essential ingredients that to gain implicit
> confidence...his tongue is to loosely hung...and too often
> runs ahead of secrecy and discretion necessary in
> delicate and perilous enterprises, however there are
> uses to be made of him and his fee is sufficiently
> detaining."[18]

But Platt was not destitute by any means, St. Leger had
allotted him a house at St. Johns. Later more was to be heard of
his finances and, later still, more of the house.

It was said that every Loyalist wanted to be an officer. There
is enough truth in that statement to justify a remark in its
qualification. Certainly, many beating orders were issued to
Loyalists who were over-confident of their abilities to raise the
numbers of recruits sufficient for recognizing the recruiter's
leadership with an official commission in the rank of captain.
Platt had obtained his warrant from Rogers, and had begun
recruiting in the Colony. However, it was a case of "too many
chiefs..." Platt succeeded in collecting only six men before a
mission took him away from the task and these men shortly
thereafter were imprisoned by the rebels.[19] Platt appears to have

---

[18]Ibid., B135.
[19]Ibid., B133/340, Oct. 22, 1780.

recruited five more men by June 1781,[20] but another mission interrupted further efforts in this direction. During his absence he was demoted from capt.-lt. to lieutenant as he had not recruited a full company of men.[21] Platt had already passed the highpoint of his army career, which is borne out by the records of the next two years.

Dr. "Hudibras" Smyth had by now escaped into Canada, and in a statement, jointly with Capt. Justus Sherwood as Director, a new phase in the operation of British intelligence began. The new system was completely antipathetic to the temperament of men such as John Platt and John Walden Myers (alias Hans Waltermeyer)[22] who were hardy independents used to exercising a great deal of freedom on their secret errands. A more formal organization was now established with its headquarters secluded on an island in the north end of Lake Champlain at the "Loyal Blockhouse." Considerable effort was made to shroud their activities in secrecy, a healthy warning to indiscreet couriers like Platt, who were now required to sign oaths of absolute secrecy.[23] The desirability of general planning, and increasing the efficiency of intelligence operations is unquestionable, yet there are many times when being an irregular is necessary though perhaps not as much as the spies themselves would have wished.

The decline in Platt's fortunes began before Smyth's arrival, but it was Smyth who completed his eclipse and nearly ruined him. Smyth sent him on a mission into the Colony from which he returned to report on rebel troop movements, supply depots,

---

[20]Ibid., B134/66, June 22, 1781.

[21]Memorial, B214/212.

[22]His complaint, B161/303, Aug.1, 1781.

[23]On Myers' secret service see Mary Beacock Fryer, **Loyalist Spy.**

suttlers and the state of morale and loyalism.[24] In addition he
had sad news of the capture of the dashing, reckless Loyalist Lt.
Bettie. Thereafter Platt seems to have been kept in idleness,
possibly deliberately. In June he pleaded to be sent out alone on
a mission,[25] but when he did receive orders he believed that
they were designed to shut him up and keep him out of the
way.[26]

Hostility between Platt and Smyth reached its climax in late
1782 and early 1783. For some time Smyth had been trying to
induce Platt to vacate the house St. Leger had allowed him to
use. Messengers, letters and personal meetings were intended
by the spymaster to make plain to his subordinate that he must
move out. Platt obtained St. Leger's certificate proving that he
had been granted the house,[27] and told Smyth bluntly that only
a direct order from the brigadier would be obeyed. However, he
would move if paid the sum of 100 guineas, which he later
claimed to be the value of repairs he had carried out while
living there. Smyth threatened to have the house confiscated,
while the animosity between them came to a head in a heated
argument in public on Christmas Day when they chanced to
meet at the house of Lt. Johns. The next day an anonymous,
insulting notice was pasted onto Smyth's house.

The rage and vindictiveness of Dr. Smyth had now been
brought to the point of charging Platt with libel, and requesting
that the military authorities courtmartial him.

General Riedesel, a devoted professional soldier,
recommended a court martial for the reason that Platt was a

[24]Platt's oath, B137/34, March 12, 1782.

[25]Ibid., B177/168, April 3, 1782.

[26]Ibid., B161/441, June 29, 1782.

[27]Platt's petition, B215/216, undated, but after his removal to Montreal.

military man and had committed a serious offence.[28] He may well have favoured Smyth, as the Doctor was in a post of importance. However, Haldimand, cautious to condemn any Loyalist prematurely, ordered that an enquiry be held to determine whether more drastic measures were called for.[29]

The court met on Jan. 23, 1783, under Capt. Dixon of the 29th Regt. and clearly established, without making a judgement, two essential points.[30] There was a continuing hostility between the two parties which resulted in a liberal exchange of insults on Christmas Day. Second, it could not be proven that Platt was the author of the anonymous libel pasted to Smyth's house the next day, although the insult bore language previously used by Platt. The incident on the 25th was largely composed of the use of heated words and Smyth's challenging Platt to step outside for a fistfight. Platt is reported to have called the other "a Rebel Doctor, and a Rebel Rascal." A second witness inserted the abusive adjective "Yankee" into these expressions when testifying while a third claimed that Platt had said that because Smyth "was at present employed by the secret service that he thought himself a great man and was above everybody else, or something to that purpose." On the other hand, Platt's witnesses testified that the Doctor had used much the same sort of expressions about Platt:

"...a damned rascal, a damned villain, a damned scoundrel and a damned liar, and goddamned him."

It was also said:

---

[28]Ibid., B134/227, Jan. 14, 1783.
[29]Ibid., B138/4v, Jan.9, 1783.
[30]Ibid., B139/270, Jan. 13, 1783.

"That as Dr. Smyth was going away he said that he (Platt) was a damned bound slave and that he (Smyth) would have his sweet pension cut off."

Sending the Governor the court's findings, Riedesel suggested that Platt be removed from St. John's for the good of the service,[31] foreseeing that the hatred between the two men could easily lead to a division of sympathies within the settlement, and hence become a public cause detrimental to the secrecy and morale of the intelligence agents. Haldimand, agreeing with Riedesel's reasoning, did not believe Platt should suffer a dismissal, another trial or public disgrace. He therefore ordered Platt to be transferred to Montreal, and that his privileges be gradually reduced or removed.[32] Previously arrested, Platt was now placed under open arrest, while his quarters at St. Johns had been given to another Loyalist.[33]

In Montreal, Platt was placed under the command of Lt.Col. Abraham Cuyler, the new Director of the Loyalists, to whom Platt was ordered to report daily, thus Cuyler functioned as a sort of parole officer.[34] In a letter to Haldimand dated April 30 of that year Cuyler stated that his charge was reporting daily, and seemed to be quite chastened.[35] It is not unlikely that, given a few more months of punitive idleness, Platt would have reinstated himself in the governor's grace, but it was not to be. Platt was continually requesting new assignments, but does not

---

[31]Ibid., B134/234-237, St. John's.

[32]Platt's petition, B138/35, Jan. 30, 1783.

[33]Ibid., B139/279, March 3, 1783.

[34]Ibid., B215/216; 260 petition of Samuel Hindman, who received Platt's house.

[35]Ibid., B165/31, Feb. 3, 1783.

seem to have received any. With the war virtually over, little was to be gained from missions of his sort.

Dr. Smyth, in contrast, continued to be unpopular in St. Johns. After the charges against Platt had been dropped, Smyth denied all of Platt's allegations,[36] and warned that unless strong action was taken against Platt, other people would carry on such behaviour. In this regard he was not mistaken. Before long a petition against Smyth and his co-director Sherwood was in circulation and by August an enquiry into their activities was begun.[37] However, with the removal of Platt from St. Johns there is little more that need be said about Dr. Smyth.

The Platt family led an unsettled life for many months during the last year of the war and the first period of peace. Having no home, they appear to have been separated for a while. Platt was on the strength of Capt. Drummond's company,[38] while later Mrs Platt and her young son were at Lachine.[39] No doubt shortly after arriving in Montreal Platt petitioned the governor for a trial,[40] aggrieved that he had suffered various penalties without knowing why, nor granted an opportunity to defend himself against the charges. He suspected that his "inveterate Enemy Doctor Smith Agent" had secretly accused him of "something criminal." Platt had already paid dearly as he was not reimbursed for house repairs and had not received promised rewards for earlier service, including a mission he had carried out for Smyth and Sherwood, which led to domestic difficulties. While confined in Montreal he had

---

[36]Ibid., B165/71, April 30, 1783.

[37]Ibid., B178/53, Feb. 2, 1783.

[38]Ibid., B178, August passim, and corresponding volumes.

[39]Ibid., B167/330.

[40]Ibid., B166/84, July 24, 1783.

been unable to attend the burial of his mother elsewhere. In order to support his family he sold his property at St. Johns.

The Platt name occurs a few more times in the Haldimand papers after this point, while members of the family appear on various muster rolls and land records. In 1784 we find "Mr. John Platt" at St. Johns with his wife and son, who had recently had his tenth birthday.[41] John "can not go on the King's Lands on account of his dist(resse)d circumstances." In later years he received a number of land grants, which no doubt helped to renew this situation and soothe his feelings.[42]

John Platt's daring missions faded as he proceeded, with the help of his son George, to begin building a commercial business in the hardware trade. In addition to resourcefulness and independence, he also had ambition and self-confidence. Financial success brought him to the level of Montreal society in which it was not considered an extravagance to have his portrait painted. The painting, executed ca.1800, does not show the blacksmith, nor the adventurous secret agent of 20 years earlier, but John Platt, gentleman, dressed in the current fashion of high-collared coat worn over a white shirt and stock, a full-faced sober man with a cool, direct gaze.[43]

His place of business in Montreal was on St. Paul Street, while his home, a property that included a garden, was located at no.70 Sherbrooke St. West. Ownership passed through Platt's descendants: the Geddes, Skaife and Rolland families. It was finally sold in 1908 to make way for a technical school. Platt lived to the age of around 61, dying on August 1, 1811, and was

---

[41] Ibid. B215/216, n.d.

[42] Ibid., B168/52.

[43] The painting was reproduced along with an article on the Platt family "Sale of Skaife Property," **Montreal Daily Express,** May 4, 1908.

buried in the Old Protestant Burying Ground which now lies levelled under Dominion (Dorchester) Square.[44]

---

[44]Report of 1889, NAC (pub. 1890). The cemetery was at the corner of Dorchester and Urban Streets.

CHAPTER 8

Loyalists in Maritime and Commercial Affairs

by John Ruch

Maritime transportation was extremely important to Canada as a means to convey imported goods and export products beyond our frontiers. In time of war it served as a communications system and a highway along which troops and supplies were moved.

Loyalists were numerous among the Montreal merchants and shippers from the end of the 17th century to the 1820s. While rarely members of sea-going crews, they were more apt to be among the builders, craftsmen and labourers ashore in the employ of the Provincial Marine during the Revolution. From 1783 on, their activity increased, with most of the merchants pooling their interests in trade and shipping while involved in more than one enterprise. In the early development of the Canadian economy, their occupations often overlapped as merchant, shipbuilder, owner, banker and land developer, much of which was on a relatively small scale. Three of the first vessels registered for a Montreal merchant were built by the Loyalist, Elias Smith, and two of the first three shipyards established in Montreal after 1800 were run by the Loyalist James Dunlop, and Hart Logan, the son of a Loyalist. Logan and George Platt, another Loyalist's son, collaborated with Molson in building Canada's first steamboats. Others were partners or shareholders in syndicates which built, owned and operated river and seagoing vessels, or involved in the triangular trade between Canada, the Caribbean and Britain.

During the American Revolution and throughout the period ending with the War of 1812, Loyalists helped build and man the vessels used by government and the military forces. In the late 18th and early 19th centuries they were numerous among the builders and owners of local merchant ships, and were some of the foremost developers of Montreal as a port, and gateway to the Loyalist settlements on the upper lakes.

PROVINCIAL MARINE

The waters of the St. Lawrence River were plied by Provincial Marine vessels from 1760 to 1813. Until the early years of the American rebellion it was not of very great strength.[1] Governors Carleton and Haldimand improved this naval effort that was essential for wartime duties as well as for practical use in peacetime. It was independent from both the Royal army and navy, having its own commissioner of the Lakes, appointed by the governor, and its own captains, seamen and vessels as well as shipyards and tradesmen. Êhis force was responsible for maintaining communications between posts, serving in offensive and defensive military operations, and for the transportation of troops, supplies, traders and merchandise.

During the Revolution, under its commissioner John Schank, the Provincial Marine grew considerably in size and importance and by 1783 it engaged 300 seamen who operated 37

---

[1]W.A.B. Douglas, "The Anatomy of Naval Incompetence: The Provincial Marine in Defence of Upper Canada before 1913," Ontario History (Toronto, Ontario Historical Society, March 1979), LXXI, 1, 3-25.; see also Mary Beacock Fryer, **King's Men** (Toronto 1980), "The Naval Establishment," 302-306.

large vessels and many smaller craft.[1] Like the land forces in Canada, the majority of experienced men were from overseas. There were, however, both skilled and inexperienced Loyalists serving among them, with the carpenters and artificers working in the shipyards. Schank's command was divided into two districts: Lake Champlain and the Great Lakes. Both districts in turn had separate commanders. Lake Champlain's senior officer was Capt. Thomas Pringle until 1780, when he was replaced by Capt. William Chambers, who controlled ten large vessels. Names of some Loyalist provincial mariners are known and it seems probable that many continued in seafaring, rather than settle as farmers. Indeed a number of mariners returned to New York City at the end of the war.[2] As for Loyalist carpenters and shipwrights, one group was recruited in Philadelphia in 1777.[3] Hiring such men from the American side was a practice that continued after the war as skilled workers were scarce in Quebec.

The largest expansion in the inland marine strength occurred in 1777 on the heels of the American invasion. Measures had to be adopted to ensure that the naval services would be adequate to support the British army's move up Lake Champlain. Vessels were built or pre-fabricated in England and shipped out to Quebec followed by reinforcements and stores in the spring. A shipyard was re-established at St. John on the Richelieu, above the rapids, that blocked direct passage to the St.

---

[1]Return of the Naval Dept., Quebec Dec. 31, 1783 (NAC: **Haldimand Papers** (henceforth HP), B190/112-114.

[2]Haldimand to Carleton, Sept. 15, 1783, **ibid.**, B148/192. They were looking for employment since they had been discharged.

[3]These 50 carpenters delayed en route at Skenesborough early 1777, Harrison Bird, **Navies in the Mountains** (New York 1962), 189.

Lawrence. Fourteen imported gunboats 36' long with 16' beams were hauled overland from Chambly to deep waters. Three larger vessels also had to be transported overland, but rain-sodden roads delayed the operation so long that the only possible alternative was to dismantle them and cart the sections across to the shipyard. This is exactly how the 14-gun schooner *Lady Maria* and the 6-gun gondola *Loyal Convert* were transported, while the unfinished 18-gun, 300 ton schooner *Inflexible*, on stocks at Quebec, was disassembled and the whole rebuilt at St. John. Finally the 12-gun schooner *Carleton*, which had been precut in England, was assembled and sheathed.

This operation was a remarkable feat, and could not have been accomplished as quickly without the careful planning, direction and close co-operation of the commissioner and a Royal Engineer, Lt. William Twiss, head of the shipyard. Both contributed to the improvements of existing water-craft: Schank's "drop-keel" for shallow-water boats, and Twiss' "drop-front" landing barge.[1] Twiss, with a reputation for solving practical problems, in 1776, while supervising the building of a dozen gun-boats, also directed the preparation of stocks for the construction of larger ships, the assembly of gear and materials for moving others overland, and the building of slipways for completed ships. One of the most speedy achievements of the operation was the reconstruction of the *Inflexible* at St. John, where the ribs and planking were put together in one day! And within four weeks, 16 shipwrights had completed the assembly and outfitting. Gov. Haldimand had relied heavily on Schank and Twiss and gave them a free hand in the performance of

---

[1]**The Old United Empire Loyalists List** (Toronto U.E.L. Assoc., 1884, reprint Baltimore 1976), passim; henceforth cited as **UE List**.

their duties to the limit of his powers. He obtained promotions for Schank to commander, and later to post captain.

Schank, like Twiss, was formerly in the Royal Navy, unlike others in the marine, who were Colonials whose names appear in the incompleted Old Executive Council List of Loyalists, which lists men who were connected with this service.[1] They ranged from two commodores down to about 36 seamen, a third of the latter appearing not to have been American Loyalists. Eleven officers and non-commissioned officers, eleven craftsmen and a gunner or two complete the roll. John Ferrier was a master shipwright serving at Quebec, St. John, Carleton Island and Kingston,[2] while John Bryant served twenty years on Lake Ontario, retiring as a Master.[3] Although not listed as an artificer, but as a carpenter who had served in Gibraltar with the Royal Ordnance, George Gibson had probably belonged to the first company of Royal Military Artificers formed, and would have been with Twiss in 1772.[4]

The most used inland craft was the standard bateaux which, if quickly built of unseasoned wood, as they usually were in the later stages of the war, did not last long. In 1776 alone, some 560 bateaux were to be built,[5] and by the end of the war, even more were needed. Some Loyalists became adept in their construction while serving with artificer companies at posts such as

---

[1]Bird, 186-7, on both, Douglas, 23, sliding keel, 20.

[2]UE LIst, 174.

[3]Ibid., 285.

[4]Ibid., 299; on early artificers Glenn A. Steppler,"British Military Artificers in Canada, 1760-1815," **Army Historical Research** (London 1982), LX, 243, 150-163.

[5]Bird, 188.

Yamaska.[1] Herkimer's Bateau Company was formed in late 1780 to employ Loyalists with transport duties between Coteau du Lac and Carleton Island.[2] While Twiss was in charge of the construction of the craft they used, the supervision of the boats' use was the responsibility of Capt. Jacob Maurer, Inspector of Bateaux, stationed at Montreal. Maurer managed the storage, repair and issuing of the bateaux, as well as keeping record of their whereabouts. As these were the 18th century counterpart of today's railway freight cars, Maurer was the equivalent of a modern yardmaster. It was just as essential then as now to keep the moveable vehicles efficiently employed throughout the waterways, not bunched together empty and idle at distant places.

The preparations for Loyalist settlements along the upper St. Lawrence and its lakes necessitated the making of many more bateaux to transport them. At Lachine, Maj. Edward Jessup had such boats built in early 1784,[3] which, after transporting their passengers to their destinations during the summer, were supposed to return to Montreal. However, as the only link with the outside world and the only vehicles available in the wilderness, some bateaux were forcibly retained by the settlers, impeding the forwarding of more settlers and supplies upstream.[4] The crews were mainly French-Canadian civilians, and the bateau service was in constant use.

---

[1] Lt. William Fraser's Company, K.R.R.N.Y. sent to Yamaska to build a blockhouse in 1780-81, and continued to serve there cutting wood etc., corresponding with Twiss (NAC: HP, B154).

[2] John E. Ruch, "Late 1780 in Quebec: Season of the Three Commanders," **Loyalist Gazette** (Toronto Autumn 1981), 7-8. Herkimer and 32 of his men are named in the **Return of the Families**, Nov. 1780 (NAC: HP B166/33-38v).

[3] Mary Fryer, **Buckskin Pimpernel** (Toronto 1981), 210.

[4] Ibid.

The John Grant family of Lachine dominated this important commercial centre which was dependent on the bateaux. Here were fused the trade routes between Lower and Upper Canada and the northwest country. Grant, a merchant, owned a local inn, which was also a clearing house for mail sent from Europe and eastern Canada to western settlers whose addresses were unknown or frequently changing. By 1812, Grant, with a fleet of 40 to 50 bateaux employed in transporting goods and passengers on the St. Lawrence and the Ottawa,[1] took Robert Grant, likely his son, into partnership for the Lachine-Kingston service. The Grants' Lachine operation included twenty houses plus storehouses, and a drydock. John died in 1818, at which time Robert became a partner of his brother-in-law Donald Duff, controlling some eighty bateaux,[2] while Hezekiah Wing ran a smaller service between Lachine and Argenteuil.[3] Grants were numerous in the fur trade, and among the Loyalists there are six Johns on the old U.E. Loyalist List. The Quaker family of Wing, while numerous in New York, were few among the Loyalists, Abraham Sr. and Jr., for example.[4]

The bateau was larger than the canoe but smaller than the Durham boat which came into service a quarter century after the Loyalists' arrival. Known for its stability, it was 30' to 40' in length, beams 5' to 8', depth 4' to 5', with very angular lines, a flat bottom and slab side.[5]

---

[1]Douglas, 8; UE List, 164.

[2]Douglas, 6; UE List, 285.

[3]Simcoe's proposals 1794, Douglas, 10.

[4]Commission as Superintendent of Bateau Construction Ile aux Noix, Aug. 12, 1813; NAC: RG8 (military "C" Ser.), C730/85-88.

[5]Henry R. Howland,"A British Privateer in the American Revolution," **American Historical Review**.

The Provincial Marine built and operated the larger ships which sailed the open lake waters in contrast to the bateau service, which, under the Quarter Master's Department, provided links over the difficult passages between the lakes. After the Revolution, the marine continued to operate but on a reduced scale, lapsing into peacetime duties of communications and transport, now under control of the military following Schank's departure from the Province in 1784. It experienced periodic fits of activity whenever the United States displayed greater belligerence than usual. In Upper Canada in the 1790s the Lieutenant-governor made considerable efforts to build his forces, including the local marine, into strong defensive arms. He turned to former marine personnel, one of whom was Loyalist John Dennis, a shipwright in the war, who had settled in the Toronto area building the occasional boat, and at least one "neat" yacht,[1] sending him to the Kingston shipyard as a master shipwright. William Baker, another Loyalist, who had served since 1773, was employed as assistant Master-Builder at the Amherstburg shipyard on Lake Erie.[2] Several types of vessels were built, those on Lake Erie were generally smaller than those built on Lake Ontario, all of which weighed between 100 and 300 tons.

At the first threat of hostilities with an inadequately-armed marine, the solution was to "build gunboats." Although some effort had been made during the two decades 1790-1810 to

---

[1]UE List, 214; possibly the man mentioned as ready to embark at New York, June 1783 in Lorenzo Sabine, **Loyalists of the American Revolution** (Boston 1864, 2nd ed.), II, 558.

[2]James Sullivan ed. **Minutes of the Albany Committee of Correspondence 1775-178** (Albany 1923), I, French, 905; Hoaksley, 771, 804; Huffnagel (Huffnail), 833-834, 842, 905. Smith, Sherwood and Badgley, NAC: HP, B148/173.

utilize the marine as a naval defence force in an emergency, the government had to set its yards to the production of gunboats, as a stop-gap measure. The boats were small, cheap, simple and quick to build, and required a small crew to operate them. There construction began during the Revolution, continuing on in peacetime, and during the War of 1813.[1] When the old Provincial Marine was finally disbanded in 1813, some of its men, and all of its vessels joined the Royal Navy which replaced it. In Lower Canada, the governor's plans for offensive operations toward the south along the Richelieu-Champlain Valley necessitated the expansion of his naval force. Gunboats were to be built at Ile-aux-Noix in 1813, and in August that year Maj. James Dunlop, the merchant ship owner, was ordered to supervise their construction.[2] Unfortunately, late in the year he was relieved of his command, and shortly thereafter dismissed from the service for disobedience to Gov. Prevost.

With the mention of Dunlop and the other Loyalists connected with commercial shipping, it becomes necessary to refer to their marine services rather than with the local Provincial defence. Their experiences were diverse as seamen, shipowners, merchants and seafighters. While the large increase in naval activity in Canadian waters during the Revolution was largely due to the military presence, the steadily growing expansion of shipping-related trades thereafter was mostly the work of these Loyalists.

PRIVATEERS

[1]**Losses Claim**, James Frost from Rhode Island, May 29, 1787, pub. **Ontario Archives Report** no.2, 1904, 918-919.

[2]Frederick W. Wallace, **Wooden Ships and Iron Men** (London & Toronto 1920) ,7-10.

During the Revolution and 1812 wars, Loyalists had served on "privateers," fast-sailing merchant vessels licensed by the government to prey on enemy ships. These craft were often manned by their owners and shareholders, who stood to profit well from the sale of any ships and cargoes they captured. The seized property was sold at public auction, and the "prize-money" was divided among the Crown, crew and shareholders. Before putting to sea on their patrols, the ships were usually refitted, armed with a number of fighting-men added to their complement. The best documented example of a Montreal Loyalist who served as captain of Marines on a privateer was John Richardson, who as a young man had worked for John Porteus, merchant in New York and Philadelphia.[1] In trade in Detroit and Montreal by the outbreak of the war, Porteus obtained business through his brother in New York, who was Assistant Commissary General, where he and other Loyalists outfitted the *Vengeance*, their "snow", a three-masted vessel, as a privateer which saw action in 1779. Richardson was on board as supercargo and Captain of Marines, his adventures on this voyage are told in his biographical sketch below. The craft was ugly but fast, overtaking and capturing several ships. In the thick of the action was Richardson, who led boarding parties onto the enemy ships under heavy fire, until the *Vengeance's* return to port for repairs, ending a five-month tour in late May. Twice again that year she set sail on expeditions southward along the American coast, but Richardson, with other duties on shore, stayed behind. On her third mission, she was last heard from in January 1780 before disappearing with her crew. Whether she sank in a storm or from enemy action is not

---

[1]NAC: Quebec Shipping Register, RG12/A1/183 (1787-1823).

known, indeed she could have been sunk by a friendly vessel. On her first outing a British warship had mistaken her for a rebel, and fired on her even after she had been recognized as a Loyal privateer. Such was the obstinacy and ill-will of some naval officers towards Colonials.

Richardson later settled in Montreal and became a prominent businessman. Another was Archibald Montgomery, who had been master of the *Black Snake* privateer.[1] The experience which these men and others had must have been invaluable to their friends who took to privateering in the next conflict as well as those outfitted for offensive action during the Napoleonic period. However, Dunlop's and Richardson's greatest contribution to the seafaring life in Canada was in commerce, rather than in battle.

MERCHANT SHIPS AND SHIPPING

The presence of large numbers of Loyalists in Canada immediately after the Revolution caused an increase in commercial activity, and as a consequence, the country acquired a noteworthy merchant fleet. For years Loyalists were the main customers and suppliers of the Montreal merchants who imported manufactured goods and raw materials. As the fur trade waned, the agricultural and forest industries flourished, eventually replacing the former. Loyalists were among the merchants, owners, operators, builders and crews of the vessels which were essential to these economic developments. By the early 1800s, Montreal had outgrown Quebec City in population and importance, and was dominating the trade of the upper

---

[1]*Ibid., Sarah,* Oct. 28, 1795, 37; *Sisters,* Oct. 13, 1796, 40; *Catharine,* Feb. 21, 1799, 155.

regions of the Great Lakes which Donald Creighton dubbed the "commercial empire of the St. Lawrence."

Until now historians have searched for "English," "Irish," "Scottish," or "French" participation in various aspects of Quebec's history. The presence of the Loyalists were mainly portrayed in the role of producers at the agrarian level, and consumers on all levels. However, they also constituted a substantial proportion of the mercantile and marine community. Many had owned shares in vessels, a few of whom had managed to save their crafts by sailing them to the Maritimes. Elias Smith and his partner, Moses Sherwood, were among those who brought their ships to Quebec, but those who had lived in the Albany area were less fortunate. The sloops owned by Benjamin French, Richard Hoaksley, and Michael Huffnagel were seized by the rebels.[1] James Frost, a ship master from Boston, had sailed his ship to many foreign ports in peacetime and at the onset of the Revolution, while in Quebec on business, he volunteered for service and turned his vessel over to the government for official use. From 1776 he served with the Provincial Marine on Lake Champlain until in 1782 he was called to Quebec City to become captain of the Port. His appointment to this civil post symbolized the beginning of a new age of shipping on the St. Lawrence.[2]

---

[1]Ibid., 21. Richardson in syndicate owning *Marie*, 1790; schooner 1790, 246, Stephen Sewall (sic) and Edward Hartley owned *Prudence*, 1816, 146.

[2]Partnership of McDenzie & Bethune, Newton Bosworth, **Hochelaga Depicta, or the History and Present State of the Island and City of Montreal** (Montreal 1839, reprint Toronto 1974), 177; Henry Atkinson, Gale & Hoffman at Quebec in mid-century, F.W. Wallace, **Wooden Ships,** 94; Luke Shay (Shea) & E.D. Merritt, successors of Canada Ship Building Co., Montreal, Bosworth, 177-178.

The different circumstances which led to the development of shipping in Montreal between the 18th and 19th centuries stand in sharp contrast to each other. There had been some shipbuilding activity during the French regime, particularly on the lakes above Quebec City, but the capital controlled the greater part of the industry, which flourished for a century, with the skills of craftsmen trained by shipwrights from France, and were highlighted by increased activity, around 1715 and again in ca.1730. Ocean-going vessels up to 700-tons were built in Quebec City which could not pass through the shallower waters further upstream.[1] During the American Revolution all shipbuilding was carried out for the government, traders were not permitted to have vessels on the lakes which lasted for a few years after the War, forcing the traders to use the services of the Provincial Marine.

The Quebec Shipping Register, beginning in 1787, shows a number of significant trends in the Province's marine activity.[2] First, the number of registrations for owners who have non-French surnames, few at first, increases steadily until they outnumber the French. Secondly, the number of registrations for vessels owned by residents of Montreal also increase considerably, compared to those for Quebec. Thirdly, the early Montreal registrations include many "foreign" built vessels. Builders' names are not normally included, but among the owners can be found quite a few Loyalists: Elias Smith prominent among them. Among the first half-dozen Montreal registrations in the late 1790s were three of his vessels: *Sarah,*

---

[1]"employing bad artificers, at a high rate," Twiss to Haldimand, June 12, 1779 (NAC: HP, B154/ 147-148.

[2]Douglas, **Provincial Marine**, 10-11.

the brig *Sisters*, and the schooner *Catherine*,[1] the latter purchased as a prize of war, while the others were "plantation-built," probably in Jamaica where his ships frequently traded. In the next decade the name of James Dunlop is often listed, but by the 1810s the Logans take a prominent place, particularly Hart Logan, who, like Dunlop, built many of their vessels in Montreal. Loyalists are also found among members of partnerships or syndicates which owned various vessels, such as Richardson and Sewell,[2] and later into the century among the partners owning shipyards were Loyalist family names: Bethune, Gale, Merritt and Shay.[3]

The increase in commercial activity in the late 1780s and 1790s increased the demand for skilled craftsmen of all kinds as the Loyalist tradesmen were not numerous enough to satisfy the need. Consequently their services were expensive. Government and military officials complained about the high wages they expected for indifferent or inferior workmanship,[4] while local merchants often had to look elsewhere for tradesmen who charged more reasonable prices. When shipwrights were scarcest, employers always had to bring them over from abroad, this was also true of both the French and

---

[1]Ernest A. Cruikshank, "The John richardson Letters," Papers and Records (Ont. Hist. Soc., Toronto 1905), VI, 20-36, see Richardson to Porteus, May 31, Dept. 23, Sept. 1789 and April 1790.

[2]Ibid., Sept. 23, 1789.

[3]Ibid., 24,25, Richardson to Porteus, June 14, 1789, before the Revolution Phyn, Ellice & Porteous had built two vessels at Detroit and during that war the organization acquired an ocean-going vessel, replace in 1781 and again in 1792, Merrill Denison, **Canada's First Bank** (Montreal 1966), I, 434, 437.

[4]Elias Smith to David Smith, Dec. 5, 1799, **Elias Smith's Letterbook 1799-1800**. (NAC: MG23), Original in Baker Library, Harvard Sch. of Bus. Mrs. Sue Jackson, Glen Ellyn, Ill. supplied photocopies for our study.

British governments. By the 1790s Simcoe could borrow craftsmen from Lower Canada for the Provincial Marine shipyards in Upper Canada, but he still had to rely on men from New York to fill the void.[1] Not long after, James Dunlop brought over Scottish ship designers, shipwrights and craftsmen to establish his own yard. Even so, he still had to summon others from New York, eleven of whom soon deserted him and returned home. Those who remained in Montreal were the builders of the early merchant fleet, and teachers of the next generation of shipbuilders.

The concentration of later writers on the period of shipbuilding from the 1840s on, when the industry was at its peak in Quebec, led them to neglect the poorly documented but essential activity of the era preceding it.

The construction of vessels at Montreal was limited to those which could navigate the lower St. Lawrence through the shallows at Lac Saint Pierre. Rapids above Montreal blocked the passage to the west while similar limitations affected vessels built on the upper lakes. As an eleven-foot depth was the maximum between Montreal and Quebec City, an eighty-foot depth held for the passage between lakes Erie and Huron and until these natural obstacles could be circumvented, the inland shipping trade was severely impeded. Ships which otherwise would have been built downriver in Montreal or Quebec City had to be constructed on the spot in the upper country. There was a closer relationship with the builders at St. John, but the Richelieu Rapids still barred the river to Montreal.

Changes in the shipping laws in the late 1780s greatly benefited trade and commerce, by permitting the traders use of their own bateaux and canoes followed by the use of privately

---

[1]Ibid., same to same.

owned larger vessels. In 1789 Robert Ellice & Co. sent John Richardson with a work crew from Montreal to Detroit to build a schooner for use on Lakes Huron and Michigan. Under the direction of a master carpenter, three French-Canadian and three Irish craftsmen worked on the *Nancy* from late June until November 24 when she was launched.[1] Richardson considered the expense of her construction "great", but was pleased enough with the results to call her "a perfect masterpiece of workmanship and beauty."[2] She plied the lakes for 24 years, being destroyed in 1814 to prevent her capture by the Americans. The firm of Phyn & Ellice had a smaller craft already in service on Lake Erie at the time of Richardson's journey.[3]

Another change in legislation in 1788 which encouraged the Canadian merchant shippers opened the coastal routes to the Caribbean. The fur traders were mainly interested in east-west routes, while merchants like Elias Smith and James Dunlop, who had coastal trade experience in the American Colonies, were quick to enter it now. Cargoes of lumber, grain and fish were exported from Lower Canada and Newfoundland to the south, while imports included molasses, rum and sugar. These cargoes were also shipped to Britain and continental Europe, vessels registered in Quebec were often sent to Britain for re-registration to take advantage of the trans-Atlantic routes.

Some documentation regarding shipping survives from the years 1799-1800 which illuminate the state of shipbuilding at

---

[1]Elias to David Smith, Jan. 19, 1800, Smith's **Letterbook.**

[2]Land Petition of Elias Smith, received and read late June 1797 at York (Toronto) pub. by Ernest A. Cruikshank, in **Papers and Records,** Ont. Hist. Soc., XXVI (Toronto 1930), 325-326.

[3]Peter Smith died in Jamaica, his epitaph ordered by Elias, **ibid.,** Dec. 8, 1799.

that time. David Smith of New York, son and partner of Elias, asked his father to enquire bout the possibility of having a 200-ton schooner built in Canada.[1] Elias' letterbook contains his correspondence in reply, in which he focused on builders in the Maritimes whom he engaged more experienced and reliable than those in Montreal. But much to his surprise he learned that construction in Lower Canada was cheaper, done in about the same time, and had a better reputation: "Canada built Vessells are in better repute in England and will sell for 25 per cent more than a Vessell built in any part of Nova Scotia."[2]

His search in Quebec narrowed down to two builders, one the French-Canadian, François Cormier dit Rossignol, who was established below Quebec at Lac Saint Paul; the other, an American trained in Boston, at Trois Rivières. Smith had probably seen the 145-ton brig built at Trois Rivières in 1798 by the same man which he reported was "handsome,"[3] David Smith had specified the vessel should be 64' long by 24' in the beam with a draught of 12' and the cost of the hull in Quebec would be $2,800 to $3,000 compared to about $7,000 in the Atlantic provinces. Elias did not compare the abilities of the two shipwrights, but implied that the American had the best training. Both would have used the same kind of wood while the American would have insisted on seasoning them for at least one year. White and red oak did not last long in ships, being subject to dry rot in as short a time as five years.[4] Elias believed that waiting for the drying of the green wood was worth while.

---

[1]Bosworth, **Hochelaga**, 177.
[2]Hugh Gray, **Letters from Canada** (London 1809, reprint Toronto 1971), 213.
[3]Mary B. Fryer, **Buckskin Pimpernel**, 248.
[4]Merrill Denison, **The Barley and the Stream** (Toronto 1965), 52-54.

Smith was not a novice in building, he had served as a master carpenter and a contractor in the British Army in Boston and New York during the Revolution,[1] and, as captain of a company of artificers, he had been engaged in various construction works, especially building bridges. Having obtained a seaworthy hull, he was prepared to complete the superstructure and rigging with his own crew. Not all ship owners could cut costs of building and outfitting a vessel as sharply as the Smiths, who owned a rope-walk in New York which could supply the necessary cordage for rigging at cost plus cartage. Further, they used their ships returning from England to bring in tackle and other special hardware items not obtainable in Lower Canada or the northern U.S. Elias, however, was growing old and had lost interest in the Jamaican trade, which claimed the life of one of his sons.[2] New business ventures in the Orient in land and mills to the west occurred at the very moment when a new marine age was dawning for Montreal.

The early years of the 19th century saw the establishment of several shipyards. Bosworth, writing three decades after the event, states that in 1806 David Munn constructed the first ships built in Montreal.[3] His yard continued to produce vessels for some time, and about 1808-9 he took Rob Robert Hunter into partnership. At the same time, two Loyalists also went into the shipbuilding business in Montreal — James Dunlop and Hart Logan. A fourth builder of the time was J. Storrow & Co. It was the vessels made in these and other yards which Hugh

---

[1]Gazette (Montreal), Feb. 6, 1796.

[2]Dunlop to Macnair, Oct. 15, 1810, **Dunlop Papers**, 1/52.

[3]Wallace, **Wooden Ships**, 90; **In the Wake of the Wind Ships** (Toronto 1927), 71 on Munn's philanthropy. For Alexander esp. **Dict. Can. Biog,** V.

Gray described at the time as "some very handsome ships ... annually built at Quebec and Montreal."[1] The industry, he wrote, was an "immense advantage" to these centres for it employed many workers year round, and contributed about £20,000 annually to the provincial economy. Indeed, his noting that work proceeded "summer and winter" indicates that it was thriving. In less prosperous years, construction was usually done during the winter when many workers were looking for employment. Although the season was harsh for outdoor labour, a vessel could be built and launched by early spring, when waters of the St. Lawrence were high, presenting fewer problems.

Economic benefits from the increase in shipbuilding and shipping were not confined to Lower Canada. The timber used in the construction of these vessels, and later the lumber which they carried as cargoes, came from both Upper and Lower Canada. Rafts of logs were floated down the upper St. Lawrence from the pioneer settlements captained by Loyalist owners such as Joel Stone and Justus Sherwood, the latter dying in 1799 while rafting near Trois Rivières.[2] The yard on Monarque St. near Molson's Brewery purchased rafts from Philemon Wright (the American founder of Hull, Quebec) sent from around Chaudière Falls, and from Alexander Simpson at Beauharnois.[3] Merchants in need of timber at reasonable prices sometimes advertised in the papers as did Elias Smith. In the Montreal *Gazette* Feb. 6, 1796 it read:

---

[1]**Register,** (Quebec), July 25, 1815, 135.

[2]The first *James Dunlop* was declared a total wreck. **Gazette** (Quebec) Nov. 27, 1812. His sloop the *Peggy* was grounded, broke up and burned some time after its registration in May 1792, **Register,** 25.

[3]Dunlop to Mrs. Macnair, May 10, 1811, **Dunlop Papers,** 1/59.

Wanted for building a vessel of one hundred and eighty
tons. A quantity of white oak, red cedar and pine timber
to be delivered in the raft at Montreal in all July and
August next...[1]

Carpenters were fairly well paid by contemporary standards,
those contracting for the building of Smith's schooner in 1799
would have charged between $14 and $15 per ton for the hull.
In the Maritimes, if the estimate for construction did not
include rigging etc., then the rate would have been about $35
per ton. Gray stated in 1809 that carpenters charged about £10
per ton, a rate considerably higher than the others, but it could
have included more than the bare hull. Shipyard owners paid
their men according to the worker's skill and experience. In
1810 James Dunlop employed 30 to 40 men in his yard. Their
wages ranged from 10 shillings per day for the best carpenters
down to 4 pence per day for common labourers.[2]

Before locally-built ships were being produced in any
number,vessels could be obtained downriver, or outside the
province. Secondhand craft of many types could also be
purchased, often at bargain prices, when they were auctioned as
prizes of war in the courts of Vice-Admiralty.

A profitable alternative was to commission the construction
from the better workman even if it meant waiting longer. But
in the interim another vessel could be purchased at auction,
preferably a British-built one. This could carry on the business
until a new schooner was ready and then, under a British
registry, could be sold abroad at profit.

Ship building in Montreal during the period 1800-20 was
dominated by Scots: Munn, Dunlop and Logan. Besides David

---

[1]Same to same, Aug. 22, 1812, **ibid.**, 1/83.
[2]**Gazette** (Quebec), March 2, 1809.

Munn in Montreal there was Alexander Munn (1766-1812), probably his brother, in Quebec City who was important to the industry.[1] Dunlop and Logan went into shipbuilding as an extension of their other businesses, and at times they were rivals although they were of different generations, and the directions of their efforts tended to differ. While both produced sailing vessels of large tonnage, Logan turned his attention to steamboats when the first such commercially successful craft came into service in the U.S., while Dunlop continued his business ventures on the high seas until his death in 1815.

In the Lower Canada registrations, Dunlop's vessels indicate that he acquired craft that were progressively larger and faster. One was built at Bécancour, and five more at Montreal, the successive measurements of these were nearly always larger. Tonnages mounted from 332 to 482, lengths from 84' to 115' and beams from 23' to 32'. The last and largest of his vessels was the Earl St. Vincent built at Deptford, Eng., and was sixteen years old when he registered her in 1815 as the flagship of his large fleet. At that time the ship could only have sailed up the St. Lawrence as far as Quebec City where she would have been based.[2] Shallow water was always troublesome to his vessels, and several of them ran aground, as did the first *James Dunlop*, which had to be abandoned and wrecked while grounded near Anticosti Island.[3] Others were saved by a high tide, or were unloaded and rose sufficiently in the water to be freed. Dunlop's vessels were launched in the spring, which grew to be

---

[1]**Register** (Quebec) resp. 99 (twice), 107, 108, 117.

[2]Ibid., 165. Holt's partnership with Watt established in 1803, R. Campbell, **History of St. Gabriel Street Church** (Montreal 1887), 131.

[3]James was eldest son of Hart's brother, William, whose younger son became the great natural historian Sir William, **ibid.**, 132-133.

a very festive social occasion - it was reported that 5,000 people gathered to watch the *James Dunlop* slide into the river, after which he held a ball for 150 friends and workers.[1]

Little is known of the appearance of these early vessels built in Montreal, contemporaries commented on some that they were handsome or beautiful or swift in the water. Dunlop once made a general comparison of a trio of his three-masted ships registered between 1806 and 1812. The main difference he noted was that, as far as inner furnishings went, the *George Canning* was not so "fine" as the *Dunlop* and *James Dunlop*.[2] Exterior ornament was sparse, vessels often had the simplest of figureheads — a knee or scroll, a few had a male or female figure. Richardson and his master-carpenter were adamant that the schooner *Nancy* would not be complete without a well-carved female figure for its bow as did Dunlop's *Janet Dunlop*, while the *Earl St. Vincent* had a male figurehead.

Hart Logan, son of James, the Loyalist baker who settled in Montreal after the Revolution, had been a merchant for several years before building ships. His partnership with George Watt was dissolved early in 1809 at which time he began to work for John Molson building the first steamboat ever to navigate the St. Lawrence.[3] He did not, however, devote all his attention to this revolutionary type of craft but also built traditional sailing vessels until after the War of 1812. From 1810 to 1812 he built

---

[1]Holt marr. Elizabeth Cuyler at New York July 30, 1818, having resigned his lucrative office nine days earlier, and been placed on half pay. Elizabeth Cuyler Hold, **Petitions for Relief**, 1827-1828. (NAC: RG8 (Mil. "C" Ser.) 634a/77-78. See also Sabine, **Loyalists**, I, 539, and Ernest A. Jones, **Loyalists of New Jersey** (Newark 1927, reprint Boston 1972), 99.

[2]Denison, **Barley**, 38. There were Loyalists Insleys (and Ammesleys) and Vaughns in this province.

[3]Denison, **Barley**, 61-63; Wilson, **Steam**, chap. 1.

the snow *St. Lawrence*, the brig, *Janet*, and the ships *James and Agnes* ,the *William* and the *Sterling*, all destined for the Atlantic trade.[1] Of these ships, the *William* was the largest, measuring 115' by 30'4" in the beam and 455 tons burden. Another ship, the *Nancy*, built in 1819, was nearly as big but was about 15% lighter in weight.[2] By this time Hart Logan had moved to London. Eng., and placed his Montreal business in the hands of his nephew James,[3] who with John Fleming, also of Montreal, were part owners of the *Nancy* along with Hart himself.

The locations of Dunlop's and Logan's shipyards were partly dependent on natural geographic features of the Montreal waterfront. For many years vessels experienced great difficulty in traversing St. Mary's Current southeast of the town, while the rapids farther upstream, between Montreal and Lachine, prohibited passage in manned vessels. Dunlop established his yard at Pointe-à-Callières at the foot of the rapids, for his craft could go no further. All west-bound cargoes had to be transshipped here, from vessel to wagon, for the Montreal-Lachine portage, then back on board a vessel. Raw materials arriving along the inland route were vast so the placement of shiploading facilities as near to the portage as possible meant less lengthy cartage and quicker turn around of transport vehicles. Close by was the office of the Inspector of ashes, a remunerative by-product of land clearance. Pot and pearl ashes were a source of income for pioneers. Great amounts of these ashes were shipped overseas to ready markets, causing controls

---

[1]Denison, **Barley** 63-64; also Wilson, **Steam,** 9-13; George also supplied metalwork for the *Swifrsure* in 1812, ibid., 26.

[2]Ibid., 12/3; 16/3.

[3]Ibid., 48/2.

to be implemented as to quality and the payment of duties. For many years one of the senior inspectors was William Johnson Holt (1762?-1826), formerly an ensign in the Pennsylvania Loyalists Regiment.[1]

Hart Logan's venture into the development of Canada's first steamboats was instigated by the founder of Molson's Brewery. John Molson had settled as a young English immigrant in Montreal in 1782 and later married Sarah Insley Vaughan, probably of a Loyalist family.[2] With a keen interest for improved technologies, after receiving the news of Robert Fulton's successful operation of a steamboat on the Hudson River in 1807, Molson did not lose time in journeying south to see it. He examined the vehicle and its power plant and spoke with the inventor. On his return to Montreal, he at once set about the creation of his own steamboat, to be called the *Accomodation*. He commissioned Hart Logan to build the boat under the direction of two experienced craftsmen, John Bruce and John Jackson, and contracted with several others for the supply of the various parts of metalwork for the engine and driving mechanism. It took from March to May 1809 to build, many of the workmen were either sons of or kin of Loyalists. George Platt, who supplied the iron parts, had been trained by his blacksmith father, Loyalist John Platt, who had one of the earliest machine shops in Montreal. Andrew White, a joiner,

---

[1]Wilson, **Steam**, 112-113, ref. Canadian Courant, Aug. 22, 1822.

[2]Register (Quebec), 170, 40 (June 3, 1820) shows that David Genovoly's widow Agathe Genovolly (sic), inherited his share. Gionovelly (sic) of Montreal subsequently married the widower Augustin Perrault, of the same town, **Gazette** (Quebec) Aug. 5, 1822. David may have been the son of Samuel Jionovelly (sic) who married Josepha St. Medard, at Montreal in July 1778 (Anglican). Margaret Gionovaly (sic) Widow of Loyalist Samuel from Savannah, Ga., was in Halifax, N.S. in the late 1780s .

built the cabin, while William Griffin, head shipwright, had eleven carpenters working under him, among whom was William Boyce. Most, if not all, of these latter-mentioned, served as crew on the boat when she was completed, Boyce acting as steward. The combination of talents on Molson's team made steam-powered vessels on the St. Lawrence the phenomenon of the age in Canadian transport. The *Accommodation* was a success insofar as it actually worked, and therefore was able to demonstrate the use of the vessel, but it was very slow and inefficient. James Dunlop actually travelled by land from Quebec City to Montreal in less time than this steamboat took to do the same trip. Having learned many lessons from the construction and operation of this first boat, the team set to work on a second, the *Swiftsure*, built in 1811-12. This was more satisfactory in its performance, and with increasing experience and knowledge, three more steamers were built for Molson: the *Malsham*, 1817-18, the *Lady Sherbrooke*, 1816-17 and the *New Swiftsure* 1817-18. The speed, reliability and regularity of this type of transport made it the standard method of communication between Quebec City and Montreal. During the 1812 War the *Swiftsure* was of great service to the government in carrying troops and supplies.

Other patrons of the steamboat were not far behind once Molson had proven their practicability. The new form of propulsion seemed to promise great rewards to those who could exploit it, and they began to challenge Molson's monopoly on the regular shuttle service between Montreal and the capital. A syndicate of thirty members commissioned Logan to build the *Car of Commerce*, a caravel, and the largest steamboat of its time in Montreal. Built in 1815-16, the vessel continued in service until it was holed and sunk in 1822. Among the shareholders were: Jabez and Jacob De Witt, David

Genovoly, Jacob Hall and Samuel Sherwood. Logan also built the *Telegraph* in 1818 for another syndicate, which was launched in May, two months earlier than his next steamboat, Molson's *Swiftsure*.

This next great era in inland shipping began about 1810, which saw an enormous increase in traffic and commerce on the St. Lawrence. After 1814, European emigrants arrived in hundreds and thousands, leading to strong competition between the operators of the various carriers for the greater share of passengers moving from Quebec westward. More attractive vessels were needed to appeal to travellers, decorative and comfortable accommodations were becoming essential. The *Accommodation* was a fairly simple and practical vehicle, little more than a solid, floating platform for the machinery, with a cabin constructed by Andrew White. However, he excelled himself in the joinery for the next steamer, the *Swiftsure*, The interior was New-Classical in style with architectural elements: pilasters, cornices and medallions. Additional ornamentation included paintings, drapery and furniture and dining facilities were provided with crystal and china. Only written descriptions of the earliest such vessels are known to survive, although some of the moveables were taken ashore when the occasion was offered. The small cabin which covered the stairway of the *Car of Commerce* was removed while she was still aground in 1822, and reputed to have served as a summer house on the slopes of Mount Royal late into the 19th century.

Besides the 140-mile steamboat service between Montreal and Quebec City, there existed the short-haul and ferry services between Montreal Island and the surrounding mainland. Steamers began operation on these routes in the late 1810s and were common by the 1820s. Many syndicates formed to build these vessels, among whose members were a substantial proportion of people who were of Loyalist origin. The Johnsons, Waits and Whites. Sir John Johnson's sons, Archibald Kennedy and John Jr., each held a share in a different company. Likely related to Loyalist John Wait, Molson's first brewer, were Oliver, who supplied logs to Molson, and a R. Wait who was a shareholder in two ferries. John White of Quebec owned interests in the *Car of Commerce* in 1814, the *Lauzon* in 1817, and the *Quebec* in 1818. Andrew White, Molson's joiner, together with Stanley Bagg, owned share of the *William Annesley in* 1825. The Montreal advocate Stephen Sewell headed the group of 32 men who commissioned the *Quebec* and Norman Bethune acted as its attorney, while Robert and J. Jones were also among its members.

Perhaps the largest syndicate of all was that formed in 1822 to build the ferry *Laprairie*. It numbered over fifty members including many merchants and small tradesmen, such as Daniel Fisher, Richard and Robert McGinnis, Benjamin Holmes and James Scott. Robert McGinnis was a malter, and Scott a labourer, while the others were merchants. Samuel Hatt, of a Loyalist family that settled in the Niagara District, became a resident of Chambly. He was a partner with Charles Adolphus Holt and Dr. Wolfred Nelson in another syndicate which built the *Richelieu* in their own area. He also owned a share in the ill-fated *De Salaberry*, named after the hero of Chateauguay.

In the early 1800s Montreal was the only centre of the steamboat building industry in the Canadas. In 1816 Lake Ontario had her first steamer, but it was not until eight years after the *Accommodation* was launched that Quebec City had her first. Shipyards around Montreal were also engaged in this work. The *Perseverance*, in which the engineer, William Brackenridge (sic) owned a share, was launched from William Grant's slip at Lachine in 1812. Three years later the *Richelieu* was built at Chambly Basin. One of the leaders in designing the mechanism of Molson's early vessels, John Bruce, built the *Ottawa* at the Long Sault on that river in 1819, shortly before his death.

A further step in the development of steam-powered vessels at Montreal was taken by a syndicate formed of major business firms. A special boat was created for the purpose of assisting larger vessels, particularly sailing craft, to ascend the river's swift currents and to power them in contrary winds or in windless conditions. The result was a tug or "steam-towboat" called appropriately the *Hercules*. About a dozen companies were represented in what became the Montreal Tow Boat Co., owners of the *Hercules*, including Richardson, Forsyth & Co., Hart Logan & Co., and Peter McGill & Co. who suffered most when their inbound cargoes from Europe were delayed for days or weeks in passing upriver from the Atlantic by unfavourable weather. The tug was built in 1823 by David Munn & Co who had, like Logan, also built steamers. Together with his widowed sister-in-law and son James, he owned shares in another steamer, the *Caledonia*.

The age of the sailing vessel on the high seas continued for many years to be the principal carrier of trans-ocean freight and passengers. John Richardson's firm, descendant of Phyn, Ellice & Co., dedicated the use of its ship the *Eweretta* to the fur trade, which made two urgent demands on its vessel, which were dependent on the speed of its inland cargo fleets. Indian trade goods had to reach Montreal early enough in spring so that they could be included in the cargoes destined for western posts. As well, the ship had to be ready to load and sail to England once the bales of fur reached Montreal in late fall. Speed in reaching the London market with the furs was essential, for prices tended to drop when the supply became more abundant as other ships arrived. So the *Eweretta* remained idle most of the year only to make two trans-Atlantic voyages. Other ship-owners could not afford the extravagance of holding a vessel empty over such a period of time. In the coastal and ocean trade, waters were open year round. Three or four-cornered voyages could be made, discharging cargoes in one port and replacing them with different goods destined for the next port and so on. Smith advised his son, David, in New York in Dec. 1799, that the *Catherine* was taking codfish from Newfoundland "...to be at Jamaica in June... at the time the Rum, Sugar, Coffee, etc is at the Lowest Price." He was aware of a temporary glut of all liquors in Britain at the time, but expected to have a good market at Montreal for rum in the spring when the fur traders would be "fixing out for the North West." He suggested to his son to "send the *Union* to Georgia, from that to England with Cargo of Cotton, Rice, etc. If the Markets are good at Cadiz send the *Elias* back with Cargo of Rice, Tobacco etc."

Smith never gave orders to his son, but relied on David's judgement of where the market would yield a greater profit.

This was the transport system on which the Loyalists as well as the balance of the population of the Canadas depended for their purchases of manufactured goods. Although the Loyalists were generally impoverished by their losses to the rebels and had to depend on credit, within a few years they were in a position to pay cash for merchandize. At first they had bartered for goods, which helps to explain the odd lots of agricultural and other products the merchants found on their hands from time to time. Hundreds of Loyalists were awarded compensation by the parliamentary commissioners who held an enquiry into these losses claims in Montreal in 1787-88. There not being a Canadian bank, the settlements were deposited to the respective Loyalist's credit with some of the larger merchant houses, such as Robert Ellice & Co. Merchants tried to persuade these individuals to use their credit by purchasing their goods, although some were adamant on receiving their money.

The great age of shipping and shipbuilding on the St. Lawrence dawned about 1840, after nearly all of the original Loyalists had died, leaving grandchildren such as the shipbuilders Luke Shay and E. D. Merritt, who took over the Canada Ship Building Co. in 1829, four years later producing the steamer *Montreal* for James Wait, to leave their mark. In Quebec City ocean vessel production was growing in size and in numbers, where in the 1850s Edward Sewell and Henry Atkinson, Gale & Hoffman were well-known builders. Thus Loyalist family names continued to be found in the industry eight decades after the Revolution.

CHAPTER 9

Occupations of Loyalists

by John Ruch

The increase in population after the American Revolution in the Province of Quebec was largely due to the presence of thousands of British troops to which the Loyalists added their thousands. Among the refugees were educated officials, trained craftsmen, semi-skilled artisans, farmers and labourers. There was a constant demand for the skills, services and products necessary to establish frontier settlements. While in the towns, Loyalists worked for either government or in the private sector helping to train a new generation of workers in their crafts and arts.

Professions, Offices & Vocations

Many well-educated, and talented professionals were among the Loyalists exiled from their native land due to the Revolution, few of whom settled in the Province of Quebec. For those who did, they represented the legal, medical, military and religious professions, as well as merchants and farmers. They were essential to the development of this only recently acquired Province and to its rapidly increasing English-speaking population. The institution of English law and landholding systems necessitated the presence of men experienced and trained in these disciplines and practices, which were different from the French systems. The diverse Protestant groups required religious leaders and institutions, men of sound training and ability. The Loyalists took part in the foundation and development of public and private projects, which gathered momentum in the 1790s and reached fruition in the early 1800s.

Clergy

In North America as in Europe the more prosperous families and those with upper class pretensions sent their sons into the time-honoured professions represented by the Church, the sword and the bar. There were several Protestant clerics of continental French origin already in the Province by the time of the Revolution. However, the Loyalist clergymen who arrived during the war were more popular with the English-speaking population due to their fluency in the language. They included: John Bethune, John Bryan(t), John Doty, George Gilmore and John Stuart, some of whom resided in Montreal for several years, but none permanently. While in Montreal, Rev. Bethune organized the first Presbyterian congregation and Rev. Stuart the first academic school,[1] both leaving an important legacy to the community through their work, as well as through their descendants who returned to Montreal, gradually becoming prominent citizens. They were educated in the professions of medicine, law and religion. Two sons of Bethune's and one of Stuart's became distinguished Anglican clergymen[2] under the influence of Rev. John Strachan, who had assumed a position

---

[1] R. Campbell, **The History of the Scotch Presbyterian Church on St. Gabriel Street** (Montreal 1887), 25-38, for Bethune; also H.C. Stuart, **The Church of England in Canada 1759-93** (Montreal 1893), 49-50; for Gilmore, 56; for Stuart, 50-55, 109-111.

[2] John Bethune Jr. (1791-1872) eventually Anglican Dean of the Diocese of Montreal; his younger brother Alexander Neil (1800-79) was Bishop of Toronto. George okill Stuart (1776-1862) died as Anglican Dean of Toronto, his son was the first English-speaking mayor of quebec City. See **Dict. Can. Biog., X.**

of importance in Upper Canada after his arrival from Great Britain. Rev. Doty, probably because of his relationship with the wealthy Ellice family, moved to Sorel, later settling at Three Rivers.[3] The most stable congregation was that of the established Anglican Church, its status and social importance attracting many members who were well aware of one of the requirements to win government contracts and commissions — to be Anglican. The Scottish immigrants however, were mostly Presbyterians, a number of whom, through the fur trade, were extremely wealthy. The Scots were the first Protestants to build their own church in 1792.

A small but spiritually strong group was formed by the Methodists, survivors and offspring of the founders of their faith in America. Descendants of Barbara Heck and her family, who were in Montreal during the war years, remained, as did younger generations of the Embury, Fisher and Lawrence families.[4]

The absence of trained clergy in many groups meant that they had to rely heavily on lay ministers and assistants. Until it was possible for the clergy to be trained in Canada, men of the cloth had to be persuaded to emigrate, or the young had to be sent abroad to study for the ministry. Out of 12 Protestant ministers (nine Anglican, three Presbyterian) receiving government support in 1790, four were Loyalists, of whom three had served as military chaplains.[5]

The Church of England in Quebec found itself in competition not only with the previously-established Roman

---

[3]On Doty, see Stuart **op. cit.**, 45-48, 108-109; related to Ellices, 45-46.

[4]Yula C. Lapp, **To Their Heirs Forever** (Belleville), 197, passim on Methodist families.

[5]Stuart, 87-88.

Catholic Church, but with numerous, rapidly growing, dissenting Protestant congregations. Possibly its clergy envied the vice-like grip of the Catholic Church on its adherents, and in common with some local politicians, saw themselves in the role of a new Hercules contesting the territory with a near Antaeus represented by the churches. Believing that victory would ultimately be theirs, if they could hold the opposition from its source of strength, which meant keeping it isolated from its European roots. To help the Protestants, Anglicans received special land grants, the "Clergy Reserves," in every township but, even with these, they never grew to the proportion that Bishop Mountain had hoped for. In education, the dream of the Protestant church to assume a dominant position in Canada was thwarted by the historical development already underway, as much as by the opposition of dissenting leaders such as Chief Justice William Smith, who in Canada carried on a struggle already begun in the American Colonies prior to the Revolution.[6]

Military

Although a great many Loyalists, approximately 25,000, had served in provincial regiments during the war, comparatively few chose the military for a permanent career. For those who did, they were often moved with their units, and were subsequently stationed in various parts of the British Empire. Officers from well-known Loyalist families served and often died abroad (particularly in the Napoleonic Wars) or in the

---

[6]Smith's opposition to the donation of land for King's College by Trinity Church, New York, L.F.S. Upton, **The Loyal Whig** (Toronto 1969), 26-34; his legal actions against this are summarized in Thomas Jones, **History of New York**.

tropics. Among those who had fought in the American Revolution, some attained high rank in later years as did the Cuylers, Coffins, De Lanceys and Johnsons. Col. Abraham Cuyler, a merchant before the war, elected to return to civilian life after the conflict, but his brother continued in service, advancing to the level of General and died as Sir Cornelius Cuyler Bt.[7] Garret Fisher, also of Dutch ancestry in upper New York, ended his career as lieutenant-general.[8] Of the Coffins from Boston, three excelled in service: John, a veteran of the Battle of Bunker Hill, was promoted to full General in 1819,[9] another served for a time as private secretary to Lord Dorchester, and a third, a Harvard graduate, was Secretary and comptroller of Accounts in Lower Canada in the early 1800s. He died in 1810 as Sir Thomas Aston Coffin Bt. former Commissary General of the Royal Army.[10]

Sons of Loyalists who had been officers often joined the army. A survey of Lorenzo Sabine's book on the Loyalists reveals dozens of these young men, and in turn their sons, who served in various regiments of the regular army or with the Canadian militia, being very active in the 1812 war. Outstanding among the families who took part in defence were the Johnsons and McDonells. Brigadier-general Sir John

---

[7]D.N.B.; Lorenzo Sabine, **Loyalists of the American Revolution**, (Boston, 2nd ed. 1864), I, 356.

[8]William D. Lighthall, "Lieutenant-General Garret Fisher: A Forgotten Loyalist," **Proceedings**, Royal Soc. of Can. 9922, 65-72.

[9]Coffin genealogy, A.P. Burke, **Colonial Gentry**, aIII (London 1895, reprint 2 vols in 1, 1970), 699-700.

[10]Sabine I, 327. John's brother Sir Isaac, and two of his sons, John Townsend and Henry Edward, became admirals; his eldest, Guy Carleton, became a general, Burke, 699-700.

Johnson commanded the regiments of the Eastern Townships, while those of his sons who were not already serving abroad joined the militia. Of his eight offspring, five eventually attained the rank of field officers, while those who did not had died.

Among Montreal Loyalist soldiers who held key positions during the period 1812-15 were James Dunlop as major commandant of the volunteer artillery company which he raised. And as a shipbuilder and owner, he superintended construction of gun-boats at St. John's shipyards. Others were Capt. John Richardson and Lt. Hart Logan, the latter a son of a Loyalist, as was Capt. George Platt, who recruited and led a volunteer cavalry company. The vigour and forcefulness with which these men realized their plans had an important influence on local militia development in the middle years of the century. In particular, the cavalry company is now recognized by military historians to have been the nucleus from which the group of cavaliers sprang who formed the cavalry company during the 1837-38 Rebellion.[11]

With regard to the 1812 War, it is interesting to note that a heroic French-Canadian leader was posthumously related by marriage to a Loyalist family. Two sons of Jacob Glen (an ensign in the K.R.R.N.Y.), John and Jacob Jr., married respectively, Marie-Anne-Julie née Hertel de Rouville, widow of Col. Charles-Michel de Salaberry in 1840 and her daughter, Marie-Anne-Hermine de Salaberry in 1836 at Chambly.[12]

---

[11]Elinor K. Senior, "The Provincial Cavalry in Lower Canada, 1837-1850," **Canadian Historical Review**, vol. 57 (march 1976), 1-24.

[12]Thomas A. Ramsey, "La famille glen de Chambly," **Les Cahiers de la Seigneurie de Chambly**, IV, 17 (Feb. 1982) La Société d'histoire de la Seigneurie de Chambly, Chambly, Québec.

The regular army was important to Quebec in the late 18th and early 19th centuries for matters in addition to defence, such as the works of the Royal Engineers. Before the rise of civil engineers in Quebec, the military was responsible for planning and advising on the construction of numerous public works from the Anglican Cathedral in Quebec City to bridges and canals throughout the Province. Of the Loyalist contribution in this field, the most outstanding was that of Maj. Philip Durnford, R.E., who was active in many projects concerning the construction and repair of fortifications. After marrying Augusta Sewell, daughter of Stephen, the attorney general and niece of the chief justice,[13] Durnford settled in Quebec.

The Royal Engineers were later replaced by trained Canadians. During the middle and later years of the 19th century the surname Keefer was associated with major engineering works, whose roots can be traced to an Alsatian who settled near St. Catharines, Upper Canada and was among the promoters of the first Welland Canal. His descendants, Samuel and Thomas C. Keefer, took a keen interest in the construction of this work, and were later acknowledged for their designs and executions of Quebec canals and bridges.[14]

The military also maintained law and order until a regular police force was established in the mid-19th century. During this time Loyalists such as James Dunlop, Stephen De Lancey and John Richardson were among the magistrates who tried offenders. The role played by Loyalist descendants in the police

---

[13]Durnford family papers held by the heirs of the late Elliot Durnford of Mtl.

[14]The Keefer's engineering works were of major importance. For Samuel Keefer (1811-90) see **Dict. Can. Biog.,** XI. T.C. Keefer was engineer of the Montreal Water Works.

forces is somewhat obscure apart from that of the Starnes family.

Nathanial Starnes left a Loyalist refugee camp in the Montreal area to settle in the Gaspé[15] for a brief time before returning to Montreal where his son, Nathan, became a recognized silversmith. Nathan's son Henry became the tenth mayor of Montreal 1856-7, and served again in 1860 until his election to the Legislative Council.[16] As mayor, he was also first magistrate and commissioner of police. Another member of the family became a commissioner in the Royal Canadian Mounted Police, and in more recent years another, John Starnes, acted as chief of security for Prime Minister Pierre Elliot Trudeau.

Medicine

Loyalist doctors were less influential than the retired military surgeons. There were six or more refugee doctors in Quebec, the most prominent were Charles Blake and his German partner, Henry Loedel, both of whom left their regiments to settle in Quebec. Samuel Adams, John Connolly, Isaac Moseley, Josiah Pomeroy and George Smyth were all more notable for their activities as Loyalists than for their professional work. The war took its toll on them: Smyth (c.1789?) and Connolly suffered poor health on arrival, Adams retired to keep an inn, and Moseley became involved in projects to recoup his lost fortunes and went to England.[17] Only Pomeroy continued to practice in Quebec as a licensed

---

[15]Nathaniel Starnes was in the Montreal district in late 1783 (NAC: Haldimand Papers (henceforth HP), B166/144).

[16]J.D. Borthwick, **History and Biographical Gazetteer of Montreal to the Year 1892** (Montreal 1892), 63-64.

[17]Sabine, **Loyalists**, II, 109.

apothecary. Ådams and Connolly had served during the war as military leaders, Pomeroy as a medical officer. Smyth was appointed medical officer of the Loyal Rangers after his escape to Canada in 1781, which was actually a front for his regular function as deputy chief of the newly formed intelligence unit.[18]

In the history of medicine in Quebec, the Loyalists contributed primarily to the founding of medical institutions rather than producing doctors. However, a number of Loyalist descendants in the second half of the 19th century pursued medical careers of distinction in Montreal: Rev. John Bethune's line produced two doctors whose radical behaviour shocked their contemporaries. Bethune's grandson Dr. Norman Bethune (1822-92) was a founder and dissolver of the Trinity Medical School in Toronto.[19] Norman's grandson, Dr. H. Norman Bethune (1890-1939) became internationally famous.[20] Both displayed powers of invention, imagination and artistry and were rebellious wanderers. Both opposed the conservatism of the establishment, while, on the other hand, another Loyalist descendant practising gynecology at the Montreal General was of a very different sort. Dr. A. L. Lockhard was among the founders of the United Empire Loyalists' Association of Quebec in 1895.[21]

Law

In this domain, the Loyalists had an effect on the Province of Quebec. As the first, large, English-speaking group of

---

[18]Mary B. Fryer, **King's Men** (Toronto, 1980), 273-294.

[19]Roderick Stewart, **Bethune** (Toronto 1973), 194-196.

[20]**Ibid.**

[21]J. Cooper, **Men of Canada**, 1901-02, 120.

immigrants, they necessitated that the British government make considerable changes in the *status quo*. To accommodate the many refugees who had settled on the shores of the upper St. Lawrence River, the old Province of Quebec was divided into Upper and Lower Canada in 1791. In both the new provinces the Loyalists caused the system of land tenure to be changed, and the English legal system established.

These exiles from the once British American Colonies brought with them lawyers, William Smith, Isaac Ogden and William Dummer Powell, who were more competent in English legal matters than the average local magistrate. The blatant partiality and ignorance of the latter had become so scandalous that the new chief justice, William Smith, instigated a public enquiry into the practice of law shortly after his arrival in 1786, which he chaired.[22] As a result of this inquiry, new regulations were formulated to assure that, in the future, detailed court records would be kept of evidence presented in legal cases, which were the basis for the magistrates' decisions. One of the principal witnesses was Powell, who had already been in practice in Quebec for the better part of a decade. His extensive knowledge of the law, coupled with his familiarity with the French language, would have led him ultimately to a chief justiceship in Lower Canada had he not been promoted to the bench in 1788 and sent to Hesse District, near Detroit, where there were many French settlers. As it was, he rose to become chief justice in Upper Canada later.[23]

---

[22]L.F.S. Upton, **The Diary and Selected Papers of William Smith 1784-1793** (Toronto); Champlain Soc. 1965, II, 24 n.2.

[23]William R. Riddell, **William Dummer Powell**, Lansing, Michigan Hist. Commission, 1924.

Smith and Ogden both served on the bench in Montreal on the regular semi-annual occasions when superior proceedings were heard.[24] In his short period as chief justice for Quebec 1786-91, of Lower Canada 1791-93, Smith indulged in a flurry of activity in public affairs, an effort which probably hastened his death. In his earlier years he had made a notable contribution in New York to advocacy, politics, journalism and history.[25] Ogden, on the other hand, held a number of different appointments in various courts during his years in Canada, beginning in Quebec City and ending there some years later after being promoted from his post in the Montreal district. Of his children ,one son became a provincial attorney general, and another, sheriff of Three Rivers.[26]

In certain areas of 19th century Quebec, the name "Stuart" was synonymous with "lawyer." During this period that family alone produced 18 lawyers.[27] Indeed, during 67 years dating

---

[24]He was judge of the Court of King's Bench, Montreal 1796-1811, Macmillan Dict. Can. Biog., W.S. Wallace ed., and Pierre-G. Roy, Les Juges de la Province de Québec, 1933, 395.

[25]L.F.S. Upton, The Loyal Whig (Toronto 1969), bibliography of Smith's unpublished writings and unpublished manuscripts, 225-228.

[26]Isaac Gouverneur Ogden was sheriff of Three Rivers 1827-67, Mac. Dict. Can. Biog. His brother Charles Richard (1791-1866) became Solicitor General in 1824, Attorney General in 1833 for this Province. He m. 1st a daughter of Gen. John Coffin, m. 2nd a daughter of Isaac W. Clarke, Dict. Can. Biog., IX.

[27]P.G. Roy, Les avocats de la region de Québec (Lévis, Québec 1936) details nine of them. An article in L'Opinion Publicque Jan 10, 1879, spoke of "ce beau nom de Stuart, la gloire incontestée de notre barreau" (this fine name Stuart, the unmatched glory of our Bar), according to Pierre Bullac and E. Fabre Surveyer, Le Centenaire du Barreau de Montréal, 1849-1949 (Montreal 1949), 44, "Henry Stuart 1815-71."

from Smith's appointment, Loyalists and their descendants occupied the chief justiceship for over 50 years.[28]

Loyalist lawyers, trained in the English convention, were among the prime influences on those who wished to learn the profession. In 1798 Jonathan Sewell charged a fee of 100 guineas in Quebec for anyone intèrested in articling under his auspices.[29] Responsibility toward their students is evident through a student John Henry of Montreal, taken on by Sewell. In 1806 Sewell was appointed to another post which forced him to find another placement for the young man. Samuel Gale Jr., also a Loyalist's son, and later a judge,[30] accepted Henry into his practice.

An example of the leadership shown in contemporary affairs by Loyalists and their children is in the protracted lawsuit over James McGill's estate.[31] This was a *cause célèbre* of the second and third decades of the 19th century. McGill, a successful fur trader and public spirited citizen, was not strictly speaking an "American Loyalist." He was, however, an active member and leader of the local militia for nearly 40 years when he died in 1813. In his will he bequeathed his Burnside Estate and an endowment of £10,000 for the establishment of a college, to take place within 10 years of his death, failing which the

---

[28]These included: William Smith Sr. (1786-93), Jonathan Sewell (1808-38), Sir James Stuart (1841-71).

[29]Jonathan Sewell, Quebec to Stephen Sewell, Sept. 27, 1798 and same to same, Oct. 18, 1798, in A.E. Patrick Buchanan, **The Bench and the Bar of Lower Canada Down to 1850** (Montreal 1925), 145-148.

[30]Contract transferring from Stephen Sewell Esq. to Samuel Gale Jr., Esq. the articles of John Henry Esq. of Montreal, 1806, Archives Nationales de Québec, Montreal: the **Greffe** (Notarial records) of J.G. Beek.

[31]Stanley B. Frost, McGill University, I (Montreal 1980), 52-54.

estate would pass to his widow and her heirs. Among the executors of his will were James Dunlop and John Richardson, both Loyalists. Dunlop did not long survive McGill, dying in 1815, while Richardson lived until 1831, taking a strong interest and firm hand in executing his charge.

The will was contested by the Desrivières family, which McGill was connected to through his marriage with the widow Charlotte Trottier Desrivières, née Guillimin. Although a committee had been set up under the name of the Royal Institution for the Advancement of Learning to found the college, it did not act within the time frame specified in the will. The family was therefore correct in its argument that literally interpreted, the will's provisions had been ignored. On this technical point the Desrivières won but were, in turn, sued, and lost in four successive attempts to regain the estate. The final decision was rendered in 1828.

In the second attempt by the Desrivières to overturn the decision, Loyalists were representing both sides. Two judges, including the Hon. George Pyke, heard the suit,[32] while the attorney for the Committee was Stephen Sewell, son of the Boston Loyalist Jonathan Sewell, and brother of the chief justice of Lower Canada. For the Desrivières family, the principal attorney was James Stuart, son of Rev. John Stuart, a Loyalist from Williamstown. Prominent among the witnesses was John Richardson, executor of the will. The Desrivières had been advised to employ Stuart, as he had drawn up McGill's will and was therefore considered to be the best qualified to speak on its contents. Sewell, however, was able to turn this fact to the Committee's advantage. In his own arguments he dwelt upon the nature of McGill's original intention rather than on

---

[32]Ibid., 53.

technicalities. He praised Stuart's drafting of the document which demonstrated the testator's desire to found a college, thus proving the Committee's contention.

The judges agreed with Sewell and the Committee. The Royal Institution had been remiss in acting tardily, but this did not alter its responsibility or deny the validity of its object.

In Quebec, semi-feudal French law co-existed with the more advanced English system. A number of French-Canadians were trained in their own discipline, while English-speaking professionals were few until after the Revolution. Merchants in particular favoured the use of English law which was adapted to a post-feudal commercial state. Quebec proposed the office of *notaire* (notary public), a system based on Roman law that saw the notary responsible for all legal papers. The office was often combined with that of the advocate until the 1785 ordinance which permanently separated the two occupations. Later, merchants would protest that by increasing the professionals' knowledge of the law the new system increased their ability to manipulate clients and ultimately increase the number of legal actions and their income. The length of training also impeded many candidates, limiting the number of new professionals which produced a more exclusive and monopolistic brotherhood than before.

By 1812, out of 29 advocates (15 English) at least five were of Loyalist origin: Alexander Elliott, Samuel Gale, Jr., Charles Ogden, D. Ogden and Stephen Sewell. By 1837 the proportion had changed noticeably, with only a dozen English names out of a total of 71. On this later roll were at least two more Loyalists mentioned: Duncan Fisher and John Pickel.

Many members of this body of lawyers took a prominent part in community affairs, and in the establishment of their own professional associations. Not until the 1820s and 30s, however, did their own professional entity begin to be asserted and objectives realized. Raising and maintaining the standards of the occupation through adequate training of students, the provision of research facilities, and the creation of a regulating body occupied much of the attention of some well-known men. Initial efforts to create an association failed in the short run, but did result in the establishment of a Law Library in 1828, whose first board included Stephen Sewell.[33] At their instigation a new law on educational requirements for their profession was passed in 1836. With these goals achieved, they proceeded four years later to found the Bar Association of Montreal. It was not until 1849 that the Lower Canada Bar Association was finally formed at Quebec City, of which the president from the outset has taken the title *batonnier*, a 700-year old French title befitting the conservative nature of the profession.[34]

Education

The arrival of the Loyalists had a direct effect on the introduction of a public school system in Quebec as well as in other areas of Canada. They wanted their children to attend similar schools to those they had supported in the American Colonies. Nothing of the kind existed in Quebec, where the Catholic Church conducted schools for the training of an elite class of "petit bourgeous functionaries:" advocates, notaries, doctors and clerics. Loyalists played a strong role in building and supporting an educational system, while some individuals had already set up their own private schools. Two Loyalists in

---

[33] Atherton, **Montreal**, II, 421.

[34] The *batonniers* in the 19th century included Henry Stuart (1856-58), grandson of Rev. John Stuart, and Strachan Bethune (1859-60, 1862-62) son of Rev. John Bethune Jr.; Beullac and Surveyer, **Le Centenaire**, 17.

particular began to plan for advanced education here, William Smith and Isaac Ogden. Smith in fact drew up a complete plan for the structure and administration of a three-level system from primary school to university on a non-sectarian basis.[35]

One English school was in existence at the time the refugees arrived. John Pullman had been persuaded to come here from New York by Rev. John Ogilvie in 1773. With no organized public system instituted, he depended on the Governor and parents for support in founding his school, with a committee of local residents set up to aid and advise him. Later when a new Governor arrived, the committee supported his petition to Haldimand for continued economic help. Among the Loyalists who signed this 1779 petition were Isaac W. Clarke and John Porteus. Competition from Loyalist schoolmasters who arrived about this time soon proved too much for Pullman, who moved to St. Maurice Forges in 1782, where he was employed as a clerk.

The Loyalists not only brought large numbers of school-age children, but also several teachers. The more adequate in this field were the ministers Bethune, Gilmore and Stuart. The clergy, however, arrived a little later than the laymen John Adams, Josiah Cass, Finlay Fisher and John Grout, who had preceded them by some years. Adams and Cass served at Machiche in the refugee camp, while Grout was destined for Three Rivers, where his help had been solicited by the refugees. He might have made a good teacher, but tragic events overtook him. In Oct. 1780, while travelling by boat with a certain Mr. Greaves and an unidentified man, the two were robbed and murdered by the unknown traveller.[36]

---

[35]Upton, **Loyal Whig,** 193-197.
[36]Savine, **Loyalists,** I, 501-502.

The Scots in their homeland had an enviable school system which was esteemed above that of England's. Finlay Fisher, a Scottish immigrant, arrived in Canada with a number of relatives after Gen. Burgoyne's disastrous defeat in 1777.[37] He opened a school in Montreal shortly thereafter, which became most popular, allowing him to claim in 1790 of having 42 pupils.[38] He continued in education until his death several decades later. About the same time as Fisher opened his school, Mr. Christie opened his in Montreal, until the arrival of Rev. Stuart, who founded his own teaching establishment and invited Christie to collaborate with him. The latter agreed, but soon was found capable only of teaching the rudiments of reading and arithmetic, to Stuart's dismay, who was compelled to replace Christie by another more competent teacher.

Rev. John Stuart's Academy was an institution in which the classical subjects of that time were taught. Beyond the primary subjects available in ordinary schools, the proverbial three Rs, Stuart's Academy progressed to Latin, English grammar and mathematics. Children of a somewhat higher class were in attendance such as Capt. Justus Sherwood's children.[39]

---

[37]Haldimand to Stuart, Nov. 3, 1781 (NAC: HP, B159/65) granting permission for Stuart and Christie to set up the academy; Stuart to Haldiman, Dec. 17, **ibid.**, B158, 257.

[38]Memorial of 1790 lists of teachers in Montreal with the number of their pupils, Atherton, **Montreal**, II, 296, 347-348.

[39]Loyalist children were also in the French Catholic schools, e.g. from the prize lists 1773-1803 of the College de Saint Raphael as cited by Atherton, **Montreal**, II, 347-348.

More advanced learning was not available for many years,[40] thus William Smith's concern that a complete educational system be established, up to and including the junior college level. Unfortunately, he died in 1793, before any substantial move could be made in this direction. However others, including Loyalist Isaac Ogden, argued cogently for the creation of such an educational system. Ogden, in 1790, drafted a charter for a university,[41] his ideas were along similar lines as Smith's. Many citizens were aware of this effort including the wealthy fur trader and philanthropist, James McGill, who was thought to have been inspired by Rev. John Strachan's effort to found such a college. Strachan, however, only arrived from Britain in 1799, and it is more likely that he only enhanced McGill's objective.

Among those Loyalists' descendants who contributed to McGill's development was Rev. John Bethune Jr., first Anglican rector of Christ Church, Montreal, later chosen as an early principal of McGill (1835-45). His brother Alexander, who eventually became Bishop of Toronto, was a product of Rev. Strachan's rigorous Anglican training, as John was. As principal, John Jr. was embroiled in the religious feuding over which church, if any, should control the university, thus much of his time was filled with "bickering, frustration and debt."[42]

---

[40]Many Loyalist children were educateed abroad, e.g. the sons of William Smith and Jonathan Sewell. However, due to high costs, parents tended to bring their children back to Canada after grammar school and send them into a profession.

[41]Stanley B. Frost, "Mr. Isaac Ogden," McGilliana, (a leaflet) no.5, (March 1978), 2.

[42]Frost, McGill, I, 70.

Many descendants of Loyalists are noted for their efforts and support in the founding of various departments of McGill. The University's faculties were established in the following order: Medicine 1829, Arts 1843, Law 1853, Applied Science 1856 (actually a part of Arts until 1870), Comparative Medicine and Veterinary Science 1889. As the original medical school evolved out of a project of the Montreal General Hospital, the scientific departments grew out of the interests of several groups of researchers. One such body was the Natural History Society, founded in 1827 by five men, including Stephen Sewell and John Bethune. In the next generation the most brilliant was Sir William Logan, a British-trained geologist, and grandson of a Montreal Loyalist. He was an international leader in his discipline, and a fellow of the University, who with his brother endowed the Chair of Palaeontology and established the Logan gold medal.[43]

Another benefactor of the University was the daughter of Loyalist Samuel Gale Jr., who endowed a chair in the faculty of Law in memory of her father, a noted judge.

Most munificent of all 19th century contributions to education in Quebec were those of Sir William Macdonald, grandson of Capt. John of the 84th Regt. (8th Chief of the Clan Macdonald of Glenaladale) who founded a Scottish settlement on Prince Edward Island in 1772. William amassed a fortune in the tobacco industry and believed it could be best put to use in the advancement of learning. His gifts to McGill included Macdonald College, and the Macdonald Physics, Chemistry and Engineering buildings. Among several chairs of learning which he endowed was the Macdonald Chair of Physics, of which the

---

[43]Ibid., I; E.A. Collard, Oldes McGill (Toronto 1946), 97-105; Mac. Dict. Can. Biog.

first holder was Prof. Ernest (later Lord) Rutherford, whose research on atomic structure in Macdonald's physics laboratory, then the best in the western world, opened the door to the nuclear age.

Macdonald's tradition of philanthropy has been carried on in the later 20th century by his successors and spiritual heirs. It began with Walter Moncreif Stewart and his wife, May B. (née Sharp) through Macdonald Tobacco and continued on with the establishment of the Macdonald Steward Foundation by his son, David Macdonald Stewart, who not only supported historical projects financially, but took an active, personal role in the founding groups. When there was no existing organization suitable to carry on an urgent project, he was instrumental in forming a new one to fill the need. In this way, the Foundation has taken a positive and constructive role in rescuing and preserving our heritage, both here and abroad. These range from the formation of the Lake St. Louis Historical Society, the Society of the Montreal Military and Maritime Museum (now the David M. Stewart Museum), La Compagnie Franche de la Marine and the Decorative Arts Museum (Chateau Dufresne) to Les Amis de Jacques Cartier which has restored the explorer's farm house near St. Malo, France.

Crafts

During the Revolution the skills of craftsmen were of great value to the government in both military and civilian projects. Of prime importance was the defence of the Province, which required large and well-equipped armed forces mostly brought in from Europe. These thousands of soldiers had to be fed, clothed and housed, as well as transported. The same was true for the hundreds of refugee Loyalists, and the additional hundreds of their Provincial regiments. The massive problems presented the government by their requirements could be solved only by employing more-or-less skilled people to assist. Men from the building trades were put to work constructing barracks, houses, fortifications, boats and ships. Teamsters and cattle-handlers as well as blacksmiths and wheelwrights were essential companions to armies on the march. Tailors, shoemakers and even hatters could perform the tasks necessary to keep people clothed, although this was largely confined to repairs and adjustments.

Most of the repair or adaptation of equipment which did not require special tools was probably carried out by the common soldier. For him it was much the same as for a settler on virgin land, having to make do. The ability of one particular Loyalist to jump from one craft to another as required prompted one scholar to comment that he was "versatile as only pioneer can be."[44]

Often skilled craftsmen were brought over from Britain or Europe as in the case of Col. Gabriel Christie, who brought a group of artificers to Quebec in July 1776.[45] In the army there were platoons of "pioneers," semi-skilled blacksmiths, carpenters, leather-workers etc., who became known as artificers. Many Loyalists enlisted in or were transferred to artificer companies, while others, such as Elias Smith, active as a captain with the British forces, first in Boston, later in New York, was commissioned to take charge of such a group on

---

[44]Helmut Kalmann, **A History of Music in Canada 1534-1914** (Toronto 1960), 43, referring to Stephen Humbert, a Loyalist from New Jersey at St. John, N.B.

[45]List of Artificers 1776 (NAC: Francis Goring mss. MG24/D4/5-8).

various works of construction.[46] Aside from a core of men who had served apprenticeships in their crafts in civilian life, most were self-trained.

Of the Loyalists troops in Quebec, a great many needed thorough military training before they were on a par with the British and German units. Thus, except for those who were particularly resourceful as scouts and raiders, where they far excelled the European soldier, they were condemned to drill or work on government projects closer to the settlements, of which there was an abundance. Lt. John Twiss, an engineer, wrote on July 11, 1779, of the sawmills to be built, roads to be repaired, rivers to be bridged and bricks to be made.[47]

Gov. Haldimand ordered the formation of two artificer companies to carry out these projects. The men were recruited by Twiss and by Capt. Robert Leake from the King's Royal Regt. of New York, and from the Unincorporated Loyalists under Maj. McAlpin's command. In recruiting from this latter pool of manpower, they had forestalled the efforts of other officers who were looking for the same skills. Thus in the mid-1780s Capt. Hanyost Herkimer was unable to form another company.[48] In this case, the men were expected to function as a transport unit in the summer and as artificers in winter. Some were sent in 1781 to Fraser's Company at Yamaska to build a blockhouse and bateaux. Another blockhouse also built by Loyalists was on an

---

[46]Smith, Land Petition, 1797, Ernest A. Cruickshank, **Papers and Records,** Ont. Hist. Soc., XXVI (Toronto 1930), 325-326.

[47]Corresp. between Haldimand and Twiss (NAC: HP, B154 (Brit. Lib. Add. ms. 21.814); construction to be done Twiss to Haldimand, July 12, 1779, 189, (bricks of), 186.

[48]John E. Ruch, "Late 1780 in Quebec: Season of the Three Commanders," **Loyalist Gazette** (Toronto, Autumn 1981), 7-8.

island in Lake Champlain, which housed the Secret Service. The considerable numbers of men required for construction works are illustrated by Twiss' request on April 3, 1783, for 400 "fatique" men.[49] By May 2 he had received 150 men, taken mainly from Jessup's Loyal Rangers.

Numerous Loyalists served as artificers or craftsmen in the "King's works." There are a number of muster rolls for these companies, with some 18 names found on the old U.E.I. List. In the Losses Claims the individual Loyalist usually mentioned his wartime occupation. Qualified craftsmen were identified by their craft, as Richard Wragg Sr. was listed as master blacksmith at St. John and not as an artificer.[50] John Platt, another blacksmith, posed as a suttler at St. John while actually functioning occasionally as a secret service agent.

After the war the presence of so many Loyalist craftsmen was felt in the Province, they having a higher proportion of skilled workers than the French-Canadians.[51] Although many of the civilian Loyalists were already working at their trades and supporting themselves by 1783, the extraordinary conditions imposed by the circumstances of war scarcely allowed their contribution to be noticed at the time. Some were on subsistence lists, but the inspectors were ordered to be quick in removing the names of those who no longer were in need. Some inspectors were slow with the paperwork while others

---

[49]NAC: HP, B154 (Yamaska blockhouse), 325-328; two letters dated March 1, 1781; (Labourers) and May 2, 381-,387-, resp.

[50]Old United Empire Loyalists List (Toronto: United Empire Loyalists' Assoc. 1884, many reprints).

[51]Fernand Ouellet, Lower Canada 1791-1840 (Toronto 1980), 9, notes that the number of Loyalist craftsmen was disproportionately high for an agricultural colony.

were always clear whether or not a craftsman was rightfully on the list.

There are indications that between 25 per cent and 50 per cent of Loyalist craftsmen moved from the Montreal area after 1783, many settling on new lands on the upper St. Lawrence, later known as Upper Canada (Ontario). Others, who in some cases had to wait years before obtaining land grants south of the river, moved to pioneer settlements between Montreal and the U.S. border. Of those who made Montreal their permanent residence, many had occupations which were useful in a "civilized" setting. While carpenters, blacksmiths and masons were in demand at developing settlements, painters, paper-stainers and potters found the most encouragement in older communities.[52]

The most common occupations given were farming and labourer. Those with other occupations numbered just over 190, representing about 30 trades and professions. The latter, over a dozen in number, included justices of the peace and two sheriffs. Of men trained in trades, we find 40 each of carpenters and shoemakers, about 30 each of blacksmiths and tailors, 14 weavers, 9 each of coopers and butchers and 7 bakers. There were 9 merchants, 5 innkeepers and a few who possessed miscellaneous skills.

Few of these craftsmen outside the armed forces or government employ were able to exercise their skills immediately on arrival. Many destitute had lost their tools and materials to the enemy, which was the basis of many of their claims for compensation after the war. Pastorius lost his

---

[52]NAC: HP, B155 (painters), Daniel Smith 149, Francis Waggoner 145; (paper stainer) surname Lieson, 148v; (potters), Lt. Samuel Humberstone, 147v. John Clucke (Kluck), 148v.

saddler's tools and his leather tanning materials, which were confiscated in 1778 at Germantown.[53] Platt's smithy was another casualty at Saratoga in 1777 of the war.[54] Other more fortunate saved their equipment from the enemy, and were able to bring it with them to Quebec. Elias Smith, described as a master carpenter, and his partner Moses Sherwood, a mariner, brought about 36 people with them in their sailing vessel *Industry* from New York City in August 1783.[55] Among the passengers were a carpenter, Andrew Abrahams, and a tailor, Cornelius Ryan. Another ship brought a mixture of people including "several Europeans that cannot be called refugees, some of whom trade," who wanted to pursue their endeavours at Quebec City. [56] Of the Loyalists, some remained in Quebec City while others chose Sorel or Montreal and thus were listed on the "Great Roll."

Officers and official Loyalists were placed where they could be most useful, consequently merchants or shopkeepers were often employed in the quartermaster or Commissary departments as were former merchants Isaac and Jonathan Clarke, who were made assistant commissaries. Gershom French, another merchant, became a jack-of-all-trades concerned with the welfare of the Loyalists at Sorel and was sent on one occasion to make a preliminary survey of lands for settlement in the Ottawa and Rideau River valleys. On the other hand, Samuel Gale, a surveyor, served as paymaster to troops in New York and Florida.

---

[53]Inventory of Pastorius' Estate, **Pennsylvania Archives**, 6th Ser., XII, 363-365.

[54]**Losses Claim**, June 22, 1787 (NAC: A.O. 12/26/157-165).

[55]Busby was a veteran soldier and the former barrack master, **Dict. Can. Biog.** IV, was allied to the Loyalist Wragg family.

[56]John Franks, a Jewish Freemason, **Gazette** (Montreal June 5, 1778).

Craft Training

Before the opening of specialized schools for the professions, training was given on the job through the traditional apprenticeship system. Lawyers accepted youths who had received an academic education as articled clerks, while physicians and craftsmen hired boys of 12 or 13 years of age as apprentices. The clerks were indentured for five years, the apprentices for seven or eight. A child often followed a parent's craft, as in the Platt and Wragg families. Trades with the greatest prospects for profit and employment were much sought after, allowing the masters of these crafts to charge the highest fees. Women took girls as apprentices, particularly in the millinery and dressmaking businesses, as did Amelia Perry, a milliner, who took on Mary Dies and Jane Mittelberger for four years each, in 1789 and 1794 respectively.[57] French-Canadian families took advantage of the numerous Loyalist craftsmen to have their children trained by them. John and Richard Wragg, for example, accepted Baptiste Rivert in 1794, who was joined by the Wragg's nephews Richard and John Gr(e)aves the next year.[58] These teenagers were expected to do a man's work as Wolfred Nelson shortly attested to when shortly after being apprenticed to a military surgeon, Nelson was treating wounded soldiers during the 1812 war.[59]

---

[57]Atherton, **Montreal**, III, 54-58 on Gale; Alfred Sandham, **Ville Marie** (Montreal 1870).

[58]George Platt, Richard Jr. and John Wragg all followed their fathers' craft.

[59]ANQM: Greffe (Notarial Records) of J.G. Beek.

Teachers, Merchants and Innkeepers

There is an extensive compilation of late 1783 which contains names of refugees. For convenience we refer to it as the Great Roll.[60] It is a list of civilian to which have been added muster rolls for some units of the King's (Rogers) Rangers, the 1st K.R.R.N.Y. and the Loyal (Jessup's) Rangers. A fair impression of the number and character of the Loyalists in the province at that time can be obtained by analysis of this Roll.

Not all merchants were in need of government assistance on reaching Canada. In late 1783 there were eight merchants and three traders on the Great Roll with a number already engaged in business here whose names are only found in records such as applications for land petitions. The Clarke brothers were employed in the Commissary as early as 1776 while others had formed their own companies with or without partners. James Dunlop, on having been exiled from Virginia, transferred his activities to Quebec in 1777 and built a large trading company over the next 40 years. Robert Ellice arrived from New York shortly after Dunlop and continued his connection with the various partnerships which evolved out of the Phyn & Ellis firm.[61] John Richardson, who had served on a privateer, stayed on in New York City for some years after the Revolution, arriving in Canada about a decade after the other two, when he became a partner of Forsyth, Richardson & Co. until 1831.[62]

Merchants who needed government protection rather than immediate contracts in 1783 were placed on subsistence lists.

---

[60]See n. 64.

[61]Dict. Can. Biog., IV.

[62]Newton Bosworth, **Hochelaga Depicta** (Montreal 1839); Merrill Denison, "The Phyn-Ellice Story," **Canada's First Bank,** I (Montreal 1966), 431-442.

Names more familiar later in Upper Canada were those of Richard Cartwright (listed as an innkeeper), and Patrick McNiff, who was engaged in survey work.[63] Gershom French and Alexander Hall were among those who remained in or around Montreal.[64] Elias Smith, described as a master carpenter on his embarkation list, was actually in business with his eldest son David, who remained behind in New York to manage the firm.[65] Elias set up shop in Montreal, along with many other merchants, on St. Paul Street. That his real occupation was not stated on the Great Roll shows that the compilers were not exhaustive in their enquiries, a fact that suggests that other Loyalists' real professions were overlooked as well.

In the late 18th century the fur trade was still the great magnet for the young and adventurous immigrants. As the principal source of Canada's wealth it dominated commercial activity, attracting many Loyalists' children into its service through the North West Company. Two of the most famous are certainly Sir Alexander Mackenzie and Simon Fraser, after whom a mighty western river was named. Fraser eventually retired to Upper Canada, while Mackenzie left for Great Britain after a lengthy association with Montreal. They were both the sons of soldiers who died as Loyalists in military service during the Revolution. Two others, Peter Skene Ogden, the son of a judge, and John Clarke, the son of an interpreter in the Indian Dept., entered the fur trade and had remarkable careers with the Hudson Bay Company. Ogden spent many years exploring uncharted country, as had Fraser and Mackenzie, and similarly

---

[63]NAC: HP, B166/143-170 (separately numbered as 1-55).
[64]McNiff, ibid., 152.
[65]Hall, ibid., 152.

wrote lengthy accounts of his travels.[66] Ogden's association with the legendary John Jacob Astor was recorded by Washington Irving in his book *Astoria*.[67]

Many merchants and traders were already active in Canada prior to the Revolution, whether they should qualify as United Empire Loyalists is a debatable point to be decided in each individual case by the man's own record. Many, like Benaiah Gibb and Peter Pangman, as well as Jacob Schieffelin, who fought both at St. John, Quebec and at Detroit[68] married Loyalist women, thus their children would be considered of Loyalist descent in virtue of their maternal roots.

In textiles, the leader in Montreal was Benaiah Gibb, a pre-war immigrant from England, who established a merchant/tailor shop which was regarded for over a century as the most respected in Canada.[69] The majority of Loyalist tailors, however, found it difficult to compete in this specialised area of the market, but were quite able to supply serviceable clothing. Richard Mandeville, William McCormack and Michael McMullen were, according the the Great Roll, leather-breech makers, while the solitary hatter was Michael Dedrick.[70] In

---

[66]Smith, **ibid.**, 144v.

[67]P.S> Ogden (1784-1854) after whom Ogden, Utah was nambed, **Dict. Amer. Biog., Mac. Dict. Can. Biog.**

[68]Mac. Dict. Can. Biog.; Adele Clarke, **Old Montreal: John Clarke: His Adventures, Friends and Family** (Montreal 1906).

[69]On Gibb's firm see Lorenzo Prince, C. Gordonsmith et al. **Montreal Old and New (Montreal 1914**, 88, 312.

[70]Dr. Blake's Accounts show one Mandeville at the Quebec Suburb and another at Sault-aux-Recollets, ANQM: Beek's Greefe; NAC: HP, B166/159 (Mandeville), 159 (McMullen), 158 (McCormack).

addition, there were 25 other Loyalist tailors and 40 shoemakers listed, substantially enhancing their craft in Canada.

The presence of thousands of soldiers in the Montreal area during the war assured that certain occupations would be in demand, particularly the vendors of alcoholic spirits. In 1779, 167 persons were licensed to sell liquor in this district, of whom 57 had non-French names.[71] They were mainly Scottish or English surnames, a number of Loyalists were among them, including Samuel Adams. A farmer from Vermont, Adams had volunteered in Burgoyne's army in 1777, and after the defeat withdrew to Canada, where he became an innkeeper and was eventually struck off the subsistence list once he was self-supporting. In Montreal, there were 27 licencees, compared to between one and three in each of its surrounding settlements.

It is likely that there were also a number of sellers who did not obtain a licence, but for some who were prosecuted we have little information about them.

It was well known by the governors that the lot of most Loyalists was particularly hard, and they thus treated them more lightly than the usual offenders. Haldimand advised officers to permit Falkner to sell drink at an outpost, but was very annoyed when there were complaints later that the man had sold some to Indians.[72] People found guilty of selling without a licence were fined £10. Gov. Dorchester's policy was to relinquish the Crown's share or "moiety" which thus reduced the Loyalist's fine to £4.8.11d. Refugees who were charged and found guilty included: Thomas Waywood in 1780,

---

[71]Dedrick, NAC: HP, B166/149.

[72]Complaints against Faulkner from Father Denault at Cedars referred to Capt. Maurer, May 3, 1781, and from Isaac Mann to Robert Mathews, May 7, 1781 in NAC: HP, B188, resp. 137-, and 156-157.

Adams in 1781, Hermanus Flaak and Andrew Waggoner in 1786-7.

Alcoholic beverages were cheap and plentiful. Public demand made the sellers' trade an attractive one to the refugees who may have been unable or unwilling to re-establish themselves in their former occupations. Local magistrates granted licences in towns and suburbs while in the countryside an applicant had to be approved by the parish priest. It was believed by the magistrates that the priests were prejudicial to the "many old subjects, Protestants who gain a decent living by means of keeping public houses." Justices of the peace in a report of 1787 advised that the recommendation of a Quarter Sessions court should be sufficient to permit the issuence of licences and also suggested that the number of licences be increased on the basis that the population had increased while the number of licences had not.

Dorchester was very much concerned with the problems caused by the importation, manufacture and sale of alcohol. Several inquiries were held during his term of office 1786-96, during which time large quantities of molasses was imported from the West Indies and locally distilled into rum. One committee suggested that 200,000 gallons per annum were being produced in Quebec's four commercial distilleries (three in Quebec City, one in Montreal[73]) although their potential was 420,000 gals. per year if sufficient molasses could be obtained.

Finally, some legislation was needed to regulate this industry, that included a number of family stills in operation in various places.[74] An enquiry was held into the production and sale of the liquor from Montreal and western districts. By

---

[73]Report, vol. 1347, **ibid.,** vol. 34, 11088-11093.

[74]Order for enquiry (draft), **ibid.,** vol. 40, 13004.

August 1788 the government agent, Mr. Valentine, had seized a family still belonging to Patrick Chambers of Oswego.[75]

Among the Loyalists on the Great Roll only one, James Plant from New York, was identified as a distiller. John Wait, who arrived with his family and friends from the Mohawk Valley a year or so earlier, was hired by Loyd & Molson late in 1782 as a maltster and brewer, but this occupation was not noted on the subsistence roles.[76] The brewing industry was introduced in Quebec during the French regime, but despite all efforts to promote it, it never flourished due to a preference for more refined spirits such as wine. Those with British and Germanic backgrounds were regular consumers of ale and beer, and wanted the brewers to succeed. Officials like Sir John Johnson saw in beer a cheap spirit, which could be easily made available in large quantities, while offering a healthy alternative to the stronger liquors.[77] The pernicious effects of intemperance among their charges, not the least of whom were the Indians, had long been observed and deplored. John Molson bought Loyd's share of the brewery before long, and while Wait died soon after, the business prospered.

Leisure Occupations: Formal and Informal

From refined entertainments of the arts to the more common level of dancing, drinking, gaming and feasting, Loyalists patronized and participated in all such local gatherings. As fur traders, some were members of the legendary

---

[75]Registration, Chambers' Memorial, Aug. 9, 1788 (NAC: RG4/A3/II/314).

[76]Merrill Denison, The Barley and the Stream (Toronto 1959), 27, 30; Shirley E. Woods Jr. The Molson Saga (Toronto 1983), 11, 14; HP: B166/134v.

[77]Denison, The Barley and the Stream, 45; Woods, Saga, 21.

Beaver Club. Troops from the east end barracks gathered at Thomas Busby's Tavern just outside their gateway. Several miles farther west the Scots were drawn to John Grant's Inn at Lachine, a rendezvous for immigrants and travellers to the upper country, as well as a clearing house for their mail. In Montreal were a number of hotels and coffee houses, and numerous taverns. Merchants in particular tended to frequent the same few places, such as the Montreal (Dillon's) Hotel, the old Coffee House and the Exchange Coffee House, where apart from socializing they learned the latest news and gossip. Other groups formed, inspired by religion or heritage to carry out philanthropic works. Such was the Female Benevolent Society, founded in the 1810s, preceding all others by two decades.

Another group established in 1760 that sometimes met in John Frank's Tavern in the 1780s was the Order of Freemasons,[78] that permeated the English-speaking population regardless of class or rank.

Both the military and Loyalists helped in the development of the Freemasons in Quebec. Benevolent and fraternal, it was based on ritual and terminology fashioned after the mediaeval craft guild of the stonemasons, in which Judaeo-Christian religious symbolism was omnipresent. The objectives of the old guilds were roughly equivalent to those of today's trade unions and industrial security agencies combined. By the late 18th century the Freemasonry had expanded the scope of their ideas. Current philosophic attitudes toward universal brotherhood, humanitarianism, science, political and social reform were voiced in the privacy of their meetings under the protection of an oath of secrecy which permitted even the most radical

---

[78]A.J.B. Milborne, **Freemasonry in the Province of Quebec 1759-1959** (privately printed 1960).

notions to be heard and discussed without fear of public castigation, thus attracting intellectuals. Artists in particular were drawn toward the Craft, including Beethoven, Haydn and Mozart. In addition were the poets Burns and Coleridge.

Participating in the philosophical enlightenment of the time, Freemasonry incurred the wrath of the Roman Catholic Church, which abhorred the Society's oath of secrecy, and was enraged that the Order's national patrons were members of Protestant Royal families. Secrecy within the brotherhood ran counter to the Church's cherished ambition to dominate through the institution of the confessional. Thus from the Roman Catholic point of view, Freemasonry was obstructive and subversive, attitudes which were shared by some Protestant church leaders.

The dominant position of the Roman Catholic Church in Quebec did not prevent Freemasonry from being introduced in New France by French Protestants or Huguenots, nor from flourishing after the Conquest.[79] Among the men of the British armed forces, many were members. Meetings were first organized shortly after the capture of Quebec City, followed by another lodge or chapter formed by the merchants.[80] Other lodges sprung up in towns and settlements, including Montreal. Most members were British or English-speaking, but others of different races and religions were accepted on complying with the standard requirement. Among the Jewish

---

[79]Pemberton Smith, **Research into Early Canadian Masonry**, Montreal.

[80]Milborne, table p.42, Quebec City 1759, Montreal (military) 1760, (St. Paul's) 1770; Detroit 1772, Niagara 1780, Cataraqui (Kingston) and Sorel 1781; of these St. Paul's survives as the oldest existing Masonic Lodge in the Province of Quebec, 24.

members were John Franks and Meyer Solomon,[81] while honourary members included the German officers Gen. Riedesel, Brig. Speht and Lt. Graefe.[82]

During the American Revolution the membership is said to have dwindled until the arrival of the Loyalists, who not only repaired the losses, but brought with them one of its most noteworthy leaders, Sir John Johnson, whose father was a Provincial Grand Master of what is today the State of New York in 1771-81.[83] On his arrival in Montreal Sir John joined a lodge, eventually becoming Provincial Grand Master of the Grand Lodge of Quebec (Moderns) in 1788.[84] The international scope of the brotherhood is illustrated by the fact that certain adjacent areas of the United States fell within his province, which saw him grant a warrant for the formation of Dorchester Lodge at Vergennes, Vermont in 1791.[85]

A complete roll of Loyalist Freemasons would be very long if it could be compiled. The late A.J.B.Milborne collected many names which he recorded in his various manuscripts and publications of: Joseph Chew, William Coffin, Alexander Cruckshank, Rev. John Doty, Alexander Ellice, Sampson Fleming, Capt. Normand McLeod, Robert Picken, Henry and Philip Ruiter, Jacob Schiefflin and Joel Stone, most of whom had some connection with Montreal.[86]

---

[81]J. Hamilton Graham, **Outlines of Freemasonry in the Province of Quebec**, 1892, 59.

[82]Milborne, 93.

[83]Ibid., 38-40.

[84]Ibid., 38.

[85]Ibid., 40.

[86]Milborne's manuscripts, NAC: MG23/H II ser., ; Milborne's **Loyalist Masons** (typescript) 1974, NAC: MG 24/L 15/705.

Our knowledge of their contemporary activity is largely confined to scattered records and newspaper announcements; attendance at meetings, public functions and names of elected officers. Loyalists generally adhered to the Modern rite, which was popular in the colonies, while British immigrants, particularly the Irish and Scots, adhered to the Ancient rite. Inasmuch as the rebel Americans rejected their principal authority and patron, the British monarch, the Modern was therefore in the opinion of the Ancients unpatriotic. In the contest for supremacy the Ancients prevailed, outweighing the Loyalists' preference resulting in the disappearance in Quebec of the Modern sect, of which Sir John was the last P.C.M.[87]

The officers of various lodges were often functionaries on public occasions, the supposed origin of the Masons causing them to be invited to lay numerous foundation stones, for which the tools of their rituals were well suited. Two such events concerned the Montreal General Hospital — the inauguration of the new hospital in 1821 at which Sir John was the principal figure,[88] and at the laying of the foundation stone of the Hospital's Richardson Wing in 1831.[89] Montreal artist Adam Sheriff-Scott was commissioned to paint two murals for the Masonic Hall on Sherbrooke St. in Montreal, illustrating the history of Freemasonry in the city.[90]

As Montreal's population increased in the early 19th century, it fast overshadowed Quebec City. Its English-speaking citizens were also increasing in proportion to the Canadien representing 61 per cent of the heads of families in the city by

[87]Milborne, **Freemasonry**, 41.

[88]Bosworth, **Hochelaga.**

[89]Milborne, **Freemasonry**, 79.

[90]Funeral of Johnson, 79; Laying Cornerstone, 80.

1841.[91] Unstable economic conditions during this period produced friction between these two linguistic groups where little or none had existed earlier.[92] The resultant insular behaviour among the Canadien resulted in a similar attitude on the part of smaller ethnic groups. It precipitated the formation of a number of nationalistic societies of which common objectives were to be protective of and benevolent toward fellow members of the respective group.

The societies crystallized around the nuclei of people who for years had annually celebrated the feast days of their national patron saints. The French had long celebrated St. Jean Baptiste Day, while the Scots St. Andrew's, the Irish St. Patrick's the English St. George's and the Welsh St. David's. On such occasions of celebration nationalistic sentiments were high pitched. Consequently it was on June 24, 1834, during a St. Jean Baptiste Day banquet at John McDonell's on St. Antoine St., Montreal, that the St. Jean Baptiste Society was founded,[93] McDonell serving as a member of the first executive.

The political situation in the Province at this time was critical, and minority groups began to think defensively. Four other Societies rapidly formed, which were the St. Andrew's, St. Patrick's, St. George's and the German Benevolent.[94] Among the first officers of the St. George's Soc. were John Platt Jr., John

---

[91]Ouelet, **Lower Canada,** 162.

[92]Ibid., 173.

[93]Atherton, **Montreal,** II, 370-373. On McDonell, son of artillery officer Lt. Agnus, see **Dict. Can. Biog.,** IX. He originally studied law under James Sutart in Montreal and as a conservative professional joined the moderate faction of the Society when it divided from the radicals in 1836. His wife was Elizabeth Pickell, daughter of John, a member of the legislature.

[94]Ibid., II, chap. XXX, 369-396.

Jones and Thomas B. Wragg and its presidents included Hon. William Badgley, W. F. Coffin, John and Dr. T. W. Jones.[95] The St. Andrew Soc. was very popular with a membership of nearly 300 in its first season,[96] among whom were sons or grandsons of Loyalists. At a meeting on March 9, 1835, after several preparatory discussions, the Society's first officers were elected on the premises of John Fisher, St. Paul Street.

The Irish were able for a period of a generation to contain the differences between Catholic and Protestant compatriots, but in 1856 a division became necessary, which saw the St. Patrick's Soc. become a Catholic organization which the Irish Protestant Benevolent Association was founded.[97]

The Welsh did not organize into an incorporated body until 1884-5 when the St. David's Welsh Society was established.[98]

The fifth such society to be founded, chronologically, was that of the Germanic people,[99] as a considerable number of American Loyalists were of Germanic descent. The first two presidents were from families which settled in this province at the time of the Revolution, or before. The founding father, Louis Gugy, 1835-9, was a nephew of Haldimand's friend, who housed the first group of Loyalists on his seigniory at (Ya)Machiche.[100] Further, there were numerous descendants of soldiers from the German regiments (Hessians) who had remained in this district following the Revolution. The second

---

[95]Ibid., 373-376.
[96]Ibid., 376-381.
[97]Ibid., 381-385, (Protestants), 385-386.
[98]Ibid., 387-388.
[99]Ibid., 386-387.
[100]Dict. Can. Biog., IV.

to serve as President in 1839-49 was Dr. Daniel Arnoldi of a well established Montreal family.

These nationalistic benevolent societies eased the burden previously carried by religious and other groups. Many churches promoted a sense of social responsibility among its better-off classes toward the impoverished such as the Calvinists and Presbyterians, but not all were as active as the Methodists, Quakers and Mennonites in assisting. Now the "societies of saints" concentrated on the relief of destitute immigrants, fellow countrymen.

While these associations formed as a result of political and economic influences, professional and earned societies began to be established in the 1820s to affirm their needs. In 1827 the first learned organization, the Natural History Society, was founded by, among others, Dr. Stephen Sewell and Rev. John Bethune.[101] The next year the Law Library was established, followed by the formation of the Bar Association. Self-improvement was fostered among the working class with the founding of the Mechanic's Institute in 1828, the promoters of which included many names familiar with the period.[102] Those who established the Montreal Medico-Chirurgical Soc. in 1843 reflected Loyalist surnames: Hall, Mount and Sewell.[103]

In addition to the formal associations whose purpose was of a serious nature, there were others whose aims were of a purely social or sporting nature. The Montreal Hunt Club emerged ca.1826 and was composed mostly of young army officers, and

---

[101]Atherton, **Montreal,** II, 352-353.
[102]**Ibid.,** 353.
[103]**Ibid.,** 452-453.

was supported by the Forsyth family for many years.[104] Typically, a Canadian method of transportation, snowshoeing, developed into a sport with the Snow Shoe Club founded in 1840. Among its executive members were Alexander Fisher and P. W. Dease.[105] The Scots introduced their favourite winter game which saw the advent of the Thistle Curling Club in 1843 with Rev. John Bethune listed on its membership roll.[106]

---

[104]John Irwin Cooper, **History of the Montreal Hunt** (Montreal 1953). The 3rd master of the Club was Col. Thomas Walker Jones, M.D., grandson of the first English child born in Montreal after the conquest.

[105]Hugh W. Becket, **The Montreal Snowshoe Club** (Montreal 1882).

[106]**The Montreal Thistle Curling Club, 1843-1943.** In 1844, this group joined with the Royal Caledonia Curling Club of which Alexander Cassels became secretary.

CHAPTER 10

The Loyalists and the Arts in Montreal

by John Ruch

Until recently, little attention has been given to the Loyalists' contribution to the development of art in the Province. Reasons for this include: early integration with other English-speaking immigrants who arrived directly from Britain who were all labelled "English" or, if a southern connection was established, they were simply referred to as "American" without discrimination.

Unlike those Loyalists who settled the areas which later became New Brunswick and Ontario, those entering Quebec found themselves in a long-established colony with a foreign culture. Once their basic needs were attended to, the Loyalists in Quebec adapted to their new Province and began to prosper.

The Fine Arts

The few artists among the Loyalists were from the old towns on the American eastern seaboard. Two of the most prominent were in Europe at the outbreak of the Revolution, where they remained: West and Copley.[1] Initially, Quebec did not attract

---

[1]The Pennsylvania Quaker Benjamin West (1738-1820) settled in London in 1763, becoming painter to George III and President of the Royal Academy. He was the first American artist to gain an international reputation. His best know

the refined Loyalist artist, owing to a population composed mostly of illiterate farmers and frontiersmen, whose needs depended on the more practical crafts. The difficulty of earning a living in this field, therefore, was a deterrent to many.

Fine art was more popular in Canada than sculpture. Many landscapes of the late 1700s and early 1800s were painted by military personnel, a number of whom were Royal Engineers, trained in topographical drawing. Among these scenes were Loyalist settlements, subject of Lt. James Peachey, a surveyor, who also drew a panoramic view of Montreal in October 1784.[2] Another military artist, at the request of Gov. Haldimand, was commissioned to paint Niagara Falls, just as the Governor's

---

work is the **Death of Wolfe** (Nat. Gallery, Ottawa); others include **The American Loyalists, Representing their Gratitude to Britannia,** and the portrait of the Losses Claims Commissioner John Eardley-Wilmot (Paul Mellon Collection). Gilbert Stuart (1755-1828) famous for his portraits of George Washington, was a student of West from 1775 for several years, returning to America in 1792. In portraiture, Stuart excelled his master as did the third American, John Singleton Copley (1738-1815), a protégé of West and Sir Joshua Reynolds. Copley's special talent for certain styles of portraiture led to his success in the 1780s. He had many Loyalist connections in London, including Brook Watson, and his father-in-law, Richard Clarke, from Boston. Clarke's son was the noted jurist Lord Lyndurst, who hired as his secretary, his cousin, the only son of Isaac Winslow Clarke of Montreal. Copley's step-brother Peter Pelham is most notable in the case against Paul Revere, who was accused of plagiarizing Pelham's **Boston Massacre.** Both West and Copley remained in London.

[2]Peachey, **Dict. Can. Biog.,** IV. The original watercolour is in the British Museum.

contemporaries in Europe ordered "souvenir" paintings of Tivoli or the Roman ruins.[3]

Portraiture was very popular in Europe in the 18th century, but only those Loyalists who travelled abroad had the opportunity to be painted by a Reynolds, or a Gainsborough, if they could afford the luxury. Dazzling feats of bravura in paint were inspired by wars and their generals, while Loyalists, who had performed daring and dramatic exploits went largely unrecorded. About 400 paintings of Loyalists are known, representing approximately one in every 200 refugees.[4]

In Montreal it was quite common for the Loyalist to have posed for local artists, once a certain level of prosperity had been attained. Of the silhouettes, several are of the Sewell family, another of Ephraim Jones.[5] The cost of oil portraits was out of reach for most, who could just afford these profile portraits.

The attainment of affluence and status was often marked by the commissioning of a portrait, which usually occurred later in life, the majority of Loyalists depicted were of middle-age or elderly. A remarkable collection of pendants of John Platt's family through four generations survived intact into this century, but was dispersed shortly thereafter.[6] The earlier pairs,

---

[3]NAC: Haldimand Papers (henceforth HP), Vol. B.

[4]Information from Victor Suthern, Asst. Curator, War Museum, Ottawa.

[5]Silhouette of Ephraim Jones is in possession of a descendant. A reproduction was supplied by the late Grant Smart. Some of the Sewells are portrayed in Hector L. Duff, **Sewells in the New World,** Exeter, Eng., including one of the chief justice's grandson, Stephen Clarke Sewell.

[6]The Platt family paintings were among those ordered photographed in the 1900s by Adam Skaife, the negatives of which are in the Notman Archive, McCord Museum, Montreal.

John and his wife Ann (nee Wragg), their son George and his wife Elizabeth (nee Mittelberger) are especially impressive. The unknown artist caught his subject's characteristics in minute detail. It is believed that either Louis Dulongpré or his friend, William Berczy, or possibly both were the artists of these works, as both were in Montreal at the time.[7] John, the elder Platt, had gone from blacksmith to ironmonger and was serving on the committee overseeing the construction of the new Anglican church.[8] His son, George, was an effective militia officer, businessman, and a member of the legislature, whose wife, through her interest in literature, was a patron of the Theatre Royale.

The finest portraits of Montreal Loyalists were commissioned in Britain, representing subjects of various ages. The most impressive was that painted by Sir Thomas Lawrence, in romantic style, of a young Sir Alexander Mackenzie.[9] A number of others of the closely-related Claus and Johnson families are known to have survived, but their whereabouts are unknown. Those who sat were generally highly cultivated, and patronized a number of artists. With the possible exception of Chief Joseph Brant, Sir John Johnson was the most portrayed Canadian Loyalist during various stages of his life. Curiously, there does not seem to be an equivalent wartime portrait of him to match those of his brother-in-law and Joseph Brant by

---

[7]Berczy, in Montreal 1805-13, shared a dwelling with Dulongpré, who had arrived in 1792 and was active in the city until 1815.

[8]John E. Ruch, "Warm and Bold Hearts: The Montreal Platts," **Canadian Genealogist,** Agincourt, Ont., V, 1 (March 1983), 30-43.

[9]National Gallery of Canada, Ottawa.

Benjamin West.[10] Sir John had the advantage of wealth, and opportunity of frequent trips to Britain to pose for such works — including those done of himself and his wife in the 1790s.[11] Their daughter, Marianne, later wife of Gen. Bowes, was charmingly painted in the Regency period, depicting her as a vivacious and pretty young lady.[12] This work is in miniature, as are several others of the family. Other miniatures include three of the younger generation of the Claus family that are preserved in the N.A.C.[13]

Sculpture was an art form supported by few Montreal Loyalists, the most prominent pieces being the pre-Revolution head of George III, the Coade stone ornaments and the statue of Lord Nelson, all of which were imported from England. Except for a sculpture of Jonathan Sewell in Quebec City, no other work is known.[14]

Decorative wood sculpture in Quebec was a tradition. Trained local craftsmen were adept in interior adornment of stately buildings and churches, religious statues as well as ship figureheads and interiors. Indeed, wood panelling and

---

[10]**Johnson and Brant** by Benjamin West, Mellon Coll., National Gallery, Washington, D.C.

[11]Francis L. Abbott's **Sir John Johnson** is known through an engraving by Bortolozzi. Lady Johnson's was drawn by the French emigré artist C.BJ.F. de St.Menin. There is a life-size chalk drawing on pink paper from a private collection on loan to Fort Johnson, N.Y. The miniature engraving, in reverse, was published in 1797.

[12]A photo of the miniature is in the Notman Archives.

[13]One of the two young men is clearly not to be identified as Christian Daneil Claus, who would have been older at the time of this work.

[14]The marble was commissioned for the **Church** of which the chief justice had been patron.

architectural decoration for ships assumed nearly as much importance for joiners, carvers and native *menuisiers* as did work ashore. Shipping merchants such as Dunlop, Logan and Richardson liked their ships to be handsomely embellished, but were usually satisfied with competent woodwork. Dunlop went as far as hiring a nephew, an amateur sculptor, to "chop" a figurehead for one of his ships, although this was more of an economic move and a help to the boy.[15] The market for figurative sculpture, however, was not large, and Canadians such as François Baillargé easily dominated the craft.

Literature

The Loyalists' emigration to Quebec marked the period with a noticeable growth of interest in the written word. Indeed, most were literate and demanded books on all subjects, not being as fortunate as those who were able to bring their libraries, in whole or in part, with them.

Of those who managed to retain their collections, Chief Justice William Smith was a true bibliophile who treasured his books with an intensity that closely rivalled the love he held for his family. It is on record that a prime consideration affecting his choice of home in Quebec City was that the house should have a study large enough to contain his library.[16] For professionals, their libraries were an assortment of works helpful in their business. In the absence of public libraries the only resort to both the professional and student was his own bookcase.

---

[15]Scottish Record Office, Edimburgh: Dunlop Papers.

[16]L.F.S. Upton ed. **The Diaries of William Smith** (Toronto, Champlain Soc. 1969), II, 195.

Two important libraries in the Eastern Townships belonged to Loyalists Samuel Gale, a surveyor and public official, and Samuel Willard, a land agent and merchant. These collections were open to local children to satisfy their own "taste for reading" as well as to their parents who "felt the cultivation of their minds to be essential to their well-being in life."[17] Gale particularly had "a choice, valuable and, for those days, extensive assortment of books." Several leading citizens of Montreal, such as Col. Daniel Claus, had lost their possessions to the rebels, and were forced to restock their libraries with purchases made here and abroad.

The English-speaking community of Montreal recognized the need for a lending library, since the existing collections, outside of personal holdings, were institutional libraries, controlled by the Catholic Church. Gov. Haldimand became a patron for a new lending library in Quebec City in 1779-80.[18] Sixteen years later prominent Montrealers established a library fund, in a "typically British" fashion, by forming a joint-stock company for the new Montreal Library.[19] The money raised was invested to cover current expenses and the purchase of books described as being "a judicious selection of the best works recently published in England..."[20] Forty years later the Library

---

[17]C(atherine) M. Day, **Pioneers of the Eastern Townships** (Montreal 1863, reprint 1973), 133.

[18]Jean McIlwraith, **Sir Frederick Haldimand** (Toronto 1906), 190-191, based on Haldimand's letter to Gen. Budé, March 1, 1779.

[19]William Atherton, Montreal (Montreal 1914), II, 350, based partly on Bosworth, see below. Information from Yvan Lamode, McGill University, and Edward C. Moodey, Fraser-Hickson Library, London, Eng., 1977, 15-62.

[20]Newton Bosworth, **Hochelaga Depicta** (Montreal 1839), 172.

had grown to 8,000 volumes, 25 per cent of which were in the French language.

The Library moved several times, not having a building of its own, until its relocating in the Fraser-Hickson Library. Today Montrealers can enjoy a literary legacy from the old Library, the founders of which included a number of Loyalists.[21]

The conventional preferences of the Loyalists can be gauged from a few contemporary references, such as in newspapers. Classics of 17th and 18th century English literature were held in high regard, including works of a historical, philosophic and religious nature, and current popular poetry and fiction. James Dunlop, for example, brought many of his books from his brother, Alexander, a bookseller in Glasgow.[22] Occasionally he referred to titles in his letters: Addison and Steele's *Spectator*, Bibles and Prayer Books, "but no psalms please."[23] Local newspapers, such as the Montreal and Quebec *Gazettes*, included a "poet's Corner," that ran conventional verses such as "The Fate of Gaming,"[24] to the latest poems of Robert Burns.[25]

Prior to 1775, specialized booksellers did not exist in Montreal, which was a void hard felt by the Loyalist reading public on their arrival. Biographies, histories and fiction, while generally available in the Old World, were luxuries here, with most scholarly material having to be imported.

Educated Loyalists took books very seriously, mourning the destruction of their libraries, "the greatest loss was a box of two

---

[21]Atherton, II, 350-351.

[22]**Dunlop Papers,** letter no. 1, June 29, 1773.

[23]**Ibid.,** 1,9, Oct. 25, 1798; 1,11, Dec., 16, 1798.

[24]**Gazette,** Quebec, July 8, 1789.

[25]Atherton, II, 124.

books...to a young family this loss was irreparable," wrote Amelia (nee Ryerse) Harris.[26] Her family managed to save four volumes when their log house burned in 1804: some works by Pope, poetry by Milton, a medical book and a New Testament. Susan (nee Burnham) Greeley recorded of the "few very good ones" her family had saved, "we studied (them) over and over (until) thoroughly acquainted with the information they contain, and can never forget it."[27] She compared their lot to the Scottish peasants as Sir Walter Scott had observed them: they had a few good books, and they knew them well. Indeed, some Loyalists carried books with them wherever they went, such as Richard Cartwright Jr., when fleeing from his home in Albany, N.Y. had a book of poetry in his pocket. During a two-day rest at Fort St. John, Quebec, Cartwright found the book an agreeable companion, or, as he referred to it, "those friends of all hours, the Muses."[28]

What few Loyalists who could be deemed "authors" were actually amateurs who wrote purely for their own enjoyment, and on occasion, for the pleasure of their peers. There were also the "pamphleteers" or polemicists, who were preoccupied with examining current ideals and events for public entertainment, through day-to-day publications.

Among these writers was William Smith, who produced a voluminous *oeuvre* for which, in part, he might be called the undisputed author for his moment and place in history. Much of his work consists of unpublished committee reports, one of which is contained in 13 volumes, while his diaries and some other writings have been published, including a *History of New*

---

[26]J.J. Talman ed. **Loyalist Narratives**, (Toronto, Champlain Soc., 1946), 135.
[27]Ibid., 78.
[28]Ibid., 45.

York.[29] But for his literary labours, Loyalist chronicles would have been more rare. His son, William, followed in his footsteps, writing the first general history of Canada in the English language.[30]

Generally, the published writings of the period were concerned with practical matters: land surveying, the economy and jurisprudence, although some publications did include controversies such as the castigating of government and local officials. Letters, written anonymously or under pseudonyms such as "Veritas," (thought to be James Dunlop), who criticized Gov. Prevost's policies.[31] The incendiary letters of "Nerva" have lately been attributed to Samuel Gale Jr.[32] These printed outcries belonged to a Loyalist tradition of political partisanship in journalism which can be traced back to William Smith's first essays, published in New York. Smith became a prolific author among the Quebec Loyalists, even though he was not highly regarded by his peers. Much of his writings, which were not purely reportorial, included essays in persuasion, outlines of policies, programmes and systems for government that were circulated among influential politicians and officials, as he was

---

[29]L.F.S. Upton, **The Loyal Whig** (Toronto 1969) bibliography of Smith's works, 225-28.

[30]He advised Lord Dalhousie on the formation of the Quebec Literary and Historical Society in surviving correspondence between them, Karl F. Klink ed. **Literary History of Canada** (Toronto, 2nd ed. 1976), I, 142.

[31]Dunlop wrote directly to Prevost, and later sent his letter to the newspaper according to a letter to his sister, **Dunlop Papers**, 1.101, July 12, 1814. He also wrote to George Canning to complain about Prevost, ibid., 1.108, March 12, 1815. "Veritas" has also been believed to have been either Gray or Skakel, Atherton, **Montreal**, II, 130.

[32]Atherton, **Montreal**, II, 129.

Gov. Dorchester's adviser for many years. His insistence on the importance of the English-speaking world, "Unity of the Empire," ensured him of a secure place in Loyalist history.

The "best sellers" among the books published by Loyalists or their children included Sir Alexander Mackenzie's *Voyages from Montreal*, a narrative of his adventures and explorations in the north west during the 1790s, that was published in England in 1801. This effort was valued for its factual description of the west, its revelations of discovery, and for its tales of high adventure, simply told.[33] Contrary to Mackenzie's recollections, the journals of Simon Fraser, another remarkable explorer of Loyalist parentage, lay in obscurity, unpublished for years.[34] The historically significant record of western exploration, written by Peter Skene Ogden, which contained observations of native people, also took time to be published.[35]

Loyalist contributions to Canadian poetry was limited to their descendants. In Quebec, books of verse often published privately, appeared occasionally in the early 19th century, among the poets was William Fitz Hawley, whose writings today are regarded as derivative from British poets, but at the time won Hawley a gold medal for verse.[36]

Theatre and Music
The advent of the British in 1760 led to a variety of presentations, and to the development of preference on the part of the local citizens. French plays previously banned by the

[33]Smith, James K. **Alexander Mackenzie, Explorer** (Toronto 1973), 148-49.

[34]W. Kaye Lamb, **Simon Fraser: Letters and Journals 1806-1808**, 148-149.

[35]Dict. Amer. Biob.; Mac. Dict. Can. Biog.

[36]**Oxford Companion to Canadian History and Literature** (Toronto); Mac. Dict. Can. Biog.,; Klink op. cit., 144.

Catholic Church, particularly those written by Molière, were now permitted to be performed by the new regime.[37]

When the Loyalists arrived, theatrical activity in Montreal increased considerably, as seen in 1784 by the number of light pieces, farces and moralistic plays that were performed.[38] Two years later, an American stock company spent the entire summer season in the City, giving presentations of French and English classics: Molière (in English), Goldsmith and Shakespeare. Early Canadian audiences were subjected to a medley of talents: short acts, acrobatics and musical recitals, performances somewhat akin to "vaudeville." In the early 1800s, John Lambert, whom Willy Amtmann aptly characterized as "un homme difficile à satisfaire," witnessed a performance of the *Taming of the Shrew* by a local company that was complemented by a small troup from Boston, which Lambert found contemptibly acted.[39]

The interest in Montreal theater caused John Molson to found the Theatre Royal in 1825. A number of Loyalists became patrons, including George Platt's wife Elizabeth, who assisted in purchasing 10 per cent of the shares, while Molson held 22 per cent.[40] The new theatre attracted noted British actors,[41] and during its 19-year existence, the performing celebrities included Charles Dickens. Amateur performances, organized by army officers and civilians, which had previously been held in

---

[37]Molière plays were not permitted in Quebec from 1694 to 1765, Willy Amtmann, **La Musique au Québec** (Montreal 1976), 310.

[38]Titles of plays performed 1783-86, **ibid.**

[39]Among the rooms used were those at John Franks' Vauxhall in 1782, and Levy Solomon's Ginseng Hall in 1786, Amtmann, 291.

[40]Merrill Denison, **The Barley and the Stream** (Toronto 1956), 151.

[41]Shirley E. Woods, **The Molson Saga** (Toronto 1983), 84.

various make-shift quarters, found a home here. But due to losses caused by fires, Molson sold the property in 1844.

Children of Loyalists who found themselves attracted to a career on the stage would almost certainly have been discouraged by their parents. To some it would have been immoral, to others unprofitable, while for others unbecoming as a career, depending on their religious, economic or social prejudices. Thus the Loyalist or his descendant's contributions to this field is obscure, apart from the fact that William Johnson Holt built a playhouse in 1817, of which little is known.[42]

Music has always flourished in Quebec, be it in the French or British periods, being a source of inherited folk culture. From the Loyalist time, forms of music were introduced and developed more quickly than at any other previous time. The military introduced regimental bands while throngs of Loyalists brought with them an assortment of music stemming from a diversity of European traditions unknown in Quebec.

The vast influx of Loyalists had a more marked effect on Quebec than did the small number of English-speaking arrivals after the conquest in 1760. In the Maritimes there were many Loyalists with a tradition based on musical literacy, and personal performance using published music. The first music book published in Canada was written by Stephen Humbert, a Loyalist from New Jersey. The work was printed at St. John, New Brunswick, in 1783. In the late 18th century the local population eagerly accepted the new musical spheres introduced by the Loyalists. At times enthusiasm for non-French fashions was so pronounced that critics satirized the

---

[42]Holt's playhouse, Franklin Graham, **Histrionic Montreal**, (scrapbook) 1896, Fraser-Hickson Library.

trend which they termed *anglomanie*.[43] Nevertheless, the strongly conservative habitant helped them to maintain their own traditions. Visitors to Canada often delighted in the musical abilities displayed by the Canadien and Indian — the tireless dancing of the Natives and the passionate singing of the habitants and voyageurs. Entertainment of British derivation, however, with which they were more familiar, was not commented on.

The Loyalists' folk music, although more varied than that of the French Canadian, was virtually ignored by writers of the day. Tunes of British origin were accepted as ordinary and "lower class" or *démodé*. In America, music was enjoyed everywhere, except among a few religious sects which prohibited it, such as the Quakers. Amtmann noted that the Swedes, Germans and Moravians had rich musical traditions which they brought to America along with their instruments. In Philadelphia, for example, the English Quakers were neighbours of the German Pietists of Germantown, which led to an active musical life from ca.1700 on. From this background, people such as Abraham Pastorius, who settled in Montreal, emerged.

As education became increasingly important to the Loyalists, their folk music suffered as oral tradition decreased and dependence on the written word or note increased. In contrast, the Roman Catholic Church's suppression of general education for the French Canadians kept many illiterate and thus their folk music flourished, preserving old French songs,

[43]Joseph Quesnel (1749-1809) satirized the imitation of English fashions in his theatrical peice "L'Anglomanie, ou le Dîner à l'Anglaise." He had, like Lambert, a somewhat sour view toward Canada. Amtmann, 321-26.

of which had come to Canada with the settlers of 1665-73 period.

Professional musicians were in evidence in Quebec towns in the 1780s-90s, although few in number. They included a German regiment's veteran bandmaster, Frederick H. Glackemeyer, (1715-1836), who imported instruments and sheet music for sale in Montreal.[44] Previously keyboard instruments were rare, but once Glackemeyer opened his shop in which he also taught, competitors quickly surfaced, namely the Europeans Berczy and Dulongpré.[45]

Music composition in England was waning at this time, thus the presence in Quebec of a number of German bandmasters and musicians. During the next half century they served to introduce and consolidate the influence of a deep musical culture very different from that of the French court, or that of the English comic opera. Along with these Germans, the educated Loyalists shared an interest in secular art music, such as the Sewell family who had a long tradition of playing musical instruments in their Massachussets homes.[46] It is not surprising therefore, that the young Jonathan Sewell was a talented violinist, who purchased sheets of chamber music from Europe, composed by Haydn and Mozart, as early as 1791.[47] That same year, under the patronage of Prince Edward, a music lover, Sewell formed a group in Quebec City in which

---

[44]Frederick Henry (Frédéric-Henri) Glackemeyer Sr., Amtmann, 272-77.

[45]French music teachers included Dulongpré, Duplessis, and Quesnel; their English counterparts included Charles Watts and John Bentley; see Amtmann, respectively 295, 294; 304 and 314.

[46]Ibid., 28-29.

[47]Kalmann, 31.

the flautist was Frederick H. Glackemeyer Jr. They performed quartets and quintets of high quality.[48] The Prince also sponsored the band concerts with Glackemeyer Sr. as bandmaster.

Sir John Johnson's family in Montreal was also interested in chamber music. In letters between Sir John and Daniel Claus, his brother-in-law, it is evident that both were great lovers of music. Claus had encouraged Sir John, as a youth, in his endeavours while in England, advising Sir John to take advantage of the opportunities that London afforded him of improving his skill on the harpsichord. Claus also asked him to purchase a number of musical works by such composers as Boyce, Handel, Corelli, Giardini and Campioni, in addition to a variety of books. Claus, a fiddler, bought a violincello which he looked forward to playing with Sir John and other friends as a "Most agreeable refreshment of the mind," after a full day's work.[49]

Public concerts became popular in the late 1780s, and apart from the private entertainments there were public balls, assemblies and theatrical programmes that included recitals and comic and dramatic operas. The military bandsmen were ubiquitous, providing music at various military and civic functions, as a complete unit or in small groups or mixed with civilian musicians.[50] Songs written for popular dances did not need translation, and were performed by all groups in Quebec. Civilian musicians occasionally included Blacks, many of

---

[48]Ibid., 50.

[49]Milton W. Hamilton, "An American Knight in Britain: Sir John Johnson's Tour 1765-1767," New York History, April 1961, info from an offprint.

[50]Kalmann, 45.

whom had come with the Loyalists, although some had lived here before the Revolution.[51]

An example of a prominent Loyalist's appreciation of music is seen through the efforts of James Dunlop, the Montreal merchant, who paid for the education of his nieces and nephews in Scotland including the "handsome accomplishments" of music, dancing and drawing.[52] For Dunlop, a lady pianist was one of the three essentials of any successful gathering: "handsome room, handsome company and good music."[53] Boys, he stressed, should not devote too much time to such arts, rather they should concentrate on disciplines such as scholarship, penmanship and accountancy.[54] Had these relatives resided with him in Montreal, he would certainly have economized and sent them to a "very good Music Master" in Montreal.[55]

Dunlop's fondness for music caused him to import two "Forte pianos" for his won house in 1802.[56] Most of the sheets of music, no doubt, were ordered through his brother's bookshop in Glasgow. The "newest and most approved" sheets of music, however, were probably obtained in London.[57] When

---

[51]Thomas Anderson encountered a black fiddler playing for a dance at Brockville in 1799-1800, Talman, **Loyalist Narratives,** 15. There is a black tambourine player in George Heriot's picture "Minuets of the Canadians," dated 1807, used to illustrate his book **Travels Through the Canadas,** 1807.

[52]**Dunlop Papers,** 1.51, Dec. 18, 1802, J. Dunlop to Mrs. Mcnair.

[53]Ibid., 1.55, Feb. 5, 1811, same to same.

[54]Ibid., 1.49, Nov. 15, 1802, same to same.

[55]Ibid., 1.51, Dec. 18, 1802, same to same.

[56]Ibid., 1.5.

[57]Ibid., 1.42, Aug. 25, 1802, J. Dunlop to Alexander Dunlop.

ordering his two pianos, he also imported for sale German flutes "ivory tipt and (in) salon keys."[58]

In the social whirl of the 1811 winter season, Dunlop noted that there was a "Country Dance," that ended at 10 p.m., every other week, and an assembly every second Tuesday,[59] that included supper at 1 a.m., then resumed throughout the small hours. Obviously these latter affairs were not for the shopkeeper or labourer.

---

[58]Ibid., 1.9, Oct. 25, 1798, same to same.

[59]Ibid., 1.55, Feb. 5, 1811, J. Dunlop to Mrs. Mcnair, cf. the Grand Ball mentioned, 1.102, Aug. 16, 1814. Dunlop wanted his employees to enjoy special occasions too, and gave a ball for them and a few friends to celebrate the launching of his new ship, the James Dunlop, 1.59, May 10, 1811, same to same.

CHAPTER 11

The Montreal Loyalists:
What Kind of People Were They?

by John Ruch

On a cold January day in 1830, a flotilla of Indian canoes crossed the frigid St. Lawrence River. They were following the bier of their lamented Superintendent from Montreal to Chambly, where he was to be buried with Mohawk honours. Most of these braves had been born in the five decades since the end of the American Revolution. To them, Sir John Johnson, son of the legendary Sir William, was an ancient warrior, veteran of ancient wars. Half a century later, after they too had been gathered to their ancestors, the United Empire Loyalists' Association of Quebec was founded. By then the stories of Loyalists' exploits and adventures had passed from living memory and went unrecorded. At that time the following appeared in a national magazine:

> The biographies of some of these Loyalist settlers in British North America would be full of instruction. But records of family movements and vicissitudes are very rarely kept... most rarely in those cases in which adventures are most frequent and the course of events most changeful. I have however, seen accounts...which were full of the romance of

faith, of courage and of perseverance.[1]

For still another century, writers continued to complain that no history of Quebec Loyalists had been written. This is the situation which this Heritage Branch has been trying to rectify: Attempting to find out who the Loyalists were, what they were like, and what they did.

This effort begins with some contemporary 18th century opinions of the refugees who came here to escape the oppression and terrorism of the self-righteous "Sons of Liberty."

Col. Maclean of the 84th Regt., Commanding Officer of the Montreal district, exploded in a letter to the Governor's secretary in 1779:

> "I am so plagued with those Royalists real and pretended that I wish to God the General would be so good as to order...them all down to Mashish or Pointe Claire for they are doing no good here."[2]

But a year leter, Maj. Nairne, Officer Commanding the Unincorporate Loyalists at Verchères told his superior officer:

> "The inhabitants of this Parish...will acknowledge that these people are perfectly quiet and orderly."[3]

---

[1]Mr. Reade, "British Canada in the last Century," quoted from the **New Dominion Monthly** by J.M. Le Moine, **Picturesque Quebec** (Montreal 1882), 47.

[2]NAC: Haldimand Papers (henceforth HP), B129/56, Maclean to Mathews, Mov. 18, 1779.

[3]NAC: Nairne Papers, MG23/GIII/23/3/281-282, Nairne to Riedesel, Dec. 16, 1781.

Both officers were writing about different groups of Loyalists. The irate Colonel was referring to an obstinate party, which preferred to live idly and comfortably in town than join refugee camps where they could be housed more economically and be useful to the government. Nairne was writing about soldiers quartered with their families in the homes of French-Canadians.

The most accurate, brief description of Loyalists I have read is the statement of the German Gen.Von Riedesel calling them "so singular a medley of people."[4] And so they were. As Prof. H. Senior discovered, the study of Quebec Loyalists is "a study in diversity."[5] There were the quiet and long-suffering, and those who Dr. Earle Thomas calls "fractious and demanding."[6] They ranged from the most noble old soldier, Daniel McAlpin to the sleazy keeper of a disorderly house, James Seabrook.[7] Before getting too involved with personalities, however, let us examine their origins both ethnic and colonial, their relative proportions according to race can now be fairly quickly approximated.

The Scots were predominant, at around 20 to 25 per cent, and in some areas much higher than that. Everywhere in the Colonies they were regarded as potential Loyalists, so much so

---

[4]NAC: HP, B137/387, Riedesel to Haldimand, Dec. 11, 1782.

[5]Title of a paper he read to Heritage Branch (Montreal), U.E.L. Assoc. in June 1981.

[6]In "The Loyal Americans of the Montreal Region 1775-1784" from our forthcoming history.

[7]Register. RG4/A3/2/146, a reference given to his "Memorial" to Gov. Dorchester.

that the rebel committee in Albany advised its agents that
anyone whose surname began with "Mac" was suspect.[8]

The next largest groups in descending order were the
Germans and Dutch (together), the Irish, then the English.
Below 10 per cent in representation were each of the small
minority groups: American Indians, Blacks, the French, Jews
and Scandinavians. Most of these ethnic groups were present in
Quebec, but the Mohawks nearly all moved westward to settle
at various locations in Upper Canada. The French should have
felt more at home in Quebec than elsewhere in Canada, except
for two circumstances. Many were Protestants (loosely called
"Huguenots" today) who were refugees from their land of
origin due to religious persecution. Many stemmed from
families which had endured exile in Germanic states or in
Britain, thus, being somewhat Anglicized or Germanized they
felt more at ease with these cultural groups. Catholics with
French-Canadian roots, who had lived at Detroit, were more
comfortable in Western Ontario. Nevertheless, some members
of both groups (Indian and French) settled in or around
Montreal.

Like the Montreal English merchants who had close
connections south of the border, the Jews had to be careful in
Montreal, particularly during the American invasion 1775-76.
About a dozen Jewish families were among the earliest English-
speaking settlers in the city after the British conquest. At least
one of these families, the Franks, was divided by the political
troubles,[9] while another, Levy Solomons, was ruined by the

[8]J. Sullivan, **Minutes of the Albany Committee of Correspondance**, I
(Albany 1923) Again "the removal of the Scots Inhabitants" was under
consideration on May 23, 1776, 410.

[9]R.G. Sack, **History of the Jews in Canada** (Montreal 1965), 61-65.

impositions of the invaders on him, and of subsequent ostracism in the community for this enforced and unwelcome fraternization with the enemy. Aaron Hart of Three Rivers was forced to provision rebel troops for six months, a debt which was never repaid. He too would have been ruined had he not enjoyed the position of paymaster to the British troops. His family later became one of the most distinguished in the province in the 19th century. Capt. Jacob Maurer of the Quarter-Master Dept., and the 2nd King's Royal Regt. of New York, occupied the post of Inspector of Bateaux in Montreal during the early 1780s.[10] As with all minority groups in America, the interest of the Jews was best served by a tolerant and stable authority such as the British Crown. After the war the constant movement of merchants and their agents makes it difficult to place their former allegiance. It is known that a number of Jews in New York City served with De Lancey's Brigade.[11] And Jewish sounding names are found in the muster rolls of Carleton's militia in 1775 as well as in other units.

Another small band of dispossessed Loyalists bore names with a definite Latin or Mediterranean flavour. Of the three which can be cited (Gionovale, Roca and Triest),[12] Gionovale may have been related to a Montreal family whose name occurs in various forms in records: Samuel Jionovelly had arrived in

---

[10]Jacob Maurera was listed as one of the Jews who signed a petition for a legislative assembly, Nov. 29, 1773, Sack, 57.

[11]Mary B. Fryer, **Loyalist Spy** (Brockville, Ont. 1974), 76.

[12]Joseph Roca was starving in London in the post-war period; Wallace Brown, **The Good Americans** (New York 1969) cites his letter to Lord Sydney, Dec. 12, 1784 (F.O.4/1). Brown also mentions one Triest who attempted to return to Connecticut in May 1783, **op cit.** 176.

Montreal by the late 1770s.[13] Forty years later David and Agathe Gionovale (Jenovolly) owned shares in one of Montreal's earliest steamboats.[14]

The secondary origin of the Loyalists, (their Colonial Home), is known in many cases, understandably, those Colonies closest to Canada are the most commonly represented. The majority came from New England and New York, and since Vermont was not then a recognized Colony, many from New York or the New Hampshire Grants would now be classified as Vermonters. After the Revolution there must have been Loyalists in Quebec from each of the Thirteen Colonies and the annexed territories. Even tiny Rhode Island was represented by Mrs. Gershom French and Catherine Destailleur, daughter of Colonial Governor Wanton.[15] But sometimes the stated origin can be misleading as with the Samuel Gale family, which is sometimes said to have been "from Florida." While he was on duty there at the time of the British evacuation, his permanent connections were in Vermont with the Wells

---

[13]Samuel Jionovelly married Josepha St.Medard in Montreal, July 1778 according to Rev. J. Chabrand de Lisle's Church Register (Anglican) (NAC: **Report 1885,** xxxii. Widow Margaret Gionovaly from Savannah, Ga., was in Halifax, N.S. March 25, 1784, **Losses Claim,** A.O. 26/138.

[14]Agathe Jenovolly, widow of David, took over his share in the steamboat "Car of Commerce," see resp. in **Shipping Register of Quebec,** RG12/A1/184/170. She later re-married.

[15]Mrs. French mentioned by Robert Hunter, **Quebec to Carolina in 1785-1786,** quoted in Wm. Toye ed. **A Book of Canada** (Toronto 1962), 77. Ref. to Catherine Wanton Destailleur's petition received Jan. 14, 1787, **Register** RG/A3/2/28.

family, which emigrated to Shefford County, Quebec, after the peace.[16]

An ethnic group which can easily be singled out for consideration is the Blacks. It might be thought that the majority of these would have come from the south where slaves were most numerous. The fact is that in Quebec most Blacks were from the border Colonies, as was the case with Indians and Whites. In 1780 a list of recently arrived "Negroes and Negro wenches" was compiled,[17] of whom 43 were from the Mohawk area, nearly all of whom were, or had been, slaves. Twenty five of these were owned by Loyalist masters, while others on the list are later found in military or support units such as the bateaux companies. At first no surnames were recorded but service records required them, thus they usually took the name of the families which they served: Fonda, Herkimer, Johnson.[18] There were a number who came by sea from New York at various times as well.[19]

By recounting the adventures of Montreal Loyalists, the general history of the Revolution is exemplified through them. Some of the leaders' experiences in chronological order are:

1774   William Smith was a Whig in New York politics and hostile toward the Tory Government Party. Isaac Ogden, in 1775, was a member of the New Jersey Provincial Congress. Both men recanted.

---

[16]**Losses Claim,** A.O. 12/24/305-306, May 8, 1787.

[17]NAC: HP, B103/369.

[18]**Ibid.**, B166, names scattered through **Return of Families** for Nov. 1780, 33-38v.

[19]**Return** for Capt. Alexander White's Co. Aug. 17, 1783, Quebec, HP:B148/178, containing four free Negroes: Richard, Nelly, Sealy and Nancy.

1775   While rebel forces swarmed north to invade Canada,
        John Platt of Saratoga infiltrated their camps, then sped
        to Montreal to inform Gov. Carleton. That same year in
        the south, Gov. Dunmore sent John Connolly to the
        Virginia frontier to raise a militia force, but rebels
        captured him in the cat. James Dunlop served in several
        "bloody encounters" and escaped.

1776   Joseph Anderson of Vermont travelled north to Quebec
        early in the year, gathering intelligence from the rebel
        besiegers of the city. He secured details of Gen. Benedict
        Arnold's proposed attack, which he had sent to Gov.
        Carleton. On the King's birthday that year, Abraham
        Cuyler, Stephen de Lancey and other members of
        Albany's civic government were seized
        and imprisoned for toasting the Royal health. Some
        local Loyalists such as Daniel McAlpin went into hiding
        and secretly recruited companies to join the army. Still
        others like Dr. Samuel Adams took their units straight
        to Canada.

1777   The great Burgoyne offensive united these groups, but
        the resounding defeat brought on by the Commander's
        demoralized advance only served to dispirit these
        provincials. Jessup, Sherwood and Adams remained
        with the General until the bitter end while in New York
        City Cuyler and others were pleading with Gen. Clinton
        to rush to Burgoyne's aid. The tattered remnants of the
        Loyalist units straggled back to the Montreal district for
        protection until they could rise and strike again.
        Loyalists such as Jonathan Clarke, brother of the

Montreal Commissary, who had been captured were sent to prison camps in the south. Joseph Chew and Elias Smith were among those active in New York on services such as administration, building and supply, while Stephen de Lancey was farming on Long Island under constant threat of rebel raids.

1778   saw the withdrawal of Gen. Howe's forces from the Philadelphia area, and with them went Samuel Lindsay and Abraham Pastorius...Pennsylvanians who had been principal guides to units such as the Queen's Rangers.

1779   John Richardson and Thomas Swan took to the seas on privateers which captured a number of enemy ships.

The years between 1777-1780 were spent rebuilding the decimated units grouped under larger formation. McAlpin, Leake, Peters, Jessup, Adams, Rogers, Butler and Johnson all sought recruits from the floating population of Quebec. Experienced parties of men went south on raids and numerous scouting missions.

1781   was the most critical year in the second half of the war, which saw the Loyalist secret serviced become formally established with its headquarters on an island in Lake Champlain. From there Sherwood and his Deputy Spymaster, George Smyth, directed clandestine operations including the negotiations with the Allens for the return of Vermont to the British side. Intelligence from several networks of spies was channelled from New England through Vermont via the Wells family, and from the Mohawk via James Ellice

at Schenectady, and from Smyth's contacts in Albany
extending north to Canada and south to New York City.

1782-83brought more refugees to Canada. While   hostile
activity was winding down, the job of receiving   and
settling the victims was becoming more difficult.
Inspectors were appointed to supervise these tasks, first
Cuyler and then De Lancey. Isaac Clarke was heavily
involved in arranging for their supplies, and William
Dummer Powell was useful in providing legal
aid and in arbitrating their disputes.

This review of Loyalist services indicates how thoroughly
involved the residents of Quebec were. Some Loyalists left
Montreal after a decade or more, when they obtained land or
appointments elsewhere, such as Dummer Powell, who became
a justice in Upper Canada.

Women were not mentioned in their own right, records of
their services are much rarer than those for men. It is supposed
that many were either left behind with their children to run the
family farm or business, or camped in groups of refugees spread
out along the St. Lawrence River. Theirs were the unsung
stories of hardship, harassment, flight and disappointment.
They are found sewing, and laundering the soldiers' shirts at 4
pence per shirt; jobs less trumpeted in history than those of the
rebels' legendary Molly Pitcher and Betsy Ross.

The Loyalists can point with pride to several ladies of even
greater romantic appeal than the rebels' two, of whom Flora
Macdonald is one. Her heroic rallying of Loyalist soldiers in the
south is less known than her rescue of Bonnie Prince Charlie a
generation earlier. Another was Lady Johnson, who escaped
from rebel captors at dead of night over the broken ice of the

Hudson River, carrying her new-born child. This escape has dramatic power far beyond the fictional flight of Little Eva from Simon Legree in *Uncle Tom's Cabin*,[20] yet it never inspired a novel, poem or even a short story. Her sister-in-law Polly, wife of Guy Johnson, died at Oswego on her flight north to Canada.[21] Their relatives in the De Lancey family fled clad only in nightclothes when rebels vindictively burned their Westchester home.[22] Like Lady Johnson, Mary McAlpin had continued to manage a large estate with many servants and slaves after her husband joined the British side. She provided fugitive Loyalists with food, shelter, clothing and money until rebels victimized and robbed her before finally imprisoning her with her three children. They were kept in an unfurnished, unheated room with little to eat for several weeks, in the hope that she would persuade her husband to return and join the rebels, but she refused. Finally she was expelled to Canada, and her husband Daniel died in Montreal shortly thereafter, leaving the family impoverished.[23]

Added to the sad tales of Loyalists' widows and orphans are those of the Revolution's elderly victims. There were dozens on subsistence lists of the Montreal district, who were from

---

[20]Thomas Jones, **History of New York** (New York 1879, reprint 1978), I, 79-81, the sleigh ride from Coldenham, Dutchess Co. To Paulus Hook. The last stage on foot and by boat is in (Sir) John Johnson, **The North American Johnsons** (London 1963), 55-56.

[21]"Guy Johnson," **Dictionary of Canadian Biography,** IV.

[22]They were Gen. De Lancey's wife, his daughter Charlotte (later Mrs. Dundas), and Mrs. Cruger, as well as an infant, and a visitor, Miss Elizabeth Floyd, Jones, **op cit.,** 185-187 and 669-670.

[23]Petitions to the Governor, HP B214/311; B215/58; **Losses Claim** A.O.12/22/430-431; 99/45.

different rungs on the social ladder, from the Johnsons at the top, down to the Andersons, Fishers and Barnetts. Some widows remarried, often simply as a matter of convenience or necessity, while men were moved by both self-interest and compassion to take on ready-made families. One elderly bridegroom confessed to the Commissioners of losses, that pity for a struggling young family led him into matrimony. On the other hand, the Commissioners suspected that James Molloy had married John Amory's widow as much for her claims on the government as for her personal attractions.[24]

Many families suffered similar hardships in their journeys from the Colonies. Both Alexander Anderson and Conrad Barnett escaped from the Mohawk Valley, each with a wife and three children, and both were captured by Indians, who killed Anderson while Barnett survived only to die of his exertions three months later in Montreal.[25] Both widows settled in the city to raise their children. Ann Scott Barnett did washing and sewing for a number of prominent local families.[26] She married a shoemaker toward the end of the war, who was able to teach her boys his trade.

The once independent and proud elderly unable to earn their daily bread had to depend on the governor for help. "Mr. Ranald McDonell, Loyalist residing at Lachine, is by birth and education a gentleman." runs one petition, explaining that he had served as a sergeant in the 84th Regt. until discharged as old and unfit. What moved him to ask for assistance was the

---

[24]Molloy would receive an allowance for his wife only if he had her brought to join him in England, A.O.12/100/176-182, **Losses Claim**.

[25]Losses Claims, Ontario Archives **Report** No.2, 1904, Mary Anderson, 387, Ann Barnett, 931.

[26]Certificates of Character in **Losses Claim,** A.O.13/11/209-211.

unhappy sight of his wife, an "old gentlewoman unused to most pitiful distress."[27] The services, sacrifices and losses of the entire McDonell clan are remarkable. Old John McDonell had seven sons in the army and two others in government service,[28] while the elderly Allen McDonell's three sons, all of whom were officers, were killed in action.[29] Occasionally an old Loyalist swallowed his pride completely and took up a questionable trade such as old Faulkner who became a "bootlegger."[30]

Montreal was a good place for the more affluent English and French children who could afford to attend the schools founded by the Loyalists. The poorer youths were apprenticed to the many Loyalist and local craftsmen, both male and female, as well as joining the rapidly-expanding businesses in the burgeoning town.

In the chronicles of Montreal, the Loyalists rank as one of the three groups which in the half-century 1775-1825 prepared the way for the modern industrial city. The fact that another of these groups, the Scots, which also included a sizeable proportion of Loyalists, led later generations to discount the "Loyalist" character of our early community. Against the French background of agriculture and the fur trade, the Scots provided the business drive and genius, the Loyalists the

[27]Petitions in HP, B214/311/260-262.

[28]Letters, **ibid.**, B188, (Mathews) to Maurer, May 3, 1781, 137, and Mann to Mathews, May 7, 1781, 155.

[29]Dunlop Papers, 71, Dunlop to Macnair, Sept. 27, 1811 (Scottish Record Office, Edinburgh, microfilm NAC).

[30]Foundation of the Hospital, and the Orphan Asylum were described by N. Bosworth, Hochelaga Depicta (Montreal 1839), 124-136, 182-185, without naming the ladies. Their executives were named in contemporary newspapers.

professionals to see the visions through. The Loyalists appeared to have monopolized particular areas in business, owing to their education. On nearly every government commission in those first fifty years was at least one Loyalist, in fact in the Montreal area the two most active of the period were Isaac Clarke and John Richardson. Sir John Johnson headed many committees as well, including one for the granting of lands, on which Abraham Pastorius, whose great-grandfather founded Germantown, Penn., also sat. Others were commissioners of the peace, such as De Lancey.

Apart from their common interest in the Community's welfare and development, they greatly differed as individuals. At one pole was James Dunlop, a flamboyant extrovert, and at the other was Isaac Clarke, who was quiet and retiring. Most Loyalists accepted Montreal as their new home and practical people made the best of it, such as Dunlop who wrote: "I prefer this Country and climate beyond Scotland...I certainly never would once think of quitting my home here to go there to reside."

Few tangible accomplishments of the first generation of Loyalists are visible in Montreal now. Of the buildings they helped to build most have been destroyed. Perhaps only in the monument to Admiral Nelson near City Hall can we see something of their efforts. This commemoration was conceived by a group led by Sir John Johnson, commissioned by a triumvirate in London which included Sir Alexander Mackenzie and erected and protected by a committee on which John Richardson served.

Loyalists were numerous in founding social and other organizations. The women, through the Benevolent Society, built a hospital for sick and poor immigrants of a later generation and created facilities for unwed mothers and orphans. Clarke and Richardson both served as presidents of the Montreal General Hospital as well as being deeply involved in the founding of financial institutions. Other Loyalists contributed to industry such as the brewer, John Wait, whom John Molson first employed in 1782 to help him run his brewery. Later when Molson commissioned the construction of Canada's first steamboat, it was built by Loyalist Hart Logan while Loyalist George Platt supplied machine parts. Of the two other shipyards then in operation in Montreal, one was owned by Loyalist James Dunlop.

Only in a few cases do we know what our Loyalist ancestors looked like. Their portraits are fairly rare and widely scattered. The National War Museum has located about 400 pictures which represent only a fraction of a percent of all Loyalists. For Montreal the number of portraits is very small, of which some remain captured by the camera - the original painting having disappeared.

What kind of people were our Loyalists? They were black, white, red and olive-skinned. They came from Great Britain, from the Six Nations of the Iroquois, from the many nations of Europe, and from Africa. They came from the Thirteen Colonies and then some. They were Catholic, Jew, Protestant, and none of the foregoing. They were Tories, Whigs and in-betweens. They were young and old, ambitious and lazy, healthy and gouty. In short they were a cross-section of the contemporary American population.

POSTCRIPT ON REVISIONIST HISTORY

The misguided nationalists of Quebec would like to obliterate most traces in the Province of non-French pioneering, tradition and culture. Much of what the nationalists of today believe was taken from them by force, was, in many instances created by newcomers, such as the Loyalists.

APPENDIX 1

The Inventory of Joseph Chew's Possessions

One of the most interesting documents uncovered by our researchers is the inventory of Joseph Chew's personal possessions made after his death in 1798.[1] It sheds great light on the domestic circumstances of a middle-class, Loyalist official residing in Montreal after the American Revolution. Room by room the contents of a small family home are revealed in this list, along with a contemporary estimate of their value.

Joseph Chew (c.1725-1798) was a Virginian who served as a militia officer in several wars. As a civilian, he was a merchant who held various minor official posts, active in Maryland, Connecticut, and later New York. In the latter city, he befriended Sir William Johnson, who appointed him as justice of the peace. This close association with the Johnson family continued until after his death. Chew became Secretary to the Superintendent of Indian Affairs, first to Guy Johnson and later to Sir John Johnson. By the mid-1780s, he had become Sir John's right-hand man as Administrator of the Indian Department.[2]

---

[1]Inventory and Appraisal of the Goods and Chattels of the late Joseph Chew, Nov. 3, 1798, **Greffe** (Notarial Papers) of J.G. Beek, no,1244, Archives Nationales, Montreal. Located by Margaret S. Stead.

[2]**Dict. Can. Biog.**, IV, "Joseph Chew," by Douglas Leighton.

The Chews' home consisted of three rooms on the ground floor and two more on the upper landing as well as having the use of a basement and yard. Furnishings were modest and serviceable while enhanced by paintings, and in the far end of the dining room, china and tableware were displayed.

On this Third day of November in the Year of our Lord one thousand seven hundred and ninety eight at the request of Mrs. Grace Deshon (?) widow of the late Joseph Chew of Montreal of the Province of Lower Canada Esquire deceased of John Chew of said Montreal Esquire, and Grace Chew son and daughter of the said Deceased being of age of majority stipulating as well for themselves as for and in the name of Joseph Chew, Eldest son and William Johnson Chew, second son of the said deceased both absent out of this Province. By us the subscribing notaries residing in the City of Montreal in the Province aforesaid was taken and made the following inventory and apprizal of all and singular the goods and chattles belonging to the Estate of the said Deceased Joseph Chew as found in the dwelling house wherein he died on the twenty fourth day of September last past situate in Notre Dame Street in the said City and as the same were shown to us by the said widow after having taken the customary oath and were apprised by Messrs Benaiah Gibb and John McKinstry of the said Montreal, gentlemen being first duly sworn to apprise the same to the best of their knowledge and conscience, and which property was left in the said house in the possession of the said widow. And signed the said parties with us notaries these presents after being duly read and also the said apprisers.
(signed) Benaiah Gibb, John McKinstry, B. Deseve, Notary, J. Beek, Notary, Grace Chew, Jno Chew, Grace Deshon

as follows:

Six green winsor chairs valued at twenty five shillings	£1.5
A traveling cantine not compleat at two pounds five shillings	£2.5

Two window blinds at three shilling & nine pence	£ 3.9
One looking glass gilt frame at thirty shillings	£1.10
A mahogany desk & drawers at four pounds	£4.0
A small pine table at five shillings £ 5	
A stove and four links of pipes at five pounds ten shillings	£5.10
Tongs shovel and hand irons at twenty shillings	£1
A pair old window curtains at seven & six pence	£ 7.6

In the Backroom

Six green winsor chairs at twenty five shillings	£1.5
Two mahogany dining tables at two pounds fifteen shillings	£2.15
A pair common curtains at five shillings	£ 5.
A looking glass at twelve shillings & six pence	£ 12.6
An old carpet at twelve & six pence	£ 12.6
Four dozen plain white plates, one dozn soup ditto, two dozn desert do, thirty five large dishes, three pair butter boats, two soup tureens, four pitchers, two washband basons, six small white bowls, three green leafs, three blue & white do, three china dishes at forty shillings	£2.00
One pr flower pots, four egg cups, one dozn blue & white coffee cups & saucers, ten blue & white breakfast ditto, five ditto larger, at twelve shillings & six pence	£ 12.6
Six dark Ground tea cups & saucers, two blk tea pots, one sugar dish, a milker, two small bowls, ten cups & saucers, two bowls, two white sweet meat pots, nine small plates at twelve shillings & six pence	£ 12.6
Nineteen wine glasses, six ale glasses, ten tumblers, four salts, three quart decanters, three pint ditto, at twenty five shillings	£1.5

Twelve silver table spoons wt	24 oz
Six ditto ditto smaller	6-1/2
one soup spoon	5-1/4
twelve tea spoons)	
one pr sugar tongs)	7-1/2

four salt spoons)
three silver casters   33-1/4
a silver teapot stand   11-1/2
one marrow spoon   1/2
Eighty eight and one half ounces valued at five shillings per ounce   £22.2.6
A cocoanut spoon edged with silver at three shillings nine pence   £ 3.9
A tea pot sugar dish milk pot Wedgewood ware & a salad dish at
five shillings   £ 5.
A mahogany teaboard four small Jamand ditto at two shillings &
six pence   £ 2.6
Eleven old framed pictures at thirty shillings   £1.10
Four large tin canisters at fifteen shillings   £ 15.
A plate warmer at five shillings   £ 5.
A fuzil at seventeen & six pence   £ 17.6
A marble mortar at ten shillings   £ 10.

In the Kitchen
Two pewter basons at four shillings   £ 4
Four pair brass candlesticks at twenty shillings   £1.0
Six dish covers at seven shillings & six pence   £ 7.6
Two funnels, twelve skewers, two clevers, a house bell, four pair
snuffers at seven shillings & six pence   £ 7.6
Two iron pots, one fish kettle, five sauce pans, two baking pans,
one grater, one skimmer, two cheese toasters, a tin save, and old
coffee pot & pitcher, two gridirons at fifty shillings   £2.10
A pair bellows at two shillings & six pence   £ 2.6
A pair handirons, shovel, tongs, rack, two pair flat irons, two tin
fenders at seventeen shillings & six pence   £ 17.6
A morter & pestel metal four shillings   £ 4.
Three chafin dishes, one spider, two Trammels, two iron tea
kettles and a spit at seven shillings & six pence   £ 7.6
Two knife strays, half doz odd knives, a pewter cullender, an iron

trivet at five shillings	£ 5.
A large old copper kettle at ten shillings	£ 10.
A ditto do. brass ditto at two shillings & six pence	£ 2.6
A toasting iron, a pair stillyards and old coffee mill at five shillings	£ 5.
Two dozn pewter plates & six ditto dishes at fifteen shillings	£ 15.
Two water bottles, one bread basket, four bottle stands, two tin sugar canisters and three blue bowls at ten shillings	£ 10.
A castor of Queens Metal compleat at thirteen & four pence	£ 13.4
Eleven blk handle knives & forks, six ditto smaller, two knife trays at five shillings	£ 5.0
A knive case with a dozn knives & forks at twenty shillings	£1.0
Six straw matts at two shillings & six pence	£ 2.6

In the Vault

An old Harness at five shillings	£ 5.
A wheel barrow at four shillings	£ 4.
Two hoes, watering pot, two rakes, a spade at five shillings	£ 5.
A frame saw, handsaw, beetle & wedges & and axe at fifteen shillings	£ 15.0

In the Yard

An old water cart at ten shillings	£ 10.
Snow box at five shillings	£ 5.
A gin case with twelve bottles at ten shillings	£ 10.
Twelve dozn empty bottles at twenty shillings	£1.0

In Mrs. Chew's Room

A bedsted and beddings compleat not valued	
Two old pictures at one shilling	£1.0
A silver watch at thirty shillings	£1.10
Six common chairs at two shillings & six pence	£ 2.6

A small stove with twelve links of pipe at three pounds	£3.0
Two swords & a poweder flasks at twenty five shillings	£1.5
Twelve table cloths at three pounds	£3.0

In Mr. Chew's Room

One looking glass at ten shillings	£ 10.
A hat case at one shilling	£ 1.
A traveling chest at two shillings and six pence	£ 2.6
A camp chair at one shilling	£ 1.0

£76.18.4

Amounting the whole of his inventory and apprizal at the sum of seventy six pounds, eighteen shillings and four pence current money of the Province of Lower Canada aforesaid and a pew in Christ Church in Montreal valued at eight pounds. Thus done inventorized and apprized as aforesaid and declared the said widow that in case any article should appear wherewith this inventory ought to be augmented, she will give duly notice thereof to whom it appertains and signed the said parties present and apprizers with us notaries after being duly read the day and year first above written.
Benaih Gibb
John McKinstry, B. Deseve, Notary, Grace Deshon, John Chew, Grace Chew, J.G. Beek, 1798.

On this twenty sixth day of August one thousand seven hundred and ninety nine appeared before us the subscribing notaries, the within named Grace Deshon, widow of the late Joseph Chew Esquire, who declared that since the date of the foregoing inventory, she has found the debts owing by her late husband to stand in manner following, vizt -

To Forsyth Richardson and Co.	£82.12.10
Colonel McKee	100.00.00

John McKinstry	32.9.10
James Dunlop	12.9.6
Benaiah Gibb	15.14.11-1/2
James Caldwell	8.12.5
Logan & Watt	5.11.8
Auldjo & Maitland	3.1.6
James Robertson & Co.	3.18.9
John Lees Esqre	40.0.0
Doctor George Silby	18.8.0
Maoella Noel for house work	8.10.0
Joseph Brant	30.0.0
Funeral Expences	25.0.0
	————
	£386.9.5-1/2

Thus the amount of debts due by the Estate are three hundred and eighty six pounds nine shillings and five pence half penny current money of the Province of Lower Canada aforesaid.

And further that a claim is made on the said Estate by the widow of John Temple Esquire of New York for the sum of five hundred & five pounds three shillings and four pence Sterling money of Great Britain in consequence of a certain note of hand dated in New London, January 6th, 1766, signed by the said Joseph Chew deceased.

Thus done and having found nothing worth wherewith this inventory and apprizal ought to be charged, all the above mentioned articles of plate, household furniture and utencils where left and remain in the possession of the said widow of the late Joseph Chew, who has willingly charged herself with them to represent same at all times when it shall appertain. And signed with us notaries after being duly read.

(signed) B. Deseve Notary.   Grace Deshon   Widow Che w   J. Beek Notary
1799

APPENDIX 2

Quebec Loyalists 1784

These are names selected from the contemporary alphabetical index of muster rolls numbers 1 to 21, compiled by Elizabeth Ruch.

The index is in the Ontario Archives, Toronto, and a copy is in the National Archives of Canada (RG 1, A IV, vol. 80).

It appears that the rolls referred to are those which Maj. John Barnes compiled in September and October, 1784, and deposited with the Quartermaster General's office (cf. British Museum Add. ms. 21,828 Haldimand Papers. N.A.C. Microfilm reel A.752; comparable to transcript of the same volume B.168). In any case, the index must date from before the division of Quebec Province into Upper and Lower Canada.

The first column of numbers refers to the location on the muster roll. The final column refers to the number of the muster roll.

	Name	Located	
28	Richard Abbot	Douglas Town, Gaspé Bay	20
3	Wm. Allen	"	"
8	Wm. Anderson	"	"
77	Int. Henry Ansum	Sorel	1
116	Chas. Arkinson	"	"
80	Jesse Armstrong	"	"
22	Jesse Armstrong	Douglas Town, Gaspé Bay	20
110	Wm. Armstrong	Sorel	1
60	James Astles	Carlisle, Chaleur Bay	21
114	James Astles	"	
37	John Bailley	Douglas Town, Gaspé Bay	20
36	David Beaty	Sorel	1
87	John Beck	Carlisle, Chaleur Bay	21
58	Benjn Belts	"	"
156	Wm. Bennett	Carlisle, Chaleur Bay	21
36	Patrick Berry	Douglas Town, Gaspé Bay	20
69	S. Bibill	Carlisle, Chaleur Bay	21
46	Michael Bilby	Sorel	1
106	John Black	"	"
123	Wm. Black	Carlisle, Chaleur Bay	21
29	Peter Blass	Sorel	1
52	Wm. Bolster	Carlisle, Chaleur Bay	21
6	Robert Boyl	Douglas Town, Gaspé Bay	20
14	John Bracking	Montreal, Lachine & Coteau du Lac	2
165	Casar Brash	Carlisle, Chaleur Bay	21
111	John Brooks	"	"
14	John Brooks	Douglas Town, Gaspé Bay	20
94	Widow Brookes	Sorel	1
26	Alexr Brotherton	Carlisle, Chaleur Bay	21
107	Widow Brouster	Sorel	1
29	Abram Brown	Carlisle, Chaleur Bay	21

22	Jesse Brown	Sorel	1
93	Widow Brown	"	"
36	James Bruntsman	Carlisle, Chaleur Bay	21
99	John Bryan	Sorel	1
65	Daniel Buck	"	"
64	Samuel Buck	"	"
56	Mathew Buckley	"	"
33	Aaron Bull	"	"
50	Wm. Buntan	Douglas Town, Gaspé Bay	20
32	Thomas Burrows	Carlisle, Chaleur Bay	21
72	Julius Bush	Sorel	1
73	Wm. Busleed	Carlisle, Chaleur Bay	21
27	Robt. Caldwell	Carlisle, Chaleur Bay	21
43	Allan Cameron	Douglas Town, Gaspé Bay	20
54	Dougal Cameron	Sorel	1
112	John Cameron	"	"
23	John Cameron	Douglas Town, Gaspé Bay	20
28	George Campbell	Sorel	1
21	Wm. Cample	Carlisle, Chaleur Bay	21
114	John Cardoss	Sorel	1
158	James Carr	Carlisle, Chaleur Bay	21
17	Wm. Carrot	Douglas Town, Gaspé Bay	20
61	Josiah Cass	Carlisle, Chaleur Bay	21
34	David Castles	Sorel	1
129	Charles Catchback	"	"
41	Richd Chamberlain	Carlisle, Chaleur Bay	21
80	Hiram Chapple	"	"
29	James Cheesborough	Douglas Town, Gaspé Bay	20
145	John Chisholm	Carlisle, Chaleur Bay	21
52	Hans Christian	Douglas Town, Gaspé Bay	20
121	James Cinquontron	Carlisle, Chaleur Bay	21
126	Wm. Clark	Sorel	1
100	Nicholas Claus	"	"
102	John Clow	"	"
90	John Cole	"	"
144	Heny Colliford	Carlisle, Chaleur Bay	21
91	Michl Coner	"	"
101	Patk Connel	"	"
59	John Conor	"	"
62	Philip Cook Sr.	Sorel	1
51	Philip Cook Jr.	"	"
134	Widow Cook	"	"
31	John Cordue	Carlisle, Chaleur Bay	21
13	Andw Couller	Carlisle, Chaleur Bay	21
1	Lt. Govr Cox	"	"
68	Peter Cramer	Sorel	1
6	Thos. Cromps	Montreal, Lachine & Coteau du Lac	2
108	Danl Cronin	Sorel	1
1	Mrs. Crookshancke	Montreal, Lachine & Coteau du Lac	2
96	Widow Crosier	Sorel	1
51	Chas. Cunning	Douglas Town, Gaspé Bay	20
139	Christr Curtis	Sorel	1
81	Thos. Darcy	Carlisle, Chaleur Bay	24
137	John Davey	Sorel	1

77	Abel Davis	Carlisle, Chaleur Bay	24
69	John Dawson	Sorel	1
35	John Dawson	Douglas Town, Gaspé Bay	20
109	A. Dayle	Carlisle, Chaleur Bay	24
16	Louis Decoigne	Montreal, Lachine & Coteau du Lac	2
5	Stephen Delancey	"	"
63	Henry Dellenback	Sorel	1
59	Jacob G. Dies	"	1
141	Chas. Dobson	Carlisle, Chaleur Bay	24
139	John Donaldson	"	"
53	Daniel Dorge	Sorel	1
52	Rev. John Doty	"	"
32	Cornelius Driskell	Douglas Town, Gaspé Bay	20
76	John Driver	Sorel	1
39	John Dunn	Douglas Town, Gaspé Bay	20
19	Mr. Dunn	Montreal, Lachine & Coteau du Lac	2
31	Patk Dunwan	Douglas Town, Gaspé Bay	20
86	James Durward	Carlisle, Chaleur Bay	24
162	Henry Echelle	Carlisle, Chaleur Bay	21
10	Thos. Edrington	"	"
137	James Edwards	"	"
16	Joseph Element	Douglas Town, Gaspé Bay	20
84	Joseph Elsworth	Sorel	1
132	Edward Elveston	"	"
103	Charles Evans	"	"
88	Charles Fielding	Sorel	1
26	James Fitzgerald	Douglas Town, Gaspé Bay	20
53	Wm. Fitzgerald	Carlisle, Chaleur Bay	21
40	Lauchn Flanighan	"	"
151	John Fleetwood	"	"
127	Robt. Flowers	"	"
82	George Foedle	Sorel	1
86	Andrew Forrester	"	"
93	Thos. Foster	Carlisle, Chaleur Bay	21
14	Jera Frances	"	"
18	Donald Fraser	"	"
47	Jera Fraser	"	"
17	Lt. Wm. Fraser	Lachine & Coteau du Lac	2
37	Thos. Freeman	Sorel	1
2	Gersham French	"	"
16	Lt. Gersham French	Lachine & Coteau du Lac	2
6	Isaac Friot	Sorel	1
122	John Gallon	Carlisle, Chaleur Bay	21
74	Benjn Galloway	Sorel	1
118	Wm. Garret	Carlisle, Chaleur Bay	21
67	George Gelker	"	"
16	John Gilles	Sorel	1
138	John Golass	Carlisle, Chaleur Bay	21
5	Robt. Goodwill	Douglas Town, Gaspé Bay	20
66	Josh Goodwillie	Carlisle, Chaleur Bay	21
142	James Grant	"	"
92	John Grant	"	"
49	John Gray	Sorel	1

3	Mrs. Gray & Mrs. Farel	Montreal, Lachine & Coteau du Lac	2
105	John Greaves	Sorel	1
20	Edw'd Greenwood	Douglas Town, Gaspé Bay	20
40	Joseph Greers	Sorel	1
11	Joseph Grooms	Douglas Town, Gaspé Bay	20
33	Hugh Hacket	Douglas Town, Gaspé Bay	20
50	John Hall	Sorel	1
122	Joseph Hambeck	"	"
11	Silas Hamlin	"	"
97	Pat Haneberry	Carlisle, Chaleur Bay	21
133	William Harlow	"	"
138	John Harris	Sorel	1
27	Rich'd Harris	"	"
164	Jack Harrison	Carlisle, Chaleur Bay	21
79	E. Hawley	"	"
7	Reuben Hawley	Sorel	1
71	George Haws	"	"
7	Barl Hayze	Lachine & Coteau du Lac	2
100	Pat Hays	Carlisle, Chaleur Bay	21
107	John Hegans	"	"
10	Abrm Heleaker	Sorel	1
8	Jeremiah Heleaker	"	"
9	John Heleaker	"	"
20	Nat Hillyers	Lachine & Coteau du Lac	2
76	Sam'l Hindman	Carlisle, Chaleur Bay	21
50	Benjn Hobson	"	"
89	Henry Hogland	Sorel	1
38	Frances Hogle	Sorel	1
136	John Hogle	"	"
92	Elias Holmes	"	"
82	Philo Holybatt	Carlisle, Chaleur Bay	21
152	Charles Hoslop	"	"
45	Awariah Howe	Sorel	1
19	James Howood	Douglas Town, Gaspé Bay	20
49	Isaac Ives	Carlisle, Chaleur Bay	21
166	John Jacobs	Carlisle Chaleur Bay	21
48	John Jafferes	"	"
35	Simpson Jenny	Sorel	1
1	Joseph Jessup	"	"
30	Mayor Jessup's family	"	"
133	Widow Johnson	"	"
128	Geo. Johnston	Carlisle, Chaleur Bay	21
55	John Jones	Sorel	1
35	Thos. Price Jones	Carlisle, Chaleur Bay	21
131	Simon Jordan	"	"
116	William Kamp	Carlisle, Chaleur Bay	24
34	James Kelly	Douglas Town, Gaspé Bay	20
146	M. Kelly	Carlisle, Chaleur Bay	24
25	John Kennedy	Douglas Town, Gaspé Bay	20
24	Willm Kennedy	"	"
161	James Keys	Carlisle, Chaleur Bay	24
160	John Keys	"	"

85	John Klurk	Sorel	1
120	James Lamberet	Carlisle, Chaleur Bay	21
98	David Lauch	"	"
22	John Lane	"	"
11	Capt. Geo. Law	"	"
12	I.T. Law	"	"
25	Daniel Lighthart	Sorel	1
127	Derby Lindsie	"	"
128	Widow Lindsie	"	"
15	Thos. Lister	Carlisle, Chaleur Bay	21
83	Geo. Longmore	"	"
68	John Loverell	"	"
89	Wm. McAdams	Carlisle, Chaleur Bay	21
21	Charles McBean	Douglas Town, Gaspé Bay	20
22	John McBean	"	"
90	A. McCambridge	Carlisle, Chaleur Bay	21
105	Chas. McCarty	"	"
23	John McCarty	"	"
9	John McCraw	Douglas Town, Gaspé Bay	20
11	Mrs. Allen McDonald	Montreal, Lachine & Coteau du Lac	2
4	Capt. Angus McDonald	"	"
148	R. McDonald	Carlisle, Chaleur Bay	21
120	Robt. McDonel	Sorel	1
48	Ronald McDonell	Douglas Town, Gaspé Bay	20
14	Mrs. McDougal	Montreal, Lachine & Coteau du Lac	2
8	Robt. McGannis	"	"
16	Dond McGill	Carlisle, Chaleur Bay	21
163	Peter McInnes	"	"
111	Danl McIntosh	Sorel	1
84	Alexr McKay	Carlisle, Chaleur Bay	21
33	L. McKenzie	"	"
87	Alexr McKinzie	Sorel	1
147	R. McKutchen	Carlisle, Chaleur Bay	21
136	Dunn McLellan	Carlisle, Chaleur Bay	21
157	John McLellan	"	"
12	John McLod	Montreal, Lachine & Coteau du Lac	2
119	Mary McMullen	Sorel	1
15	Alexr McNeil	"	"
45	James McNivem	Carlisle, Chaleur Bay	21
7	Daniel McPherson	Douglas Town, Gaspé Bay	20
98	Widow McPherson	Sorel	1
4	Hugh McQuarters	Douglas Town, Gaspé Bay	20
167	John Maclauchlan	Carlisle, Chaleur Bay	21
32	Wm. Mallory	Douglas Town, Gaspé Bay	20
7	Ann Mann	Carlisle, Chaleur Bay	21
9	Barba Mann	"	"
10	Edwd Mann	"	"
2	Isaac Mann Sr.	"	"
3	Isaac Mann Jr.	"	"
13	John Mann	Montreal, Lachine & Coteau du Lac	2
5	John I. Mann	Carlisle, Chaleur Bay	21
4	Thos. Mann	"	"

6	William Mann	"	"
110	John Manning	"	"
129	John Mattellizie	"	"
85	H. Maxwell	"	"
108	Saml May	"	"
32	Garret Miller	Sorel	1
8	Hannh Miller (orphan)	Carlisle, Chaleur Bay	21
153	Stephn Miller	"	"
121	John Mobus	Sorel	1
131	Frances Moore	"	"
1	Joseph Morrel	Douglas Town, Gaspé Bay	20
2	Thos. Morris	Douglas Town, Gaspé Bay	20
75	D. Munro	Carlisle, Chaleur Bay	21
2	Mrs. Munro & Chr.Bruce	Montreal, Lachine & Coteau du Lac	2
69	Felix Myers	Sorel	1
42	John Myers	Carlisle, Chaleur Bay	21
118	Henry Mynard	Sorel	1
56	Andw Naughton	Carlisle, Chaleur Bay	21
109	Bastian Navarre	"	"
104	Chas. Nicholas	"	"
18	Azer Northrup	Sorel	1
17	Elihu Northrup	"	"
17	Patk Nugent	"	"
55	Thomas Orr	Carlisle, Chaleur Bay	21
78	Eze Ouserhout	Sorel	1
132	John Pamphry	Carlisle, Chaleur Bay	21
83	Augn Parodice	Sorel	1
44	Willm Paterson	Carlisle, Chaleur Bay	21
53	James Paxton	Douglas Town, Gaspé Bay	20
65	Chr. Pearson	Carlisle, Chaleur Bay	21
57	Saml Perry	"	"
117	Robt. Petegrew	Sorel	1
19	Jonah Phelps	"	"
154	Willm Phillips	Carlisle, Chaleur Bay	21
143	Willm Powell	"	"
11	John Powers	Sorel	1
44	John Prentice	Douglas Town, Gaspé Bay	20
45	Saml Prentice	"	"
74	Azr Pritchard	Carlisle, Chaleur Bay	21
30	Edmund Purcel	"	"
113	Christr Quinn	Sorel	1
42	John Renney	Sorel	1
125	Saml Richardson	"	"
13	Thomas Richardson	Carlisle, Chaleur Bay	21
121	Thos Richardson	"	"
130	John Ritchie	"	"
61	Dun Robertson	"	"
10	John Robertson	Douglas Town, Gaspé Bay	20
115	Wm. Robertson	Carlisle, Chaleur Bay	21
81	John Robinson	Sorel	1
99	David Rogers	"	"

20	John Rogers	"	"
75	Widow Rogers	"	"
21	Willm Rogers	"	"
15	John Rose	Douglas Town, Gaspé Bay	20
3	Samuel Rose	Sorel	1
113	John Rosendall	Carlisle, Chaleur Bay	21
135	John Ross	"	"
135	Mrs. Ross	Sorel	1
66	George Rowse	"	
78	E. Russell	Carlisle, Chaleur Bay	21
70	Stafford Russell	Sorel	1
121	John Rustle	Carlisle, Chaleur Bay	21
62	Aaron Sampson	Carlisle, Chaleur Bay	24
18	Robt. Sawyers	Douglas Town, Gaspé Bay	20
23	Daniel Scott	Sorel	1
24	David Scott	Carlisle, Chaleur Bay	24
72	John Scott	"	"
48	John Scully	Sorel	1
13	Hermon Sea	Sorel	1
12	James Sea	"	"
14	John Sea	"	"
104	John Selfrige	"	"
17	James Shaw	Carlisle, Chaleur Bay	24
34	Simon Shearer	"	"
51	Thomas Sherar	"	"
63	John Sibie	"	"
73	Gody Siebert	Sorel	1
13	Robt. Simpson	Douglas Town, Gaspé Bay	20
5	Mar Skimming	Montreal, Lachine & Coteau du Lac	2
16	John Slitt	Carlisle, Chaleur Bay	24
49	Capt. Smith	Douglas Town, Gaspé Bay	20
124	John Smith	Sorel	1
40	John Smith	Douglas Town, Gaspé Bay	20
58	Patk Smith	Sorel	1
9	Mrs. Stanley	Montreal, Lachine & Coteau du Lac	2
7	Nat. Sterns	Carlisle, Chaleur Bay	24
20	James Stone	"	"
38	Patk Sullivan	Douglas Town, Gaspé Bay	20
27	Magnus Sunholm	"	"
43	James Sutherland	Sorel	1
26	Joseph Sutherland	"	"
25	Jacob Teague	Carlisle, Chaleur Bay	21
117	Richd Thomas	"	"
88	Willm Thompson	"	"
21	George Thomson	Douglas Town, Gaspé Bay	20
91	John Thorn	Sorel	
1			
102	John Thully	Carlisle, Chaleur Bay	21
135	George Tilford	"	"
101	John Time	Sorel	1
31	Israel Tompkins	"	"
96	Pat. Tool	Carlisle, Chaleur Bay	21
124	John Travers	"	"
18	St. Gerson Trenche	Montreal, Lachine, Coteau du Lac	2

		(French)	
91	Pat. Trener	Carlisle, Chaleur Bay	21
30	Robert Trippe	Douglas Town, Gaspé Bay	20
99	Nat. Triseal	Carlisle, Chaleur Bay	21
38	John Tuttle	"	"
39	S. Tuttle	"	"
37	Willm Tuttle	Carlisle, Chaleur Bay	21
76	William Tylor	"	"
24	William Upton	Sorel	1
150	Willm Vondervelden	Carlisle, Chaleur Bay	21
95	Edward Wall	Carlisle, Chaleur Bay	21
94	Nic. Wall	"	"
29	Jas. Waller	Sorel	1
140	Fredk Wearing	"	"
115	Nichs Weaver	"	"
112	John Whichsibie	Carlisle, Chaleur Bay	21
37	Alex White	Sorel	1
106	Willm Whitemore	Carlisle, Chaleur Bay	21
60	Fredk Williams	Sorel	1
119	Robt. Williamson	Carlisle, Chaleur Bay	21
12	Willm Wills	Douglas Town, Gaspé Bay	20
75	Anty Wilmot	Sorel	1
54	Edwd Wilson	Carlisle, Chaleur Bay	21
1	John Wilson	Sorel	1
5	John Wilson Junr	"	"
109	Aaron Wimple	"	"
140	Saml Winterbottom	Carlisle, Chaleur Bay	21
123	Widow Wood	Sorel	1
47	John Wright	Douglas Town, Gaspé Bay	20
130	Alexr Young	Sorel	1
28	Geo. Young	Carlisle, Chaleur Bay	21
134	Christ. Zime	Carlisle, Chaleur Bay	21

Claimants for Losses in the Province of Quebec

The names of individuals who appeared before the Losses Claims Commission are contained in a volume of the Commission records, classified as A.O.12, vol. 120. Heritage Branch (Montreal) members compiled the names of those people who appeared before the commissioners in cities of present day Quebec. The original volume is actually a register of the order in which Loyalists were heard. Thus the number is that of the person's place in line, and does not refer to the serial number of his or her claim. The claims published in the Ontario Archives Report No. 2 are only a fraction of those preserved in the Commission records, and many claims heard in Quebec have never been printed. This list is therefore a quick guide to the names of Loyalists who appeared to plead their own cases. As related in the Fall 1983 issue of Loyalist Gazette, "When Loyalty Was Not Enough," the commissioners sat in Quebec City, Three Rivers and Montreal, amongst others which are now in the Province of Ontario.

N.B. In a number of cases, several claimants' names were listed under one number by the Commission clerk. They have been compiled on the following list as 1301A, 1301B etc.

Hearings in the Province of Quebec 1787-1788

The following list is given in Audit Office Records, A.0.12, vol. 120, ff.23-50. (N.A.C. Microfilm B.1181). Muster Roll Number (MR); Origin (ORG) in the Colony; Site (LOC) where the claimant was heard in Canada; date of claimant's hearing.

SC=South Carolina
GA=Georgia
NY=New York
MD=Maryland
VA=Virgina
RI=Rhode Island
PA=Pennsylvania
NJ=New Jersey
NH=New Hampshire
VT=Vermont
CN=Connecticut
DL=Delaware
MS=Massachussetts

Location:
Q=Quebec City
TR=Trois Rivières
M=Montreal

MR	Name	ORG	LOC	DATE
683	McNAIGHTON, Annabella	SC	Q	5 May 1787
684	" , Alexr.	GA	"	" "
685	MILLER, Wm.	NY	"	16 "
686	HOLLAND, Samuel (Maj)	NY	"	21 "
687	COFFIN, John	MD	"	" "
688	ROCHEBLAVE, Philip	NY/VA	"	22 "
689	McNEILL, Archd.	MD	"	29 "

690	FROST, James	RI	"	"	"
691	HARRIS, Jane	PA	"	31	"
692	MILLER, James	NY	"	2 June 1787	
693	MILLER, Wm. Jr.	NY	"	"	"
694	ROGERS, Mary (wid)	NY	"	6	"
695	PERRY, Samuel	NY	"	8	"
696	ORR, Thomas	NY	"	"	"
697	MORRIS, Lt.Col.John	NJ	TR	10	"
698	PRIOT, Isaac	NY	M	13	"
699	CAMPBELL, Elizth.	NY	"	16	"
700	CRUICKSHANK, Alexr.	NY	"	"	"
701	SNYDER, Wm.	NY	"	"	"
702	HOWARD Matthew	NY	"	"	"
703	FISHER, Donald	NY	"	"	"
704	MUCHMORE, Jonathan	PA/MD	"	18	"
705	POMEROY, Josiah	NH	"	"	"
706	COX, John	NJ	"	"	"
707	BARNET, Ann	NY	"	"	"
708	SMITH, Alexr.	PA	"	"	"
709	McILMOYL, James	NY	"	19	"
709a	WAITE, John	NY	"	20	"
710	MILLER, Garrett	NY	"	"	"
711	ADAMS, Saml.	NY	"	"	"
712	MENARD Henry	NY	"	"	"
713	HARKAMER, Joost	NY	"	21	"
714	SCOTT, Walter	NY	"	"	"
715	MOLLOY, Nelly	NY	"	22	"
716	DERICKS, Philip	NY	"	"	"
717	PLATT, John	NY	"	"	"
718	HYATT, Abraham	NY	"	"	"
719	MOCK, John	NY	"	"	"
720	SWAN, Thomas	MD	"	"	"
721	BRIANT, Rachel	NY	"	"	"
722	BEST, Harmanus	NY	"	23	"
723	RUITER, John	NY	"	"	"
724	HENDERSON, James	VT	"	"	"
725	CAMERON, Duncan	NY	"	"	"
726	RUITER, Henry	NY	"	"	"
727	WEHR, (WEBER) Christian	NY	"	"	"
728	TEBARE, Joseph	NY	"	"	"
729	HOGLE, Francis	NY	"	25	"
730	JONES, David	NY	"	"	"
731	JONES, Capt. John	NY	"	"	"
732	STEWART, William	NY	"	"	"
734	MERKLE, Jacob	NY	"	26	"
735	MUNRO, Hugh	NY	"	"	"
736	FROOM, James	NY	"	27	"
737	HUFFNALL, Michael	NY	"	"	"
738	WRAGG, Richard	NY	"	"	"
739	DUNHAM, Daniel	NY	"	"	"

739a	SKIMMING, John	NY	"	"	"
740	McINTOSH, Donald	NY	"	28	"
741	McCLERIN, Mercy	NY	"	29	"
742	ROGERS, William	NY	"	"	"
744	WEYWOOD, Thomas	NY	"	"	"
745	PARROTT, James	NY	"	30	"
746	ADAMS, John	NY	"	"	"
747	McGUIN, Daniel	NY	"	"	"
748	KIRBY, John	NY	"	"	"
749	GILL, Richard	NY	"	"	"
749a	MARSH, Abraham	VT	"	"	"
750	WRIGGS, Alexander, John & Abraham	NY	"	"	"
751	BRANT, Children of Mary	NY	"	2 July	
752	ROGERS, Maj. James	NY	"	"	"
753	CAMERON, Alexander	NY	"	"	"
754	SMITH, William	MD	"	"	"
755	ROBERTSON, Thomas	NY	"	"	"
756	MILLS, Abel	NY	"	"	"
757	CARRIGAN, Patrick, Peter & Paul	NY	"	"	"
758	HUNTINGTON, Simon	NY	"	3	"
759	BUSH, Julius	NY	"	"	"
760	SIBERT, Godfrey	NY	"	"	"
761	GROUT, Henry	NY	"	"	"
762	STEVENS, Roger	VT	"	"	"
763	ROUSE, George	NY	"	"	"
764	BROWN, Andrew	NY	"	4	"
765	McPHERSON, Alexander	NY	"	"	"
766	EVERTS, Oliver	VT	"	"	"
767	WRIGHT, Ebenezer	VT	"	"	"
768	DELANCEY, Stephen	NY	"	5	"
769	BUELL, Mary & Timothy	NY	"	"	"
770	LIGHTHARD, Daniel	NY	"	"	"
771	HOGEL, Elizabeth, James & Busteyon	NY	"	"	"
772	FRENCH, Jeremiah	VT	"	"	"
773	SHERWOOD, Justus	VT	"	6	"
774	WOOLCOTT, Abner	VT	"	"	"
775	ROSE, Samuel	VT	"	"	"
776	HAWLEY, Abijah	VT	"	"	"
777	BRISBIN, William	NY	"	7	"
778	GRAVES, John	NY	"	9	"
779	LINDSAY, Derby	NY	"	"	"
780	GLENNY, James	NY	"	"	"
781	McDONELL, Capt. John	NY	"	10	"
782	SMITH, Benoney	NY	"	"	"
783	ADAMS, Samuel	VT	"	"	"
784	HAWLEY, Reuben	VT	"	11	"
785	SCOTT, Daniel	VT	"	"	"

786	LEE, James	NY	"	"	"
787	HOLMES, Elias	NJ	"	"	"
788	CHESSER, John	NY	"	"	"
789	MABUS, John	VT	"	"	"
790	FILER, Samuel	VT	"	"	"
791	DEWAR, John	NY	"	"	"
792	CHISHOLM, John	SC	Q	"	"
793	YOUNG, Alexander	NY	M	12	"
794	HELIKER, John	NY	"	13	"
795	McNIFF, Patrick	NY	"	14	"
796	McGUIN, Sarah & George	NY	"	"	"
797	McDONELL, Enos Ranald	NY	"	16	"
798	CAMPBELL, Alexander	NY	"	17	"
799	OVERMOUTH, Zachariah	NY	"	"	"
800	WILSON, John	NY	"	18	"
801	GORDON, Robert	NY	"	"	"
802	WILLIAMS, Frederick	NY	"	"	"
803	WEARING, Frederick	NY	"	"	"
804	KAZEBACH, Henry	NY	"	"	"
805	SPOONER, Ralph	NY	"	"	"
806	VAN KOUGHNET, Michael	NY	"	19	"
807	STINSON, John	NH	"	"	"
808	MATTICE, Nicholas	NY	"	"	"
809	BOUCK, Frederick	NY	"	"	"
810	MOSELEY, Isaac	CN	"	20	"
811	GALLOWAY, Benjamin	DL	"	"	"
812	HOW, Amariah	VT	"	"	"
813	JENNE, Simpson	VT	"	"	"
814	JOHNSON, Mary (widow)	VT	"	"	"
815	WOOD, Rebecca (widow)	NY	"	"	"
816	RICHARDSON, Samuel	VT	"	"	"
817	SMITH, John	VT	"	"	"
818	BUCK, Samuel	VT	"	"	"
819	NORTHRUP, Keria (widow of Elihu) VT	"	"	"	
820	MOORE, Francis	NY	"	"	"
821	DRIVER. John	NY	"	21	"
822	PHILLIPS, John	NY	"	"	"
823	CASTLES, David	VT	"	"	"
824	CURTIS, Uriah	VT	"	"	"
825	MATTHEWS, William	NY	"	23	"
826	PROCTOR, William	NY	"	24	"
827	BOYLE, George	NY	"	25	"
828	McDONELL, Allan	NY	"	26	"
829	CASS, Josiah	VT	Q	31	"
830	CALDWELL, Robert	VT	Q	"	"
831	SCOTT, David	VT	"	"	"
832	LANE, John	VT	"	"	"
833	McKENZIE, Lawrence	VT	"	"	"
834	PEARSON, Christopher	VT	"	"	"
835	PEARSON, Mary	PA	"	"	"

836	TAGUE, Jacob	NY	"	1 August	
837	PATERSON, William	NY	"	"	"
838	MAN, Isaac Sr.	NY	"	"	"
839	MAN, Isaac Jr.	NY	"	"	"
840	McGEAR, Mary	NY	"	2	"
841	COULTER, Andrew	NY	"	"	"
842	SHERMAN, Simeon	NY	"	"	"
843	NAUGHTAN, Andrew	NY	"	"	"
844	SHERAR, Thomas	NY	"	"	"
845	BETTS, Ben Jr.	NY	"	3	"
846	PHILLIPS, William	NY	"	9	"
847	CARMAN, Michael	NY	"	"	"
848	GRYFFIN, Joseph	NY	"	13	"
852	LEWIS, David	NJ	Q	16	"
881	STERNS, Nathan	NY	Q	"	"
1005	HOLMES, James	NY	M	11	"
1006	WEEJARS, Jacob	NY	"	12	"
1007	CHISHOLM, Alexander	NY	"	20	"
1008	SANFORD, Ephraim	NY	"	22	October
1009	MEYERS, John W.	NY	"	"	"
1010	FLAAKE, Harmanus	NY	"	23	"
1011	WHITE, Alexander	NY	"	24	"
1012	SMYTH, Patrick	NY	"	25	"
1013	McBAIN, Angus (McBean)	VT	"	26	"
1014	PRITCHARD, Azariah	CN	"	29	"
1015	TYLER, William	NY	"	"	"
1016	FRASER, William Sr.	NY	"	30	"
1016a	FRASER, William Jr.	NY	"	"	"
1016b	FRASER, Thomas	NY	"	"	"
1017	McGRUER, John	NY	"	"	"
1018	ROSS, Donald	NY	"	"	"
1019	HUNTER, David	NY	"	"	"
1020	SHAVER, Philip	NY	"	"	"
1021	SHELL, John	NY	"	"	"
1022	COONS, John	NY	"	"	"
1023	FROST, Edward	NY	"	"	"
1024	WALLISER, Anthony	NY	"	"	"
1025	FRASER, John	NY	"	31	"
1026	MacLEAN, Murdoch	NY	"	"	"
1027	MacLEAN, Donald	NY	"	"	"
1028	ROSE, William	NY	"	"	"
1029	McKAY, John	NY	"	"	"
1030	CHYSLER, Philip	NY	"	"	"
1031	McDONELL, Ronald	NY	"	"	"
1032	MURCHISON, Duncan	NY	"	"	"
1033	MURCHISON, John	NY	"	"	"
1034	MURCHISON, John, Jr.	NY	"	"	"
1035	McDONELL, Donald	NY	"	"	"
1036	GRANT, Archibald	NY	"	"	"
1037	CALDER, Janet	NY	"	1 November	

1038	SNYDER, Jacob	NY	"	"	"
1039	ROSS, Finlay Sr.	NY	"	"	"
1040	McGILLIS, Donald Jr.	NY	"	"	"
1041	McKAY, Hugh	NY	"	"	"
1042	GRANT, Peter	NY	"	"	"
1043	McDONELL, John	NY	"	"	"
1044	CAMERON, John	NY	"	"	"
1045	McKENZIE, Duncan	NY	"	"	"
1046	CAMPBELL, Alexander	NY	"	"	"
1047	FISHER, Alexander	NY	"	5	"
1048	FISHER, Finaly	NY	"	"	"
1049	CLAW, John W.	NY	"	6	"
1050	LINDSAY, Abigail (widow of John)	NY	"	"	"
1051	HAWS, George	NY	"	"	"
1052	HANES, Joseph	NY	"	"	"
1053	McGREGOR, Daniel	NY	"	7	"
1054	FINNY, Peter	NY	"	"	"
1055	HINDMAN, Samuel	NY	"	8	"
1056	SMYTH, Dr. George	NY	"	"	"
1057	VAN DUSEN, Conrad	NY	"	9	"
1058	McDONELL, Kenneth	NY	"	12	"
1059	McGREGOR, John	NY	"	"	"
1060	GORDON, Robert	NY	"	"	"
1061	CLARK, Francis	NY	"	"	"
1062	CALDWELL, John	NY	"	"	"
1063	WHAILEN, David	NY	"	"	"
1064	McDONELL, John Sr.	NY	"	"	"
1065	McDONELL, Allan	NY	"	"	"
1066	McDONELL, Alexander	NY	"	"	"
1067	McDONELL, Roderick	NY	"	"	"
1069	McARTHUR, Duncan	NY	"	12	"
1070	McGREGOR, Peter	NY	"	"	"
1071	CLARKE, James	NY	"	"	"
1072	GRANT, Allan	NY	"	"	"
1073	McLEOD, William	NY	"	"	"
1074	McDONELL, Ronald	NY	"	"	"
1075	BANGELL, Adam	NY	"	13	"
1076	GRANT, Donald, Jr.	NY	"	15	"
1077	GRANT, Donald Dr.	NY	"	"	"
1078	GRANT, Angus	NY	"	"	"
1079	McINTOSH, John	NY	"	"	"
1080	McDONELL, Kenneth	NY	"	"	"
1081	CAMERON, William	NY	"	"	"
1082	BETHUNE, Angus	NY	"	"	"
1083	GRANT, Finaly	NY	"	"	"
1084	LIVINGSTON, Flora	NY	"	"	"
1085	McDONELL, John	NY	"	"	"
1086	McDONELL, Roderick	NY	"	"	"
1087	MILROSS, Andrew	NY	"	19	"
1088	EMPEY, Philip Sr.	NY	"	6 December	

1089	HOFFTALIN, James	NY	"	7	"
1090	McBEAN, Isabel	NY	"	"	"
1091	QUINN, John	NY	"	14	"
1092	FRASER, Isabel (widow of Simon)	NY	"	18	"
1093	GRANT, William	NY	"	24	"
1094	YUREX, Isaac	NY	"	29	"
1095	JESSUP, Joseph	NY	"	9 January, 1788	
1096	BENDER, George	NY	"	10	"
1097	HORN, Henry	NY	"	"	"
1098	FERGUSON, Israel, Richard, & Farrington	NY	"	11	"
1099	McINTYRE, Duncan	NY	"	"	"
1100	McARTHUR, Donald	NY	"	"	"
1101	McDONELL, Alexander	NY	"	"	"
1102	CHISHOLM, Hugh	NY	"	"	"
1003	McLENNAN, John	NY	"	"	"
1104	CHISHOLM, Alexander	NY	"	"	"
1105	McGRIGOR, Jugh	NY	"	"	"
1106	McKAY, Angus	NY	"	12	"
1107	McPHERSON, Alexander	NY	"	"	"
1108	FITZPATRICK, Peter	NY	"	"	"
1109	McNAUGHTAN, John	NY	"	"	"
1111	McLAREN, Even	NY	"	"	"
1112	JONES, John	NY	"	"	"
1113	HAMBLIN, Silas	NY	"	14	"
1114	URQUHART, William	NY	"	"	"
1115	McLEOD, Isabel	NY	"	15	"
1116	STEWART, David	NY	"	"	"
1117	MUNRO, Hugh	NY	"	"	"
1118	BEAN, Thomas Ross	NY	"	"	"
1119	TAILOR, Thomas Ross	NY	"	"	"
1120	McKAY, Donald	NY	"	"	"
1121	McGEOAH, William	NY	"	"	"
1122	GLASFORD, James	NY	"	"	"
1123	BARBER, Abraham	NY	"	"	"
1124	McMARTIN, Malcolm	NY	"	16	"
1125	McMARTIN, John	NY	"	"	"
1126	BEST, Conrad	NY	"	"	"
1127	BEST, Hermanus (per widow of Jacob	NY	"	"	"
1128	DEAL, Adam	VT	"	"	"
1129	PRENTICE, Daniel	NY	"	18	"
1130	ANDERSON, Mary (widow of Alexander)	NY	"	19	"
1131	REED, Duncan	NY	"	"	"
1132	TOWNER, Ithiel	NY	"	"	"
1133	GRANT, John	NY	"	"	"
1134	CAMERON, Christian (widow of Donald Ross)	NY	"	"	"
1135	WILTSEE, Benoni	NY	"	22	"

1136	KELLEY, James	NY	"	"	"
1137	LEAKEY, William	NY	"	23	"
1138	FENNELL, John	NY	"	24	"
1139	LANDON, Asa	NY	"	"	"
1140	McDONELL, Alexander	NY	"	25	"
1141	McDONELL, Hugh	NY	"	"	"
1142	KENNEDY, Alexander	NY	"	"	"
1143	GRAHAM, Thomas	NY	"	"	"
1144	McGILLIS, Donald	NY	"	"	"
1145	FERGUSON, Alexander	NY	"	"	"
1146	DINGWELL, James	NY	"	"	"
1147	DINGWELL, John	NY	"	"	"
1148	McPHERSON, Murdoch	NY	"	"	"
1149	McDONELL, Donald	NY	"	"	"
1150	SHERWOOD, Thomas	NY	"	"	"
1151	CASWELL, Samuel	NY	"	"	"
1152	CARLEY, Barholomew	NY	"	"	"
1153	CLOSSON, Caleb	NY	"	"	"
1154	GRANT, Alexander	NY	"	"	"
1155	CAMERON, Alexander	NY	"	26	"
1156	CHISHOLM, William	NY	"	"	"
1157	FERGUSON, Peter	NY	"	"	"
1158	CAMERON, Angus	NY	"	"	"
1159	McDONELL, John of Inverness	NY	"	"	"
1160	McDONELL, John of Tomachrackie NY	"	"	"	
1161	McDONELL, John of Doldgreggan	NY	"	"	"
1162	CAMERON, Alexander	NY	"	"	"
1163	McDONELL, Duncan	NY	"	"	"
1164	GRANT, Duncan	NY	"	"	"†
1165	GRANT, Duncan (per late Alexander Grant)	NY	"	"	"
1166	McPHERSON, James	NY	"	"	"
1167	McDOUGAL, John	NY	"	"	"
1168	FERGUSON, William	NY	"	"	"
1169	McDONELL, John of Fort Augusta	NY	"	"	"
1170	ROBERTSON, Donald (by William Berguson)	NY	"	"	"
1171	SUTHERLAND, Jean	NY	"	"	"
1172	McDONELL, Alexander (by his son Jonathan)	NY	"	28	"
1173	McDONELL, Duncan	NY	"	"	"
1174	McDONELL, John of Cornwall Township	NY	"	"	"
1175	McDONELL, John of North Uist	NY	"	"	"
1176	McDONELL, John of Auchingtun	NY	"	"	"
1177	McMULLIN, Donald	NY	"	"	"
1178	HAGART, John	NY	"	"	"
1179	CAMERON, John of Corwall Township	NY	"	"	"
1180	CAMERON, Donald	NY	"	"	"

1181	McGRUER, Catherine (widow of Donald)	NY	"		"	"
1182	McDONELL, Angus	NY	"		"	"
1183	McDONELL, Alexander of Cornwall Township	NY	"		"	"
1184	FRASER, Donald	NY	"		"	"
1185	GRANT, Alexander of Strathspey	NY	"		"	"
1186	MARKLY, Jacob	NY	"		"	"
1187	LOUCKS, George	NY	"		"	"
1188	SHAVER, John	NY	"		"	"
1189	MARLKLY, Henry	NY	"		"	"
1190	WALKER, Philip	NY	"		"	"
1191	BURRITT, Stephen & Daniel	NY	"		"	"
1192	CAMERON, late John (by Alexander Grant for widow Ann Cameron	NY	"		"	"
1193	WALLACE, William	NY	"	29	"	
1194	BARNHART, George	NY	"	"	"	
1195	CAUER, (CARN?), Jacob	NY	"	"	"	
1196	JONES, Daniel	NY	"	30	"	
1197	BEVERLY, David	NY	"	"	"	
1198	BREMNER, George	NY	"	31	"	
1199	McCAFFERY, John	NY	"	1 February		
1200	TEEPLE, John	NY	"	2	"	
1201	ROSS, John	NY	"	4	"	
1202	ROBLIN, Philip	NY	"	"	"	
1203	VAN CAMP, Peter	NY	"	5	"	
1204	LEAHY, William Jr.	NY	"	"	"	
1205	VAN CAMP, Jacob	NY	"	"	"	
1206	WIST, John	NY	"	6	"	
1207	DULMAGE, John	NY	"	6	"	
1208	HECK, Paul	NY	"	"	"	
1209	LAWRENCE, John	NY	"	"	"	
1210	CONTERMAN, Jacob	NY	"	"	"	
1211	STUART, James	NY	"	8	"	
1212	ROBERTSON, Joseph	NY	"	"	"	
1213	FOYKE, Daniel	NY	"	"	"	
1214	STONEBURNER, Jacob	NY	"	"	"	
1215	TOMKINS, Israel	NY	"	9	"	
1216	BAKER, Henry	NY	"	"	"	
1217	SOMMERS, Andrew	NY	"	"	"	
1218	McNARIN, John	NY	"	"	"	
1219	FORSYTH, James	NY	"	"	"	
1219a	McINTOSH, Alexander	NY	"	11	"	
1220	CRYDERMAN, Catherine	NY	"	"	"	
1221	MORDEN, Joseph	NY	"	"	"	
1222	McINMOYL, Hugh	NY	"	"	"	
1223	ANNABLE, John	NY	"	12	"	
1224	GLASFORD, John Sr.	NY	"	"	"	

1225	GLASFORD, John Jr.	NY	"	"	"
1226	CROWDER, James	NY	"	"	"
1227	STARING, John	NY	"	"	"
1228	SELLECK, Dayle	Ny	"	13	"
1229	MERSELTS, John	NY	"	"	"
1230	FRASER, John (Boleskin)	NY	"	"	"
1231	ROSS, Thomas (Dunwich?)	NY	"	"	"
1232	RYCKMAN, Widow	NY	"	"	"
1233	WAGGONER, Jacob	NY	"	14	"
1234	ALGIER, Martin	NY	"	"	"
1235	WARNER, Michale	NY	"	"	"
1236	SCHICK, Christian	NY	"	"	"
1237	BREADY (BRODY?)	NY	"	"	"
1238	EAMER, Philip	NY	"	"	"
1239	FARLINGER, John	NY	"	"	"
1240	COLLINGER, Michael	NY	"	"	"
1241	PICKLE, John	NY	"	15	"
1242	BEAGLE, Daniel	NY	"	"	"
1243	MUNRO, Alexander	NY	"	"	"
1244	VAN ALLEN, Jacob	NY	"	"	"
1245	COOK, John Sr.	NY	"	"	"
1246	WALDECK, Martin	NY	"	"	"
1247	BOWEN, Luke	NY	"	"	"
1248	AGNEW, William	NJ	"	"	"
1249	MILLER, Peter	NY	"	"	"
1250	CLINE, Michael	NY	"	"	"
1251	TAYLOR, Jane (widow of John McCarthy)	NY	"	"	"
1252	CAMERON, William	NJ	"	"	"
1253	CROUS, Peter	NY	"	"	"
1254	PROUS, Peter	NY	"	"	"
1255	CARMAN, Michael (included in no. 847)	NY	"	"	"
1256	STREATS, Jacob	NY	"	"	"
1257	AULT, John	NY	"	16	"
1258	KINGSBURY, Joseph	CN	"	"	"
1259	EMPY, Philip Jr.	NY	"	"	"
1260	LOWNIE, John	NY	"	"	"
1261	CLOW, Henry (Plow?)	NY	"	"	"
1262	ROMBOGH, Jacob	NY	"	"	"
1263	CASFORD, John	NY	"	"	"
1264	BROOKS, Richard	NY	"	18	"
1265	McGLOUCHLONE, William (McLaughlin?)	NY	"	"	"
1266	DIXON, Robert	NY	"	"	"
1267	NICHOLSON, Alexander	VT	"	"	"
1268	BOGART, Gilbert	NY	"	"	"
1269	FALKNER, William	NY	"	"	"
1270	FALKNER, Ralph	NY	"	"	"
1271	DAFOE, John	VT	"	"	"

1272	OLIVER, Frederick	VT	"	"	"
1273	MIDDAGH, John	NY	"	19	"
1274	MIDDAGH, Stephen	NY	"	"	"
1275	MIDDAGH, Martin (for child of late Hy. Bush)	NY	"	"	"
1276	SEGAR, Adam	NY	"	"	"
1277	SMITH, Jacob	NY	"	"	"
1278	GRASS, Michael (Glass?)	NY	"	20	"
1279	BUCK, George (Bush?)	NY	"	"	"
1280	SPENCER, Jeremiah	VT	"	"	"
1281	GARLOW, Peter (Carlow?)	NY	"	"	"
1282	BLOWER, Casper	NY	"	"	"
1283	SPENCER, Benjamin	VT	"	"	"
1284	MILLER, Jacob	NY	"	21	"
1285	BUIS, Steven (Bliss?)	NY	"	"	"
1286	CHRISTIE, John	NY	"	"	"
1287	HOFFMAN, Joseph	NY	"	"	"
1288	CAMPBELL, Colin	NY	"	"	"
1289	METZ ,Henry	NY	"	"	"
1290	PICKLE, John	NY	"	"	"
1291	ANDERSON, Samuel & Joseph	VT	"	"	"
1292	ROSE, James	NY	"	"	"
1293	LOUCKS, Jacob	NY	"	25	"
1294	SILLS, Conrad	PA	"	"	"
1295	KELLER, William	NY	"	"	"
1296	DAY, Barnabas (Ray?)	NY	"	"	"
1297	LOUCKS, Abraham	NY	"	"	"
1298	PURDY, Gilbert	NY	"	"	"
1299	JACKSON, James	NY	"	"	"
1300	PALMER, David	NY	"	"	"
1301	SMITH, John	NY	"	"	"
1301a	BOGART, Gilbert	NY	"	"	"
1302	BRADSHAW, James	NY	"	"	"
1303	RUITAN, Peter	NJ	"	"	"
1304	DOLIER, Peter	NJ	"	"	"
1305	CRYSDALE, John (Drysdale?)	NY	"	"	"
1306	COLLENGER, Sarah	NY	"	"	"
1307	JACKSON, Henry	NY	"	"	"
1308	SYMMONS, Henry	PA	"	"	"
1309	KELLER, Frederick	NY	"	"	"
1310	CORNELL, Albert	NJ	"	"	"
1311	WARTMAN, Abraham	PA	"	"	"
1312	CORRY, James	NY	"	26	"
1313	HAWLEY, Jeptha	VT	"	"	"
1314	McAULEY, Robert	NY	"	"	"
1315	BRISCOE, Isaac	VT	"	"	"
1316	BENEDICT, John	CN	"	"	"
1317	EMPY, John	NY	"	"	"
1318	FRYMIRE, Nicholas (Faymire?)	NY	"	"	"
1319	SERON, Christopher	NY	"	"	"

No.	Name				
1320	GREEN, John	NY	"	"	"
1321	SHEWMAN, William (Sherman?)	NY	"	"	"
1322	WEIGAR, Everhart	NY	"	"	"
1323	FARRINGTON, Stephen	NY	"	"	"
1324	VAN ALSTINE, Lambert	VT/CN	"	"	"
1325	BOUCK, Adam	NY	"	27	"
1326	ROYS, Evan	MS	"	"	"
1327	VAN ALSTINE, Peter	NY	"	"	"
1328	SPARHAM, Thomas	NY	"	"	"
1329	CROSS, Henry	NY	"	"	"
1330	WRIGHT, Jesse	MS	"	"	"
1331	PETERSON, Abraham	NY/NJ	"	"	"
1332	FRANKLIN, Joseph	NY	"	"	"
1333	McKENZIE, Colin	NY	"	"	"
1334	SHARP, Guisbert	NY	"	"	"
1335	FITZGERALD, John	NY	"	"	"
1336	VAN DE CAR, Ralph	NY	"	"	"'
1337	HUFF, Paul	NY	"	"	"
1338	SIMPSON, Alexander	NY	"	"	"
1338a	CASSELMAN, Warner	NY	"	"	"
1339	CONNELL, Hugh	NY	"	"	"
1339a	BLAKE, Nicholas	NY	"	"	"
1340	TAYLOR, Jared	MS	"	"	"
1341	DIXON, John	NY	"	"	"
1342	PATTET, Dunham (Patten?)	NY	"	"	"
1343	BRISBANE, Robert	NY	"	"	"
1344	PLAUS, Peter (Plase?)	NY	"	"	"
1345	WOOD, Jonas	NY	"	"	"
1346	DEWIT, Garton	NY	"	"	"
1347	PARKE, Nathan	NY	"	"	"
1348	LINCH, James	NY	"	"	"
1349	GIBSON, John	NY	"	29	"
1350	RUSSELL, William	NY	"	"	"
1351	TARBELL, Samuel	MS	"	1 March	
1352	COLE, Simon	NY	"	"	"
1353	GILCHRIST, Peter	NY	"	"	"
1354	BREMER, Peter	NY	"	"	"
1355	CONCKLIN, Abraham	NY	"	"	"
1356	KNAPP, Joseph	NY	"	"	"
1357	FRYMIRE, Philip (Faymire?)	NY	"	3	"
1358	HURLBERT, Moses	NY	"	"	"
1359	MALLORY, Enock	VT	"	"	"
1360	COWDER, William	NY	"	"	"
1361	DINGMAN, Richard	NY	"	"	"
1362	CLARKE, Simon	NY	"	"	"
1362a	CARR, William	NY	"	4	"
1362b	BUTTERWORTH, James	VA	"	"	"
1363	FREDERICK, Barnet	NY	"	"	"
1364	FREDERICK, Lodowick	NY	"	"	"'
1365	CLARKE, Robert	NY	"	"	"

1366	DUNCAN, Richard	NY	"	5	"
1367	BARNHART, John	NY	"	"	"
1368	BREWSTER, Mary (Browster?)	PA	"	"	"
1369	FRANKS, William	NY/PA	"	6	"
1370	SWARTFAGER, Frederick	NY	"	"	"
1371	CHRISTIE, George	NY/VT	"	"	"
1372	HICKS, Edward	PA	"	"	"
1373	WALLDROFF, Martin & Margaret	NY	"	"	"
1374	CRYSLER, John (James Kriesler?)	NY	"	8	"
1375	CAMPBELL, Duncan	NY	"	10	"
1376	PEACOCKS, David	NY	"	12	"
1377	WHITMAN, robert	NY	"	13	"
1378	BENEDICT, Elijah	VT/CN	"	14	"
1379	FREEMAN, John	NY	"	17	"
1380	MOSHER, Lewis	NY	"	"	"
1382	ENGLAND, William	NY	"	27	"
1383	CROWSON, Abraham	NY	"	"	"
1384	OGDEN, Nicholas	NJ	Q	19	"
1385	LIDDEL, Andrew	NY	"	15	"

APPENDIX 4

Montreal's Loyalist Associations

by John Ruch and Violet Coderre-Smith

The Montreal branch of the United Empire Loyalists' Association of Canada, founded in 1973, was not the first of its kind in Montreal. An earlier organization had preceded Heritage Branch by eight decades but had disbanded shortly after the turn of the century.

The older group, or old Association, called itself the United Empire Loyalists' Association of the Province of Quebec. Centennial celebrations of the American Revolution in the late 1870s and 1880s had roused a strong reaction among Loyalists' descendants. These men and women as well as those with an interest in Canadian history, banded together in local groups dedicated to preserve and promote the Loyalists' story.

Societies formed in areas where the first Loyalist settlers had been more numerous. Provinces on the Atlantic coast had received the greatest number of refugees and, fittingly, were the first to see the permanent establishment of such a group. In 1889 the New Brunswick Loyalist Society was founded,[1] followed by Quebec's on May 2, 1895, Ontario's on Febr. 28, 1896, with Nova Scotia's being the last, on May 11, 1897. Each was an autonomous and independent organization. Leaders of the various groups did, however, maintain some links with each other in matters of mutual concern. Montreal corresponded

---

[1]United Empire Loyalists' Association of Canada, **A Position Paper on Nomenclature** (Toronto 1977), 32.

with Sir Leonard Tilley, Lt.Gov. of New Brunswick, and President of the local Loyalist Society.

Early official records of Montreal's Association cannot be traced, leaving contemporary newspaper reports, lists of executives from annual directories, and occasional private papers as the only sources for information. It is known that meetings were held in early 1895 before the founding meeting on May 2, but details remain elusive. The prime mover at the meeting which saw the establishment of the Association was Frederic Gregory Forsyth (nom de plume Viscount de Fronsac), an amateur historian, who enlisted the support of interested people for the new Society. Forsyth was chairman of the first official meeting at which time general policies were discussed and an executive board elected.

The next day the Montreal *Daily Star* published an account of the Association's "aims and objects....o weld a national and patriotic sentiment throughout the Province, and also to preserve in some tangible form the traditions of the Members' forefathers."[2] Further, members were to make an effort "to enlist the sympathy of the other organizations and, if possible, create a Dominion organization by amalgamating the different provincial associations of Canada."

From the beginning, the Society acknowledged the bicultural character of Quebec in its endeavours. A resolution was adopted that "a committee composed of members of the old French royalist families...(whose ancestors took loyal roles in military service 1775-83 and 1812-15) be added to the governing body." The result was joint honourary presidents: One representing the French families, the other, a descendant of

---

[2]"Loyalists' Descendants: A Provincial Society Organized in Montreal," **Daily Star** (Montreal, May 1895), 4/4.

a leading Montreal Loyalist family. It was also decided that the badge of membership should incorporate a fleur-de-lis or "some other emblem" indicative of the participation of the French-Canadians both at the time of the Revolution and in the Association. Many founding members had French blood, such as A.C. de Lery Macdonald. Aware of sensitivities in the community, they took part in a number of public causes, as did Macdonald, when he led the Association in opposing the erection of a monument at Louisburg by a group of Bostonians who wanted to commemorate its capture in 1745. The project was considered as "an insult" to the Acadians, "who have already suffered so much."[3] and elicited widespread protest in Canada.

Reports of its meetings were carried in both the English and French press.[4] These gatherings, held regularly from October to May inclusive on the first Monday evening of each month, were held in buildings such as that of the Natural History Society, and the Chateau de Ramezay, to which some members had an affiliation. Following the business of the meetings, a lecture on a historical topic was usually given, then patriotic or historical songs, poems and recitations by those in attendance were offered.

The Association was small in membership compared to Ontario's and New Brunswick's, but slightly larger than Nova Scotia's. By 1898 Quebec had 35 members compared to 250, 150

---

[3]Louisburg's Capture: The U.E.L. Assoc. to Strongly Oppose the Erection of a Monument Commemorative of the Event," **Gazette** (Montreal, June1895), 5/3; see also **Daily Star,** De Lery Macdonald's letter to the editor (Montreal, June1895), 4/3.

[4]"Nouvelle Association," **Le Monde** (Montreal, May 1895), 3.

and 30 respectively. The members' profiles were also similar. Social leaders, politicians, scholars and professional people headed the rosters. In Montreal, lawyers seemed to predominate the executive, which also included a priest, two doctors, a chartered accountant, and two army officers. The Hon. President Sir Henri Joly de Lotbiniere, and the President, the Hon. Jonathan Wurtele were both lawyers who had become politicians and been elected to the Provincial Legislature. De Lotbiniere had gone on to become the Lt.Gov. of British Columbia, while Wurtele had risen in the judicial system at home. William D. Lighthall, archivist of the Society, and A.C. de Lery Macdonald, also lawyers, were partners in their own law firm, and actively interested in several historical and learned societies. Wurtele was honourary president of the Association in 1899, and was succeeded as president by George Durnford, C.P.A, who remained in this capacity until the Society ceased to function. Lighthall later resigned as archivist, and was replaced by Rev. John Bruce Pyke in 1897 for the duration of the Association.

Apart from Sir William George Johnson, Bart., members' surnames give little indication of any Loyalist descent. Few of the first Montreal Loyalists' surnames were reflected in the names of this group, as the Settlers' heritage had been passed down through maternal lines. The Durnfords, for example, stemmed from Jonathan Sewell, the Skaifes from John Platt, and the Wurteles from Campbells. Some Loyalist surnames borne by a few members, such as Mount, stemmed from Loyalist families which had originally settled elsewhere than in this locality. Indeed, some of the members do not appear to have had any direct Loyalist ancestor.

Today, the Society is open to membership on the basis of hereditary qualification — proof of lineal descent from a

Loyalist ancestor. This requirement is more rigourous than that in force half a century or more ago, as prior to 1914 there was not a central authority to standardize procedures. The Heritage Branch distinguishes between direct descendants of Loyalists, who are entitled to membership, versus other interested persons including collateral descendants of Loyalists, all of whom are entitled to become associates members.

Amongst earlier members who do not appear to have had direct Loyalist connections, but who nevertheless were considered to be members of the Association, was Prof. Lighthall, whose surviving daughter Alice knows of no clear proof of such lineage. In fact their Schuyler ancestors were prominent revolutionaries. Some Lighthalls had been linked with the British, such as a William Lighthall who settled in Upper Canada, and another, Abraham, who appears to have been a courier for Loyalist intelligence agents.[5] However, they did have a collateral ancestor who was childless and whose property in the Eastern Townships was bequeathed to their branch of the family. This was Lt.Gen Garrett Fisher, a Loyalist soldier who remained in the military after the Revolution and achieved the highest rank ever attained by a Loyalist veteran in the British Army.[6]

---

[5]Abraham Lighthall appeared at St. Jean April 13, 1783 with information from James Ellice (secret agt. "Z.L.") He was known and trusted by Dr. Geo Smyth, Deputy Chief of Loyalist Intelligence (NAC: Haldiman Papers (henceforth HP), B170/134-137, ii), Geo. Smyth to Mathews and Riedesel, and John Nairne to Riedesel; Wm. Lighthall of Kingston m. Sarah Connor D.U.E. by May 20, 1817, W.D. Reid, **Loyalists in Ontario** (Lambertville, N.J. 1973), 71.

[6]Published several times, probably first in Royal Soc. of Canada, **Proceedings, 1922**, 65-72.

Frederic Forsyth's membership was based on Loyalist ancestry, but of people who had not chosen to emigrate from the new United States to Canada. His parents were from Portland, Maine, where he was born in 1856.[7] He deserves more than a passing mention, for as chairman of the founders' meeting and thereafter a member of the Association's council he has a claim to be regarded as a principal member. Talented, intelligent, and widely-travelled, he was somewhat eccentric. From his father, a strong supporter of the southern States during the American Civil War, he had absorbed an interest in "noble" causes. Unfortunately, many of these were unpopular and unpractical. His study of old laws when he was originally intended for the bar had led him to the realization that many were still valid, although long in abeyance or forgotten. Immersion in genealogical and heraldic lore had given him some authority to pursue a family claim to the title of Viscount de Fronsac, by which style he was usually known in the latter half of his life.[8] Frederic enlisted the resources of many scholarly disciplines in his subsequent efforts to establish the authenticity of his claim, and the restoration of the historic rights and privileges attached to it.

Forsyth's powers of judgement were uneven. He was enlightened enough to realize that only by uniting his cause with the interests of others could any progress be made in appealing to public authorities. Thus he became active in various groups in which he could find at least some shared

---

[7]F.G. Forsyth, bio notes, April 1886, state he was b. Portland, Me. July 1856, photocopies sent to Heritage Branch 1980 by Mary Murphy, Librarian Maine Hist. Soc., Portland. Ca. 1900 Forsyth claimed to have been born in Montreal.

[8]His claim to the title was outlined in F.G. Forsyth, **Memorial of the De Forsyths de Fronsac** (Boston 1897), 14-15, his descent 3-17.

interest. The Aryan Order which wanted to restore a hierarchical system in the U.S. was composed mostly of men descended from families who had held rank in America before the Revolution, whether of Spanish, Dutch, French or British nobility and gentry.[9] Forsyth, however, lacked a sense of political reality, and continued to persevere in such activity to the end of his life in 1925,[10] finding very little sympathy among parliamentarians whose support he solicited. He did not appreciate the fact that, whether government was willing to restore a class system or not, championing the cause would be political "suicide." Few politicians would ever be likely to fly in the face of the democratic prejudices of the electorate, either then or now.

In support of his policies, Forsyth also published writings to justify them. Several of his works refer to the history of the Loyalist period and to his association with the provincial societies in Canada. His shorter articles are scattered, but one work is wholly devoted to the Loyalist subject: *The Rise of the United Empire Loyalists*, published in Kingston in 1906, is almost entirely composed of a study of Colonial charters and the political situation (1770s-80s). Only the last chapter deals with the Loyalists in the Revolution, and their later presence in Canada. It is less a history of the people than an elaborate defence of his argument that parliament had consistently suppressed the nobility and their descendants in Canada.

---

[9]Fronsac, Viscount de (Frederic Gregory Forsyth), **The Rise of the United Empire Loyalists** (Kingston 1906), V, 110-120.

[10]He d. Nov. 2, 1925, in Toronto, and newspapers there carried his obit. We are indebted to W.H. Forsyth, Atlanta, Ga., for informaion, esp. for use of Peggy Love's transcript of the obit.

It seems clear that Forsyth was an important factor in the foundation of some Loyalist associations. He claimed to have laid the foundation for the whole Canadian association, but what is certain is that his was the first voice to be raised in the Old Association at Montreal in 1895.[11]

The next year (1896) by letters from the Viscount de Fronsac to Col. W. Hamilton Merritt of Toronto, a division was established there...in 1897 by the energy of Rev. Arthur (sic) Pyke, member of the general council at Montreal, the Nova Scotia division was established at Halifax...[12]

Forsyth evidently continued to consider the Quebec association as the mother of the other two, although the latter thought themselves wholly independent. In 1903 he claimed:

The efforts of the loyalists effaced the annexation propaganda that Yankee intrigue was fostering in Canada and did more to exalt the royalist influence and imperial connection than all the commercial schemes, preferential trade formulae and imperial league teachings combined, and which appeared only after the loyalists had led the way...[13]

---

[11]He was chairman of the founding meeting, see n. 3 above, and claimed to be the founder in his **Memorial** (1897), 17.

[12]Forsyth, **Rise** (1906), 118.

[13]Forsyth, **Memorial** (2nd ed. 1903), 76. Forsyth's view of the League was uncomplimentary, being composed of "impractical persons" who had proposed no "practical feature" for constitutional representation in its

In spite of his boasts of leadership of a strong Loyalist representation, Forsyth did not enjoy an unqualified support from them. Aside from patriotic sentiments and a desire to honour their ancestors, the greater number did not share his sympathies.

In most settings, Forsyth and his cause found limited support. Having exhausted the possibilities in one city he would move on to another. Earlier he had been active in Boston and Baltimore, and after about a decade in Montreal he moved on to lobby in Ottawa. From there he went to Halifax, where he developed a project already conceived in Montreal to form an heraldic society. Finally, in the last years of his life, he migrated to Toronto, where he died aged 68. As with so many people who labour in the cause of some unachievable goal, his solid accomplishments were by-products or "spin-offs" of his central activity. His valuable collection of historic documents was rejected by the Federal government, and he subsequently bequeathed it to an old seigneurial family of Quebec.[14]

If the Association founded in Montreal in 1895 can be regarded as one of those by-products of Forsyth's activity, then Heritage Branch has a special reason to remember him. Our precursor had an existence of something over a decade, during which time the Loyalist's history was kept alive.

Reasons for the demise of the Old Association are not clear, but appear to have been varied. The loss of several important

---

projected imperial union, Fronsac, **The Democratic and Parliamentary Usurpation** (Ottawa 1912), 86-87.

[14]Thanks to Hon. John R. Matheson of Perth, Ont., for assistance and A. Vachon, Head of Medals, Heraldry and Costume Section, NAC, for information from his biog. article on Forsyth.

and active members through death or removal from Montreal, and the diversity of interests among the remaining members may be cited as some probable detrimental influences. Forsyth and Rev. Pyke were no longer resident in the city after 1906, and the Honorary Presidents, already elderly when appointed, by this time could hardly have taken an active part in the Association's affairs. Wurtele died in 1904, Johnson and de Lotbiniere barely survived the Association, both dying in 1908.[15] Other members, especially the lively amateurs and the learned antiquaries, had diverging pursuits, while others belonged to numerous national societies which had both social and benevolent objectives in the community.

The interest in the Loyalist period did not cease among the members when the Old Association dissolved. Lighthall and Macdonald continued to affirm the place of the Loyalists in the long and varied history of Montreal. In their work with the Numismatic and Antiquarian Society, and McGill University, they tried to give each phase of history its proper weight in a balanced representation. Lighthall occasionally gave lectures on the Loyalists; his interest was of long standing. In 1889 he had championed the importance of the Loyalist migration to Canada in his book *Songs of the Great Dominion*. A recent authority has referred to this as a landmark of cultural publication which gave to his readers a new view of this country and its people.[16] It was a collection of pieces which the

---

[15]Biogs. of Wurtele and Joly de Lotbiniere in William Wood ed. **The Storied Province of Quebec** (Toronto 1931), IV, Joly de Lotbiniere, 244-45, W.S. Wallace ed. (Macmillan) **Dict. of Cdn. Biog.**

[16]Roy Daniells in Karl F. Klinck ed. **Literary History of Canada** (2nd. ed., Univ. of Toronto, 1976), I, 211-213. Two examples of Lighthall's lectures were: "The Settlement of the U.E. Loyalists," at the Soc. of Historical Studies of

compiler regarded as typically Canadian in subject matter. Lighthall eulogized the coming of the Loyalists, and saw in later generations epic virtues among the English-speaking Canadians which he asserted were derived from the heroic efforts of these ancestors.

There was close collaboration between the law partners, Lighthall and De Lery Macdonald. They formed private collections of books and documents of unusual importance, much of which was or is destined for public institutions. Macdonald was particularly interested in portraits, and helped establish such a collection for the Chateau de Ramezay, representative of prominent people of the British and French regimes. Among the portraits are those of Haldimand, Dorchester and the Johnson baronets.

Although little is known of the records of the Old Association, copies of one or two documents connected with A.D.Durnford's application are still held by his descendants.[17] Personal records of the various members are dispersed: Judge Wurtele's extensive collection of family papers was divided among three public repositories — the National Archives of Canada, and the Archives Nationales at Quebec City and Trois Rivières.[18]

It is regrettable that the old Association did not live to fulfill its self-appointed tasks. If it had, the history of the Loyalist

---

Montreal, March 7, 1888; and "Legends of the U.E. Loyalists," at the American Folklore Society, Montreal, 1896; see also Roy. Soc. of Can. **Proceedings,** 1888, xvi, and 1896, xxxii, resp. for simple ref. For Lighthall's ancestry see H.G. Todd, **The Armory and the Lineages of Canada** (1915), !!, 80-82, "Schuyler-Lighthall."

[17]Information from Mrs. Eliot Durnford, Montreal, given to Margaret S. Stead.

[18]Alfred C. Wurtele to John E. Ruch, Victoria, B.C., April 21, 1978.

settlers of Quebec would be better documented today. In addition, the role of the Loyalists and their descendants would be much more clearly defined and understood. The popular emphasis in recent years on the multi-national and multi-cultural origins of the Canadian population accords with a similar perception of the Association members: Unity arising out of diversity.

Heritage Branch — Montreal

In 1973, George Van Koughnett, a local businessman of Loyalist descent became interested in establishing a local branch of the United Empire Loyalists' Association of Canada in Montreal. He placed a notice of his intent in local papers, to which he received a small but enthusiastic response. Subsequently, a meeting of 18 individuals was held at the home of Mrs Gwendolyn Fuller on May 2 of that year, with Van Koughnett acting as chairman while Mrs. Fuller kept minutes. The group agreed to organize such a branch in the City, and proceeded to hold an election of officers: Mr. Van Koughnett, president; Mrs. Fuller, Secretary; and Mr. Frank J. Smith, Treasurer.

Rules and Regulations were then established. Membership was to be open to all interested in the Society and its aims after satisfying certain basic requirements. Associate Members were not to be required to furnish ancestral documentation. This category could include Loyalist descendants unable to prove their descent from specific Loyalists at the time of applying for membership. Full membership only to be extended to those able to furnish documented proof of their genealogical inheritance. All membership fees and donations to fund the Branch's operations.

As each Canadian branch of the Association bears a name chosen by its own membership, Heritage Branch was selected to pay tribute to those whose struggles secured a heritage for succeeding generations. The branch then applied to the Association's headquarters and obtained a Charter presented by Mr. Howard Warner of Ottawa, Dominion President U.E.L.Assoc. at a banquet held at the Helene de Champlain Restaurant on St. Helen's Island on January 30, 1974. The charter decrees:

1   To unite together irrespective of creed or political party,
    the descendants of those families who, during the
    American Revolutionary War of 1775-83, sacrificed their
    homes in retaining their loyalty to the British Crown,
    and to perpetuate this spirit of loyalty to the Principle of
    Law, Order and Justice.
2   To preserve the history and traditions of that important
    epoch in Canadian history by rescuing from oblivion the
    history and traditions of the Loyalist families before it is
    too late.
3   To collect together in a suitable place the portraits,
    documents, books, weapons, flags, monuments,
    memorials and all other articles and things relating to
    the United Empire Loyalists, which are now scattered
    throughout Canada and elsewhere.
4   To publish an historical and genealogical journal of
    annual transactions.
5   To erect, construct and repair buildings, monuments,
    memorials and also to purchase real estate and other
    objects that may be considered desirable to perpetuate
    the memory of the United Empire Loyalists.

In common with all branches of the Association, Heritage
Branch shares its coat-of-arms, a modern creation by the College
of Arms which conveys by means of clear pictorial devices the
historical distinction of the Loyalists. The Loyalist Banner, or
Flag, however, is often misunderstood. It is actually the old
Union Flag, or Jack, which was in use from 1606-1801, and
served as the rallying point for the first Loyalists. According to
heralds it is a royal badge in banner form for military use - the
Association sees in it the symbol of so much that was sacrificed
by so many.

Having no permanent quarters, Branch meetings were held
in the Advertising and Sales Executive Club's suite in the

Queen Elizabeth Hotel, of which Van Koughnett was then Club President. Subsequently, David M. Stewart, President of the Macdonald Stewart Foundation generously offered the use of meeting rooms, first at the old Fort on St. Helen's Island which housed his Museum (now the David M. Stewart Museum), then in Glenaladale, his family's former residence in Pointe Claire, and finally at the Macdonald Stewart Foundation on Sherbrooke St. in Montreal, where meetings continue to be held.

Bibliography

The most valuable sources of information are in the National Archives in Ottawa, the Provincial Archives in Quebec and Ontario, the British Library, and the Public Record Office, London, England. Among the more frequently consulted series, of which microfilm is available at the National Archives, are the **Haldimand Papers**, the **Records of the Losses Claims Commission**, the **Land Papers**, and the **British Military and Naval Records**. Complementary **Land Papers** are to be found in the Archives Nationales, Québec, and the Ontario Archives, Toronto. A typed index exists in Ottawa for the **Losses Claims**, and card indexes for the other three series, which do not necessarily account for all names to be found in the records.

I Primary Sources

National Archives, Ottawa

British Military and Naval Records, RG 8, Ser.1.
Haldimand Papers, MG 21, Add mss. 21,660 to 21, 892 (original), and B.1 to B.232 (transcript).
Land Papers, RG1, L3L (Lower Canada), RG 1, L3 (Upper Canada).
Records of the Losses Claims Commission, MG 14, AO 12 and 13.
War Office Records, MG 13, WO 17.

II Published Official Documents and Records

Losses Claims — **Report**. Ontario Archives no. 2. Toronto, 1904.
Simcoe Papers — Ernest A. Cruikshank ed. **The Simcoe Papers**. Toronto: Ontario Historical Society, 5 vols. 1923-1931.
State Papers of New York:

Minutes of the Albany Committee of Correspondence, 1775-1778. Albany: vol.I, James Sullivan ed. 1923.
Minutes of the Albany Committee of Correspondence, 1775-1778. Minutes of the Schenectady Committee, Index. Albany: vol. II, Alexander C. Flick ed. 1925.
Minutes of the Commissioners for Detecting and Defeating Conspiracies in the State of New York, Albany County Sessions 1778-1781. Victor H. Paltsits ed. (3 vols. Albany, 1909-1910) reprint 2 vols. Boston 1972.
Minute Book of the Committee of Safety, Tryon County. Samuel Frey ed. New York, 1905.
State Papers of Vermont:
vol. VI. **Sequestration, Confiscation and Sale of Estates.** Mary G. Nye ed. Montpelier, Vt. 19414.
vol. XVII. **The State Papers of Governor Thomas Chittenden.** John A. Williams ed. Montpelier, Vt. 1969.

III Calendars, Catalogues and Guides to Manuscripts

American Manuscripts Calendar — Benjamin F. Stevens and H.J. Brown eds. **Report on American Manuscripts in the Royal Institution of Great Britain.** 4 vols. London, Historical Manuscripts Commission, 1904-1909.
British Headquarters (New York) Papers or **Carleton Papers,** see American Manuscripts above.
Genealogical Records — Gregoire, Jeanne. **Guide du Généalogiste.** Montreal 1974.
Haldimand Papers Catalogue — **Reports.** Douglas Brymner ed. National Archives, Ottawa 1884-1889.
Losses Claims:
Palmer, Gregory. **Biographical Sketches of Loyalists of the American Revolution.** New Haven, 1984.
Quebec Archives — **L'Etat général des Archives publiques et privée du Québec.** Québec, Qué. 1968.

The Old United Empire Loyalists List. (reprint of The Centennial of the Settlement of Upper Canada. Toronto 1885) Baltimore 1984.
Upper Canada Land Records:
Ontario Archives: Reports nos. 17 (1919), 18 (1920).
Reid, William D. The Loyalists in Ontario: The Sons and Daughters of the American Loyalists of Upper Canada. Lambertville, N.J. 1973.

IV Secondary Sources

The Loyalists

Books
Allen, Robert S. Loyalist Literature, an Annotated Bibliography. Toronto 1982; The American Loyalists. (exhibition catalogue) Otttawa: National Museums of Canada, 1983.
Bird, Harrison. March to Saratoga: General Burgoyne and the American Campaign, 1777.
Brown, Wallace and Heward Senior. Victorious in Defeat. Toronto, 1984.
Crowley, James A. The Old Albany County and the American Revolution. Troy, N.Y. 1979.
Cruikshank, Ernest A. The King's Royal Regiment of New York. appendices by Gavin K. Watt ed. Toronto, 1984.
Fitzgerald, E. Keith, Loyalist Lists. Toronto: Ontario Genealogical Society, 1984.
Flowers, A.D. Loyalists of Bay Chaleur. Vancouver, 1973.
Fraser, J. Skulking for the King: a Loyalist Plot. Erin, Ont. 1985.
Fronsac, Viscount de (Frederic Gregory Forsyth). The Rise of the United Empire Loyalists: a Sketch of American History. Kingston 1906.
Fryer, Mary B. Buckskin Pimpernel: the Exploits of Justus Sherwood, Loyalist Spy. Toronto, 1981; John Walden Mayers:

Loyalist Spy. (2nd ed. of Loyalist Spy. 1974) Toronto, 1983; **The King's Men: The Soldier Founders of Ontario**. Toronto, 1980; and William A. Smy. **Rolls of the Provincial (Loyalist) Corps. Canadian Command, American Revolutionary Period**. Toronto, 1981.

Graymong, Barbara. **The Iroquois in the American Revolution**. Syracuse, N.Y. 1976.

Jones, Orlo and Doris Haslam ed. **An Island Refuge: Island of St. John**. (Prince Edward Island) Breadalbane P.E.I.: Abegweit Branch, U.E.L. 1983.

Lapp, Eula C. **To Their Heirs Forever**. Belleville, Ont. 1977.

Logan, G. Murray. **Scottish Highlanders and the American Revolution**. Halifax, N.S. 1976.

Mathews, Hazel C. **Frontier Spies**. (pub. privately) Fort Myers, Fla. 1971.

Mississquoi Loyalist Legacies. Mississquoi Historical Soc. vol. XIV, (Stanbridge East, Que.) 1976.

Sabine, Lorenzo. **Loyalists of the American Revolution**. (2nd ed. Boston, 1869) reprint 2 vols. Baltimore, 1979.

Sir John Johnson Branch, U.E.L. **Loyalists of the Eastern Townships of Quebec**. Stanbridge East, Que.: Mississquoi Historical Soc. 1983.

Smith, Paul C. **Loyalists and Redcoats: a Study of British Revolutionary Policy**. Williamsburg, Va. 1964.

Smith, William. **The Diary and Selected Letters of Chief Justice William Smith 1784-1793**. 2 vols. Toronto: Champlain Soc. 1963.

Thomas, Earle. **Sir John Johnson, Loyalist Baronet**. Toronto, 1986.

Upton, L.F.S. **The Loyal Whig: William Smith of New York and Quebec**. Toronto, 1969.

Walker, James St. G. **The Black Loyalists**. Dalhousie University, N.S. 1976.

Wetmore, Donald and Lester B. Sellick. **Loyalists in Nova Scotia**. Hantsport, N.S. 1983.

Wilson, Ellen G. **The Loyal Blacks**. New York, 1976.

Wright, Esther C. **The Loyalists of New Brunswick**. Fredericton, N.B. 1955, and later reprints.

Articles

Lemoine, James M. "Settlement of the U.E. Loyalists in the Province of Quebec and Elsewhere," **Maple Leaves**. ser.1862.

McCaw, Audrey M. "The Loyalists of Southern Quebec," **Loyalist Gazette**. Autumn 1983, p19.

McDougall, David J. "The Gaspé Loyalists," **Loyalist Gazette**. Autumn 1983, pp14-16.

Ruch, John E. "1779: Montreal and the Loyalists," **Loyalist Gazette**. United Empire Loyalists' Association: Toronto, Autumn 1979, pp4-5; "Project 1983, Montreal: Its Background, Aims and Progress," **Loyalist Gazette**. Spring 1979, pp3-4; "Quebec in Early 1780: McAlpin and the Loyalists," **Loyalist Gazette**. Spring 1980, pp10-11; "Late 1780 in Quebec: Season of the Three Commanders," **Loyalist Gazette**. (Pt. 1) Autumn 1980, p18; (Pt.2) Autumn 1981, pp7-8; "When Loyalty Was Not Enough: The Losses Claims Commission in Old Quebec 1787-1788," **Loyalist Gazette**. Autumn 1983, pp17-18; "Heraldry in the Loyalist Era," **Heraldry in Canada**. pub. in four parts: I. "Heraldry in Colonial America," vol. 17, no.4 (Dec. 1983) pp8-12; II. "Arms of the Pre-Loyalists in Canada; the Governors," vol. 18, no.1 (March 1984) pp4-11; III. "The Loyalist Military," vol. 18, no. 4 (Dec. 1984) pp12-18; IV. "*Foreign* Loyalists," vol. 19, no.2 (June 1985) pp7-14; "Loyalist Heraldry," **Heraldry in Canada**. vol.22, no.3 (Sept. 1986) pp46-49; "Quebec 1784: Farewell, Good Soldiers," **Loyalist Gazette**. June 1985, pp5-6; "1781 — A *Dutch Uncle* Brings Order out of Chaos," **Loyalist Gazette**. Dec. 1985, pp10-11; "Some Quebec References in Ontario Land Records," **Connections**. vol.9, no.2, Dec.1986, pp10-12.

Senior, Heward. "Why Loyalists Remained Loyal," **Canadian Genealogist**. Agincourt, Ont. vol.2, no.1 (1980) pp24-30.
Senior, Heward. "Portrait of a Quebec Loyalist: William Smith of New York," **Loyalist Gazette**. Autumn 1983, pp10-11.
Senior, Elinor K. "Loyalist Regiments After the Revolution," **Canadian Genealogist**. Agincourt, Ont. vol.2, no.1 (1980) pp31-46.
Siebert, Wilbur, H. "The American Loyalists in the Eastern Seignories and Townships of the Province of Quebec," **Proceedings and Transactions of the Royal Society of Canada**. Ottawa, 1913, Sec.II, pp3-41; "The Loyalist Settlements on the Gaspé Peninsula," **Proceedings and Transactions of the Royal Society of Canada**. Ottawa, 1915, Sec.II, pp305-405; "The Temporary Settlements of Loyalists at Machiche, P.Q.," **Proceedings and Transactions of the Royal Society of Canada**. Ottawa, 1914, Sec.II, pp407-414.

General

Dictionaries and Directories

Doidge, Thomas. **An Alphabetical List of Merchants, Traders and Householders Residing in Montreal**. Montreal, 1819.
Halpenny, Frances G. **Dictionary of Canadian Biography**. Toronto, vols. IV, 17---1800. 19--; V. 1801-1820. 1983; and VI 1821-18--. 19--.
Terrill, Frederick W. **A Chronology of Montreal and of Canada, 1752 to 1893**. Montreal, 1983.
Wallace, W. Stewart. **The Macmillan Dictionary of Canadian Biography**. Toronto, 1963.

19th Century Publications

Becket, Hugh W. **The Montreal Snow Shoe Club, Its History and Record with a Synopsis of the Racing Events of Other Clubs**

Throughout the Dominion from 1840 to the Present Time. Montreal, 1882.

Borthwick, John D. History and Biographical Gazeteer of Montreal to the Year 1892. Montreal, 1892; History of Montreal Including the Streets of Montreal, Their Origin and History Illustrated. Montreal 1897; History of the Montreal Prison from 1784 to 1886, Containing a Complete Record of the Troubles of 1837-8, the Burning of the Parliament Buildings in 1849, the St. Alban's Raiders 1864 and the Two Fenian Raids of 1866 and 1870. Montreal, 1886.

Bosworth, Newton. Hochelaga Depicta: The Early History and Present State of the City and Island of Montreal. Montreal 1839, reprint Toronto 1974.

Brown, Thomas S. Montreal Fifty Years Ago. Montreal, 1870.

Brumath, A. LeBlond de. Histoire populaire de Montréal depuis son origine jusqu'à nos jours. Montreal, 1890.

Campbell, Robert. A History of the Scotch Presbyterian Church, St. Gabriel Street. Montreal, 1887.

Caron, Ivanhoe. La Colonisation de la Province de Québec: Deputs du Regime anglais. Québec 1923.

Christie, Robert. A History of the Late Province of Lower Canada. 6 vols. Quebec, 1848-1856.

David, Laurent-Olivier. Biographies et Portraits. Montreal, 1876

Day, Mrs. C.M. Pioneers of the Eastern Townships. Montreal, 1863, reprint (n.p.) Page-Sangster, 1973.

Fraser, John. Canadian Pen and Ink Sketches. Montreal, 1890.

Garneau, François-X. History of Canada from the Time of its Discovery till the Union Year 1840-41. trans. by Andrew Bell. 3 vols. Montreal, 1862.

Graham, John H. Outlines of the History of Freemasonry in the Province of Quebec. Montreal, 1892.

Hawkins, Ernest. Annals of the Diocese of Quebec. London, 1849.

Sandham, Alfred. **Ville-Marie, or Sketches of Montreal.** Montreal, 1870.

Sellar, Robert. **History of the County of Huntingdon and of the Seigniories of Châteauguay and Beauharnois from the Earliest Settlement to the Year 1838.** Huntingdon, 1888.

20th Century Publications

Adams, Frank. **History of Christ Church Cathedral.** Montreal, 1941.

Atherton, William H. **Montreal, 1535-1914.** 3 vols. Montreal, 1914.

Auclair, Elie. Histoire de Châteauguay. Montreal, 1935.

Buchanan, A.W. Patrick. **The Bench and Bar of Lower Canada down to 1850.** Montreal, 1925.

Clarke, Adele. **Old Montreal, John Clarke, His Adventures, Friends and Family.** Montreal, 1906.

Collard, Edgar A. **Call Back Yesterdays.** Toronto, 1965.

Cooper, John I. **The Blessed Communion: The Origins and History of the Diocese of Montreal.** Montreal, 1960.

Denison, Merrill. **The Barley and the Stream: The Molson Story.** Toronto, 1955.

Devine, E.J. **Historic Caughnawaga.** Montreal, 1922.

Frank, Solomon. **Two Centuries of the Life of a Synagogue.** Montreal, 1968?

Gibbon, John M. **Our Old Montreal.** Montreal, 1947.

Graham, Franklin. **Histrionic Montreal: Annals of the Montreal Stage With Biographical and Critical Notices of the Plays and Players of a Century.** Montreal, 1902.

Jenkins, Kathleen. **Montreal: Island City of the St. Lawrence.** New York, 1966.

Prince, Lorenzo et al. **Montreal Old and New.** Montreal 1915.

Manning, Helen T. **The Revolt of French Canada, 1800-1835.** Toronto, 1962.

Milborne, A.J.B. **Freemasonry in the Province of Quebec, 1759-1959.** Knowlton, 1960.

Ouellet, Fernand. **Histoire économique et sociale du Québec, 1760-1850.** Montreal, 1966; **Le Bas-Canada, 1791-1840.** Ottawa, 1976.

Roberts, Leslie. **From Mission Colony to World City.** Toronto, 1969.

Sack, Benjamin. **History of the Jews in Canada from the Earliest Beginnings to the Present Day.** 2 vols. Montreal, 1945.

Smith, Pemberton. **A Research into Early Canadian Masonry, 1759-1869.** Montreal, 1939.

Turmel, Jean. **Police de Montréal, historique de service: Premières structures et évolution de police de Montréal, 1796-1971.** 2 vols. Montreal, 1971-1974.

Wade, F. Mason. **The French Canadians, 1760-1945.** Toronto, 1955.

Wood, W.C.H. **The Storied Province of Quebec.** 5 vols. Toronto, 1931-1932.

Acknowledgements

Heritage Branch owes a great debt to the late David Macdonald Stewart, who interested himself in its constructive historical work, and to his widow Liliane, President of the Macdonald Stewart Foundation, for her support of its Bicentennial Project in tribute to his memory. Furthermore, the publication of this volume is due to the devoted and energetic leadership of his daughter Victoria M. Stewart of the Lake Saint Louis Historical Society with the participation of her associate, Mr. Clayton Gray.

Interim support for the project was generously contributed by members of Heritage Branch, especially Phoebe Hyde, Marianne Davis, Elizabeth Ruch, and Okill Stuart after the early stages in which the project received two grants from the New Horizons Program of the Department of Health and Welfare Canada and the assistance of Charles-E. Douville and Jeanne R. Davies.

Members of the Project Committee, first formed in 1976, included Joyce Bradford, Eleanor Brodie, Violet Coderre-Smith, Marianne Davis, Alma and Roy Hayward, Ann Lachance, Alice M. Lighthall, Malcolm Loucks, Stephen Manson, Gerald Rogers, Margaret S. Stead, Okill Stuart, Earle and Faith Thomas and Gwen Trask.

During the course of this work several founding members passed away, including: Gwendolyn Fuller, Edith Loucks, Grant Smart and George Van Koughnett.

Throughout Prof. Hereward Senior and Dr. Elinor Senior were valued advisors, as well as contributors of their writings. Richard Garrity, Karen Findlay and several other members of the Québec Family Historical Society assisted in searches.

Mrs. Elliott Durnford allowed us access to her late husband's genealogical notes. Mrs Bruce Kirwin, Mansonville, Qué, lent extensive notes on the Elliotts and related families.

Genealogical information was also received from Ken Annable, Ottawa; Kenneth Annett, St. Foy; Anne Bernatovech, Levittown, Penn; Aldo Brochet, Toronto; A. R. Brooks, Verden, Man; R.N.Broadhurst, Red Deer, Alta;
Ann and Connie Champion, Québec; Sheila Fitchett, Montréal; W.H.Forsythe, Atlanta, Ga; George DeL. Hanger, Roanoke,Va; Sue Jackson, Glen Ellyn, Ill; Clive Lewis, St. Thomas, Ont; Darby G. Livingston, Bennington, Vt; Mildred R.Livingston, Prescott, Ont; Don McCallum, Noyan; Ruby Moore, Stanstead East; Ellen S. Morris, Allenhurst, N.J; Sister Marianne O'Gallagher, Québec; Florence Cunning Pearson, Victoria, B.C; Diane Sardo, Hamilton, Ont; Walter S. White, Sorel.

At the National Archives of Canada our work on Pre-Confederation Manuscripts was greatly facilitated by the constant advice and assistance of Patricia Kennedy and also on occasion by Patricia Birkett, and Bruch Wilson; on music: by Helmut Kallman and Barbara Norman; on photographic searches: Lydia Foy and Roanne Molchtar, and for much personal assistance: the staff of the search room. Many in the National Library, including Norma Gauld and Patrice Landry helped with searches for references. Also in Ottawa, Carl Christie, A.J.H.Richardson and others too numerous to mention assisted with individual enquiries. We are very grateful to them for their assistance. In the Ontario Archives, Toronto: John Mezaks and his staff.

In the Archives Nationales de Québec, Qué, we enjoyed the full op-operation of the late Roland Auger, Head of the Genealogical Section, and Raymond Gingras, then Assistant Head. Also in Québec, Cynthia Dooley, Librarian of the Literary and Historical Society of Québec.

Archivists and librarians of many institutions in Montreal were called on for assistance, and were all of great help: Conrad Graham, Pam Miller, Elizabeth Saunders and Mrs. M. Carroll of the McCord Museum; Stanley F. Triggs, Nora Hague and

Rosina Fontein of the Notman Archive; Nancy Chadwick and Mrs. D. Cole of the Montreal General Hospital Archives; Freeman Clowery, formerly of the Bank of Montreal, and Mabel Good, formerly of Molson's Brewery, Elizabeth Hale and Bruce Bolton of the David M. Stewart Museum, Nora Bryan and Rosemary Lydon of the Westmount Public Library.

In the United States the staffs of: the New England genealogical and Historical Society, Boston, Mass; New York State Archives, Albany; Germantown Museum, Germantown, Penn; New Jersey State Archives, Newton, N.J.; Pennsylvania State Archives, Harrisburg, Penn; Pennsylvania Historical Society, Philadelphia; Virginia State Archives and the Virginia Historical Society, Richmond Va.

We are grateful for donations of books and other materials by Eleanor Brodie, Rabbi Solomon Frank, the estate of the late Hazel C. Mathews, Gerald Rogers, Grant Smart, Rev. Thomas Ramsey, Annette Wolfe, and also for the loan of a microfilm reader to Messrs. Bell & Howell.

The Chew Inventory and the Blake & Loedel Accounts are published by kind permission of the Archives Nationales, Montreal, and quotations from the Dunlop Papers by permission of the Scottish Register Office, Edinburgh.

During the recent editing of this manuscript by Victoria M. Stewart, it was found that due to the long lapse since its compilation, much emendation was necessary. To readers who may still find an occasional error we echo the words Francis Parkman wrote in 1851:

If by any accident I have missed the mark I shall cordially thank any one who will set me right.

Index